CONFLICT OF THE CHURCH AND THE SYNAGOGUE

A study in the origins of antisemitism

JAMES PARKES

A TEMPLE BOOK

ATHENEUM 1969 NEW YORK

To H.E.

Published by Atheneum
Reprinted by arrangement with
The Jewish Publication Society of America

Library of Congress catalog card number 61-11472
Manufactured in the United States of America by
The Murray Printing Company,
Forge Village, Massachusetts
Published in Canada by McClelland and Stewart Ltd.
First Atheneum Edition

TABLE OF CONTENTS

INTRODUCTION THE LITERARY MATERIAL FOR THE STUDY OF JEWISH-CHRISTIAN RELATIONSHIPS *Page* IX

ABBREVIATIONS *Page* XVIII

CHAPTER I THE JEWS IN THE ROMAN WORLD *Page* 1

Origin and dispersion—first contacts with Rome, and privileges in the empire—occupations–Greek and Alexandrian opinion of the Jews—the Jews in the Greek cities—Roman opinion of the Jews—Jewish missionary activity.

CHAPTER 2 THE CLASH WITH CHRISTIANITY *Page* 27

Judaism and the Law—the teaching of Jesus in Mark—the accounts in Luke and Matthew–the crucifixion–the infant Church and the admission of the Gentiles—the activity of Saint Paul and his teaching about the Jews—the Jews in the rest of the New Testament—Jewish relationships with the early Church—Jewish attitude to Saint Paul—the issues still confused.

CHAPTER 3 THE PARTING OF THE WAYS *Page* 71

The separation, Jews and Christians in Palestine—the separation, letters to the synagogues—the separation, Jews and Christians in the diaspora—the separation, the Romans, Ramsay's view—the separation, the Romans, Merrill's view—the date of the separation—the Judeo-Christians after the separation—the creation of an official attitude to Judaism—the creation of an official attitude to Christianity—influences of Christianity on Judaism — relations between scholars—Jews and Christians.

CHAPTER 4 THE PART PLAYED BY THE JEWS IN THE PERSECUTIONS *Page* 121

View of modern scholars and their authority in Patristic literature—nature of available evidence—Jews in the Acta of the first century—stories showing Jewish initiative from Hadrian to Constantine—cases of Jewish hostility in the crowd—persecutions under Julian—persecutions under Shapur II—the mythical Acts—cases of Jewish kindness to the Martyrs—absence of any records of Jewish responsibility for the persecutions—Summary of evidence.

CHAPTER 5 THE FOURTH CENTURY *Page* 151

The problem facing the leaders of Judaism and Christianity—the Christian view of the Jews—Eusebius of Caesarea and Hilary of Poitiers and Jewish history—Chrysostom and the Jews of Antioch—Ambrose and the burning of a synagogue—Epiphanius and Jewish belief—converts, catechumens and church services—the councils of the fourth century—legislation affecting the Jews up to the death of Theodosius the Great—the treatment of heretics—events in fourth-century history—Jews and Christians.

CHAPTER 6 THE THEODOSIAN CODE IN THE WEST *Page* 197

The progress of legislation—Honorius and Valentinian III—Theodoric the Ostrogoth—the Lombards—Gregory the Great—Honorius, Gregory III, Stephen and Hadrian.

CHAPTER 7 LAW AND HISTORY IN THE BYZANTINE EMPIRE *Page* 225

The reign of Arcadius—Theodosius II and the Theodosian Code—the treatment of heretics in the fifth century—the Jews of Antioch—the legislation of Justinian—the treatment of heretics by Justinian—the council of Chalcedon—the Jews and the Persian wars—the destruction of synagogues and forced baptisms—the Legislation of Leo and later councils.

CHAPTER 8 THE JEWS IN BYZANTINE LITERATURE *Page* 271

The nature of Byzantine literature—physical, occupational and mental characteristics of eastern Jews—early eastern Christian writings against the Jews, Ephrem, Aphraates and Jacob of Serug—eastern disputations, Anastasius of Sinai—eastern disputations, Gregentius and Herbanus, the Teaching of Jacob, the Trophies of Damascus, the conversion of the Jews of Tomei, the history of Theodosius and Philip—the Jews in the Iconoclastic controversy—the miraculous conversions of the Jews—Jews in apocryphal writings—Jews in the theologians—'Jew' as a term of abuse in the Nestorian-Chalcedonian-Monophysite controversy—the ritual of the conversion of the Jews—relations between Jews and Christians.

CHAPTER 9 CIVES ROMANI, RELIGIONE JUDAEI *Page* 307

The barbarian invasions—the position of the Jews in Roman Gaul—the Syrians in western Europe—the simplification of Roman Law—the Arian period—the Jews and the Frankish councils—the Jews and the Frankish kings—compulsory baptisms in France—the Jews in literature—the laws of

Charlemagne—economic position of Jews—relations between Jews and Christians.

CHAPTER 10 THE JEWS IN VISIGOTHIC SPAIN *Page* 345

The Visigothic period—conditions of the Jews in Spain—the Breviary of Alaric—laws and councils of the first half of the seventh century—laws and councils of Recceswinth—laws and councils of Erwig—laws and councils of Egica—reasons for the persecution of the Jews in Spain.

CHAPTER 11 THE FOUNDATIONS OF ANTI-SEMITISM *Page* 371

APPENDIX 1 LEGISLATION AFFECTING THE JEWS FROM A.D. 300 TO 800 *Page* 379

APPENDIX 2 THE 146TH NOVELLA OF JUSTINIAN *Page* 392

APPENDIX 3 PROFESSIONS OF FAITH EXTRACTED FROM JEWS ON BAPTISM *Page* 394

APPENDIX 4 SPECIAL PRAYERS TO BE ADDED IN THE DEDICATION OF A CHURCH WHEN THE BUILDING HAS BEEN A SYNAGOGUE *Page* 401

APPENDIX 5 MARTYRDOM OF THE FIRST CENTURY ASCRIBED TO THE JEWS *Page* 402

INDICES *Page* 405

NOTE.—Each chapter is preceded by a short bibliographical introduction giving the sources, and the main authorities consulted.

PREFACE

The publication of a study of the causes of antisemitism needs neither justification nor explanation at the present time. But a word may be said of the material offered in the present work. The progress of events from the mediaeval ghetto to modern Europe is fairly well known. That the roots of the present situation lie in the mediaeval past is generally agreed. The present work tries to go a stage further, and to answer the question: why was there a mediaeval ghetto? In 1096 there were wild popular outbreaks against the Jews in all the cities of northern and central Europe. What made this possible? The answer could only be found by a study of the earlier period, a period incidentally which is little known by either Jewish or Christian scholars of the subject. It was necessary to begin with the Jews in the Roman world, and to trace their passage through the Roman pagan and Roman Christian civilisations into the beginning of the Middle Ages if the significance of this sudden popular fury was to be discovered.

The material to be surveyed was enormous, and needed careful selection if a book already large was not to assume impossible proportions. For this reason much has been left out. Much more evidence could be produced to support the thesis that the hostility of the Roman world to the Jew offers no explanation of the creation and survival of antisemitism. More illustrations of the attitude of the Jews could have been drawn from post-biblical Jewish literature. But, as the collection of material progressed, I became more and more convinced that it was in the conflict of the Church with the Synagogue that the real roots of the problem lay; and it seemed wiser to give the maximum material on that subject so as to allow the reader to judge for himself the accuracy of the theory.

It was necessary to attempt to present all, not a selection, of the known facts of Jewish-Christian relations. To do otherwise was to expose myself to the charge of selecting only those laws or passages in Chroniclers and Historians which supported my argument. And it was necessary to give references for my quotations, so that scholars might check them for themselves if they disagreed with my interpretations. I have at least not concealed my sources under such phrases as ' a late Arab Chronicler ' or ' an early and reliable authority ', phrases which again and again reduced me to fury in working through the modern material used in the preparation of this book. For this is neither a book of propaganda, nor an attempt to justify by any means available a particular hypothesis. It is an attempt to review with as much impartiality as possible the origins of a serious contemporary problem.

This study carries the history of antisemitism down to the beginnings of mediaeval Europe. A further volume, bringing the subject down to the end of the Middle Ages, is now in course of preparation, and will, I hope, appear within a short time.

This book was written while I was on the staff of International Student Service, for presentation as a thesis for the Doctorate of Philosophy at Oxford. I must express my deepest thanks to International Student Service for allowing me the necessary time for research, and to Exeter College, Oxford, for giving me a post-graduate scholarship during the period involved. I must also express my gratitude to the Authorities of the University of Geneva for the hospitality of their admirable library.

It would be impossible to express my thanks to all the scholars, Christian and Jewish, who have assisted me in this study. But I cannot omit the names of my two chief counsellors, Professor Powicke, of Oxford, and Mr Herbert Loewe, whose departure to Cambridge has left Oxford without a Rabbinic scholar. To them I owe a debt which cannot be measured in words. For financial assistance in publishing this work I have to thank the Committee for Advanced Studies at Oxford and Mr I. M. Sieff for their generosity.

Though I fear that there will still be found by the industrious reader errors and oversights in the text, yet that the book was finished at all is due to the continual patient work, on manuscripts, sources and proofs, of my two collaborators, Helen Ellershaw and Miles Hyatt. If, after all their work, there are still inconsistencies or errors, the fault is mine and not theirs.

JAMES PARKES

May 1934.

INTRODUCTION

ON THE LITERARY MATERIAL FOR A STUDY OF JEWISH-CHRISTIAN RELATIONSHIPS

The rejection of Christianity by the Jewish people has, inevitably, always troubled the Christian conscience, and it is natural that an immense literature has grown up around the subject. To describe in detail the whole of this literature would be an enormous work in itself. The purpose of this introduction is more modest. It is designed to supplement the detailed bibliographies given to each chapter by a general survey of the development of the controversy between Jews and Christians from the separation of the two religions up to the present time.

So long as the rejection of Christianity remained in doubt it was natural that the main effort of the protagonists of the new faith should be to explain and to justify it to their unconvinced fellow-countrymen. Their task was to prove by reference to the Scriptures which both parties accepted, that Jesus was really the Messiah. Their attitude to His condemnation by the authorities of Jerusalem was a tentative one. They were more anxious to excuse than to condemn. This is the situation at the time when the synoptic gospels were written.

But the events following the destruction of Jerusalem in A.D. 70 made the conversion of the mass of the people less likely, and there is, consequently, a change in the tone of the literature. It is designed to confute rather than to convince. To this period belongs the Gospel of Saint John, with its complete lack of distinction between parties, and its condemnation of ' the Jews ' as a whole for actions which the synoptists had more specifically ascribed to the Pharisees or to some other party. The spread of the Church among Gentiles and Hellenistic Jews, who were either totally unacquainted with the Scriptures, or at best knew them but slightly, forced the Church into the collection of the main texts from the Old Testament on which it based its claim that Jesus was the Messiah, and many editions of these ' Testimonies ' were probably in circulation at the beginning of the second century. While the problem of the Jews was of capital importance to the Christians, it is easy to see that the problem of the Christians was of but very slight importance to the Jews. Not only were they engaged in a political and religious task which taxed all their energies, but in any case the Christians must have seemed a very small and insignificant sect to the leaders of Judaism. No literature has survived, and it is doubtful if any ever existed, in which the Jews set in writing their replies to the challenge of the Christians. At most this or that paragraph of the Talmud may have been uttered with the Christian doctrine, and the reply to it, in the mind of the rabbi concerned. The main Christian document of this second period is the dialogue of Justin with Trypho, written in the middle of the second century, which not only contains the fullest statement of the Christian teaching on the authenticity of the claims of Jesus to be the Messiah, but also the beginnings of a developed doctrine of the rejection of the Jews. There must have been many other such dialogues during this period, and one is known to us by name, the *Dialogue of Jason and Papiscus*. Traces of it are to be found in two dialogues which reflect fairly early conditions, those of *Timothy and Aquila* and of *Athanasius and Zacchaeus*.

But in the main the Church of the second and third centuries was concerned with its relations with paganism more than with Judaism, and information about its attitude to the Jews has to be looked for here and there scattered throughout the writings of the Church fathers. Literature addressed to them directly has, however, always existed, and 'Altercationes' or 'Disputationes' or discourses 'contra Judaeos' are to be found in almost every century. The earliest known to have been translated into a Teutonic tongue is the *Book on the Catholic Faith* of Isidore of Seville, written in the seventh century to confute the Jews of Visigothic Spain.

A parallel literature from the Jewish side is not to be found before the Spanish controversies of the Middle Ages, but from that time onwards a number of Jewish authors have set themselves to refute the texts used by Christians to assert the truth of their religion. The most famous of the latter works is the *Strengthening of Faith*, by the Karaite Rabbi, Isaac of Troki, which, written in the sixteenth century and based largely on older materials, has enjoyed a considerable vogue in eastern Europe up to the present day, and has produced a number of Christian rejoinders, the latest being the work of Canon Lukyn Williams, *Christian Evidences for Jewish People*.

A detailed study of the literature of the Middle Ages is reserved for a later volume treating of the relations between the Church and the Synagogue during that period, and here it is sufficient to remark that works of a precisely similar character to the earlier ones existed throughout the Middle Ages, containing very largely the old texts and methods of argument.

A popularised form of this literature was the miracle play, in which the part of the Jew was, naturally, always an unpleasant one. How far back these plays may be traced is an uncertain point, but there is a *Dialogue between the Church and the Synagogue*, attached to the writings of Augustine but certainly not by him, which almost looks as if it were written for dramatic presentation. To this popular literature of attack the Jews replied by the production of scurrilous biographies of Jesus. The earliest evidence for such biographies goes back to the second century, but the one which has survived, the *Sepher Toldoth Jeshu*, is probably mediaeval. It was known in whole or in part to various Christian scholars of the Middle Ages, and was finally published *in toto* by Wagenseil in his *Tela Ignea Satani* in 1681. Since then it has provided frequent ammunition for antisemitic writers. In its essence it is a parody of the Gospel narratives, turning all the good in them into evil. It is significant primarily for the use made of it by modern antisemitic writers. In itself it cannot be considered a serious view of Jewish scholarship, and it is indeed very doubtful whether it was as widely known among mediaeval Jews as Wagenseil would claim, though it certainly enjoyed considerable currency among the folk-lore and unwritten legend of the simpler type of Jewish family.

The first field covered by this literature is, then, the interpretation of the Scriptures themselves, whether Jewish or Christian. A second subject enters into consideration with the development of post-Christian Jewish scholarship in the Talmud. Many of the early fathers show a more or less profound acquaintance with the development of contemporary Judaism and the Jewish method of interpretation of the Scriptures. The writer who devoted most attention to the matter was Jerome. He produced innumerable commentaries of the Scriptures in which he contrasts the Jewish and Christian interpretations, and also a new Latin version of the Bible, in order to give Christians, especially those who knew no Hebrew, an authoritative version for the purpose of confuting the Jews. But there are no lengthy commentaries or attacks upon the Talmud as such until a much later period. All that was done was to prohibit Christians and, where possible, Jews from reading these 'interpretations'.

The Middle Ages condemned the Talmud without trying to read it. The first attempt to secure a Christian view of its contents was undertaken by the Spanish Dominicans in the thirteenth century, and by a papal bull all passages offensive to Christianity were deleted. Similar action was taken at various other points in the Middle Ages, but more serious was the renewed attack of the Dominicans in the sixteenth century. In 1505 they commissioned a converted Jew, Pfefferkorn, to make a collection of all the offensive passages in the Talmud. This was published in 1507 as the *Judenspiegel*, and led to a great controversy between the clericals and humanists, led by the Dominicans and Reuchlin. The clericals won, but Reuchlin, though defeated, ushered in a new era by his courageous defence of the Jews and the Talmud in the *Augenspiegel*. At the end of the seventeenth century a Protestant professor, John Andrew Eisenmenger, published a violent attack on the Talmud and on Judaism as a whole under the title of *Entdecktes Judentum*, an 'Original and True Account of the way in which the stubborn Jews frightfully blaspheme and dishonour the Holy Trinity, revile the Holy Mother of Christ, mockingly criticise the New Testament, the Evangelists, the Apostles and the Christian religion, and despise and curse to the uttermost extreme the whole of Christianity'. This work was so virulent that its first edition was suppressed, and for ten years it only circulated in a few copies. But in 1711 the King of Prussia was interested in the matter, and the whole—two quarto volumes of more than a thousand pages each—was republished at the royal press at Königsberg.

These two volumes are of capital importance for the future development of antisemitism. Not only do all later antisemites, such as Rohling, plagiarise them, but they link together, as no ancient writer did, the contemporary conduct of the Jews with their theological and historical failings. In this way the hatred of the Jews for the Christians is explained as the consequence of Jewish religious teaching, and the responsibility of the non-Jewish population for its existence is kept well in the background.

The matter slumbered during the rest of the century, but it was again fanned into flame by the emancipation of the Jews and by the prominent part which they took in the economic developments of the nineteenth century. Economic and religious questions became completely intertwined with politics, and a new form of polemic was evolved, in which contemporary life was the main interest. But the old accusations still remained to explain the Jewish position in society and to deepen the new hostility of the common people to the Jews.

The literature which this new antisemitic movement produced is enormous, and it is only possible to indicate a few examples. The earliest writings came from France, where in the 'forties Toussenel produced in two volumes a work, *Les Juifs, rois de l'époque*. This was followed by *L'entrée des Israelites dans la Société française* by the Abbé Joseph Lemann, himself a converted Jew, and these two works served as a basis for the infamous attack on the French Jews of Edouard Drumont, *La France Juive*, which, in spite of being a work of two fat volumes, ran into innumerable editions and produced a whole literature of attack and defence in the years immediately preceding the Affaire Dreyfus.

In Germany a similar literature came into being with the publication by a journalist, Wilhelm Marr, of a sensational pamphlet on the *Victory of Judaism over Germanism*. The nineteenth century saw this attack developed along several different lines. Treitschke developed political antisemitism: Chamberlain embellished all the absurdities of racial antisemitism with immense learning in *The Foundations of the Nineteenth Century*: Canon Rohling in the *Talmudjude* revived ritual murder accusations and all the poison of

Eisenmenger; and finally Werner Sombart in *Die Juden und das Wirtschaftsleben* combined a serious study of the rôle of the Jews in the building up of modern society with a fantastic structure of religious and racial theory, linking the development of modern capitalism to the exigencies of the Mosaic Law.

The final stage of antisemitic development accompanied the foundation of the Zionist Organisation as a world-wide federation of Jews. Out of this fact emerged a literature representing the Jews not merely as the enemies of individual Christians, or of particular national societies, but as the enemies of the whole world, and the secret plotters of a world revolution in their own favour. Out of this approach grew the famous forgery, *The Protocols of the Elders of Zion.*

The defence of post-Christian Judaism and the re-examination of the Christian attitude to the Jew begin much later than the attack. While certain mediaeval Popes and ecclesiastical writers were not unsympathetic to them, and while the Papacy, for instance, steadily defended the Jews against the ritual murder accusation, it is not unnatural to find the first defence of the Talmud coming from a sixteenth-century humanist, Reuchlin, and the first complete examination of the history of the Jews among the Christian peoples undertaken by a Pastor of the Reformed Church, who thus did not feel personally responsible for what had happened before the Reformation. This important publication was *L'Histoire des Juifs, pour servir à continuation de l'Histoire de Flave Josephe*, published by Jacob Christian Basnage at Rotterdam in 1701. This work was considerably used by other authors in the eighteenth century, and its popularity is indicated by its appearance in several editions both in French and English, and by the appearance of a pirated edition of it in Paris, in which his texts are falsified to divert the blame from the mediaeval Church.

The eighteenth century witnessed the emergence of an emancipated literary Jewish group in Berlin under the leadership of a Jewish philosopher, Moses Mendelssohn. Frequented by many of the leading Christian intellectuals of his day, Mendelssohn inspired a new respect for the Jew, which is reflected in the play of Lessing, *Nathan the Wise*, and in the political plea of Christian William Dohm, *Upon the Civil*

Amelioration of the Condition of the Jews. In England a similar reaction took place, and a dramatist of the second half of the century, having become extremely interested in the Jewish problem, produced a play, *The Jew.* Though Lessing's work is incomparably greater as literature, the two plays have this in common, that the Jew becomes as superhumanly virtuous as society had been accustomed to consider him superhumanly evil. Lessing shows his Jew as the great philosopher of toleration, Cumberland as the generous moneylender and anonymous philanthropist. This tendency in literature produced in the nineteenth century Dickens's Mr. Riah (though his Fagin is much better known) and George Eliot's *Daniel Deronda.*

It would, however, be true to say that the literary tradition of the Jew as the evil character is by no means dead, and that when to-day a character is referred to as 'a Jew' in a book, it is usually meant as a term of dislike or contempt. This is, in fact, much the older tradition. Jews as a common subject of romances are first found in the time of the iconoclastic controversy,. and though the story usually—though not always—ends with the conversion of the Jew, it invariably begins with his misdeeds. Eastern literature is, on the whole, better disposed towards them than western, but the human side of Shylock is a witness to the genius of Shakespeare only, and has few parallels in anything written between the eighth century and the eighteenth.

A new element in what may be called 'the literature of defence' was introduced by the emergence in the nineteenth century of higher criticism. The results of the researches of German scholars into the authenticity of the New Testament were immediately known to Jewish scholars, who now had access to the European universities. This produced a demand for a re-examination of the part they were supposed to have played in the drama of Calvary—presuming it even to have taken place. In 1838 a French Jewish scholar, Joseph Salvador, produced *Jésus Christ et sa Doctrine*, which was an attempt to study critically the history of the first two centuries of Christian history. This was followed some twenty years later with a more direct attack by J. Cohen, *Les Déicides*, in which the whole responsibility of the Jews for consciously killing the Messiah was rejected. Since then many Jewish works on the subject have appeared. Among them some of the most noticeable are *As others saw Him*, by Joseph Jacobs; *The Trial of Jesus*, by an American Jewish lawyer, Max Radin; and more recently *Jesus of Nazareth*, by Joseph Klausner.

A second product of the new study of the Scriptures was a re-examination of the debt owed by Christianity to Judaism. This produced a considerable literature during the latter half of the nineteenth century. The first group to undertake such study were astonishingly little influenced by modern views of Judaism. Harnack and Schürer reproduce almost the same conception of the Jews as the theologians of the early centuries of the Church. A revision of the Gospel account of Pharisaism, and of the accepted conception of the Talmud, was made necessary by the appearance of *The Pharisees*, by Travers Herford, and by the literature arising out of the Rohling-Bloch trial. Though the actual trial never took place, since Rohling withdrew the day before it was to open, it gave the opportunity for a complete refutation of the usual calumnies on the Talmud. At the same time the re-emergence of ritual murder accusations led to the publication by Hermann Strack of *The Jew in Human Sacrifice*. Finally, in recent years, have appeared two exhaustive studies by Christian scholars on early Judaism, *Judaism of the Tannaitic Period*, by George Foote Moore, and the *Kommentar zum Neuen Testament aus Talmud und Midrasch*, by Hermann Strack and Paul Billerbeck. On the same subject, from the Jewish side, have appeared *The Synoptic Gospels* and *Rabbinic Literature and Gospel Teaching*, by Claude Montefiore. To these may be added the study of the different strata in the Gospels as they present the teaching of Jesus, *Jesus and the Law of Moses*, by B. H. Branscombe.

A third development of the nineteenth century was a new Jewish interest in secular history. This interest produced a great Jewish apologist in H. Graetz, who began his *Geschichte der Juden* about 1850, following up and surpassing such limited works as those of Depping and Bedarride on the history of the Jews in western Europe. Since the time of Graetz many Jewish historians have appeared, including Dubnow with a further complete history of the Jews, Juster with a specialised study of the Jews in the Roman Empire,

Aronius with a collection of early sources for Jewish history in western Europe, and others.

This historical work formed the basis for a new apologetic, which was made very necessary by the re-emergence of anti-semitism in the second half of the nineteenth century. This time both Jew and Gentile scholar entered the field on the same side. Among Gentiles, Leroy Beaulieu wrote *Israel parmi les Nations* in the 'eighties, and G. F. Abbott *Israel in Europe* some ten years later. On the Jewish side the outstanding work was *Antisemitisme* by Bernard Lazare, and more recently the racial aspect has been dealt with by M. Mieses in *Der Ursprung des Judenhasses*. This apologetic literature is now so enormous that it is impossible to quote examples of it. It can only be said that little of it rises above mediocrity, or tries to trace the problem to its real historical roots. It is for this reason that the present study was undertaken.

In this brief review of an immense literature, study of the Old Testament history of the Jew has been deliberately omitted; but in a survey of the numerous ways in which non-Jews have been led to a different appreciation of Judaism from that offered by the early Church, the work of Hebraists like the Buxdorf family in the seventeenth century has played no mean part.

In the whole of this account it is significant that no honourable part has been played by converted Jews, as interpreters of their old faith to their new. In the Middle Ages converted Jews were either silent or proved the sincerity of their conversion by virulent attacks upon Judaism. The sixteenth-century Pfefferkorn was an eminent example of this type. In recent centuries a number of converted Jews have written works to bring their co-religionists to conversion, e.g. *Wegweiser zum Leben für Hebräer, oder Beweggründe wegen welchen ich Thomas Neumann das Judenthum verlies und ein Katholischer Christ ward*, of 1791, or *Erreurs des Juifs en Matière de Religion* of Nicolas Léveque, 1828. The first converted Jew vigorously to undertake the defence of the Jews against unjust accusations was Daniel Abramovitch Chwolson, a Russian Jewish Christian scholar. The attempt to set Jesus in His Jewish setting was also first attempted by a Jewish Christian in the nineteenth century, in the work of Alfred Edersheim, *The Life and Times of Jesus the Messiah.*

To-day it must still be said that the popular view of the Jews has little altered through the influence of modern scholarship. But, for those who will take the trouble, it is possible at last to understand the true nature of the Judaism out of which Christianity grew, and which still exists side by side with it. But much still remains to be done, both from the religious and from the historical standpoint, if the Jewish problem of to-day is to be understood, and, on the basis of a true understanding, solved.

ABBREVIATIONS

A.B. (An. Boll.)	*Analecta Bollandiana*, periodical publication of the Bollandists.
Aronius	*Regesten zur Geschichte der Juden bis zum Jahre* 1273, Julius Aronius. Berlin, 1902.
A.S.	*Acta Sanctorum.*
Breviary	*Breviarium Alariciense.* Ed. G. Haenel. Leipzig, 1849.
C.J.	*Codex Justinianus.* Ed. Krueger and Mommsen. Berlin, 1886.
Const. Sirm.	*Constitutio Sirmionis.* See C.T.
Cor. Scrip. Byz.	*Corpus Scriptorum Byzantinorum.*
C.S.C.O.	*Corpus Scriptorum Christianorum Orientalium.*
C.S.E.L.	*Corpus Scriptorum Ecclesiasticorum Latinorum.*
C.T.	*Codex Theodosianus.* Ed. Mommsen and Meyer. Berlin, 1905.
D.C.B.	*Dictionary of Christian Biography.*
E. and H.	*Letters of Gregory the Great,* in edition of Ewald and Hartmann, in M.G.H.
Harduin	*Sacrosancta Concilia ad regiam editionem exacta,* 1728.
J.Q.R.	*Jewish Quarterly Review,* Old Series.
J.T.S.	*Journal of Theological Studies.*
L.V. (Leg. Vis.)	*Leges Visigothorum.* Ed. Zeumer, in M.G.H. quarto, Leges, I, i. Leipzig, 1902.
M. (in Ch. VI only)	*Letters of Gregory the Great,* in edition of Migne's Patrologia Latina.
Mansi or M.	*Collectio Conciliorum Amplissima.*
M.G.H.	*Monumenta Germaniae Historica.*
M.G.W.J.	*Monatschrift für Geschichte und Wissenschaft des Judentums.*
Nov.	*Novellae* of Theodosius or Justinian. See C.T. and C.J.
P.G.	*Patrologia Graeco-Latina.*
P.L.	*Patrologia Latina.*
P.O.	*Patrologia Orientalis.*
P.S.	*Patrologia Syriaca.*
R.E.J.	*Revue des Etudes Juives.*
R.O.C.	*Revue de l'Orient chrétien.*
S.A.	*Synaxaire Armenien de Ter Israel.*
S.A.J.	*Synaxaire Arabe Jacobite.*
S.C.	*Synaxarium Constantinopolitanum.*
S.E.	*Synaxaire Ethiopien.*
S.G.	*Synaxaire Georgien.*

CHAPTER ONE

THE JEWS IN THE ROMAN WORLD

BIBLIOGRAPHICAL INTRODUCTION

It is not the task of this chapter to survey the whole of the Jewish diaspora, nor to give in any detail the legal, social, and religious position of the Jews under Roman protection. For such a study the reader is referred to the works of Radin and Schürer, and, above all, to the two encyclopædic volumes of Juster, which contain an exhaustive bibliography of the ancient and modern sources of Jewish history throughout the Roman period. For the documents of the pre-Roman period Willrich may also be consulted.

The source material for all such study is mainly Jewish, for the works of Livy and Polybius both present lacunæ covering the sections in which they might be expected to give an impartial Gentile survey of the situation of the Jews. We are left therefore primarily to the Maccabees, to Josephus and to Philo.

As, however, our purpose is not so much to study the general situation of the Jews in the ancient world, as to consider the relations between them and their neighbours which existed before the coming of Christianity, it is more important for us to know the casual references to them in Gentile writers, than to follow their actual history. These references have been collected at various times, but the most complete is that of Reinach, to which reference will be made throughout the chapter. In addition to them we have also to consider the evidence coming from Egyptian papyri, to supplement the work of Philo for our knowledge of the situation of the Jews in Alexandria in the first century A.D.

The main problem set by these references is that of 'classical antisemitism'. The interest in them developed largely in Germany in the desire to prove that antisemitism was something which inevitably accompanied the Jew wherever he went, and which was due to his own racial and unalterable characteristics. This is a view which underlies the work of Willrich, Wilcken and Stähelin, and their work should be read with this in mind. The proclamation of the fragmentary accounts of law-suits between Egyptian Jews and Gentiles before the Roman authorities by Bauer and others as 'Acts of heathen martyrs' reveals this tendency sufficiently obviously, and on this subject the criticism of an expert Hagiologist like Hippolyte Delehaye should be consulted.

While, therefore, the works of the authors mentioned need to be studied for the material they contain, the works of Bell, Hild, Dobschütz, Heinemann and Fuchs provide a more objective perspective of Jewish-Gentile relationships. The work of Hild is of particular value, because of the care with which he considers the date and setting of each comment upon the Jews in Roman authors. How far racial mysticism has penetrated modern German scholarship can be seen from the work of Fuchs, who would appear from his name to be a Jewish author, and who yet states in his introduction that he is unable to find satisfaction in a completely historical account of the events to be considered.

In so far as all these studies wish to generalise on the position of the Jews in the ancient world from an examination of the hostility to which they were undoubtedly subject in certain places and at certain times, they exhibit the weakness of not taking into account the implication of contemporary Jewish missionary activity and its known success. In general they also omit the peculiar character of the Alexandrian situation, and the inevitable difficulties of adjustment of a monotheistic people in a polytheistic world. The work of Fuchs helps for a consideration of the Alexandrian situation, and a detailed consideration of the adjustments made necessary by Jewish monotheism will be found in Juster. For a study of the missionary activity of the Jews, the works of Schürer, Krueger and Foakes Jackson may be indicated. The best study seems to me, however, that of Friedländer. Further references to the missionary activities of ancient Judaism will be found in the bibliographies of the two succeeding chapters.

LIST OF BOOKS

BAUER, A. — *Heidnische Märtyrakten*. Archiv für Papyrus Forschung. Leipzig, 1901.

BELL, H. L. — *Juden und Griechen im Römischen Alexandria*. Supplement to 'Alten Orient', 1926. Jews and Christians in Egypt. British Museum, 1924.

DELEHAYE, H. — *Les Passions des Martyrs et les Genres Litteraires*. Paris, 1905: especially pages 161 ff.

DOBSCHÜTZ, E. VON — *Jews and Gentiles in Ancient Alexandria*. American Journal of Theology, 1904.

FREY, J.-B. — *Les Communautés juives à Rome aux premiers temps de l'Eglise*. Recherches des Sciences Religieuses, 1930 and 1931.

FOAKES JACKSON, F. J. — *Josephus and the Jews*. S.P.C.K. 1931.

FRIEDLÄNDER, M. — *Das Judentum in der vorchristlichen griechischen Welt*. Wien, 1897.

FUCHS, LEO — *Die Juden Aegyptens in Ptolemäischer und Römischer Zeit*. Vienna, 1924.

HEINEMANN, J. — *Antisemitismus*. Pauly Wissowa R.E. supp. 5. 1931.

HILD, J. A. — *Les Juifs à Rome devant l'opinion et dans la litterature*. Revue des Etudes Juives, Vols. VIII and XI.

JOSEPHUS — *Les Antiquités des Juifs*. Ed. T. Reinach. Paris, various dates.
Le ' contre Apion '. Ed. T. Reinach. Paris, 1932.

JUSTER, J. — *Les Juifs dans l'empire Romain*. Paris, 1914, 2 vols.

KRUEGER, P. — *Philo und Josephus als Apologeten der Juden*. Leipzig, 1926.

LA PIANA, G. — *Foreign Groups in Rome*. Harvard University Press, 1927.

PHILO — *Ecrits Historiques*, with an introduction by F. Delaunay. Paris, 1870.

RADIN, M. — *The Jews among the Greeks and Romans*. Jewish Publication Society of America, 1915.

REINACH, T. — *Textes des Auteurs Grecs et Latins relative au Judaisme*. Paris, 1895.

SCHÜRER, E. — *The History of the Jewish People in the time of Jesus Christ*. English translation. Edinburgh, 1901.

STÄHELIN, F. — *Der Antisemitismus des Altertums*. Basle, 1905.

WILCKEN, U. — *Zum Alexandrischen Antisemitismus*. Abhandlung der Kgl. Sächs. Gesellschaft der Wissenschaft, 1909.

WILLRICH, H. — *Juden und Griechen vor der Makkabäischen Erhebung*. Göttingen, 1895.
Judaica. (A continuation of the above.) Göttingen, 1900.

I. ORIGIN AND DISPERSION

Although many histories of the Jews give the impression that during the period which preceded the exiles they were a more or less definable political and racial group, this is, in fact, far from being the case. A careful reading of the Old Testament itself makes it clear that their unity was both politically and racially extremely vague. The Israelites who entered Palestine from the east and brought the religion of Yahweh with them were certainly distinct from the different Hebrew tribes of Palestine whom they subjugated, and on whom they imposed with more or less success their religion.

The boundaries of their authority depended on the prowess of their chieftains, and on the situation of the neighbouring empires. It had nothing to do either with the extent of their actual settlements or with their racial unity. Their religion, the religion of Yahweh, was not the religion of a particular geographical area : it was the religion of a military and priestly aristocracy, and was never (during the period of independence at least) the only religion to be found within the borders of Israelite domination. The Old Testament is full of accounts of the struggle waged by the Israelites against the local 'Baals'; and temples to various gods existed in Jerusalem itself throughout the period of the kingdom[1].

If the religion of Yahweh was never the sole religion of 'Palestine', neither was it ever exclusively confined to Palestine. Sinai, the chosen dwelling of Yahweh Himself, was outside Palestine, and Sinai did not lose its importance even after the construction of the Temple in Jerusalem. It is possible that the original home of the religion was at the mouth of the Euphrates, and that this continued to be a centre of some importance for a considerable period of Old Testament history. Deutero-Isaiah, who in all his prophecies makes no reference to Palestinian history, and who addresses in turn Jerusalem and the coast-lands, may have been a Yahwist from this area. But, even if Palestine was the chief centre of Yahwism, it was spread abroad long before the

[1] Cf. Godbey, *The Lost Tribes a Myth*, pp. 105-110.

Christian era by the trading and military stations scattered through western Asia and north-east Africa. Though Palestine itself was a primarily agricultural country, and though it is unlikely that many of its inhabitants were engaged in trade in the early days of its settlement by the Israelites, yet certain trade relations were cultivated by Solomon and his successors[1], and a certain number of worshippers of Yahweh would be likely to be found in the trading companies of the neighbouring mercantile states of the coast. In addition to these probable trading centres, there were certain military stations held by Israelites both in the Assyrian and in the Egyptian empires. In Elephantine and on the edge of Cyrenaica there were Israelite soldiers even before the final fall of the Jewish Kingdoms, and in the third century the Syrian Kings established others in Phrygia. The different exiles contributed to create another group of settlements in western Asia, some agricultural, some military, some of a mixed constituency[2].

In accordance with the usual practice in the ancient world, as soon as any of these settlements became sufficiently large and permanent, a cultus centre would be established[3], and the requisite privileges for worship would be obtained from the local authorities, or from the central ruler himself. If, as was the case, for example, in the military stations, the privileges obtained were considerable, there would be a steady demand from the other inhabitants of the settlement for admission to the fellowship or family of Yahweh, so that every one of these centres became also a nucleus for proselytising surrounding areas. In addition to the possible privileges which adoption into the family of Yahweh entailed, the purity of Jewish religion must have exercised a powerful influence upon the best elements with which it came into contact.

[1] I Kings ix, 26 and xxii, 48 refer to sea traffic, and x, 28-29 refers to land traffic in horses. These references are more reliable evidence of Israelite participation in the Mediterranean trade than the earlier allusions in Genesis xlix, 13, and Judges v, 17, which are not only in conflict with each other and Deuteronomy xxxiii, 18-20, but credit tribes with sea power at a period when it is almost certain that they did not possess the coast towns.

[2] For a survey of the Jewish settlements in the Roman Empire see Schürer, Div. II, Vol. II, § 31, p. 219 ff.

[3] *Ibid.* p. 253.

Relics of this proselytism are to be found even to-day in the existence of Jewish customs among many Asiatic and African peoples from China to the Gold Coast, who are certainly not Semitic ; and the famous Jewish nose seems to be of Hittite rather than Semitic origin[1].

Of the actual conditions of these settlements, and the conditions of the admission of proselytes in different parts very little is known. A detailed picture of Jewish life in the diaspora is possible only in the period in which the majority of Jews were living under Roman rule. That they were already very widely dispersed is shown by the remark of Strabo that the Jews ' have already settled in every city, and it is not easy to find any spot on the earth which this tribe has not occupied and where it has not asserted itself[2]', or that of the Jewish Sybil: ' the whole earth, and the sea also, is full of them[3]'.

II. FIRST CONTACTS WITH ROME AND PRIVILEGES IN THE EMPIRE

The Jews first came into contact with the Romans at the time of the Maccabees, and in 162 B.C. an embassy was sent to Rome to invite their alliance against Demetrius of Syria[4]. This the Romans, on the principle of *divide et impera*, were prepared to do, and Rome remained on friendly terms with Judaea until in 65 B.C. Pompey, passing through Syria after his conquest of Mithridates and Tigranes, reduced it to a Roman province and so removed the necessity of a treaty relationship with an independent people. In 63 B.C., under the pretext of settling a disputed succession, he re-entered Judaea and captured Jerusalem. Hyrcanus was made High Priest, under Roman protection, but his political power was curtailed and Judaea was placed under the general supervision of the governor of Syria. This situation lasted until

[1] See Godbey, *op. cit.*, Chapters ix-xv.

[2] Strabo, quoted in Josephus, *Ant.*, XIV, 7, 2, §115 (beginning of 1st cent. B.C.).

[3] *Orac. Sybil*, iii, 271 (2nd cent. B.C.). For a study of the work known as the ' Jewish Sybil ' see Schürer, *op. cit.*, Div. II, Vol. III, p. 271 ff.

[4] I Mac. viii, 22.

the time of Julius Caesar, when in return for the support of the Jews a certain measure of their political power was restored to them, only to disappear again with the appointment of a Roman governor by Tiberius, an event itself followed within less than half a century by the destruction of Jerusalem and the obliteration of the political separateness of the Jews altogether.

Long before this final destruction arrived, and while the centre of political relationships was still Jerusalem, the Jews in the diaspora succeeded, through the influence of the Maccabees, in securing important privileges from the Roman authorities[1]. Already in 161 B.C. they had obtained for all Jews within the Roman dominions the status of *peregrini*[2], which allowed them to be judged by their own law, and to follow their own customs in such matters as marriage or inheritance. They then asked for, and about 110 B.C. succeeded in obtaining, the same privileges for Jews resident in all kingdoms and states allied with Rome, under pain of Roman displeasure[3]. Such privileges were independent of the question of citizenship, which was already possessed by the Jews in many of the cities of Asia, Syria, and elsewhere.

All these privileges were confirmed by Julius Caesar in a general permission to 'live according to their own laws'. This formed the *magna carta* of the Jews in the Roman Empire, being frequently reaffirmed in general terms by subsequent emperors[4]. This toleration is generally expressed by historians in the phrase that Judaism was ' religio licita '. The phrase is not a legal one, and is first used by Tertullian (*Apolog*. 21). In Roman law the Jews formed a ' collegium ' rather than a ' religio '; and as such had the right to retain their own observances. There was nothing exceptional in the actual giving of these privileges, for in so doing the Romans were only following their usual custom of granting the greatest possible local autonomy to the different parts of their empire. The average minority policy of a modern European state would have appeared to any Roman statesman an incon-

[1] For the complete collection of these see Juster, Vol. I, Intro., sec. iii; also Schürer, *op. cit.*, Div. II, Vol. III, p. 257.

[2] I Mac. viii, 22.

[3] Josephus, *Ant.*, XIII, 9, 2, and XIV, 10, 22.

[4] Juster, *op. cit.*, Chapter I, sec. i.

ceivable folly. Privileges granted to the Jews, however, very soon revealed a one-sided character. To allow them to live according to their own law was in essence to allow them the undisturbed worship of their own God. A society accustomed to polytheism granted this permission without great difficulty, and even before the followers of Yahweh appeared claiming privileges already granted to others, Rome was the centre of many eastern cults which, in spite of occasional official repression, grew and flourished in mutual toleration. Such a policy was general in the ancient world, and the Jews in the days of their independence had themselves allowed foreign cults to settle in Jerusalem; and every trade agreement they made was accompanied by permission to the trader to worship his own God in the quarter of the town allotted to him[1].

But as the principle of monotheism was by this time firmly established in Judaism, the granting of toleration to the Jews became a granting of unique favours which could not be compared to those granted to others. ' The principle of religious liberty was very widely respected in the ancient world. It was not difficult, because the Gods of the nations were exceedingly tolerant of each other. It was only the God of the Jews who was haughty and aloof. The tolerance he readily received he did not extend to others. In his supreme jealousy he hindered his followers from the accomplishment of many acts which were obligatory among the different nations. To give toleration to Yahweh was to suppress in favour of the Jews the punishment to which the omission of these acts exposed them. The laws had to be suspended in their favour. Special privileges had to be granted them—for an exception in favour of a minority is a privilege. But to refuse this toleration was to run counter to the ancient principle of tolerance, and was to render the practice of Judaism impossible. This was the dilemma: persecution or privilege[2].'

The Jews had to be permitted not only not to offer sacrifices to the Gods, but also to adopt a special form for their expression of loyalty to the emperor. They could neither burn incense to his *numen* nor accept his statues in

[1] Cf. I Kings xi, 31-33.

[2] Quoted from Juster, *op. cit.*, Vol. I, p. 213.

their synagogues. Moreover, they had to ask for exemption from offices which involved them in official worship of the Gods or of the emperor. It is a much disputed question whether the Jews were ever employed by the Romans in the army. They were granted exemption by Caesar, and may have always retained it. Jerome says of them that 'it is no wonder that they have lost their manly bearing, for they are not admitted to the army, or allowed to bear swords or carry other arms[1]'. On the other hand, as independent units they were highly prized by the western Asiatic empires and by the Egyptians. In such a situation it was easier for them to observe their religion. It was the individual Jew in a non-Jewish legion who presented difficulties[2]. As to the general Jewish population in Rome itself, on occasions when bread was given out on the Sabbath they were allowed to receive theirs on the following day. When oil was distributed which was connected with idolatry, they received a money compensation.

These special privileges the Jews enjoyed throughout the empire, independent of whether they were citizens either of a particular city or of Rome itself. A large number of Jews probably did not possess the status of citizen until the edict of Caracalla extended it to all inhabitants of the empire. Wherever the individual Jew might be, these privileges depended on relations established between Rome and Judaea. Even after the destruction of the Temple, and of any form of Jewish political autonomy, the Jews still continued to be regarded as a nation by the Romans, and the authority in religious matters of the Patriarch of Jerusalem was still recognised as covering all Jews within the Roman empire. He is always called Patriarch 'of the Jews' and not 'of Judaea[3]'. Until the war of A.D. 68 he was allowed to receive the 'didrachm' from all Jews within the empire, and even at times when the export of gold was forbidden the Jews were allowed to send what amounted to considerable sums to Jerusalem[4].

[1] Jerome, *On Isaiah*, iii, 2, in P.L., Vol. XXIV, p. 59.

[2] For a full discussion see Juster, Vol. II, Ch. XXI, sec. ii.

[3] Juster, *op. cit.*, Vol. I, p. 391.

[4] Cf. Cic., *pro Flacco*, lxvi-lxix. One of the charges against Flaccus was his confiscation of this offering to the Temple.

After the destruction of Jerusalem this sum was changed into a special Jewish tax which, as a crowning insult, was paid to the treasury of Jupiter Capitolinus. Thence it filtered into a special department of the imperial treasury. It is probable that this tax was continued throughout the duration of the empire, though we only know of its existence up to the third century. In the second century the Jews were allowed to take a new voluntary collection for the authorities in Palestine, the 'aurum coronarium', which in its turn was confiscated by the Christian emperors.

In addition, the Patriarch had the right to nominate the chief officers of the different Jewish communities, and was the supreme judge in all religious matters. He was considered by the Roman authorities equivalent in rank to a high Roman official, and some Patriarchs were even on intimate terms with the emperors themselves. To maintain his contact with the widely scattered communities under his control, there was a regular system of envoys or 'apostles' who had authority to represent him and to collect his taxes. The word 'apostle' first appears after A.D. 70, and is perhaps taken from the Christians, but the office certainly existed earlier. This regularly established link between Jerusalem and the diaspora was of particular importance during the time of organised hostility to the early Church. Concerted plans could be made and consistent action followed in many parts at once.

It seems strange that this internal freedom continued after the long struggle between Rome and the Jews which, beginning with the war in Judaea, lasted with interruptions well into the second century. But apart from the confiscation of the didrachm, the Romans seem to have left the Jews scattered throughout their possessions completely in peace, and they in their turn do not seem to have taken any part in the struggle. It is not until the time of the Christian emperors that their status suffers any alteration. With their social position the situation is different. They could not expect to retain their popularity, even if the Romans were sufficiently generous to allow them their legal rights, and we shall find a new and more hostile attitude to things Jewish in the times following the war of 68.

III. OCCUPATIONS

The Jewish religion and the privileges which it necessitated naturally brought a certain prominence to the Jewish people. But it can be easily exaggerated. Their position in the Roman world had very little in common with their life in mediaeval ghettos or even in modern cities. In the main they were indistinguishable from the other inhabitants of the Mediterranean cities. They were not the only ' orientals ', and they were of the same race and appearance as the Syrians and the Phœnicians who had been dwelling in Greece, Italy and Spain for centuries. They lived in groups, for the convenience of synagogue worship and of common life, but so did the other foreign groups in all the great cities of the empire. But whereas the modern Jew is distinguished often by his profession, and the mediaeval Jew had not only profession but dress to mark him, and both often presented physical characteristics strange to all the rest of the population of the locality, none of these distinguishing marks separated the Jew of the Roman empire from the rest of its inhabitants. It is impossible to say of any profession in the empire that the bulk of those who followed it were Jews, or conversely that the bulk of the Jews followed that profession. They followed all professions. The immense majority were in relatively humble walks of society, since a large proportion of them began their life in the diaspora as slaves. A large number were occupied with agriculture, particularly in the East, in Asia, the Euphrates valley and Egypt. In Europe it was probably only slaves who followed agriculture for the simple reason that it was almost exclusively a slave occupation. But in the East there were free colonists, planted at different periods by different empires. We hear of them in all sorts of artisan occupations, especially dyeing, silk weaving and glass-making, and in various trades and commercial occupations, but the latter was not a predominantly Jewish characteristic—' Jamais un auteur païen ne les caractérisa comme marchands, jamais à l'époque païenne ces deux notions—Juif et marchand—ne vont ensemble comme de soi-même[1] '.

[1] Juster, Vol. II, p. 312. The whole of this section on the economic position of the Jews in the Roman empire is of great value.

Still less can we say that the Jews were largely occupied with finance. The kind of financial activities which were known to the Roman world were primitive and unproductive. They were for the purpose of display, and for the purchase of political favours, and not for the development of industry. The borrowers were cities and the sprigs of the nobility, and the lenders—who would certainly have welcomed no oriental rivals—were the Roman knightly aristocracy. There is one reference which is triumphantly acclaimed as the 'klassische Ausdruck' of the unchangeability of Jewish characteristics by Wilcken. An Alexandrian merchant, Serapion, writes to a friend in financial difficulties and warns him above all to 'keep clear of the Jews[1]'. It is evident that it is a money-lender who is in question, and we know from Philo that such existed at Alexandria, but the letter dates from a time of violent political feeling, and in any case it is never safe to generalise from an individual case of whose setting we are absolutely ignorant. Moreover, if the half-humorous cynicism of Hadrian is to be trusted, it would be wise to keep clear of all money-lenders in Egypt; for in asking a friend why he had imagined he would ever find religions to interest him (Hadrian) in Egypt, he summarises the Egyptian character thus: 'the one God in Egypt is money. It is worshipped by the Christians, by the Jews, and by everybody else[2]'.

From the various sources available we have collected a considerable amount of information on Jewish occupations, but it almost all comes from inscriptions, from chance papyri, and hardly ever from polemical literature. The satirists Juvenal and Martial make great fun of Jewish beggars, but their descriptions of Jews are no more comprehensive than their descriptions—equally vulgar—of Greeks and Romans, and apart from the satirists the only occupation which interested the classical world seems to have been their ardour in making converts. Jewish occupations as such were not the basis of Jewish unpopularity, where such existed.

[1] *Griechische Urkunden*, Berlin, IV, 1097.

[2] Reinach, No. 182.

IV. GREEK AND ALEXANDRIAN OPINION OF THE JEWS

The Jews were almost the last of the Semitic peoples to become known to the Mediterranean world. It is probable that it was not until the last days of the independent kingdom that they began to take any extensive part in the trade around them, and since they neither possessed the sea coast nor lay on any of the great trade routes which hugged the coast, it is not surprising that they appear to have escaped notice until the time of Alexander the Great. From then onwards there exist a considerable number of references to them, some showing actual knowledge, some none, and some showing definite prejudice and dislike.

The first thing which attracted outside attention was naturally their religion. Theophrastus, Clearchus and Hermippus, writers of the third century, consider them to be a race of philosophers. The first, after an extremely mixed and inaccurate description of Jewish sacrifices, says that the most interesting thing is that, ' being by nature philosophers, during the sacrifice, they discuss the divine nature with each other'. Clearchus relates that in India philosophers were called ' Calani ' (presumably Brahmins), and in Syria, ' Jews '. Hermippus considers that Pythagoras learned his philosophy from the Jews. The story reappears as late as Diogenes Laertius in the third century A.D.[1] This picture of the Jews as philosophers was also quoted with disapproval. For they exhibited two characteristics which easily displeased the later Greek philosophers and sophists. They were excessively intolerant, and they combined with their philosophy a number of observances which could only seem the grossest superstition to the Greek world. This disapproval was natural, for whereas the Greek intellectual stood in sharp opposition to the simple-minded Greek who worshipped the Gods, the Jewish ' philosophers ', in other words the teachers in the Jewish synagogues, believed intensely in the Jewish religion. Later sophists, therefore, found them hateful to Gods and men in their intolerance, and lent a readier ear to the tales of a very different kind which also appeared in the third century. The entire collection of stories by which the

[1] Reinach, Nos. 5, 7, 14 and 98.

negative characteristic of intolerance was transformed into a positive characteristic of hostility to all humanity can be traced to a single source, Alexandria. Thence come all the slanders which later writers repeat, and which Tacitus made familiar to the whole Roman world and to our day.

The city of Alexandria was the most permanent monument which Alexander the Great bequeathed to posterity. After his death Egypt was seized by his brilliant general Ptolemy, who shortly afterwards added Palestine also to his dominions. At the beginning of his reign Alexandria was still almost unpopulated, and as the conquerors mistrusted the native Egyptians, the city was largely settled with foreign elements, Greek, Syrian and Jewish. It appears, in fact, that the Jews were specially encouraged to settle there, and they soon filled one of the five divisions of the city, and overflowed into a second. Of these different foreign elements the Jews were the best known to the local Egyptians. Not only were there Jewish settlements in Egypt itself which had been, at intervals at least, unpopular with the Egyptian hierarchy, but Palestine was a near neighbour. The Egyptian intelligentsia must have been familiar with the Jewish story of the Exodus, which was celebrated annually in the Feast of the Passover. It was not a story calculated to flatter Egyptian pride. At what stage they provided themselves with an alternative version we do not know, but shortly after the settlement of Alexandria it appears in full detail. The first time it is recounted, by Hecataeus of Abdera, it is in no way insulting to the Jews. Its main purpose is obviously to defend the honour of the Egyptians. Egypt was suffering from a pestilence. The Gods ordered them to purify the country by expelling all foreigners. This was done, and some went to Greece under the leadership of Danaos and Cadmus, but the bulk went to the nearer country of Palestine. Offended at this treatment, Moses, ' a man distinguished by his wisdom and courage ', who led the migration to Palestine, founded a society deliberately hostile to all foreigners[1]. The story rapidly became more malevolent. Manetho, an Egyptian priest who wrote a short time later, attributes the plague from which Egypt suffered exclusively to the foreigners. The emigrants were all lepers and criminals. The Egyptians

[1] Reinach, No. 9.

themselves had not suffered from the disease[1]. In this form, as an explanation of Jewish ' misanthropy ', it is repeated by Poseidonius of Apamea[2], by Apollonius Molon[3], and is given full expression by Tacitus[4].

Having once begun, the Alexandrian writers soon found the means to embroider these stories in which the Jews were presented in an unfavourable light. The previous stories may have been originally Egyptian legends of the Exodus. The later are pure inventions. The Jews worshipped the head of an ass; and they ritually indulged in cannibalism. It is perhaps natural that Egypt, with its animal-headed deities, should have evolved the story of the worship of an ass-headed deity by the Jews. The choice of an ass is significantly Egyptian. The Greek or Roman would have found it absurd to represent a deity with the head of any animal, but nothing particularly disagreeable attached itself to the idea of an ass. In fact, the beast was held in some honour both in Rome and elsewhere. To the Jews it was an animal to be ridden by a king. But in Egypt it was considered as unclean. The story first appears in an unknown writer whose name was apparently Mnaseas, a pupil of Eratosthenes, a president of the Academy of Alexandria[5]. The story is repeated with variations some half a dozen times, and is also quoted by Tacitus. The other story is from another unknown writer, Damocritus. Once in seven years the Jews catch a Greek, fatten him and eat him. Apion makes the story more living by introducing the actual Greek victim to Antiochus Epiphanes during his visit to the Temple, and by making him himself recount his tragic fate[6].

With these stories in the air, it is easy to see how the negative exclusiveness of the Jews was attributed to malevolence and how this malevolence could be translated into active hostility, as when Lysimachus (also of Alexandria) alleges that they are commanded to overthrow and destroy all altars and temples—a charge which was true enough of

[1] Reinach, Nos. 10 and 11.
[2] *Ibid.*, No. 25.
[3] *Ibid.*, No. 27.
[4] Tac., *Hist.*, V, i. Reinach, No. 81.
[5] Reinach, No. 19.
[6] *Ibid.*, Nos. 60 and 63, D.2.

the old independent days in Palestine itself, but which happened outside Palestine on rare occasions and under special provocation. But it is evident that something more than literary activity was required to keep these stories alive. This was provided by contemporary life in Alexandria. Unhappy would be the people whose conduct had to be judged exclusively by their behaviour in that turbulent city. Neither Greek, Christian nor Jew would find his reputation enhanced by such a test. Certainly it would be an unhappy ground to choose for a defence of the Jewish character. Of the history of the city during the Ptolemaic period we have little information, but the sources, both in papyri and elsewhere, are considerable for a reconstruction of the situation in early Roman times. The Jews occupy a good deal of the foreground of the picture. The original reason for their unpopularity has already been suggested. They were a foreign element introduced at the beginning, at a time of suspicion on the part of the native inhabitants, and an element which came armed with an exceedingly unpleasant story of the past behaviour of the Egyptians. Further, they were undoubtedly prominent in the commercial life of the city. To what extent it is impossible to form an exact estimate. Many were occupied in the farming of the taxes and royal domains. At least later papyri speak of such people with names which suggest a Jewish origin. But a word of caution is necessary. Not all Semitic names were Jewish in Alexandria, and not all Jews bore Semitic names. The statement can only be a general one, and left at that.

The irritation caused by their commercial prominence was accentuated by a third factor. They were apparently not citizens of Alexandria. This is a point which has been much debated, though it is irrelevant to the present issue. But the letter of Claudius, following the troubles in A.D. 38, which has been recently discovered[1] seems to settle the question definitely against the theory that they were citizens. But in return they possessed powerful privileges, and even a senate of their own, a right denied to the city as a whole. The presence of a group, powerful both numerically and commercially, but taking no part in the common life of the city, was bound to be a source of jealousy and friction. It perpetually

[1] H. I. Bell, *Jews and Christians in Egypt*.

marked out the Jew as having interests other than those of the rest of the inhabitants, and at the same time it would give the Jews themselves a permanent feeling of malaise which would not tend to promote peaceful relations. We know that the Jews attempted to obtain both citizenship and a share of the public life of the city.

The refusal of this would have embittered the situation in any surroundings, but there was yet another reason in both Ptolemaic and Roman Alexandria to make the distinction of the Jews a source of trouble. The Jews had received many privileges from the Ptolemies and were loyal to them. The native Egyptians in Alexandria disliked the new Greek dynasty. When the Romans appeared, the Jews deserted the Ptolemies for the Romans, an action which was not necessarily dishonourable, for the Romans had always been friendly to the Jews elsewhere, and one of the difficulties of their situation in Alexandria was that, as they were not citizens, they still felt more Jews than Alexandrians. But the Romans were hated not only by the Egyptian population of the city but by all the rest, for by its conquest Alexandria ceased to be a capital city of an independent state, and became merely the seat of a governor subordinate to Rome.

For the trouble which arose in the time of Caligula our information, though still all reported through the Jewish eyes of Philo and Josephus, is extensive, and the situation which is revealed was one which the emperor Claudius could without exaggeration characterise as being a war between the Jews and the rest of the population.

While it is unquestionable that the blame lay on both sides, and that each side provoked the other, the result, even in the mouth of the great Jewish philosopher of Alexandria, Philo, is to give a thoroughly unpleasant picture of the general standard of the Jewish population of the city. The fact that the picture is unintentional gives it more significance. After describing the rioting and the appalling massacres of Jews of every age and sex, he adds: ' but what was worse than the looting was that business came to a standstill. Money-lenders lost the securities of their loans '. It is true that he adds that farmers, sailors, merchants and artisans could also not carry on their business, but the prominent place given to the first category is distressing, and gives a weight it would not otherwise deserve to the remark of Serapion to his business friend in trouble which has already been quoted. But while admitting that the picture thus given of the Alexandrian Jew is all that the most ardent antisemitic writer could demand, it must be repeated that no other group really comes out with any better reputation. Hadrian's summary gives the true perspective. But happily Alexandria is not typical of the ancient world.

V. THE JEWS IN THE GREEK CITIES

Our knowledge of the relations of the Jews with the inhabitants of the Greek cities of the eastern Mediterranean has mainly come to us through references in the *Antiquities* of Josephus. The Jews had secured that all the privileges which they possessed from the Romans they should also possess in the Greek cities allied with Rome, and here it was specific privileges rather than any general ill-feeling which seems to have been responsible for such trouble as there was. These cities were great commercial centres, and very wealthy. The Jewish immunity from sharing the burdens of offices which conflicted with their religious principles might escape unnoticed in the Roman empire as a whole. It could only arouse animosity in a city state.

But there was a second grievance, the money which the Jews of every city sent to Jerusalem, and which appears to have been by no means an ' invisible export '. From Josephus we learn that the cities of Ephesus and Sardis, the provinces of Asia, Libya and Cyrene, and the islands of Delos and Paros had prohibited this export, but without success, for on appeal the Jews obtained from Rome the cancellation of the prohibition[1]. While the edicts quoted by Josephus present certain difficulties as to text, there seems no reason for doubting the substantial accuracy of the situation they describe, and, indeed, it would be surprising if there were not resentment at the draining of considerable sums from the cities' resources for such a purpose, especially as all the

[1] Jos., *Ant.*, XIV, 213, and XVI, 160.

cases are quoted from the end of the first century B.C., when the long period of civil war must have had a serious effect upon their finances.

Apart from these cases of hostility Josephus mentions only one other. There was trouble at Caesarea, a city which the Jews considered as a Jewish foundation of Herod, but which the Syrians claimed as a much older Syrian settlement, in which, therefore, the Jews had no right to behave as though they owned it[1]. In general the Greek and oriental cities were the greatest field of Jewish proselytism, and such implies fairly friendly relations. In the second half of the first century A.D. the situation changed, but until that time we can presume that the Jews normally lived in fairly good relations with both the Greeks and the Syrians.

VI. ROMAN OPINION OF THE JEWS

It was customary among the philosophers and political thinkers of the Roman Empire, as it is among certain Hellenists of to-day, to lay the blame for the decline of Greek and Roman morality on the invasion of eastern religions which continued steadily throughout her history from the time when Rome came first into contact with the eastern world. There may be a certain element of truth in the assertion, but the Greek and Roman worlds collapsed morally through their own inherent weaknesses. Lucretius, struggling passionately to believe his own theory that nothing existed but matter—and failing to do so—owed his despair to no corrupting eastern mystery religion; and Virgil, the most spiritual and mystical of the Roman poets, shows in his gentle melancholy no trace of eastern influence. Sections of the Semitic and oriental world did introduce morally degrading religions into the west, but it was not the Jewish section. Tacitus, with his statement that the Christians distinguished themselves for their ' odium generis humani ', prevents us from taking seriously his statement that Jewish converts were taught to hate their country and their family. Otherwise the only specific accusation against the Jews is not that they were

[1] Jos., *Ant.*, XX, 173.

corrupting society, but that they were utterly exclusive. As Juvenal says:

> ' Romanas autem soliti contemnere leges
> Judaicum ediscunt et servant. et metuent jus
> Tradidit arcano quodcumque volumine Moses:
> Non monstrare vias eadem nisi sacra colenti;
> Quaesitum in fontem solum deducere verpos[1].'

This accusation is indeed constant throughout the period, but it can scarcely be called a method of degrading Roman civilisation.

It is easy enough to understand that the Romans did not at once distinguish between Judaism and the other oriental cults which had penetrated into Roman society. They appear at first to have confused Yahweh Sabaoth with 'Sabazius', a Syrian epithet of Dionysus, and to have believed the Jews to be worshippers of 'Jupiter Sabazius'. As such they were expelled from Rome in 139 B.C. by the Praetor Peregrinus, Cn. Cornelius Hispalus[2]. It seems probable that the Jews so expelled were not dwellers in Rome, but an embassy from the Maccabees. This action did not, however, change the friendship which already existed between the Romans and the Maccabeans. After these incidents silence falls for nearly a century. During this time the Jews must have established some kind of settlement in Rome, for they appear to be already powerful and organised by the time of Cicero. By this time events in Judaea had changed the whole situation. Pompey took Jerusalem in 63 B.C., and the independent relations between Rome and Judaea came to an end. But the conquerors showed moderation, and though Pompey was never forgiven by the Jews for having violated the Temple, the friendship between the Jews and the Romans persisted, and was generously rewarded by Julius Caesar.

The period of the Herods was one in which the Jews enjoyed complete security under Roman protection. Representatives of the royal house were for long periods in Rome and knew how to adopt all the popular vices of Roman high

[1] Juv., *Sat.*, xiv, 100. Reinach, No. 172.

[2] Reinach, No. 141.

society. In Palestine itself, outside Jerusalem, rose magnificent Roman buildings of all kinds dedicated to the emperor. The Jewish upper classes cultivated Roman friendship and the Roman way of life. The future seemed secure. And yet within twenty years the whole picture changed, and Rome and Judaea were engaged in a war which taxed the resources of the empire itself. To understand this change we must pass from the life and ambitions of the Romanised Jewish aristocracy to the preoccupations and longings of the rank and file and the religious leaders of the Jewish people. Whatever was the opinion of the politicians and priests, neither the Pharisees nor the ordinary people felt anything but hatred for the Roman rule. The Pharisees acquiesced because under that rule they were allowed the privileges essential for the continuation of Judaism, but they only acquiesced so long as that condition was observed. A threat to their law, and they were ready to take up the national cause at once. In fact the peace was a very brittle one. It depended on a great deal of tact on both sides, and tact was not a conspicuous characteristic either of the Jews or of the Roman governors. The New Testament records several 'incidents', and it is probable that a multiplication of these would in the end have led to war. But it was precipitated by the flood of Messiahs who sprang up in the first half of the first century A.D. The causes of the emergence of so much Messianic unrest have often been missed. It was not merely a reaction against the loss of national sovereignty. It was brought about by the fact that according to the calendar in use among the Jews at that time, the coming of the Messianic age was expected about the middle of the first century[1]. One essential factor of that age would inevitably be the disappearance of the Roman authority in Palestine. Many of the followers of Jesus expected Him to lead them against Rome, and both before and after His time there were many attempted risings which were crushed by the Romans with increasing severity. Under such circumstances, it is amazing that outside Palestine the Romans showed the moderation to leave Jewish privileges untouched, especially as the troubles in Palestine were spasmodically accompanied by

[1] See *Messianic Speculation in Israel*, by Dr A. H. Silver. Macmillan, 1927, especially p. 16 ff.

serious troubles in various other eastern provinces of the empire.

The change in the situation in Palestine itself was soon reflected in Rome. There is an immense difference in tone between the references to the Jews in the Augustan age and in the second half of the century. While Horace and Ovid laughed at them good humouredly, Juvenal and Martial found them contemptible and detestable[1]. It is very unfortunate that the references to Jewish history which existed in Livy and Polybius are in the portion of the works of those authors which are lost. But it is extremely doubtful if we should find the same bitterness in them that we find in Seneca and Tacitus[2].

VII. JEWISH MISSIONARY ACTIVITY

The general ferment in the Jewish world which this Messianic excitement occasioned both drew especial attention to the Jewish religion and accentuated among the Jews their activity as missionaries. Both were a menace to their security. We have seen that Judaism remained at best something incomprehensible to the Roman world. It would have been astonishing that philosophers did not appreciate it had they not been quite unaccustomed to the combination of ethics of which they could approve, with ritual and theological presuppositions which they associated only with superstition. The universalism of the Jewish conception of God seemed in complete contradiction with the intolerance of Jewish religious practice. As soon as the situation became troubled it was natural that it was the bad and incomprehensible side which dominated the situation. Such being the case, it was evident that once the loyalty of the Jews to Rome was doubted all the reputation which they had enjoyed in Roman estimation tumbled down like a house of cards. The glamour removed, all that the Roman saw was a people who disbelieved in the Gods, who despised Roman ways, who were gloomy and fanatical, exclusive and intolerant. The crimes of individual Jews became, as is always the case in

[1] Hild, *op. cit.*, R.E.J., Vol. XI, p. 38. Reinach, Nos. 131, 134 and 172.

[2] Hild, *op. cit.*, R.E.J., Vol. VIII, p. 11, and Vol. XI, p. 39.

such situations, the crime of the whole people. They were a rabble of aliens, fortune-tellers and charlatans, and a menace to the morality of the Roman people.

To complete the picture of the situation it is necessary to look at it from the other side, and to consider the attitude of the Jews to the Gentiles during this period. The Jews were not in an easy position. As long as they lived in an independent community it was possible for them to possess a conception of life in complete variance with that of their contemporaries without it seriously affecting the daily life of the individual Jew. It is noticeable that as long as this period lasts they are spoken of by pagan writers with admiration and respect. But for the Jews living in the diaspora the situation was different. Life was impossible without definite privileges. The demand for these privileges was the first cause of friction in the Greco-Roman world. The genius of Julius Caesar, and the continuation of his policy by Augustus, seemed at first to have solved the problem. We have already seen how brittle the solution was. Even so it might have lasted had the exclusiveness of the Jews been really a fact. If their attitude to their neighbours had been the haughty contempt for Gentiles to be found in parts of the Talmud, the Roman might have tolerated it with an amused contempt on his side also. But all that we know of the period shows that the attitude of the Jews was the exact opposite to this aloof indifference. They were enthusiastic missionaries of their religion, and this fact was the final and in some ways the most important cause of the destruction of their security. For this they were expelled from Rome in 139 B.C. They were expelled again by Tiberius, and again by Claudius. Even in the middle of the wars at the end of the first century the Flavians had to take measures to make the circumcision of Gentiles a capital offence. In the whole of Jewish history contempt for the non-Jew was never less in evidence than in the century which saw the foundation of Christianity. That the Apostles themselves, who were Jews, that Paul, who claimed to be a Pharisee, could consider as they did the question of Gentile observance of the Law is evidence of this. The references to the interest taken by Greeks and Romans in Judaism are legion[1]. The foundations of the Gentile

[1] Reinach, Nos. 51, 99, 101 and 145.

Church were laid almost exclusively among proselytes or people already interested in Judaism. The transition by which these groups passed from partial membership of Judaism to full membership of the Christian Church was an easy one. Had the synagogues of the diaspora insisted primarily on the ritual and not the moral and ethical implications of Judaism, on observance of the letter rather than the spirit of the Law, it is doubtful if this transition would ever have taken place except in a few individual cases. What Christianity offered them was not something completely different, but the same thing with, in addition, the power of Jesus Christ in place of the disadvantages of circumcision and other ritual prescriptions.

The Romans were always suspicious of the activities of eastern missionaries in Rome, and the Jews were not the only people concerned. But the Jewish proselyte seemed particularly dangerous to the security of the empire because he was an ' atheist '. This did not so much mean a believer in no God, as a disbeliever in the Gods of the state. It had nothing to do with the absence of images in Jewish worship. It was not an irreligious attitude, but one which escaped being seditious only by the granting of special privileges. All that was required for conformity to the state religion was to scatter a few grains of incense upon an altar, and to obtain a certificate, easily granted, that this had been done. To refuse so simple an act of fellowship with society, one might almost say of common courtesy to one's neighbours, seemed to show a strangely malignant character. One was not asked to believe anything. One was only asked to conform to a political convention. And the Jews, and later the Christians, were the only people who refused. Whatever Seneca or Tacitus might think of this courage from the standpoint of their philosophies, they could only condemn it as men of action and Roman officials, and consider that to allow such a religion to spread was an act of supreme folly. To chastise it with the scorpions of ridicule, to repeat the accusations of a Manetho or an Apion was an act of political wisdom, whether the accusations were well founded or not.

It was therefore not the actual principles of the Jewish religion, but the effervescence of Messianism and the missionary proclivities of the Jews in the diaspora which destroyed the peace between Rome and Judaism. The numerical and political strength of the Jews embittered and prolonged the struggle when it came. It did not cause it. The struggle left bad blood on both sides, but essentially the advent of Christianity to power removed all the causes of the conflict. For the reasons which inspired the Jews inspired also the Christians, and the victory of the Christian attitude to ' atheism ' and to missionary activity should have brought political peace to the Jews. Instead, the advent of Christianity perpetuated their tragedy. The reasons for this have nothing to do with the old enmities. They are to be found only in the conflict of Christianity with its parent religion.

CHAPTER TWO

THE CLASH WITH CHRISTIANITY

BIBLIOGRAPHICAL INTRODUCTION

The narrative of this chapter turns mainly upon the account given in Mark and in the Acts of the Apostles of the ministry of Jesus and the development of the early Church. It is claimed that these narratives give a logical, reasonable and satisfying picture of what occurred, and it cannot be too strongly urged that the main sources to be consulted are the narratives themselves, approached with an open mind instead of with some particular modern theory as to their corruption. While modern exegesis has rendered incalculable services to the elucidation of the texts, it has become so complicated and contradictory that we are in perpetual danger of forgetting that a reasonable amount of inaccuracy and forgetfulness on the part of their authors may be allowed without any need for a logical reason being given for this carelessness. The danger of the modern approach is nowhere more conspicuous than when it is the general atmosphere and picture of the original narrative which is under consideration, and not the exact implication of this or that point of detail.

This plea is urged, not with the intention of claiming any originality for my approach or conclusions, but because it is impossible to survey and assess all the different theories which might invalidate them. Something, however, needs to be said of the two books which have been mainly quoted. The essential accuracy of the historical narrative of Mark is defended by Burkitt, and I see no reason to forsake his conclusions for the new German theory of authentic scraps of teaching set in an imaginary framework, which is presented by Rawlinson. That so logical a development as Mark presents happened fortuitously seems to me impossible. And if it is not fortuitous, then, whether the author received it from eye-witnesses or together with the scraps of teaching, seems to me an utterly unimportant issue. The same is true of the narrative of Acts. In both cases to imagine the framework to be a late composition embodying older traditions is to ascribe to the authors a prophetic realisation that people would one day wish to know exactly how the opposition between Judaism and Christianity arose, and a determination to answer the question, and this seems an entirely gratuitous complication of the problem. Further to consider that authors, writing an imaginary skeleton at a time when relations between Jews and Christians were at their worst, deliberately invented for us the data for exonerating the Jews from the charge of malicious blindness which the authors themselves make against them, seems to me still more absurd.

A word must be added to explain the omission of the fourth gospel from the study of the first period. I have removed it to the following chapter, not because I do not accept the authenticity of its picture of the esoteric teachings of Jesus, but because it seems to me to contain in its attitude to the Jews far more elements of the situation around A.D. 100 than of the situation in the lifetime of Jesus. A brilliant defence of a contrary view will be found in the work of Canon Raven (especially p. 203). But I do not find it convincing, for he seems to me to be certainly wrong in speaking of a ' synoptic attitude ' as though the synoptic gospels were consistent in their picture, and he omits the speeches of Jesus to the Jews from this defence. It is, however, interesting that the reasons which he gives for accepting the Johannine picture in preference to that of the synoptists are exactly those which make me choose Mark in preference to John; in other words, that it presents a more real picture of human relationships. It may be, however, that one should accept the Johannine picture of the internal divisions of the authorities over Jesus as a valuable supplement to the general picture as sketched by Mark.

The attitude of Paul to the Law is mainly developed in his earlier epistles, which have been the object of a detailed study by Kirsopp Lake. While their dating is not an essential part of the argument, I have followed this order:

Galatians, on the journey to the council at Jerusalem mentioned in Acts, *c.* A.D. 50.

Thessalonians, during the second missionary journey, and probably from Corinth, *c.* A.D. 52.

I and II Corinthians, during the third missionary journey, *c.* A.D. 53-57.

Romans, from Corinth, *c.* A.D. 57.

The other books of the New Testament do not seem to need any special comment.

The relation of the teaching of Jesus to the currents of thought in the Judaism of His time is still a matter of controversy. We must, however, exclude those estimates of the opposition between Him and contemporary Jewish teachers which do not take account of modern researches, and which base their conceptions of Judaism exclusively on the gospel narratives. Whether they be accepted or rejected, the work of Travers Herford, Moore, Billerbeck and Strack, and Montefiore cannot be ignored. There are, however, a number of modern authors who, while recognising the inadequacy of the gospel portrait of Judaism, still hold to the traditional view of the *complete* originality of Jesus and His *entire* independence of and opposition to the Judaism of the Pharisees. The work of Bischoff belongs to this category; and Raven enunciates the view that while the teaching of Jesus is completely Jewish, it is completely ' un-Judaic '; which seems somewhat of a paradox. To a lesser extent the same view is held by Easton. The denial of originality in the teaching of Jesus will be mainly found in the Jewish biographies referred to in the general biographical introduction. An analysis of the differences in attitude revealed in the different gospels will be found in Branscombe.

The study of Saint Paul's attitude to the Law has not been undertaken with anything like the same thoroughness. An original point of view is presented in Montefiore's work on Saint Paul, but scholarship in general retains the position that the rejection of the Judeo-Christian compromise was essential to the development of Christianity, and consequently, while Saint Paul's views have been violently challenged by Jewish scholars, Christian scholarship seems to have felt little need to defend them. The theory that Christianity was founded by Paul has now too few advocates to be worth consideration.

LIST OF BOOKS

ABRAHAMS, I.	*Studies in Pharisaism and the Gospels.* Cambridge, 1917 and 1924.
ACTS OF THE APOSTLES	Commentary by R. B. Rackham, *Westminster Commentaries*, 1904.
BISCHOFF, E.	*Jesus und die Rabbinen, Jesu Bergpredigt und 'Himmelreich' in ihrer Unabhängigkeit vom Rabbinismus.* Leipzig, 1905.
BRANSCOMBE, B. H.	*Jesus and the Law of Moses.* Hodder and Stoughton, 1930.
BURKITT, F. C.	*The Gospel History and its Transmission.* 1907.
EASTON, B. S.	*Christ in the Gospels.* Scribners, 1930.
HERFORD, R. T.	*Pharisaism.* Williams and Norgate, 1903. *The Pharisees.* 1924. *Judaism in the New Testament Period.* 1928.
JONES, M.	*The New Testament in the Twentieth Century.* Macmillan, 1924.
LAGRANGE, M. J.	*Le Judaisme avant Jesus Christ.* Paris, 1931.
LAKE, K.	*The Earlier Epistles of Saint Paul.* Rivington, 1911.
MARK, GOSPEL OF	Commentary by A. E. J. Rawlinson, *Westminster Commentaries*, 1925.

MONTEFIORE, C. — *The Synoptic Gospels.* Macmillan, 2nd ed., 1931.
Rabbinic Literature and Gospel Teachings. Macmillan, 1930.
Judaism and Saint Paul. Goschen, 1914.

MOORE, G. F. — *Judaism*, 3 vols. Harvard University Press, 1927.

RAMSAY, SIR W. — *Saint Paul the Traveller and the Roman Citizen.* Hodder and Stoughton, 1895.

RAVEN, C. E. — *Jesus and the Gospel of Love.* Hodder and Stoughton, 1931.

SANDAY, W., AND HEADLAM, A. C. — *Commentary on the Epistle to the Romans.* International Critical Commentaries, 1900.

STRACK, H., AND BILLERBECK, P. — *Kommentar zum Neuen Testament aus Talmud und Midrasch.* Berlin, 1924.

WALKER, T. — *Jesus and Jewish Teaching.* Allen and Unwin, 1923.

I. JUDAISM AND THE LAW

It is not part of this study to attempt a theological estimate of the relative merits of Judaism and Christianity. We are concerned with the clash of two religious organisations, and only indirectly with the conflict of theological conceptions which was involved. It is not Christian doctrine which has been the main external influence in the Jewish life of the last fifteen hundred years, but the Christian Church. The Jewish problem to-day expresses itself primarily in economic and political phraseology. False racial theories have been substituted for false readings of the Old Testament. Jewish observances are perhaps more coloured by Roman influences than by Christianity. Sephardic Judaism owes much to its contact with Arab civilisation. But the whole of the Jewish world even to-day bears the marks of the environment, friendly or hostile, created by the Christian Church. For throughout all those centuries a large portion of the Jewish people have lived under the domination of a Christian majority. The Jews of to-day are the direct inheritors of the life of mediaeval Jewry, and the life of mediaeval Jewry was built upon foundations laid in the earliest centuries of its daughter religion.

To trace the origin of the conflict we have to pursue two lines of enquiry simultaneously, the line of the historical development of the events, and the line of the historical development of the literature in which those events were recorded. An event related in the gospel of Matthew as occurring in the first months of our Lord's ministry needs to be considered from the standpoint of the date when the gospel was written, as much as from that of the time to which the event is ascribed. The most obvious example of this contradiction is to be seen in the reference to the different groups within Judaism. In the synoptic gospels it is now the Pharisees, now the scribes, now another party which is described. In the fourth gospel all are included together under the general term ' the Jews ', and all are considered equally to be, and always to have been, the enemies of the new teaching.

It is not possible historically to trace this antagonism of the Christian to the Jew exclusively to the fact of the crucifixion. Nor can the Jewish antagonism to Christianity be traced exclusively to the teaching of Paul. The origin of the profound difference which exists between Judaism and Christianity must ultimately be related to the teaching of Jesus, although He Himself lived and died a Jew. Even if we recognise, as we are bound to do, that many of the sayings attributed to Him in the gospels are either unauthentic or coloured by memory and intention, yet we cannot eliminate all the conflicts with other Jewish teachers or the denunciations contained in them unless we are prepared to deny their entire historicity. But it is very important to know exactly the nature of the conflict and what Jesus denounced, and to distinguish this from the colouring which belongs to the period of transcription rather than to the period of occurrence. He wished to change things in current teaching, but not to abandon Judaism itself. He attacked the Pharisees unsparingly, but His greatest predecessor was the Pharisee Hillel.

In view of the fact that the Pharisees, and therewith post-Christian Judaism, are almost universally judged by Christians on the basis of the twenty-third chapter of Matthew and Paul's Epistle to the Romans, it is essential to enquire further into the scope and causes of this opposition. We have no Jewish sources of the time of Jesus, except as they are embodied in the Talmud, and we are compelled to build up our knowledge of the Judaism of the first century largely from a disentangling of the teaching of earlier rabbis from the later material contained therein. But thanks to the researches of various modern scholars we can assess the Judaism of the first century with sufficient accuracy to be in a position to deny that there was so profound a difference between the Judaism of the first century and that of a hundred years later that the New Testament picture of the one and the Talmudic picture of the other can both be taken as equally accurate. It is, however, unwise to swing to the opposite extreme and condemn the whole New Testament picture without discrimination. The picture of the Jews in the fourth gospel may be completely invented. The synoptists and Paul cannot be so easily set aside, and they describe a real conflict.

To consider that Jesus dismissed the whole of Pharisaic Judaism as simply 'hypocrisy' is to attribute to Him an impossible superficiality. He denounced what seemed to Him to be *pessima* because it was *corruptio optimi*. But if it had not been for the work of the Pharisees, Jesus would not have been born a Jew, because no Judaism would have survived until His time[1]. The Pharisees had saved it, but in the externally and internally troubled centuries which followed Ezra its development had been extremely difficult; and since it was intricately involved with contemporary political and social questions, the result at the time of Christ was a mass of ill-adjustments[2]. Fanaticism, meticulous insistence on detail, and narrow-mindedness are not the prerogative of the Pharisees, but are to be found in any intensely religious group fighting with its back to the wall, as was Judaism during these centuries. One would not go to the Scottish Covenanters or the Albigenses for a realisation of the broad charity of the Gospel. And like the Covenanters and the Albigenses, the Pharisees considered that their meticulous insistence upon certain acts and beliefs was, in the conditions under which they were living, essential for the development of the true mission of Israel, the worship of God according to Torah. The Pharisees, with their teachers everywhere, with their independence of the authorities at Jerusalem, the political and priestly leaders of the nation, wanted the *whole* of Israel to know Torah, for only in so doing would Israel be fulfilling its mission before God. In opposition to the Greek philosophers, who built their ideal city on slave labour, the Pharisees were completely democratic. Many of the most famous rabbis, especially of the earlier period, were themselves artisans. Jesus, as a village carpenter, would not inspire them with any contempt. It would not even arouse comment that He followed a trade.

The word Torah is only very imperfectly translated by ' Law '. To the Jew it has a far richer meaning, and does not in the least imply a slavish following of a written document, even if that document has final authority. ' It is near the truth to say that what Christ is to the Christian, Torah is to the Jew[3].' It also could be spoken of as an ' Incarnation '

[1] *Pharisaism*, by R. Travers Herford, Chapters I and II.

[2] *The Synoptic Gospels*, by C. G. Montefiore, Introduction, p. lxxx ff.

[3] *Pharisaism*, p. 171.

of the Divine, for it expressed the whole of the Divine will for, and thought about, man. It contained far more than mere ' precept ' or laws, although even the precepts, by being Divine ordinances, brought men to God in the performance of them. Thus to have many precepts was not a burden ; it only gave men so many more opportunities for doing expressly His will, and even if some of the precepts seemed trivial, it was not for man to judge the importance of what God had ordained. The task of the scribes was to study the written Law, which of itself was not always easy to understand in changing conditions, and to know its interpretation so that in everything which a man did he might please God. The written Law was thus the basis of Torah, but Torah itself was the complete revelation of the life of the holy community or nation through which the individual in every act could fulfil the purpose of God in His creation. Nor was this conception merely rational and intellectual, in spite of the continual emphasis on ' understanding '. It was in Christian language ' redemptive '. ' Torah ' was a living creative force expressing itself through the Holy Community to the world as a whole. The scribes were not necessarily priests. Many or most were laymen, but laymen set apart by competent authorities because of their knowledge of Torah and of the guidance which previous interpreters had found in it. Torah was divine and final, and therefore it was essential for every new precept proposed to find its authority either in the work of a previously accepted scribe or interpreter of the written Law, or else in the written Law itself. Naturally enough in times of crisis and confusion their tendency was to interpret the written and oral Law more and more strictly, and to increase the wall of legal severance which separated Jew and Gentile, or, for that matter, the righteous from the unrighteous Jew. If ' it would be unfair to say that the Rabbis deliberately extended the ceremonial at the expense of the moral Law ', yet ' it is true to say that their devotion to the non-moral side of the Law did occasionally produce evil results on the moral and spiritual side both in themselves and their followers[1] '. Wherever there are external forms in a religion there is a danger of formalism,

[1] *The Synoptic Gospels*, Montefiore, Intro., p. lxxviii.

and even a group with no external forms such as the Society of Friends is not free from the danger.

When the spiritual reasons for doing certain acts are no longer accepted it is natural for it to seem mere hypocrisy to insist upon doing them. To those who see in ' the Law ' merely ' the letter ', it is natural to call it dead and powerless. But if it is necessary to understand something of the inner meaning of both religions to understand the tragic conflict which exists between them, it is no juster to go to Christian sources to understand Judaism than to go to the Jews to understand Christianity. Even those Christians who have re-examined the attitude of Christianity to Judaism still tend to see between the two religions a gulf which is unbridgeable. Travers Herford found that ' the conflict was one between two fundamentally different conceptions of religion, viz. that in which the supreme authority was Torah, and that in which the supreme authority was the immediate intuition of God in the individual soul and conscience. The Pharisee stood for one; Jesus stood for the other[1] '.

But this opposition is only true upon the assumption of certain Protestant interpretations of Christianity. It would be truer to say that the Christian through Jesus, the Jew through Torah, sought the same thing—' the immediate intuition of God in the individual soul and conscience '—and that to preserve for succeeding generations the possibilities of that intuition each religion has ' hedged it round ' with the discipline of a system and the humility of an authority.

Jesus attacked the scribes and Pharisees because they seemed to Him to obscure that direct relationship between man and God by falsifying the nature of Torah. He went further than they would ever have allowed in claiming that the written word of the Law itself could obscure that relationship. This was a fundamental point. But it was not a rejection by Jesus of ' Torah '. It was His Gentile followers a century later who, seeing in ' Torah ' only a body of prescriptions, saw in Judaism only the observance of a dead law which Jesus had rejected.

[1] *Pharisaism*, p. 167.

II. THE TEACHING OF JESUS IN MARK

The opposition is not to be understood from a consideration of the recorded controversies alone. It lay in the manner of His teaching. Statements made by Jesus might be wise or good in themselves from the Pharisaic point of view, but He was neither a scribe nor did He quote the authority of accepted scribes for His utterances. To accept them as authoritative expressions of Torah was, in the minds of its official interpreters, to undermine the whole structure. The stages of this feeling are easy to trace in the gospel of Mark. When Jesus first preached in Capernaum the people were astonished ' for He taught them as having authority, and not as the scribes '[1]. When on that, or more likely on a subsequent, occasion He healed a man in the synagogue, they were still more amazed at His ' authority '[2]. That this ' authority ' implied to Jesus no opposition to Torah is shown by the healing of the leper which occurred some time later. The leper is sent to the priest to have his health certified, and to perform all the ritual acts required[3]. Meanwhile the reputation of Jesus grew, and the scribes were troubled at it. When He returned to Capernaum, there occurred a fresh incident. Healing a man sick of the palsy, He said to him ' Son, thy sins are forgiven '. This caused the scribes still further anxiety. ' They reasoned in their hearts, saying, Why doth this man thus speak? he blasphemeth: who can forgive sins, but one, even God? [4]' This cannot be called a hostile attitude, and the reply of Jesus is not hostile. It is plain and straightforward. He perceives they are questioning His action, and He justifies it to them.

So far it has been a question of authority, and the questioners—it is absurd to call them ' opponents ' at this stage—are the scribes. The next incident introduces the Pharisees, and it is perhaps significant that it introduces a direct question of the strict observance of the Law. Jesus was eating with publicans and sinners. The scribes and Pharisees

[1] Mark i, 22.
[2] *Ibid.* 27.
[3] *Ibid.* 44.
[4] *Ibid.* ii, 6 and 7.

remarked upon it, and again He gives them a reasonable answer, and one which they could have accepted as adequate. ' They that are whole have no need of a physician, but they that are sick '[1]. A little later the disciples of Jesus were not fasting, when those of John the Baptist and of the Pharisees were observing a fast. They ask Him to explain. He does so, but the answer contains a new note[2].

Naturally we have only the slightest summary in the gospels of a process which had been going on for several months at least. We cannot know what other conversations and discussions took place between Jesus and His disciples, and between Him and the Jewish teachers who followed with so much uneasiness His growing popularity. But we can see that there has been a change between the time when they found Him eating with publicans and sinners, and when they questioned Him about fasting. ' No man putteth new wine into old wine-skins ' could be taken to imply a complete rejection of the old Law and tradition. His previous actions, although unusual, contained nothing explicitly illegal. Though the forgiveness of sins shocked them, yet, when Jesus proved His knowledge of the man by showing them that He had cured him, they could have reconciled this with their ideas. When they questioned Him about fasting, there is nothing in their words to show that they were other than anxious for information. But His reply must have greatly increased their disquiet. It seemed an admission that He looked at the matter from a frankly novel standpoint. They soon found their anxiety confirmed. On the Sabbath His disciples ate ears of corn as they passed through the fields. Here was a straight issue. Why, they asked Him, do your disciples do on the Sabbath day that which is *not lawful*? Jesus' answer is half a justification from the Scriptures, but He adds the revolutionary words ' The Sabbath was made for man, and not man for the Sabbath '[3].

Such an answer, coming as a climax to a long development, decided them to take action. But they determined first to make sure of the correctness of their suspicion that He was

[1] Mark ii, 17. Graetz, English trans., Vol. II, Ch. 6, builds his whole conception of the mission of Jesus on this verse.

[2] Mark ii, 19-22.

[3] *Ibid.* 27.

adopting an unorthodox attitude to Torah. Jesus went into the synagogue and found there a man with a withered hand. It is quite likely that his presence was deliberate. In any case 'they watched Him, whether He would heal him on the Sabbath day; that they might accuse Him '[1]. Jesus recognised the challenge, and accepted it. 'Is it lawful to do good on the Sabbath day or to do harm?' The Pharisees did not answer. They were there to observe His action, not to indulge in a controversy. And Jesus 'looked round about on them with anger, being grieved at the hardening of their hearts', and proceeded to cure the man. 'And the Pharisees went out, and straightway with the Herodians took counsel against Him how they might destroy Him.' Jesus, on His side, withdrew from the region.

Though the question at issue seems a slight one to a Gentile, it went directly to the heart of the whole Pharisaic conception of Torah. For they did not admit that there could be a question of relative gravity in a deliberate and unnecessary breaking of its precepts.

The scribes admitted that in cases of life and death it was lawful to set aside the laws of the Sabbath. But in the first case, that of plucking the ears of corn, and in the second, that of healing the man with the withered hand, no such urgency could be alleged. The question 'Is it lawful to do good on the Sabbath day?' seemed to the Pharisees beside the point. The man could just as well be healed on the next day. He was in no danger, and therefore there was no legitimate ground for breaking the Sabbath. To postpone the cure by a day was neither 'to do harm' nor 'to kill'. From the point of view of the Pharisees Jesus was undermining the whole structure of Torah by such an action. The divergence between them in practice was slight. But so long as Jesus defended His action just on its own basis and did not interest Himself to explain it as a legitimate interpretation of the written Law, so long was He to their minds really doing harm and not good by His conduct. For however long the process of interpretation, every good thing was included in the written Law which was the basis of Torah[2].

[1] Mark iii, 2-6.

[2] Cf. *Pharisaism*, p. 152.

There follows a period when Jesus was left in peace, and He on his side seems deliberately to have avoided disturbing the authorities. Those whom He healed ' He charged much that they should not make Him known '[1]. But it was impossible that the situation could continue thus indefinitely, and it appears that the local scribes and Pharisees fearing, perhaps, to act on their own initiative against anyone who enjoyed such popularity, asked the advice of the authorities at Jerusalem. Perhaps also they attempted to persuade His friends and relations to restrain Him. In any case, at some point unmentioned, we find both His friends attempting to put Him under restraint as mad, and ' the scribes which came down from Jerusalem ' condemning His miracles as the work of the devil[2]. This attempt was felt by Jesus to be so grossly unjust that it moved Him to His severest condemnation. To cavil at His attitude to the Law was one thing. To ascribe His healings to the devil was a very different matter. It was blasphemy against the Holy Spirit. Perhaps His reply abashed them, for they left Him in peace for a long while. But it could only be a truce, and when they returned, it was again to challenge Him on the direct observance of the prescriptions of Torah[3]. This time He replied to them in detail, and opposed in formal argument their traditions with the Mosaic Law itself. He accepted their challenge, and admitted that He did not observe their prescriptions. But he did not by a single word suggest that He rejected Torah itself. It was the other way round. He charged them with nullifying it.

Into the further details of the conflict it is not necessary to enter. The other gospels add many other details, and confuse the historic development of the picture. But they do not substantially alter it. The Sermon on the Mount in the first gospel gives in much greater detail the teaching of Jesus and allows us to see His attitude to the Mosaic Law, and to its development. After insisting that He came not to destroy but to fulfil it, He goes on to interpret it. The method which He adopts, that of setting one precept side by side with another in order to mitigate the rigour of the first, is

[1] Mark iii, 12.

[2] *Ibid.* 21-29.

[3] *Ibid.* vii, 1-23.

the normal method of rabbinic teaching. But the rabbis did it impersonally. If the contrast in the sermon—'Ye have heard that it was said to them of old time . . . but *I* say unto you'—is accurately reported, and is not a Greek version of a not completely understood Aramaic original, then here also He went further than any Pharisaic teacher would permit himself to do.

III. THE ACCOUNTS IN LUKE AND MATTHEW

The gulf which was thus created was never bridged by either side. Jesus made no concession which the Pharisees might have accepted, and they on their part were not prepared to withdraw their opposition to a teacher who would not conform to the accepted rules of interpretation, and who presumed on His own authority to discriminate between what should be observed and what could be neglected. It is no part of our task to judge between them[1], and it is to-day a purely academic question whether either side could have bridged the gulf created. But it is important to attempt to define as exactly as possible the extent of the conflict, and to disentangle from the narrative what belongs to the event, and what reflects the period of the writer. This is essential from both sides, from the Christian side as it concerns the unmeasured denunciations in the later ministry of Jesus, and from the Jewish side in relation to the events leading up to the condemnation of Jesus by Pilate, and His Crucifixion.

There is an unmistakable increase in hostility in the tone of the three synoptists if they are read in the historical order of their appearance. Mark deals with explicit questions, shows a reasonable historic development, and allows the conflict to be accurately traced. There are certain difficulties, but nothing which interrupts the essential realism of the picture. Each incident related is connected with an actual example of conflicting opinion. There is no general and apparently unprovoked attack upon them. With Luke there is a frequent colouring of the incidents recorded by Mark. Mark relates that the people of Nazareth were offended at Him. Luke adds the story of their attempt to cast Him over

[1] Cf. *Pharisaism*, p. 167.

a cliff, and places it at the very beginning of His ministry, when there was no reason whatever for such hostility[1]. Additional emphasis is given to the incident of the healing of the palsied man[2]. It cannot be said that this reflects any deliberate intention on the part of Luke. He records several occasions on which Jesus was invited to a meal by a Pharisee[3], and though these occasions are used to illustrate the conflict, they imply a certain spiritual fellowship. Further, Luke alone gives the incident of the Pharisees warning Jesus of an intention of Herod to seize Him[4]. The most important addition which he makes to the Marcan narrative is the strong condemnation in the eleventh chapter of formalism and its accompanying vices.

With Matthew there is a much more noticeable bias. The gospel was written to convince the Jews that in Jesus 'the promises made to Israel' had passed from the Jews to the Christian Church. The change in tone is illustrated at the very beginning of the gospel. Luke and Matthew both record the preaching of John the Baptist. In Luke it reads:

> He said therefore to the multitudes that went out to be baptised of him, Ye offspring of vipers, who warned you to flee from the wrath to come? . . .

In the version of Matthew there is this change:

> Then went out to him Jerusalem and all Judaea, and all the region round about Jordan; and they were baptised of him in the river Jordan, confessing their sins. But *when he saw many of the Pharisees and Sadducees coming to his baptism*, he said unto them, Ye offspring of vipers, who warned you to flee from the wrath to come? . . .[5]

In all the incidents which he takes from Mark there is some slight change accentuating the opposition between Jesus and the Jewish authorities. The incident of the centurion's servant, with its condemnation of the lack of faith in Israel, is set at the very beginning of the narrative

[1] Mark vi, 4, and Luke iv, 28.

[2] Mark ii, 6, 7, and Luke v, 17 and 21.

[3] Luke vii, 36; xi, 37; and xiv, 1.

[4] *Ibid.* xiii, 31.

[5] *Ibid.* iii, 7, and Matthew iii, 5-7.

immediately after the Sermon on the Mount[1]. Even before any encounter with the scribes or Pharisees is recorded there is a strong condemnation of them in the sermon itself, although they are not mentioned by name, but only as ' the hypocrites '[2]. In the incident of the man with the palsy, the question of Jesus: ' Why reason ye in your hearts ', becomes ' Wherefore think ye *evil* '[3]. In the answer which He gives them on fasting, the words are added: ' go ye and learn what this meaneth, I desire mercy and not sacrifice '[4]. The hostility of the Pharisees is emphasised by the doubling of the accusations that Jesus healed by diabolic power[5]. No references to hospitality offered by or accepted from the Pharisees are recorded. Finally there is nothing in Mark or even Luke which corresponds to the violence, bitterness and thoroughness of the famous denunciations of chapter twenty-three, which even if it opens with the recognition that they ' sit in Moses' seat ' sees nothing but corruption and hypocrisy in all their works.

Much depends on the manner and setting of the incidents. Neither in Luke nor in Matthew have they the naturalness of Mark. There is only one passage in Mark which goes beyond a condemnation of formalism, and of the Pharisaic attitude to the Law, and that passage presents certain difficulties[6]. Jesus accuses them of rejecting the commandments of God that they may keep their traditions. The illustration which Mark proceeds to give of this is the law of ' Corban '. But the attitude which Jesus condemns was also condemned by Pharisaic Judaism, and that which He approves is the Pharisaic interpretation of the original. It is only possible to imagine that the error comes from Mark, who was not a Jew, and who confused what he received.

When the violence of the conflict between Jews and Jewish or Gentile Christians, which existed at the time when the gospels were being written down, is realised, it ceases to be surprising that there is this additional vehemence in the

[1] Matthew viii, 5 ff.

[2] *Ibid.* vi, 2, 5, 16.

[3] *Ibid.* ix, 4.

[4] *Ibid.* ix, 13.

[5] *Ibid.* ix, 34, and xii, 24.

[6] Mark vii, 9-13.

denunciations put into the mouth of Jesus. As to His own teaching, we can be certain that He did denounce unsparingly that attitude which did not discriminate between one law and another, and which demanded unquestioning obedience of the whole. He did not reject the idea of interpreting the Law, for He interpreted it freely Himself, but He did reject some of their actual interpretations, and refused to give ' their traditions ' the force of Torah itself.

IV. THE CRUCIFIXION

Jesus and the Pharisees differed on the question of authority in the interpretation of Torah. Because the attitude of each side hardened in the half century which followed His death, the separation between Judaism and Christianity became inevitable. It was the Law and not the Crucifixion which was the basis of this separation. It is only later that the words (which typically enough are to be found only in Matthew) ' His blood be on us and on our children ' came to assume their terrible importance, and that the Christian hostility to the Jews was based upon the Cross. It is evident that the Pharisees were decided not to accept the authority of Jesus. But it is a long step from the refusal to accept the teaching of a new preacher to the plotting of His death. It is to be noted that in the account from the betrayal to the Cross there is no mention of them. The ' scribes ' are included by Mark, but omitted by Matthew. But neither mentions the Pharisees. It was not the teaching of Jesus which led to His death. It was the fear of His Messianic claims by the Jewish authorities in Jerusalem, the fear that it would lead the Romans to remove what little privileges they still enjoyed.

The actual facts of the arrest and trial are exceedingly difficult to establish. Since the disciples are all recorded to have forsaken Him and fled, there is no certain basis for the narratives which follow the scene in the garden of Gethsemane. Moreover none of the evangelists were, so far as we know, experts in legal questions, and here they are describing a serious trial ending in a capital sentence. Consequently some modern writers have attempted to deny all authenticity to the gospel narratives[1]. It is true that the process related does not conform to the known juridical procedure of the time. But this would probably be so with an amateur report of any great modern trial—especially when the author was not himself present—and the existence of this confusion does not justify a total rejection of the narrative. For the main outlines are clear. The initiative was taken by the Jewish authorities at Jerusalem, though it is evident that Jesus Himself foresaw the danger in coming there, and expected His death. But while the authorities were unwilling to risk their precarious autonomy for a teacher whose teaching they did not accept, it is also clear that they did not wish to endanger their own position with the populace who thronged Jerusalem for the feast, by themselves executing some sentence upon Him. They secured themselves both with the Jewish crowd and with the Roman government by their action in first condemning Him and then handing Him over to Pilate for sentence.

Such seems to be the actual outline of the events. It satisfies the narrative and the known conditions better than either of the two alternative hypotheses, which would ascribe the whole responsibility either to the Romans or to the Jews. It would seem at first to be an argument for total Jewish responsibility that the purely Jewish story of the death of Jesus, to be found in the Sepher Toldoth Jeshu and in the Talmud[2], ascribes the whole action to the Jews, gives stoning (the Jewish punishment) as the cause of His death, and omits all reference to the Romans. But it is probable that the acceptance of responsibility (which involved no moral condemnation to the Talmudic rabbis, for they insist that He had a fair trial) is due to the frequent Christian charge that this responsibility had, in fact, been theirs. But if the whole responsibility had, in fact, been Jewish, it is incredible that the Romans were ever introduced into the narratives at all, for at the time at which they were written the Church was desirous of cultivating the friendship of Rome. If, on the other hand, the entire responsibility had lain with Rome, then the vehemence of anti-Jewish polemic in the earliest

[1] For a fully documented exposition of this view see Juster, *op. cit.*, Vol. II, p. 134, note 2. A full bibliography is there given.

[2] *Christianity in Talmud and Midrash*, pp. 78-80.

period becomes incomprehensible, because so unnecessarily offensive to the Jews. For, after all, the Church desired to win the Jewish acceptance of the Messianic claims of Jesus, and it would be the height of folly to repel them by pinning to them so terrible an accusation without any cause.

Each of the narratives presents special characteristics, and again it is Mark who gives the most reasonable account. Luke, who emphasises throughout the universal appeal of Jesus, is clearly anxious to present the Romans in as favourable a light as possible. Pilate *twice* attempts to free Jesus, and even Herod is introduced to support him. Matthew is equally interested to present the Jews in an unfavourable light, and adds the words already referred to.

V. THE INFANT CHURCH AND THE ADMISSION OF THE GENTILES

The Law and the Cross, these are the two rocks on which Christianity and Judaism divided, but it must not be thought that the separation became immediately apparent. It is possible to see the gulf widening in the Acts of the Apostles and in the Epistles of Saint Paul. In his first speech after the Resurrection Peter carefully avoids insisting upon Jewish responsibility for the Crucifixion by emphasising first the 'determinate counsel and foreknowledge of God', and then by ascribing the act itself to the 'hands of lawless men'[1]. In the second speech he goes a little further, but after saying 'whom ye delivered up, . . . when Pilate was determined to release him', he adds 'I wot that in ignorance ye did it, as did also your rulers'[2]. He uses the same guarded language in his prayer of thanksgiving after his release from his first imprisonment: 'against thy holy Servant Jesus, whom thou didst anoint, both Herod and Pontius Pilate, with the Gentiles and the peoples of Israel, were gathered together, to do *whatsoever thy hand and thy counsel foreordained to come to pass*'[3].

[1] Acts ii, 23. The latter words may be a summary in Lucan language, but they appear to reflect accurately the development of ideas.

[2] *Ibid.* iii, 13 and 17.

[3] *Ibid.* iv, 27.

The Jews also only gradually came to believe in the irreconcilable nature of the new religion. When Peter was arrested for the first time they were content to forbid him to speak in the name of Jesus, and to let him go[1]. The second time he was arrested Gamaliel undertook his defence. His speech as recorded in Acts exactly reflects what we should expect of this first contact with the leaders of the new sect. He is clearly uncertain whether their teaching is true or not[2]. We learn that at this time ' a great company of the priests were obedient to the faith '[3]. Violent antagonism did not manifest itself until Stephen began to preach. Then it was not the Palestinian Jews whom he offended, but the ' Libertines, Cyrenians, and Alexandrians ', Jews of the diaspora, who were more sensitive to the possible dangers to Judaism than were the Jews of Jerusalem. Stephen was accused of stating that Jesus would destroy the Temple and would ' change the customs which Moses delivered unto us '[4]. Brought before the High Priest, Stephen abandoned all the tact with which the Apostles had so far spoken before the authorities, and after a lengthy introduction on Israelite history, suddenly burst into a violent denunciation: ' ye stiffnecked and uncircumcised in heart and ears, ye do always resist the Holy Ghost: as your fathers did, so do ye. Which of the prophets did not your fathers persecute? and they killed them which showed before of the coming of the Righteous One; of whom ye have now become betrayers and murderers; ye who received the law as it was ordained by angels, and kept it not '[5]. What Stephen had said about the Law we do not know, and what he was leading up to before he broke off is also uncertain, except that he was obviously going to taunt them with not having kept it themselves[6]; but in any case the priests decided to take energetic measures to suppress the new heresy. The commission to do so was entrusted to Saul[7].

[1] Acts iv, 21. The idea that the two arrests are a doublet seems to me to be false.

[2] *Ibid.* v, 38, 39.

[3] *Ibid.* vi, 7.

[4] *Ibid.* vi, 14.

[5] *Ibid.* vii, 51.

[6] Cf. *Ibid.* vii, 39.

[7] *Ibid.* viii, 1-3; cf. xi, 19.

Events at the same time took place within the Christian community which were bound to strain relations still further. As a result of a vision, Peter accepted a call to go to Joppa to visit a ' God-fearing ' Gentile, Cornelius. There he became convinced that God had called the Gentiles also, and that ' he should not call any man common or unclean ', for ' God is no respecter of persons, but in every nation he that feareth him and worketh righteousness, is acceptable to him '. With the consent of the Jewish Christians present—called for the first time ' they of the circumcision '—he baptised Cornelius directly into the Christian Church. The Christians at Jerusalem, when he reported the matter to them, after some opposition accepted his action, and ' glorified God, saying: then to the Gentiles also hath God granted repentance unto life '[1].

The admission of the Gentiles inevitably brought the question of the Law into prominence, but there is as yet no question of the Law not being valid for Jewish Christians. Nor was Jewish opinion at this period itself unanimous that Gentiles ought to observe either circumcision or the whole of the Law. ' There were those who held and believed that the true circumcision was of the heart rather than of the flesh, and who were willing to argue that, for the proselyte at least, such spiritual circumcision was all that God required or that man should ask. They were anxious to throw the moral laws of the Pentateuch into strong relief, so that the dangerous multiplication of ritual and ceremonial enactments might be counteracted '[2]. The synagogue was surrounded by large numbers of ' God-fearing ' Gentiles, and so long as the leaders of the Christians remained Jews, it is possible that it was not clearly understood by other Jews that the Christians had in fact eliminated all distinction between Jews and Gentiles within the Church. They may have been aware that a conflict of opinion was in progress, but it is unlikely that they realised its outcome before the Christians themselves, and it was some time before a decisive step was taken by the Church. The Christians had clearly become a party whom they would need to watch. But they were a ' party ', not a separate religion.

[1] Acts x and xi.

[2] Montefiore, *op. cit.*, lxxix.

VI. THE ACTIVITY OF SAINT PAUL AND HIS TEACHING ABOUT THE JEWS

In A.D. 49 or 50, when Paul set out from Antioch on his first missionary journey in Asia Minor, he began his preaching quite naturally in the synagogue, and though he stated openly that Jesus had been crucified by the Jews ' that dwell in Jerusalem, and their rulers ', he was invited by the congregation to return the next Sabbath and continue his preaching[1]. During the week they apparently thought better of it, and when he began to preach on the following Sabbath there was a disturbance, attributed by the author of the Acts to the jealousy of the Jews at his influence over the Gentiles[2]. Paul replied ' seeing ye thrust it [the Word of God] from you, and judge yourselves unworthy of eternal life, lo, we turn to the Gentiles '. The importance of this statement is great. But it was not a final or exclusive decision of policy. In the next city, Iconium, He again preached in the synagogue on his arrival. Apparently his preaching caused a great division of opinion, and he was ultimately forced into flight by the opposition to it[3].

The question of the Law very soon became an internal question of the Church, affecting the relations between Jewish and Gentile Christians, and it was decided that Gentiles did not need to observe its precepts long before it was felt that they were not valid for Jewish Christians either. The Apostles took the basis on which the Jews accepted ' the proselytes of the gate ', the ' Noachian commandments ', and made them the basis of Gentile participation in the Church, but with this difference, that the observance of these regulations admitted the Gentiles to full membership and not only to partial adherence to the fellowship. But when Peter is referred to by Paul[4] as living ' as do the Gentiles ', it meant no more than that he no longer observed the rigid separation of Jew and Gentile at meals, and that he consented, as he had already done in the case of Cornelius, to eat with the Gentiles. It did not mean that he ceased to observe the Law in so far

[1] Acts xiii, 42.

[2] *Ibid.* xiii, 45.

[3] *Ibid.* xiv, 1 ff.

[4] Gal. ii, 14.

as it affected his own conduct apart from contact with the Gentiles, nor did Paul himself at this time think of laying aside his own obedience to the Law, though we should know more clearly where he stood if we had any idea of the meaning of his reference to the circumcision of Titus[1]. That he was firmly convinced that observance of the Law was in general unnecessary *for the Gentiles* is clear from the Epistle to the Galatians which was written at this period. In this Epistle he makes the definite statement that ' if righteousness is through the Law, then Christ died for nought '[2], and again ' Abraham had two sons, one by the handmaid, and one by the free woman. . . . These women are two covenants: one from mount Sinai, bearing children unto bondage, which is Hagar. Now this Hagar is mount Sinai in Arabia, and answereth to the Jerusalem that now is: for she is in bondage with her children. But the Jerusalem that is above is free, which is *our* mother. . . . Now we, . . . are children of promise '[3].

Taken by itself the whole argument would suggest that Paul himself no longer observed the Law. But we know that this was not the case. When he says that he ' through the law died unto the law that I might live unto God '[4], it would, if we had no other evidence, appear unquestionable. But, in fact, among Jews he accepted even rigid observance of the Law. Such a position could be only transitional, for as he himself says, ' every man that receiveth circumcision is debtor to the *whole* Law ', and Jewish Christians could not permanently pick and choose what they should obey of its ritual and ceremonial observances. It is evident from this epistle that many of them had not accepted the compromise for which all the Apostles had first stood at Jerusalem, and that the party which considered Christianity to be only

[1] Gal. ii, 3 ff. ' But not even Titus who was with me, being a Greek, was compelled to be circumcised; and that because of the false brethren privily brought in, . . . to whom we gave place in the way of subjection, no, not for an hour.' It is impossible to say either from this passage, or from Paul's position at this time, if he did or did not circumcise Titus. It would, of course, be known to his hearers, who would have known if the emphasis was on ' *compelled* ', meaning he was circumcised, or on ' *not even* ' (*i.e.* though he was my companion), meaning he was not.

[2] *Ibid.* ii, 21.

[3] *Ibid.* iv, 22.

[4] *Ibid.* ii, 19.

a Jewish sect was a strong one. We cannot even be sure of Paul's own attitude, in its entirety, to these Jewish Christians. We have neither sermon nor epistle to this section of the Church. Peter and James, in addressing Jews, do not raise the issue. The first writing addressed to them in which it receives full treatment is the epistle to the Hebrews written nearly twenty years later.

On both his subsequent journeys, though it is evident that the tension was growing steadily greater, Paul always began his preaching with the Jews in any centre visited, and at one, Ephesus, he was so well received that he was asked to stay for some months. But there, as at Corinth, he finally ' went to the Gentiles ' and left the Jews in open opposition to his teaching[1]. During this period he elaborated considerably his doctrine of the Law and of the relation of the Church to the Jews, which he had foreshadowed in his epistle to the Galatians. In contrast to one violent outburst to the Thessalonians (from whom he had certainly received bad treatment)[2], in which he denounces the Jews ' who both killed the Lord Jesus and the prophets, and drave out us, and please not God, and are contrary to all men, forbidding us to speak to the Gentiles that they may be saved; to fill up their sins alway: but the wrath is come upon them to the uttermost '[3], he usually speaks with great restraint and with ' great sorrow and unceasing pain '.

Since the doctrines enunciated by Paul in these epistles, particularly in the epistle to the Romans, have provided the doctrinal basis for the attitude of the Church to the Jew throughout the centuries, it is important to give them in some detail. Since Paul and Jesus are in certain schools of theology set in stark opposition to each other, it is also important to note that in this respect Paul is logically following

[1] Acts xviii, 4-7 (Corinth) and Acts xviii, 19; xix, 8-9 (Ephesus).

[2] *Ibid.* xvii, 5.

[3] I Thess. ii, 14 ff. It seems to me likely that the last verse is a gloss added after the destruction of the Temple. If it is genuine, it is difficult to see to what event it could apply about A.D. 52, unless it is a reference to their final damnation (cf. II Thess. i, 8: ' them that obey not the gospel of our Lord Jesus; who shall suffer punishment, even eternal destruction '), in which case it is an outburst of rage in complete contrast to his real view of the future of the Jews set out in his epistle to the Romans. See *infra*.

to their conclusion the denunciations of the Pharisees in the gospels.

According to Paul, the Law itself is ' holy, and the commandment holy and righteous and good '[1], and it was a privilege to the Jews to have received it—' What advantage then hath the Jew? . . . Much every way: first of all that they were intrusted with the oracles of God '[2]. All this is again summed up in the sentence ' my kinsmen according to the flesh; who are Israelites; whose is the adoption, and the glory, and the covenants, and the giving of the law, and the service of God, and the promises; whose are the fathers, and of whom is Christ as concerning the flesh '[3]. The Gospel itself was first given to the Jews[4], and only when they refused it was it given to the Gentiles[5].

The rejection of the Gospel by the Jews raised several new problems. The Jew felt that he had no need for the Gospel because he had all that he required in the Law. Paul, with his belief in the universal significance of Christ, could not possibly admit such a claim. Nor could he admit two alternative schemes of salvation. Having decided that salvation was according to Jesus, he was forced to conclude that the Law was incapable of bringing salvation[6]. Safeguarding as well as he could its holy character, he attempts to explain its failure in practice by saying that ' the Law is spiritual; but I am carnal, sold under sin '. The Law showed him what was good, but because of sin, he was powerless to do the good which he saw[7].

An alternative explanation, and one which won more general acceptance, was that the Law had not saved Israel, because Israel had never understood it. ' Israel, following after a law of righteousness, did not arrive at that law. Wherefore? Because they sought it not by faith, but as it were by works.'[8] The real function of the Law had been

[1] Rom. vii, 12.

[2] *Ibid.* iii, 1, 2.

[3] *Ibid.* ix, 3, 4.

[4] *Ibid.* i, 16.

[5] *Ibid.* ix, 19, to end of xi, especially xi, 17 ff.

[6] *Ibid.* iii, 20.

[7] *Ibid.* vii, 14-25.

[8] *Ibid.* ix, 31.

to be our ' tutor, to bring us unto Christ '[1]; and instead, the Jews had elevated into a final and eternal dispensation what was meant as temporary and imperfect[2].

Even more difficult to explain were the ' promises ', which were made both to Abraham and to later generations through the prophets. It was inevitable that Paul should claim that the promises now belonged exclusively to the Church, and that therefore Israel was, at any rate so long as it persisted in refusing to accept Christ, excluded from them. The promises of God could not lapse. The failure of the Jews could not make the word of God ineffective[3]. Nor could they claim that the promises depended on the Law, for the promise to Abraham preceded the giving of it[4]. The Gentiles, accepting Christ, became the true inheritors of them. ' They are not all Israel, which are of Israel.'[5] Here he is attacking directly a Pharisaic argument that the promises applied finally and exclusively to Israel, and that the worst Israelite was better than the best Gentile[6]. God did not cast off Israel, but Israel failed to see in Christ the fulfilment of the Law. ' By their fall salvation is come unto the Gentiles, for to provoke them to jealousy.'[7] As a result of this provocation Paul was convinced that ultimately the Jews also would be gathered in, and this he looked forward to as the culmination of the Gospel. 'For if the casting away of them is the reconciling of the world, what shall the receiving of them be, but life from the dead? And if the first fruit is holy, so is the lump: and if the root is holy, so are the branches. But if some of the branches were broken off, and thou, being a wild olive, wast grafted in among them, and didst become partaker with them of the root of the fatness of the olive tree; glory not over the branches: but if thou gloriest, it is not thou that bearest the root, but the root thee. Thou wilt say then, Branches were broken off, that I might be grafted in. . . . Be not high minded, but fear:

[1] Gal. iii, 23-24.

[2] II Cor. iii, 11 and 15. Rom. iii, 21.

[3] Rom. iv and xi.

[4] *Ibid.* iv, 10-12.

[5] *Ibid.* ix, 6 ff.

[6] See Sanday and Headlam, *Epistle to the Romans*, p. 246.

[7] Rom. xi, 11.

for if God spared not the natural branches, neither will He spare thee. Behold then the goodness and severity of God: toward them that fell, severity; but toward thee God's goodness, if thou continue in His goodness: otherwise thou also shalt be cut off. And they also, if they continue not in their unbelief, shall be grafted in: for God is able to graft them in again. For if thou wast cut out of that which is by nature a wild olive tree, and wast grafted contrary to nature into a good olive tree: how much more shall these, which are the natural branches, be grafted into their own olive tree?'[1]

While, naturally, no Jew would accept his diagnosis of their situation, yet they could not accuse him of hasty and violent denunciation. He himself was convinced of their ultimate salvation, which meant to him their acceptance of the Gospel, for salvation under any other terms was unthinkable. This he expressed in the Isaianic doctrine of the remnant. 'God did not cast off His people which He foreknew. Or wot ye not what the scripture saith of Elijah? How he pleadeth with God against Israel. Lord, they have killed thy prophets, they have digged down thine altars: and I am left alone, and they seek my life. But what saith the answer of God unto him? I have left for myself seven thousand men, who have not bowed the knee to Baal. Even so then at this present time also there is a remnant according to the election of grace. . . . Now if their fall is the riches of the world, and their loss the riches of the Gentiles; how much more their fulness?'[2] These two statements are important, for they preserved the Jews during the Middle Ages from complete extinction. For it was argued that if they were completely extinguished there would be none to provide the converted remnant which was to be the final crown of the Church.

In so far as his own position was concerned, Paul never ceased to regard himself as a Jew. 'I also am an Israelite, of the seed of Abraham, of the tribe of Benjamin'[3], but he observed the Law, not because he any longer felt it to be necessary, but in order to win the Jews. 'For though I was free from all men, I brought myself under bondage to all,

[1] Rom. xi, 15-24.
[2] *Ibid.* xi, 2 ff.
[3] *Ibid.* xi, 1.

that I might gain the more. And to the Jews I became as a Jew, that I might gain Jews; to them that are under the law, as under the law, not being myself under the law, that I might gain them that are under the law.'[1] It was on this principle that he acted during his final visit to Jerusalem, when he found the Jewish Christians very troubled by the reports which they had heard of his activities. 'Thou seest, brother,' they said to him, 'how many thousands there are among the Jews of them which have believed; and they are all zealous for the law: and they have been informed concerning thee, that thou teachest *all the Jews* which are among the Gentiles to forsake Moses, telling them not to circumcise their children, neither to walk after the customs.'[2] To show them his orthodoxy he 'took a vow', and accepted responsibility for four other men who had taken the same vow, involving particular attendance at the Temple. But there he was recognised by some Jews from Asia, and his presence caused a riot from which he was only saved by Roman intervention. There followed his arrest, his long imprisonment, and his appeal to Caesar.

If we accept the Jewish Law by its own standards, then we cannot be surprised at their refusal to accept the idea of 'becoming a Jew to save the Jews'. It is rather astonishing that the Apostle had been so long able to maintain such an attitude[3]. The Jewish Christians at Jerusalem were apparently contented when he showed his personal obedience to the Law. But those who knew him on the mission field were not so easily satisfied. In the same way, when he was brought before the council for trial, he was able to bring some of the Pharisees over to his side by raising the question of the resurrection. They protested that 'We find no evil in this man: and what if a spirit hath spoken to him, or an angel?'[4] But the majority was against him, and he remained a prisoner under the charge of the Roman authorities. We cannot be certain of the exact nature of the accusations against him. According to Acts[5], he was 'a mover of

[1] I Cor. ix, 19.

[2] Acts xxi, 20 ff.

[3] Cf. I Cor. vii, 18-20.

[4] Acts xxiii, 9.

[5] *Ibid.* xxiv, 5 and 6.

insurrections among all the Jews throughout the world', 'a ring-leader of the sect of the Nazarenes' and a profaner of the Temple. But the original charge must have been more specific.

That Paul in his attack upon the Law was doing it less than justice can be said without detracting from the greatness of the Apostle. 'The Christian will probably say in reply: Did not Paul himself know all about it? Was he not born and bred a Jew? Was he not a "Pharisee of the Pharisees"? Had he not been "zealous beyond those of his own age in the Jews' religion". Was he not "as touching the law, blameless". Who could be a better and more reliable witness upon the question of what the Jews' religion really was? Yes. And did not Paul abandon the Jews' religion? Did he not write about it long years after he had been converted to a different religion? And is it not common knowledge that a convert seldom takes the same view of the religion he has left as those who remain in it?'[1] The fact remains, however, that the Christian Church adopted without enquiry the Pauline estimate of the Jewish religion. The ultimate redemption of Israel on which Paul pinned his deepest faith was rarely referred to by Patristic writers. The inadequacy of the Law, and the forfeiture of the promises, was their continual accusation against the Jews. By the time the Book of Revelation was written at the very end of the century, it was already possible to speak of the redeemed of the Church in terms of the twelve tribes of Israel without it appearing strange[2].

[1] Herford, *op. cit.*, p. 175. Compare also *Judaism and S. Paul*, by C. G. Montefiore, where it is argued that Paul did not really know full rabbinic Judaism, or he could not have so completely misrepresented it, particularly by leaving out entirely the Jewish doctrine of forgiveness, and by ignoring the intimate and personal relationship with God under the Law in Jewish thought.

[2] Rev. vii, 4-8.

VII. THE JEWS IN THE REST OF THE NEW TESTAMENT

The epistles of Paul, even when dealing with Jewish questions, were addressed to Gentiles who were in danger of being influenced by the prestige of the Jewish Law. But the New Testament also contains letters directly addressed to Jewish Christians. The epistle of Peter is addressed from Rome to ' the elect who are sojourners of the Dispersion, in Pontus, Galatia, Cappadocia, Asia and Bithynia '. The epistle of James is addressed generally to the ' twelve tribes which are of the Dispersion ', while the epistle to the Hebrews, in view of its contents, is almost certainly addressed to Palestinian Jewish Christians familiar with all the daily ritual of the Temple services.

The epistle of Peter, while it makes hardly any reference to the Jewish origin of its recipients, condemns the whole of the old dispensation almost contemptuously as ' your vain manner of life handed down from your fathers '[1]. The right of the Christians to the ' promises ' is also clearly and exclusively stated in the emphasis of the words: ' to whom it was revealed, that not unto themselves, but unto you, did they minister these things, which now have been announced unto you through them that preached the gospel unto you '[2].

In contrast to the rest of the literature of the Apostolic Age, the epistle of James contains no polemic at all. Its calm and quiet tone, and its exclusive preoccupation with the building up of practical saintliness, impress the reader at once. The absence of Christological argument has led some scholars to see in it a Jewish epistle adapted for Christian purposes[3]. While this view is not generally accepted, it is a commentary on the self-contradiction of conventional views of Judaism that this, in many ways the most attractive of Apostolic writings, should be attributed by anyone to Jewish authorship without it being realised that such an attribution condemned the view that Judaism was arid and dead. It is

[1] I Peter i, 18.

[2] *Ibid.* i, 12.

[3] *E.g.* F. Spitta in *Zur Geschichte u. Literatur des Urchristentums*, Vol. II.

impossible to tell what was the attitude of the author to the Law. He accepts perfectly the situation of the people to whom he was writing, in so far as it was concerned. As we do not know the details of its date nor the occasion of its composition, all that we can safely deduce from it is that the question of the Law was not so universally a burning issue as we might be tempted to think from the works of Paul.

The third document addressed to Jewish Christians is the epistle to the Hebrews, and here the situation is very different. It has been conjectured, with a fair amount of probability, that it was addressed to Palestinian Jewish Christians during the war with Rome from A.D. 68 to 70. It reflects a time of crisis and of difficult decision which best fits this period. Its insistence on the priesthood and on sacrifice shows the Temple to be still standing. Its recipients were familiar with every detail of its ceremonial. The purpose of the letter is clear. It is written to convince them that they are no longer members of the Old Covenant, and that, therefore, the defence of the Temple and the Holy City is no affair of theirs. Its argument is precise. The Law made nothing perfect, and is cancelled because it is weak and unprofitable[1]. It was only the copy and shadow of heavenly things[2]. Its dignity is only stressed when the author wants to contrast the still greater dignity and glory of the New Dispensation[3]. The sacrifices and priesthood of the Old Dispensation are similarly thrown into shadow by the perfect sacrifice and priesthood of the New[4]. God's own intention to cancel the Law is proved from Jeremiah[5]. Such language is even stronger than that of Paul himself, who nowhere speaks of God ' finding fault with the Law '. To emphasise its weakness still further the author contrasts it with the faith of those who had lived before and after it had been pronounced[6]. The list goes straight on through the heroes of the Old Testament, making no distinction, and thereby implying that those who lived after the issue of the Law were

[1] Hebrews vii, 18, 19.

[2] *Ibid.* viii, 5.

[3] *Ibid.* ii, 2 and ix, *passim.*

[4] *Ibid.* x and vii.

[5] *Ibid.* viii, 8-13.

[6] *Ibid.* xi.

themselves only justified by the same faith as those whose lives preceded it. And of all alike he underlines the fact that 'all died in faith, *not having received the promises*'[1]. To make his rejection of the whole outlook of life of the Jew still more distinct, he says of these heroes of faith, many of whom, such as Gideon, Samson, David and the Maccabees, had lived and died in the struggle for national independence and for the sacred soil of Palestine, that they 'confessed that they were strangers and pilgrims on the earth', and not 'mindful of that country from which they went out'[2]. From this it was easy to deduce that the promises belong to the Christians, and refer only to a heavenly Jerusalem.

In its approach the epistle to the Hebrews belongs to the period of the first gospel. It is an argument to people not yet convinced. The insistence with which both documents build up their proofs that Jesus was the Messiah of prophecy and the High Priest of a New Dispensation imply a period when proof was still needed. Jews were shown in the gospel that Jesus was the Jewish Messiah. Jewish Christians are shown in the epistle that they are no longer members of the Jewish faith. The other book to be considered belongs to a later phase. The fourth gospel assumes without argument that the separation has already taken place. It is no further use arguing with the Jews. They are assumed to be the enemies of Christianity: and Christianity itself is a universal and not a Jewish religion. A careful reading of the book shows an amazing contrast in spiritual tone between the discourses addressed to the disciples and those addressed to the 'Jews', and while the former constitute some of the most exquisite treasures of Christian literature, the latter are unreal, unattractive, and at times almost repulsive. We can attribute the one, even if indirectly, to a personal memory. But the other is a reflection of the bitterness of the end of the first century, and will be discussed in the following chapter.

[1] Hebrews xi, 13.
[2] *Ibid*. xi, 13, 15.

VIII. JEWISH RELATIONSHIP WITH THE EARLY CHURCH

We have ample documentation for tracing in detail the growth of the hostility of the growing Church to its parent Judaism. It is more difficult to trace the estrangement from the other side. The Christians were, after all, a very small sect, and there is no reason why a contemporary Jewish writer should devote much time to them. Talmudic literature reflects the existence of early hostilities, but we cannot trace in it any exact development. We are compelled to make use of the New Testament, and in particular of the Acts of the Apostles, and we must use the evidence with caution, not because of any intentional mis-statement, but because Jewish motives and feelings were, naturally, much less known to the author than were the reactions of his Christian brethren.

It is, however, abundantly clear that it was the question of the Law which was the principal cause of conflict. It is therefore inherently probable that the first serious trouble arose over the preaching of Stephen, in which there appears to have been outspoken condemnation of its observance. In any case something compelled the Jewish authorities to see that the new movement had to be taken seriously, and the commission to root out the new sect was entrusted to Saul. It is to be noted that Stephen's preaching first aroused opposition among the Jews of the diaspora[1], and that it was to a Jew of the diaspora that the commission to exterminate the new sect was entrusted. Again, when Saul has become Paul and has returned for the last time to Jerusalem, it is the diaspora Jews who stir up the riot against him for his non-observance of the Law. The reason is probably to be found in the fact that the diaspora Jews, living among the Gentiles, were quicker to see the menace to the Law in the new teaching than were the Jews living in Palestine, where observance of the Law, by being universal, aroused less interest.

To understand the significance of the mission entrusted to Saul it is necessary to describe in greater detail the authority of the Jewish High Priest in the Roman empire. He was

[1] Acts vi, 9.

recognised by the Roman authorities as the supreme head of all the Jews of the empire, and in all matters of religion or custom he had absolute authority so far as the Romans were concerned. Even after the destruction of Jerusalem, the Patriarch had the same position.

But while Judaism was a recognised religion—or while the Jews were a recognised nation, for there was no distinction between the one conception and the other—it was not necessarily possible, without certain risks, for any Roman or other non-Jew to declare himself a Jew. The severity with which this was regarded differed at different epochs. For a short period under Hadrian, and after the time of Constantine, it became a punishable offence to become a convert to Judaism under any circumstances. The privileges given by the Romans to the Jews, though in fact given to the Jews originally as a ' nation ', were confined to practising Jews[1], so that by excommunication the Jewish authorities could deprive a Jew of his legal privileges. After A.D. 70, when all Jews were compelled to make a payment to the *fiscus judaicus*, this payment formed the recognition of the fact that an individual was a Jew.

Until the time of Constantine it was not a crime in itself to become a Jew, but to do so exposed the proselyte to a charge of atheism. In the case of a man this would not necessarily be known, so long as he did not hold any public office. As master of his household, his family worship was to some extent his own affair. But his conversion would necessarily be made known if he occupied an official position requiring participation in public sacrifice, though, probably, some proselytes took to heart the lesson of Naaman[2]. A woman could only become a proselyte with the consent or at least the connivance of her husband, since her absence from domestic worship could not be concealed from him. In the main such proselytism could only be revealed by a system of spies, and the first emperor who made use of such was Domitian[3], who extracted large fines from poor persons convicted of becoming proselytes, and executed wealthy ones

[1] Edict of Lentulus, Jos., *Ant.*, XIV, 10, § 13 ff.

[2] II Kings v, 18. Among the Egyptian papyri are a number of certificates that sacrifice had been offered, *i.e.* by either Jews or Christians.

[3] Suetonius, Domitian, xii, and Dion Cassius, lxvii, 14.

in order to confiscate their estates. His successor, Nerva, immediately stopped the work of the spies[1], and the proselytes were again left undisturbed until the time of Hadrian's law against circumcision[2]. This was repealed in favour of Jews *by birth* by Antoninus[3], but proselytes were to be punished with banishment or death, and proselyte slaves were to be set free, as having been ' mutilated ' against their will.

It was always possible for the Roman authorities, without undermining the privileges extended to genuine Jews, to punish efforts on their part to make proselytes. This they seem to have done as early as 139 B.C.[4], and the expulsions from Rome recorded by Tacitus and Suetonius in the reigns of Tiberius and Claudius were probably connected with their missionary activities[5].

While proselytes would, of course, come under Roman law, if the Romans wished to punish them, the Jewish authorities could punish Jews who offended Jewish law as did the Jewish Christians. The narrative in Acts contains nothing impossible in the statement that the Jerusalem authorities sent Paul with a mission to uproot the new heresy in certain synagogues of the diaspora. The only uncertain point is that they apparently exercised the right of extradition, since Paul was to bring his captives ' bound to Jerusalem '. Apart from this text, there is no evidence that the High Priest possessed this right, which was very rarely conceded by the Romans, and had only been granted to Herod as a special favour[6]. There is, however, no definite evidence that the right did not exist, though in this particular case it is difficult to see why the High Priest should want the prisoners brought to Jerusalem, a somewhat costly procedure, when all that was required was to give instructions that they should be punished wherever they were found. The Jews had the right of flagellation; and this is the

[1] Dion Cassius, lxviii, 1, 2.

[2] Vita Hadriani, xiv, 2.

[3] *Digest*, 48, 8, 11.

[4] Valerius Maximus, I, 3, 3: ' Judaeos qui Sabazi Jovis cultu Romanos inficere mores conati erant, repetere domos suas coegit '.

[5] *Annals*, II, 85. Suetonius in Reinach, 185-186.

[6] Juster, Vol. II, p. 145, and note 5.

punishment which would probably have been applied in this case, since it is extremely unlikely that they would have thought of putting a large number to death, even if they had the power to do so[1], as they seem to have had. If it had seemed sufficiently grave it is more likely that they would have been excommunicated and thereby lost the privileges they enjoyed as Jews.

It will be thus seen that at the beginning Judaism had the whip hand of Christianity, in that it was the Jews who decided what a Jew was, and who had the right to be admitted to the privileges they enjoyed. By the simple act of excommunication they could expel a Christian from these privileges and report against him as an atheist. Moreover, so long as the Christians chose to remain—officially, at least—a Jewish sect, they were subject to the discipline of the synagogue. How rigidly this discipline was applied we have no means of knowing, but that more happened than is recounted in the Acts of the Apostles is seen by Paul's declaration in the second epistle to the Corinthians (xi, 16-29) 'in prisons more abundantly, in stripes above measure, in deaths oft. Of the Jews five times received I forty stripes save one. Thrice was I beaten with rods, once was I stoned, . . . in perils from my countrymen, in perils from the Gentiles, in perils in the city, in perils in the wilderness, in perils in the sea, in perils among false brethren '[2].

IX. JEWISH ATTITUDE TO SAINT PAUL

Both the information we possess and a consideration of the circumstances would lead us to expect hostility at this stage to be directed against the leaders of the new sect. The sudden dispersion which followed Stephen's murder seems to have been an isolated incident. The real danger lay with the ringleaders, and as long as the issue lay in the question of the Law, the most dangerous man was Paul. At first the opposition manifested itself in sudden violence, which was rather

[1] The question of whether the Jews at this time had the right to administer capital punishment depends on the credibility given to the narrative of John (xix, 31) that the Jews delivered Jesus because they could not execute Him themselves. This is not mentioned by the synoptists, or by any other authority. See Juster, *op. cit.*, Vol. II, p. 133.

[2] See also Ch. IV, section III, and Appendix Five.

mob action than official condemnation. On the first journey, at the Pisidian Antioch, 'the Jews urged on the devout women of honourable estate, and the chief men of the city, and stirred up a persecution against Paul and Barnabas and cast them out of their borders'[1]. At Iconium the 'Jews that were disobedient' stirred up the souls of the Gentiles and 'made an onset both of the Gentiles and of the Jews with their rulers to entreat them shamefully and to stone them'[2]. At Lystra they actually did stir up the mob to stone them[3]. The same 'mob violence' stirred up by the Jews is reported on the second journey at Thessalonica[4] and at Corinth[5]. At Philippi they got into trouble, as Jews with the Roman colonists, but there is no statement that the Jews had any hand in their arrest. But at Corinth the Jews bring them before Gallio the proconsul.

This incident has been almost as much disputed as the trial of Jesus Himself. Those who for one reason or another doubt the credibility of Acts point out quite logically that, as the Jews had their own jurisdiction, they had no reason for bringing Paul before the Roman authorities. But Luke clearly realises this also, for in his account Gallio refuses to hear the charge on exactly this ground. Luke's accuracy might have been suspect had Gallio acted differently, but as Luke shows himself aware that the Jews were not *compelled* to bring Paul before the Roman court, there seems little reason for doubting his narrative when he states that they did so. Actually it seems not to have been the first time that the Jews brought Christianity to the notice of the Romans, though they do not figure in the story of the trial and imprisonment at Philippi. If when in writing to the Corinthians Paul says that he has thrice been 'beaten with rods', then it must be assumed that, apart from Philippi, he had twice appeared in a Roman court. In other words, though Acts makes no reference to them, it seems that there had been other incidents similar to that at Corinth at other periods of his missionary journeys. Nor is this inherently unlikely

[1] Acts xiii, 50.
[2] *Ibid.* xiv, 5.
[3] *Ibid.* xiv, 19.
[4] *Ibid.* xvii, 5.
[5] *Ibid.* xviii, 6 and 12 ff.

if there is any probability in the statement that the Jews of Corinth dragged Paul before the Romans. The charge they brought was that Paul was trying to persuade them to ' worship God contrary to the Law '. This is certainly a charge with which they could technically have dealt themselves. The situation is the same as it was in the trial of Jesus. The New Testament in both cases informs us that the Jews preferred to lay the responsibility on the Romans for deciding what to do.

In the first case it has been suggested that they did so in order to transfer the odium, which they might incur from the crowd, from themselves to Pilate. This can scarcely be the reason in this case. There is, however, a possible explanation. The teaching of Paul had both in Corinth and elsewhere been attracting a good deal of attention, and had been making ' proselytes ' to Christianity. These were not ' proselytes ' in the Jewish sense that they thereby became circumcised or observed the Law without performing that rite. But the Church itself was still a Jewish sect in the minds both of Jews and Romans. Though the Jews were tolerated, though becoming a proselyte was not in itself a crime, yet it is evident that it was not officially looked on with favour by the Romans. It was not so many years since the Jews had been turned out of Rome because of their proselytising activity. The Roman colonists of Philippi, as soon as they found that Paul was trying to make proselytes of them, raised a disturbance, and though the magistrates could not find it to be a crime, they asked him to leave the city.

It seems legitimate to assume that Paul was felt by the Jews to be endangering their position with the Roman authorities at Corinth. He was attracting more attention than they desired. If this be so, then it was natural that they should attempt to dissociate themselves from him, not by the privacy of a condemnation in their own courts, but by the publicity of denouncing him to the proconsul. There is all the more ground for saying this if we realise that already on five occasions Jewish communities had—without the slightest success—attempted to silence Paul by condemning him in their own courts. Nor can it be said that the fact that Paul had already left them and ' turned to the Gentiles ' in any way freed them from the embarrassment in which he placed them. Paul himself was still a Jew, and, moreover, he was elaborating a doctrine that those who believed his teaching were the true Israel. He was making the situation altogether too complicated, and the best way out was to show the Romans that they at all events had nothing to do with him.

Their attempt failed, because actually it was difficult for them to make a precise accusation against him. Beneath the brief words that he taught men to ' worship God contrary to the Law ', almost any complaint that they could make would be included. Their speech might have been something like this:

> ' This man is causing a great deal of trouble to our loyal Jewish community. He calls himself a Jew, and has been preaching here for some time, both in the synagogue and outside; but his teaching is absolutely unorthodox, and he has five times been condemned by different synagogue courts for it. Our Law is the basis of the privileges which we enjoy under your beneficent rule, and you know well that the Law enjoins us to be good and obedient citizens. But this man preaches an incomprehensible rigmarole against the Law itself, and is perpetually claiming his privilege as a Jew to do it.
>
> ' There is another point. We are a peaceable community, and if a proselyte does join us from time to time, you have always kindly looked the other way, for you know that by making him observe the Law we guarantee that he will remain a good citizen. But this man spends all his time making proselytes out of anyone he meets, and does not enjoin upon them the keeping of the Law, in addition to the fact that they are not taken from the most reputable elements among the population[1], and some of them lead lives which we should never allow. When these people get into trouble, as they are sure to do, it is we who will be blamed for it, for they will call themselves Jews, and claim our privileges. But they know nothing about the Law on which these privileges are based and are even taught to despise it. We beg you to forbid this Paul to call himself a Jew, and to go on abusing

[1] This is based on the evidence of the character of the early Church in Corinth as revealed in the epistles.

our Law, and also to recognise that neither he nor his precious following have anything to do with us. We might mention that we understand that there would be some precedent for scourging him.'

Such an accusation, which seems to me to represent the attitude of the Synagogue to the Church as it was beginning to define itself, might well have been dismissed by Gallio as nothing to do with him; for actually they could not accuse Paul of any legal Roman crime. Why they took and beat Sosthenes at the conclusion of the proceedings we shall never know; perhaps because he was a Christian, and is the same as the Sosthenes who greets the Corinthians in the opening salutation of the first epistle; perhaps because he put their case badly.

In the narratives of the imprisonment and trials of Paul before different Roman-Palestinian authorities there is little new to be learnt. Evidently, in spite of his declaration that if he had committed any crime he was prepared to die for it[1], he preferred to be judged by Rome and not by his own courts. The accusations of the priests have somewhat the same vagueness, in so far as actual crime is concerned, as those at Corinth. The most noteworthy point of the whole affair is the passion with which Paul insists that he himself had done nothing against the Law[2].

X. THE ISSUE STILL CONFUSED

It is made evident that the Jewish authorities had not worked out a concerted plan for dealing with the new sect by the reception which Paul received at Rome. The local Jewish leaders were aware that Christianity was ' everywhere . . . spoken against '[3]. But they had received no instructions about it, and had heard no evil of Paul himself. On the contrary, they express a desire to hear Paul's own view of the matter. The original mission of Saul was local, and of short duration. The enemies of the Church were also local—or

[1] Acts xxv, 11.

[2] *Ibid.* xxii, 3; xxiii, 1; xxiv, 14; xxvi, 5, 22; xxviii, 17.

[3] *Ibid.* xxviii, 22.

parties within it[1]. The Jewish people might approve when Herod killed James, the brother of John, and attempted to seize Peter[2], but here also it was an attack upon the ring-leaders, not upon the rank and file that was made.

It was possible for either side to seize upon single points or persons, but neither had yet a general policy towards the other. Though a mediaeval Christian, if he were asked what was the substance of his hostility to the Jews, would undoubtedly place first the Crucifixion, yet in the conflicts of this period it lies outside the field of debate. Even before a developed Christology arose it was felt to be part of the 'fore-ordained purpose of God'. It was always spoken of by Jesus Himself as a necessity for the accomplishment of His mission. Paul only once accuses 'the Jews' of responsibility for His death[3], and that in a moment of anger. In the whole of the long argument in Romans there is no single verse which ascribes the death of Christ to the Jews. Foakes Jackson, in summing up the period, says: 'What the apostles are said to have preached is that His Resurrection proved His Messiahship. This was a cause of offence to the ruling priestly aristocracy, on grounds purely political; the people seem to have received the message with some approval. The impression left by a candid perusal of the Acts is that the Judaism of the time was not intolerant of opinions. The real battle was the question of observing the Law. The least weakening on this point aroused a storm of indignation, as it had done during the ministry of Jesus'[4]. But on the Law also neither side occupied a consistent position towards the other. A Jew could not easily condemn outright a sect which contained so many blameless followers of all its prescriptions, and the Judeo-Christians had not yet sunk to the unhappy position which they occupied in the second century. Nor did all Christians go so far as Paul appeared to do—indeed, it was difficult for them to do so in view of his inconsistency. The time had not yet come when Christians felt so strongly about it that they could doubt whether a Christian who

[1] Cf. I Thess. ii, 14.

[2] Acts xii, 1-3.

[3] I Thess. ii, 15.

[4] *The Rise of Gentile Christianity*, p. 83.

observed the Law had any chance of salvation[1]. So far, Gentile and Jewish Christians lived in mutual toleration.

External events were soon to compel a clearer attitude on both sides. The generation of Jews and Christians which followed the destruction of Jerusalem, not the generation which first heard the preaching of Christianity, is responsible for the completion of the separation. That accomplished, it still required several centuries for the beliefs of each party to crystallise into the forms which they have historically assumed.

[1] Justin, *Dialogue with Trypho*, xlvii.

CHAPTER THREE

THE PARTING OF THE WAYS

BIBLIOGRAPHICAL INTRODUCTION

The material for this chapter is taken from the patristic literature of these centuries. For English readers most of these are to be found in convenient form in the collection of Ante-Nicene Fathers, though in some cases the editions are not complete. This is particularly so for Origen, the most copious of the early writers. Together with patristic literature has been included the gospel of Saint John, to which reference is made in the bibliographical note of the previous chapter. There are also various writings of importance which are not included in the patrologies, in particular the early apocryphal gospels and certain heretical works, such as the Clementine Recognitions and the Didascalia Apostolorum.

To comment on all the fathers quoted is impossible in this note. There are, however, three classes of literature and certain special writers who deserve a remark.

The most important of all early sources is the Dialogue of Justin with Trypho the Jew, a work of the middle of the second century, by one of the most brilliant of the early Christian apologists. This dialogue, though perhaps not the first (the lost dialogue of Jason and Papiscus is probably earlier) is the model from which all later examples of this class of literature spring.

A second class of literature of particular importance is the ' Testimonies ', collections of texts of the Old Testament to prove different claims connected with the person of Christ and the call of the Gentiles. For this the work of Rendell Harris will need to be consulted, though many scholars do not wholly agree with the early date to which he traces them back.

The third group of writings calling for special consideration are the sermons or homilies especially directed against the Jews. Of these there are a considerable stream. In most cases they were not spoken *to* Jews, and in general it is not to be presumed that Jews were present at all at their delivery. They were warnings to Christians of the danger of intercourse with the Jews. Inevitably they all recall each other, for the ground to be covered in such addresses was relatively restrained. It is significant that without exception none of them are primarily, or in most cases at all, interested in the doings of contemporary Jews.

For our knowledge of actual relations we are therefore thrown back upon chance quotations in other writings. And for all our knowledge of the development of a theological attitude to the Jews we must look to the same sources, and not to the homilies expressly devoted to them. For this reason no special list of these homilies is included. It would be entirely deceptive.

Five writers deserve special mention, Justin, Tertullian, Hippolytus, Cyprian and Origen. The first was a native of Shechem in Palestine, and was trained as a philosopher, the second was an African and a lawyer, the third apparently a Roman, the fourth an African and teacher of rhetoric, and the fifth an Egyptian. They thus represent not only geographically but also in their trainings an astonishingly varied range of interests. Their different writings are of capital importance for the development throughout the Church of the absolute condemnation of the Jews which is characteristic of patristic literature as a whole.

In the list of books given below a number of local monographs are of particular interest for a more detailed survey of Jewish Christian relations in the centres with which they deal.

Finally there is the question of the Judeo-Christians. A number of books are quoted dealing with the rise of the Gentile Church, but I doubt whether full justice has yet been done to this section of the early Church. At least, I have not been able to find an adequate study of the subject.

LIST OF BOOKS

Ancient Sources

PATROLOGIA LATINA
PATROLOGIA GRÆCA — For convenience all quotations are made from these two collections.

(The Vienna Corpus of Ecclesiastical writers should be consulted on questions of texts, for it embodies more modern discoveries and corrections.)

THE APOCRYPHAL NEW TESTAMENT — Ed. M. R. James, Oxford, 1924.

DIDASCALIA APOSTOLORUM — In *Horæ Semiticæ*, No. 2. English trans., London, 1903.

THE ANTE-NICENE FATHERS — T. & T. Clark. Edinburgh, n.d. 20 vols.

Modern Works

SYMPOSIUM — *Judaism and the beginnings of Christianity: a course of Lectures delivered at Jews' College.* Routledge, 1924.

BONWETSCH, N. — *Die Schriftbeweise für die Kirche an den Heiden als das wahre Israel bis auf Hippolyt.* Theologische Studien, Leipzig, 1908.

FOAKES-JACKSON, F. J. — *The Rise of Gentile Christianity.* New York, Doran, 1927.

FREIMAN, M. — *Die Wortführer des Judentums in den Aelteren Kontroversen.* M.G.W.J., 1911 and 1912.

GINZBERG, L. — *Die Haggada bei den Kirchenvätern. Erster Teil.* Amsterdam, 1899. 2nd, Berlin, 1900. 3rd, Poznansky Memorial, Warsaw, 1927. 4th, Studies, New York, 1929. 5th, Chajes Memorial, Wien, 1933.

GOLDFAHN, DR. A. H. *Die Kirchenväter und die Agada.* M.G.W.J., Vol. XXII.

HAAS, MAX *Die Makkabäer als christliche Heilige.* M.G.W.J., Vol. XLIV.

HARRIS, RENDELL *The Early Christian Testimonies.* Expositor, 1906 and 1910.

HERFORD, R. TRAVERS *Christianity in Talmud and Midrash.* Williams and Norgate, 1903.

HORT, F. J. A. *Judaistic Christianity.* Macmillan, 1894.

HULEN, A. B. *The Dialogues with the Jews as sources for the early Jewish Arguments against Christianity.* Journal of Biblical Literature, Vol. LI, i.

KITTEL, G. *Paulus im Talmud,* in *Rabbinica.* Leipzig, 1920.

KRAELING, C. H. *The Jewish Community at Antioch up to* A.D. 600. Journal of Biblical Literature, Vol. LI.

KRAUSS, S. *Jews in the Works of the Church Fathers.* J.Q.R., Vols. V and VI, Old Series.

LAGRANGE, M. J. *Le Messianisme chez les Juifs.* Paris, 1909.

LAIBLE, H. *Jesus Christus im Thalmud.* Berlin, 1891.

LE BLANT, E. *Le Controverse des Chretiens et des Juifs aux premières Siècles de l'Eglise.* Memoires de la Société Nationale des Antiquaires de France, 6me serie, No. 7, 1898.

MERRILL, E. T. *Essays in Early Christian History.* Macmillan, 1893.

MIESES, M. *Der Ursprung des Judenhasses.* Harz Verlag, Wien, 1923.

MONCEAUX, P. *Les Colonies Juives dans l'Afrique Romaine.* R.E.J., Vol. XLIV.

RAMSAY, SIR W. *The Church in the Roman Empire before* A.D.170. Hodder and Stoughton, 1893.

STRACK, HERMANN L. *Jesus, die Häretiker und die Christen nach den ältesten jüdischen Angaben.* Schriften des Institutum Judaicum, Berlin, No. 37, 1910.

TURNER, C. *The Testimonies in the early Church.* Journal of Theological Studies, 1905 and 1908.

WERNER, KARL *Geschichte der Apologetischen und Polemischen Literatur*, Vol. I. Schaffhausen, 1861.

I. THE SEPARATION: JEWS AND CHRISTIANS IN PALESTINE

At the death of Paul, Christianity was still a Jewish sect. In the middle of the second century it is a separate religion busily engaged in apologetics to the Greek and Roman world, and anxious to establish its antiquity, respectability and loyalty. To decide on the date at which the separation took place is no easy task, for there are so many parties to be considered. When the armies of Titus approached Jerusalem, the Judeo-Christians retired to Pella. At the same time the rabbinical leaders retired to Jabne. The defence of Jerusalem was undertaken by the political and not by the religious leaders of the people. The fall of the city, however, reacted differently upon the two different groups. The rabbinical leaders might consider it to be a punishment for the sins of the people. But the Judeo-Christians went further, and saw in it a final ' departure of the sceptre from Israel '. The loss of the Temple meant that Judaism had now only the Law as a basis for its continued independence. Had the Judeo-Christians been the only members of the new faith, the breach between them and the Jews might have been healed, for they also desired to observe the Law. But the rabbis at Jabne were not unaware of their contact with Gentile Christians who did not observe the Law at all. They knew the teaching of Paul, and condemned it utterly[1]. It was only a step from this condemnation to the refusal to accept as orthodox the conformity of the Judeo-Christians.

This step was taken by the insertion into the daily Blessings recited in the synagogue of a declaration about heretics so worded that the Judeo-Christians could not pronounce it. This declaration, the Birkath-ha-Minim, was composed by Samuel the Small, who lived in the second half of the first century. His exact date we do not know, but he was a contemporary of Gamaliel II, who presided at Jabne from 80 to 110, and was also acquainted with two rabbis who were killed in the capture of Jerusalem in 70. We may therefore conclude that he was somewhat older than Gamaliel, and date the malediction which he composed to between

[1] Kittel, *op. cit.*, Chapter I.

80 and 90[1]. Of the actual wording of the original malediction we cannot be certain. Later forms only contain the word 'minim' or 'heretics', and it now only refers to 'slanderers', but according to Jerome[2] it contained the express condemnation of 'Nazarenes'—a word which may well have been erased in the many censorings to which Jewish literature has been subject at the hands of Christian authorities. The purpose of the malediction is to detect the presence of Minim, for if they were invited to pronounce the Eighteen Benedictions they would inevitably omit that particular paragraph from them. The fact that the test was a statement made in the synagogue service shows that at the time of making it the Judeo-Christians still frequented the synagogue. There would be no point otherwise in trying to prevent them from leading the prayers. In other words, at the time when official Judaism, represented by the rabbis at Jabne, had decided that the presence of these people could not be tolerated, the Judeo-Christians, however much they disagreed from other Jews on the question as to whether the Messiah had or had not come, still considered themselves to be Jews; and it is not too much to suppose from this that there were also Jews who considered that a disagreement on this point did not make fellowship with them impossible. They must have been generally accepted, or it is incredible that they should have continued to frequent the synagogue. They were evidently there as ordinary members, since it needed the introduction of this formula to detect them.

A breach would, however, from their point of view, occur if the rest of the Jews decided definitely on another Messiah, and this is what happened in the time of Barcochba. Even though all the Jews did not by any means accept his claim, yet it was accepted by very influential leaders such as Aqiba, and the discussion round it would inevitably bring into relief the fact that they were at least agreed in refusing to accept Jesus as Messiah, whatever was thought of Barcochba. This would give a date well into the second century for the break from the side of the Judeo-Christians. So late a date would not, however, apply to all of them—and, indeed, there is no reason to suppose that all simultaneously came to the

[1] Travers Herford, p. 125.
[2] Jer., *On Isaiah*, v, 18. P.L., XXIV, 87.

same conclusion. Some had evidently come to it much earlier, even as Paul and other Jewish apostles had done. We may, however, accept the date of the malediction as that affecting the majority of those concerned. This would fit in with the addition in the first gospel of the words ' His blood be on us and on our children ', which implies a final separation ; and the date usually given for this gospel is between 80 and 90.

It is important to add that even if dates round the end of the first and the beginning of the second century are given for the official break between the two religions, yet, as long as there were any number of conversions from Judaism to Christianity, there were many places in which it would be difficult to draw the dividing line. The existence of much of the anti-Judaic literature of the early Church, and in particular such courses of sermons as those of Chrysostom at Antioch in 387, show that respect for the synagogue was by no means dead among some Christian groups. It was, however, regarded by orthodox theologians with absolute disapproval, and was also so regarded by the central authorities of Judaism. But these had moved before the end of the second century to Babylon, where their contacts with Christians were fewer than in the west.

II. THE SEPARATION: THE LETTERS TO THE SYNAGOGUES

It is reasonable also to date the letters and 'Apostles' sent out to the Jews of the diaspora to the end of the first century. Through his emissaries the Jewish Patriarch of Palestine was able to keep in fairly close touch with the Jews in the rest of the world because of the annual collection which was made by all the synagogues to the central organisation. The decision which is marked by the inclusion of the test malediction on the heretics into the Eighteen Benedictions was an important one. The matter touched the diaspora even more closely than Palestine itself. We may therefore presume that before the end of the century all the synagogues of the diaspora had been informed of the new malediction and warned to have no dealings with the Christians.

It is important to attempt to define exactly the nature of the official instruction issued at this time. The frequent references in patristic literature make it certain that some such step was taken, but they differ in the contents which they ascribe to the letters sent. It is difficult, but necessary, to try to distinguish what was sent out officially from Palestine from what was spread abroad unofficially by individual Jews.

If we take the substance of what is told us by Justin, Eusebius and Jerome, we can make a fair reconstruction of the letter. It contained a formal denial of the truth of the Christian account of the teaching and resurrection of Jesus. Christianity was a denial of God and of the Law[1]. It was based on the teaching of Jesus, who was a deceiver, and who had been put to death by the Jews. His disciples had stolen His body, and then pretended that He had risen again from the dead and was the Son of God. It was therefore impossible for Jews to have anything to do with such teaching, and His followers should be formally excommunicated[2]. Jews were to avoid all discussions of any kind with the Christians[3]. It is probable that the letters also contained a copy of the Birkath-ha-Minim, with instructions to include it into the Eighteen Benedictions. For the daily cursing of Christ in the synagogue is very closely associated with the letters[4]. All three writers insist on the official character of these letters, and on their wide dispersion.

Many modern writers would have us also include in the official letters the broadcasting of slanders against both the person of Christ and the morals of Christians[5]. They accuse the Jewish authorities of spreading officially the stories to be found in the Sepher Toldoth Jeshu as to the illegitimacy of Jesus, and His evil ways. They believe that from this source came also the rumour of Thyestean banquets and Oedipean intercourse at the meetings of the Christians[6].

[1] Justin, *Dialogue*, cviii, and Eusebius ,*On Isaiah*, xviii, 1; P.G., XXIV, p. 213.

[2] Justin, *ibid*., and Jerome, *On Isaiah*, xviii, 2; P.L., XXIV, p. 184.

[3] Justin, xxxviii, and Origen, *Celsus*, VI, 27; P.G., XI, p. 1333.

[4] Justin, xvi, xlvii, xcv, cxxxiii.

[5] *E.g.* Harnack, see below, Ch. IV, Section I.

[6] Cf. Origen, *Celsus*, VI, 27, and Section VIII below.

This seems exceedingly unlikely. It is natural that the step taken was bitterly resented by the Christians, but at the same time we cannot be surprised at its being considered necessary. The Church still contained many Jewish members who considered that belief in the Messiah could be reconciled with membership of the Synagogue, and the Gentile Christians were still probably largely recruited from the group of the ' metuentes Deum '. To make accusations which could easily be disproved would have been very bad policy. It would have discredited the entire letter, for those who received it would inevitably know that Christians might be in error, but were not leading immoral lives. If we exclude the charges of immorality, the charges against the personal character of Jesus fall also, for the two come from the same source. We can, in fact, legitimately conclude that it was a dignified but firm denunciation of the Christians, accompanied by an order to have no fellowship with them, and a copy of the new passage to be included in the service of the synagogue. For more than this we cannot hold the authorities responsible; and for acting thus we can neither blame them nor be astonished at them.

III. THE SEPARATION: JEWS AND CHRISTIANS IN THE DIASPORA

Before considering the effects of the receipt of this letter upon the synagogues of the diaspora, we must consider what the general situation was in the communities which received it. It is natural to assume that the initiative in the development which took place was due to the Christians. When they denounced, the Jews reacted. To suppose an initiative on the part of a majority, which was very occupied with other matters, is to suppose an unnatural order of events. The Church has never declared a movement heretical until the movement has made a statement which is unacceptable. To propose the contrary order in this case is to propose something inexplicable and unique. But, in fact, we know that the Christians gave continual provocation. The whole development of teaching in the sub-apostolic period was inevitably infuriating to the Jew. The fact that the Christians considered it essential to the explanation of their position does not alter this truth.

Although Judaism rallied with extraordinary speed from the blow struck at the Jewish religion by the destruction of the Temple and of all the ceremonial of which it was the centre, and though the Jews in the diaspora had long been accustomed to centre their religion round the synagogue, yet it cannot but have left a sense of tragedy and humiliation upon the generation which witnessed it. It was a point which they would have liked to pass over in silence, until time had healed the scars. But the Christians never allowed them to forget it. In all the literature of the period there is only one reference in which the destruction of the Temple is not cast up at them as a gibe, as a proof that their glory had departed. This one reference is in the Didascalia Apostolorum, a work remarkable throughout for the lack of hostility which it shows to the Jews. It calls Christians also to fast over the fallen city: 'for their sake we ought to fast and to mourn, that we may be glad to take our pleasure in the world to come, as it is written in Isaiah, "rejoice all ye that mourn over Zion" . . . so we ought to take pity on them, and to have faith, and to fast and to pray for them '[1].

The more usual attitude to the Jews is that expressed in the addresses to them in the fourth gospel, or, fifty years later, in the *Dialogue of Justin with Trypho*. It is possible to read the beginning of the gospel of Mark without knowing how the discussions with the Pharisees are going to end. The fourth gospel opens with a statement of the rejection of Jesus by the Jews. 'He came unto His own, and they that were His own received Him not.'[2] On His first visit to Jerusalem He cleanses the Temple, and thereby puts Himself openly in opposition to the authorities[3]. Nicodemus the Pharisee is afraid to come to Him by day[4]. Jesus is afraid of their possible interruption of His ministry as soon as He knows that they have heard that His disciples are baptising those who come to Him, and withdraws from Judaea[5]. The

[1] See *Horae Semiticae*, II, xxi, p. 96.
[2] John i, 11.
[3] *Ibid.* ii, 13 ff.
[4] *Ibid.* iii, 2.
[5] *Ibid.* iv, 1, 3.

first Sabbath controversy leads to a persecution, and immediately after it the Jews seek to kill Him[1]. Then follows one of the long and unsympathetic denunciations of the Jews which mark the gospel, and which contain words which accurately reflect the situation at the time when they were written, but which would seem strange in one of the earlier gospels: ' ye search the scriptures, because ye think that in them ye have eternal life, and these are they which bear witness of Me and ye will not come to Me '[2]. The speech continues: ' think not that I will accuse you to the Father. There is one that accuseth you, even Moses, on whom ye have set your hope. For if ye believed Moses ye would believe Me, for he wrote of Me '[3].

From this moment onwards every time that Jesus is made to speak to the Jews He appears deliberately to mystify and to antagonise them. He does not attempt to win them, for He knows His own, and treats the rest with hostility and unconcealed dislike. The Jews themselves are represented as perpetually plotting to kill Him, and afraid to do so, because of His moral power[4]. Even when Jesus addresses those Jews ' which had believed on Him ', He says of them that they are of their ' father the devil '[5]. In the middle of His ministry the Jews decide to expel from the Synagogue any who believe in Him[6], so that people are afraid to speak openly of Him[7]. All this is redolent of the atmosphere which must have existed at the end of the century, when, indeed, confession of Christianity meant expulsion from the Synagogue, and exposure to the unknown dangers of Roman persecution. The whole content of the addresses to the Jews is self-justification to those who have already made up their minds, and not pleading with those who are not yet enlightened. The temper is fundamentally different from that shown by the synoptists, or by Paul, but it is very close to the gibes of Justin: ' circumcision was given you as a sign,

[1] John v, 16 and 18.
[2] *Ibid.* v, 39 and 40.
[3] *Ibid.* v, 45 and 46.
[4] *Ibid.* vii, 1, 19, 25, 30, 45; x, 31, 39; xi, 53.
[5] *Ibid.* viii, 44.
[6] *Ibid.* ix, 22.
[7] *Ibid.* vii, 13.

that you may be separated from other nations, and from us, and that you alone may suffer that which you now justly suffer, and that your land may be desolate, and your cities burnt with fire. These things have happened to you in fairness and justice '[1].

It is not surprising that such an attitude caused acute resentment, and it is equally to be expected that resentment, would quickly develop into violence. But these attacks were merely the surface expression of a more deep-seated contradiction. With the destruction of the Temple the Christians were convinced that all that there was of promise and encouragement in the Old Testament had passed to them[2]. They disinherited the Jew from his own sacred books at the very moment when these provided his only comfort. All the Law and the promises led on to Christ the Messiah. Rejecting Him, the Jew lost also all share in them. ' Judaism ', says Ignatius, ' is nothing but funeral monuments and tombstones of the dead.'[3] The Christian did not even allow him any further merit in the actual observance of the Law. It was only a mass of frivolities and absurdities, except as a preliminary to the Gospel[4]. By some mysterious process all that was good in Judaism had become evil. To Ignatius it was merely human ideas, for on its ' funeral monuments ' were human names alone[5]. The whole of the epistle of Barnabas is an exposition of the Church as the true Israel. It is heresy even to try and share the good things of promise with the Jews. In tones of unusual gravity, and with a special appeal, the author warns his hearers against such mistaken generosity: ' This also I further beg of you, as being one of you, and loving you both individually and collectively more than my own soul, to take heed to yourselves, and not be like some, adding largely to your sins, and saying: " the covenant is both theirs and ours " '[6].

[1] Justin, *Dialogue with Trypho*, Chapter xvi.

[2] See further, Section IX.

[3] Ignatius, *To the Philadelphians*, vi, 1.

[4] *Epistle to Diognetus*, Ch. iv; P.G., II, p. 1172.

[5] Ignatius, *Epistle to Philadelphians*, Ch. vi, 1. The shorter version calls them ' monuments '.

[6] Ch. iv.

If such was the attitude of the Christians, we cannot be surprised if Tertullian is right in saying that the Jews attached infamy to the name ' during the interval from Tiberius to Vespasian '[1]. The evidence of violent hostility on the part of the Jews of the diaspora belongs almost exclusively to this period. The actual content of the persecution of the Christians by the Jews will be considered later[2], but it is evident that the temper on both sides was such that in the diaspora also we may date the separation to the generation following the destruction of Jerusalem. From this time onwards Christianity would have to make its own peace with Rome, and would be little likely to be protected by the Synagogue in case of trouble with the Roman authorities.

IV. THE SEPARATION: THE ROMANS, RAMSAY'S VIEW

In the consideration of the date of the separation between the Church and the Synagogue, we have to consider not only the parties already discussed, the Palestinian Jews and Judeo-Christians, and the diaspora Jews and Gentile Christians, but also the Romans. As long as Christianity was a Jewish sect it enjoyed the protection extended to Judaism, and the attitude of Gallio was the only one possible. When they were recognised as separate, the Christians were exposed to the possibility of suppression. The whole question of the beginning of the persecution of Christianity by the Romans is involved in violent controversy. It turns on two points: when did the Romans first become conscious of the organised existence of Christian Churches, and, when they did, for what precise crime did they persecute them? It is impossible to state all the different opinions which have been expressed. It will be of more value to the present purpose to summarise somewhat fully two contrasting points of view, that of Dr Ramsay, which is exposed in *The Church in the Roman Empire before* A.D. 170[3], and that of E. T. Merrill in *Essays in Early Christian History*[4].

[1] *Answers to the Jews*, Ch. xiii; P.L., II, p. 637.
[2] See Ch. IV.
[3] Hodder and Stoughton, 1893.
[4] Macmillan, 1924.

Dr Ramsay, basing his main argument on the efficiency of the Roman provincial organisation, decides for a very early recognition of the existence of the Christian Church. Starting from the fixed point of the correspondence between Pliny and Trajan, of which the date is 112, he states that ' Trajan clearly regarded the prescription of the Christians as a fundamental principle of imperial policy which he did not choose, or shrank from altering '[1]. The question to decide is the date from which this policy became ' fundamental '. Some say from the time of Domitian, but this is to ignore the full account of the persecution under Nero, which is given by Tacitus and confirmed by Suetonius. The theory that Tacitus is only describing a single isolated event is contradicted by the form of mention in Suetonius, who refers to the persecution of the Christians among other acts, not of a temporary character, but ' of the nature of permanent police regulations for maintaining order and good conduct '[2]. The fair and natural interpretation is that Suetonius considered Nero to have maintained ' a steady prosecution of a mischievous class of persons ', which ' implies a permanent and settled policy '. Properly considered, the account in Tacitus also shows more than casual action. The first charge was incendiarism, but when the public got disgusted at the cruelty inflicted on the prisoners they were charged with *odium humani generis*, which was not an abstract charge, but meant an attempt to destroy Roman society. This is supported by the first epistle of Peter[3]. Moreover, Tacitus speaks of an *ingens multitudo*, which must mean more than a short attack on a few incendiaries. ' On these grounds we conclude that if Tacitus has correctly represented the authorities, the persecution of Nero, begun for the sake of diverting popular attention, was continued as a permanent police measure under the form of a general prosecution of Christians as a sect dangerous to public safety.'[4]

The charge was not yet ' the Name ' as it was in Pliny's time, but *flagitia cohaerentia nomini*, the accusations of disgraceful immorality and cannibalism, to which the

[1] *Op. cit.*, p. 226.

[2] *Ibid.* p. 230.

[3] I Peter ii, 12: ' they speak against you as evil doers '.

[4] Ramsay, p. 241.

apologists constantly refer. When Nero had once established the principle in Rome it would be naturally followed in all the provinces. ' There is no need to suppose a general edict, or a formal law. The precedent would be quoted in every case where a Christian was accused.' But ' between 68 and 96, the attitude of the state towards the Christians was more clearly defined, and the process was changed, so that proof of definite crimes committed by the Christians was no longer required, and acknowledgement of the name alone sufficed for condemnation. Nero treats a great many Christians as criminals, and punishes them for their crimes. Pliny and Trajan treat them as outlaws and brigands, and punish them without reference to their crimes '[1].

The Flavians continued the policy laid down by Nero, and Ramsay accepts the authenticity of a council held by Titus before the capture of Jerusalem[2]. ' In Titus' speech the difference between Judaism and Christianity is fully recognised, but the fact was not grasped that the latter was quite independent of the Temple, and of Jerusalem as a centre.'[3] When this latter fact was recognised, ' the enmity which underlies the speech of Titus would be carried into vigorous action '—action based on the extensive reports on the Christians which Ramsay assumes would exist in the imperial archives.

The policy of Titus was naturally followed by Domitian, and it is only because of his anti-Christian bias that Dio Cassius says that Clemens and Domitilla, whom Domitian exiled, were Jews, whereas really they were Christians. It is quite impossible that the government could still be confusing the two, and the treatment of Jews was quite different.

The silence of Christian writers about this steady and continual persecution is to be referred to their lack of interest in history at this early period. There has also been misrepresentation of the references which are to be found. The author of the first epistle of Peter says to his readers: ' Let none of you suffer as a murderer, or a thief, or an evil-doer,

[1] Ramsay, p. 245. Ramsay argues that the persecution in Bithynia had nothing to do with the law against *sodalitates*, as the Christians, by giving up their common meal, had conformed. *Ibid*. p. 213.

[2] Sulpicius Severus, *Chron.*, II, xxx.

[3] Ramsay, p. 254.

or as a meddler in other men's matters: but if a man suffer as a Christian, let him not be ashamed, but let him glorify God in this name '[1]. This implies official action, since only the governor could execute capital sentence. The Apocalypse of John refers to Rome as 'drunk with the blood of the saints', and is full of references to persecution[2]. Clement refers to 'the examples which belong to our generation' as 'a vast multitude of the elect'[3], and Ignatius speaks of Ephesus as the highway of the martyrs to Rome'[4].

It is evident that persecution could not have preceded the separation of the Church and the Synagogue, so that, on Ramsay's view, we should have to date this separation back to the time of the Apostles themselves, and presume that the attitude taken by Paul was both understood and followed by the immense majority of his converts.

V. THE SEPARATION: THE ROMANS, MERRILL'S VIEW

E. T. Merrill, writing as a classical scholar and not as a Church historian, finds that there has been a perpetual tendency to exaggerate the persecutions altogether, and to accept as evidence statements which would not be accepted in any other branch of research. He considers that the Church historians have come to believe in persecution 'for the Name' because of its 'persistent affirmation'; and in spite of the fact that, firstly, such a condition would be inexplicable in Roman law, and that, secondly, other explanations are possible. 'In the presence of a considerable number of isolated but evidently cognate phenomena there is a natural tendency in the trained human intellect to relate them together into a system, and to find a single rule to explain all the allied cases, a single cause to account for all results.'[5] As we know of no Roman legislation condemning 'the Name', modern scholars invent the theory that Christians

[1] I Peter iv, 15 and 16.

[2] See *e.g.* vi, 9; vii, 14; xii, 11; xiii, 15; xvi, 6; xvii, 6; xviii, 24; xx, 4; etc.

[3] 1st Epistle of Clement, vi; P.G., I, p. 220.

[4] Epistle to the Ephesians, xii.

[5] *Op. cit.*, p. 132.

were treated as wild beasts, enemies of humanity, outlaws and so on. Further confusion has been created by the statement that Christianity was *illicita*, and this has been taken to correspond to the modern idea of *illegal*, whereas it only means *unincorporated*. It is quite absurd to think that all members of such groups, of which many existed, were treated as outlaws.

It is equally incredible to suppose that the high officials of the empire were aware of the existence of Christianity until the middle or end of the second century[1], at which time a concerted policy began to appear. But even then persecution was not for 'the Name', but for the crimes which these particular *collegia* were alleged to practise.

As to the persecution under Nero, there is no evidence in pagan or Christian writers that it extended outside Rome, or that an *ingens multitudo* perished in it. Tacitus was fond of such rhetorical exaggeration, and in another passage he has an even stronger phrase to describe an event in which we know from Suetonius that there were twenty victims[2]. The persecution in Rome arose from the need of finding a culprit for a particular event, and Christians were selected because it was known that they were unpopular with the masses. Jews might have equally well been taken had they not had influence at court, in the person of Poppaea. The account in Tacitus makes it quite clear that arson was the legal charge, and the *odium humani generis* only added to give it plausibility. The crisis once over, Nero had no further interest in the sect. Turning then to examine the accounts said to exist in Christian documents, Merrill notes that no details would be known to us at all of this persecution, if it were not for the pagan writer Tacitus. Evidently, therefore, it did not make so profound an impression upon the Church as is supposed. The evidence of I Peter and the Apocalypse he considers to be 'misinterpreted and sometimes misdated'[3].

Sporadic action in different provinces was all that took place for many years. Pliny's action in Bithynia was obvi-

[1] *Op. cit.*, p. 56 ff.

[2] *Ibid.* p. 101. The twenty victims are described as 'immensa strages, omnis sexus, omnis aetas, illustres, ignobiles, dispersi aut aggerati'.

[3] *Ibid.* pp. 113-124 for a discussion of the texts.

ously such, for Mellito, Bishop of Sardis in the vicinity, writing more than fifty years after it had happened, had never heard of it. 'When all possible concessions have been made regarding the influence of precedent in Roman legal procedure, there is to be found in all the history of Roman law and administration no precedent that would justify the assumption of a pronouncement or other action that could possibly be regarded as putting any class of Roman citizens or subjects once for all outside the pale of the law. The whole spirit and tendency of Roman law and administration was in precisely the opposite direction.'[1] As a matter of fact, even the rhetorician and lawyer Tertullian makes no such absolute charge as modern writers have attempted to do[2].

The persecution under Domitian he discredits entirely. The opening of Clement's letter to the Corinthians, on which so much is built, is absurdly exaggerated in its interpretations. Clement says that he has been delayed in writing 'through unexpected and repeated troubles and hindrances'. 'The language sounds curiously like an apologetic introduction to a modern letter—"I really meant to write you long ago, but all sorts of bothering things have interfered".' The allegation that Clemens and Domitilla were Christians, and that Dio Cassius concealed the fact through prejudice, is absurd, and Dio's prejudice a myth. There is no reason why he should have had much information about an obscure sect, and still less why he should conceal it. Dio's supposed statement apart, the first evidence of persecution is seventy-five years later, and unconvincing. As to the Apocalypse, it can only be said that historical data cannot be studied in such poetical and apocalyptic dreams[3]. In dealing with the Bithynian persecution, he replies point by point to the argument of Ramsay[4], and finds that it was, and was considered by Pliny and Trajan to be, simply a question of the existence of a *sodalitas*, when such had been forbidden. It was so far from being a crime to be a Christian apart from

[1] *Op. cit.*, p. 143.

[2] *Ibid.* p. 134.

[3] *Ibid.* pp. 158-159.

[4] *Ibid.* p. 199 ff.

other evidence, that Trajan, hearing of the nature of this particular *sodalitas*, gave it special favours.

Merrill is not concerned with the date of the separation between the two bodies. His interest is the persecution of Christianity by the Romans, and his conclusion would be that we cannot get any useful evidence from Roman action for settling the date of the separation, whatever we may deduce from the internal relations of the two groups.

VI. THE DATE OF THE SEPARATION

In the light of the previous discussion it is possible to conclude that the definite separation into two religions took place towards the end of the first century. Some of the leaders on either side had decided upon its inevitability, or necessity, much earlier. In some cases the link was kept much later, but in general we can say that at the end of the first century Christianity began to stand upon its own feet theologically and socially. Such a conclusion is supported by the appearance of the Birkath-ha-Minim, and by the development of the attitude of the Gentile Christians to Judaism. The only arguments against this date are those of Ramsay. For it is clear that however excellent the Roman State Archives, and however much time the emperors spent in studying them, it is somewhat extravagant to assume that the Romans were aware of the emergence of a new cult before its own sectaries, and before its parent body had realised it. A number of Christians were certainly executed by Nero. But it was not a persecution of the Church or of Christianity. It was an isolated event, even if Suetonius thought that it was a declaration of routine policy. If we recognise this, then we can also recognise that Titus, if he really held a council before Jerusalem in which he declared that the destruction of the city would lead to the destruction of Judaism and Christianity, did not recognise that two different faiths were involved, and that he still considered Christianity merely to be a Jewish sect. In the same way all argument for the bias of Dio Cassius disappears, and we can accept at its face value his statement that Clemens and Domitilla were Jews. Whether Domitilla became a

Christian later in life does not concern us. Robbed of all the supports which ultimately rest on a persecution under Nero of Christianity as such, the arguments of Ramsay collapse, for the references in epistles and in the Apocalypse are not enough by themselves to prove a persecution of *Christianity* in the first century.

But we need not go as far as Merrill and suppose that the high officials were unaware of the existence of Christianity before the middle or end of the second century. The references in the epistles and Apocalypse do mean something. Christians were looked on with disfavour, from whatever source that disfavour came. The second century apologists clearly felt the need for a defence of Christianity to the pagan world. Disturbances within the Jewish community took place as far west as Rome as early as the days of Claudius. They were aroused by the missionary journeys of Paul, and doubtless of other Apostles. These would demand no more than police action to preserve order. But if we imagine them to have continued, as they probably did, throughout the half-century in which the separation was taking place, then we can safely say that the evidence of the epistles and Apocalypse is adequately accounted for, and that so far as the Roman evidence is concerned, the end of the first century is the time of the definite emergence of Christianity as a new religion.

VII. THE JUDEO-CHRISTIANS AFTER THE SEPARATION

There is one group to whom it has been already implied that the preceding argument does not wholly apply—the Judeo-Christians. There is no more tragic group in Christian history than these unhappy people. They, who might have been the bridge between the Jewish and the Gentile world, must have suffered intensely at the developments on both sides which they were powerless to arrest. Rejected, first by the Church, in spite of their genuine belief in Jesus as the Messiah, and then by the Jews in spite of their loyalty to the Law, they ceased to be a factor of any importance in the development of either Christianity or Judaism. It is conventional to state that they would have permanently confined

Christianity to the Jewish world, that they wished to impose conditions which were impossible for the Gentiles, but we only possess the evidence against them. And they on their side might well say—paradoxical as it may appear to us now—that the Gentile Church by its attitude made the acceptance of the Messianic claims of Jesus impossible to the Jew; and that the perpetual statement of the Gentile leaders that the Jews continued to reject Christ was fundamentally untrue, because they were being offered Him only upon conditions which were false and impossible for a loyal Jew to accept—in other words, an attitude to the whole of Jewish history and to the Law which was based upon Gentile ignorance and misunderstanding, and was quite unsupported by the conduct of Jesus Himself.

Though thus isolated, they lingered on in Palestine for centuries. For them, the critical years were not so much from A.D. 70 to 100, as from 70 to 135, and the final destruction of Jerusalem under Trajan. Until the Jews had in large numbers decided for another Messiah, they might continue to hope that they would accept Jesus. But when, led by the famous Aqiba, the bulk of the population followed Barcochba, then the position became hopeless. Though the Birkath-ha-Minim dates from thirty or forty years before these events, yet we know of no actual persecution of them by the Jews between the death of James and the outbreak of the revolt in the time of Trajan. Then indeed they suffered severely for their refusal to accept Barcochba, and to share in the defence of the city, and many were put to death[1]. After the defeat of the revolt, when the Jews were formally prohibited from entering Jerusalem, for the first time a Gentile bishop was established in the city. As the choice of Barcochba confirmed the refusal of the Jews to accept Jesus, so the presence of a Gentile bishop emphasised the break from Judaism of the new religion.

Just as it is conventional for Christian historians to consider that the history of the Jews up to the Incarnation is to be considered as a preparation for the Gospel, and that Jewish history in some way stops when Christian history begins, so also the Judeo-Christians are regarded as ceasing to be of importance when their defeat by the Gentile

[1] Justin, *First Apology*, Chapter xxxi; P.G., VI, p. 375.

Christians was assured. But the Church of the second century was no more the Church of the fourth than was the Judaism of the second century the complete Judaism of the Talmud. Neither had yet absorbed or rejected various intermediate groups which existed at the earlier period.

The interesting fact about this period is that from the two poles of Catholic and Rabbinic orthodoxy stretch an unbroken stream of intermediate sects. For there were some groups which had both Christian and Jewish representatives, such as the Gnostics and the Ebionites, and among the Jewish believers in Christ there appear to have been a number of different groups varying in their conception of the amount of the Law which should still be obeyed. We shall see when we come to consider the action of the councils, and the denunciations of the fourth century, that there is every reason to believe that the common people were much more friendly with each other than the leaders approved of, and this is reflected in some of the popular literature which has survived, and which lacks the bitterness of the more intellectual theologians.

The disputation between Peter and the Apostles on the one side and representatives of the different Jewish parties on the other, which is related in the *Clementine Recognitions*, shows no special bitterness towards the Jews, and the discussions themselves are said to have taken place at the request of the High Priest[1]. Even more striking are the Acts of Philip[2], a production of the third century. Philip goes to a town called Nicetera in Greece, and when the Jews hear of his presence there ‘ they say hard things of him as of a corrupter of the Law ’. They agree, however, readily to the proposal of the chief among them, Hiereus, that he should undertake to argue with Philip. Hiereus does so with much courtesy, and is converted by Philip, and after some resistance on the part of his wife, from whom Philip demands that he shall live separated, she is converted also, and Philip makes his home with them. This situation lasts for some time, and then when Philip preaches again, the Jews and pagans get very angry, and summon him to the court. Philip appears, and the mob wish to stone him. But again a Jew intervenes

[1] *Clementine Recognitions*, I, liii; P.G., I, p. 1236.
[2] *An. Boll.*, Vol. IX, 1890.

and undertakes to argue with him. He questions Philip on the interpretation of the Prophets, and on the virgin birth, and professes himself satisfied with Philip's replies. He then takes the credit to himself for Philip not being stoned by the mob, and for this presumption Philip afflicts him with a number of ailments, of which Hiereus subsequently heals him in the name of Jesus. This double miracle instils fear, if not affection, into the Jews, and they make no objection when Philip proceeds to convert and baptise all the inhabitants, themselves apparently included.

The hostility of the Jerusalem authorities was always presupposed, but the apocryphal Acts, which began to appear in the second and third centuries, saw nothing strange in the general conversion of the Jewish people. In another version of the Acts of Philip[1], he goes to Athens, and is pursued thither by Ananias and an army of five hundred men. These are converted by Philip's miracles, while Ananias himself, for his refusal to be so, is swallowed up in the ground—by stages—bravely protesting his refusal at each stage. In the Acts of Peter[2], of the second century, there is the strange contrast of the fourth gospel repeated. 'The Jews' believe, but are afraid to confess it for fear of 'the Jews'. In the later apocryphal works the hostility is much more marked, and no Jewish conversions are expected.

While, therefore, we may correctly date the actual separation from the end of the first and the beginning of the second century, we should be wrong to assume that the distinction which we can now observe between Christians and Jews represents the situation as it appeared to those living at the time.

VIII. THE CREATION OF AN OFFICIAL ATTITUDE TO JUDAISM

If there be any justification to be found for the picture of the Jews and of their history drawn in the writings of the Fathers, it would be that they believed the influence of the Jews to be a perpetual and present danger to their flock,

[1] *The Apocryphal New Testament*, p. 439.

[2] *Ibid.* p. 90.

that they saw in the Jews the opponents of orthodoxy, and the deceivers of the simple. It must be admitted that very little evidence of the truth of this supposition is to be found in the literature remaining to us. We hear of heretical Christian sects influencing the orthodox, but we hear nothing about such influence being exercised by Jews. It is not a charge made by Justin, or in any writing deliberately addressed to them. The usual charge is inveterate hostility, which is something essentially different. But in view of the fact that such a situation did apparently occasionally exist in the fourth and fifth centuries[1], it is, perhaps, reasonable to believe that it existed in the second and third centuries also.

By the second century the controversy over the Law had ceased to play the rôle which it had played at the earlier period. The Church had become predominantly Gentile in membership and almost exclusively so in leadership. Justin refers pityingly to some few Gentile Christians who, from weakness, still observed the Law, and as a magnanimous concession on his part admitted that they might be saved[2], but he adds that other Christians would not venture to have any intercourse whatever with such persons. The compromise arranged in Acts, and the concessions made by Peter and Paul, had absolutely no further validity[3], and the actions of the Apostles, approved in the first century, would, as Jerome and Augustine later agree, have been the rankest heresy once the Church was properly established. The field of controversy has shifted from the Law to the 'promises', in other words, to the whole question of the fulfilment of all prophecy in the person of Jesus Christ.

We may at first wonder why the attempt to prove the reality of the Divinity of Christ made it necessary to falsify the whole of Jewish history, as the Gentile Church undoubtedly did, but if we study their approach to the problem we see that they were led on inescapably by the method of their own argumentation from the first legitimate assumption to

[1] See Ch. V, Section VII, on the influence of Jews on catechumens.

[2] Justin, *Trypho*, Ch. xlvii.

[3] Cf. the correspondence between Jerome and Augustine on this point. Letters 28, 40, 75, 82 in the Edition of Augustine's letters by Marcus Dodds, or P.L., XXXIII, same numbers.

the last and most extravagant fabrications. Unhappily, historical criticism did not exist for either party in the struggle, and the system which the Church used to support her claims was in manner, though naturally not in matter, the same as that used by the Jew to refute them. Historically, Jesus during His earthly life was linked to Jewish history and to the Jewish scriptures. The Church, in spite of all its philosophising, never lost sight of the actual historical reality of the Incarnation, and unhesitatingly rejected all those views which tended to reduce to a plane of secondary importance the events of the earthly life of Jesus. The Fathers insisted on His relation to Jewish prophecy and the divine history of His people. But in safeguarding themselves against an identification of Jesus with a Greek demigod, or with the mythical saviour of a mystery religion, they were compelled to interpret the whole of the Jewish scriptures in such a way as to support their own view[1]. We have already seen how the writer of the epistle to Barnabas feared that his readers would be tempted to share the scriptures with the Jews. The only alternative was to claim the whole of it for themselves and to antedate the rejection of the Jews and the emergence of the Church to the beginning of revealed history, by emphasising the position of Abraham as the father of many nations, of whom only one, and that themselves, was chosen.

It is therefore not surprising to find Justin saying of the Bible to Trypho: ' your scriptures, or rather not yours but ours, for you, though you read them, do not catch the spirit that is in them '[2]. The writer of the epistle to Diognetus, in speaking of the spirit of the Church, says, in the most natural way possible, ' the fear of the Lord is chanted, the grace of the prophets is recognised, the faith of the gospel is established, the tradition of the apostles is guarded, and the joy of the Church rejoices '[3], without any feeling of break between the first two clauses and the rest. Lactantius, the most Greek of the early fathers, speaks casually of ' our

[1] This action apparently attracted the comment even of certain pagans. Cf. Eusebius, *Prep. Evan.*, I, ii-v; P.G., XXI, p. 28 ff.

[2] *Trypho*, xxix.

[3] Ch. xi; P.G., IV, p. 1184. Actually this chapter seems not to be by the author of the rest, but it is contemporary.

ancestors who were the leaders of the Hebrews '[1], and every martyr refused to dishonour his obedience to the God of Abraham, of Isaac and of Jacob. Tatian, who lived about the middle of the second century, in his *Address to the Greeks*, claims Moses as proof of the antiquity and respectability of Christianity[2]. That he should wish to claim such antiquity is perhaps natural when we remember that Josephus wrote the whole of his *Antiquities of the Jews* to disprove the pagan gibe that Judaism was an upstart faith. Antiquity appeared to have been highly valued in the ancient world. Theophilus, bishop of Antioch from 168 to 181 (or 188), in his letters to Autolycus, after relating the story of creation, and of the flood, and after pointing out pagan ignorance of these events, adds ' and therefore it is proved that all others have been in error, and that *we Christians alone have possessed the truth* '[3]. He also is distressed by the accusation that Christianity ' has but recently come to the light '[4].

But it was not enough to make a general claim to the whole of the Scriptures. It was necessary to claim each particular advantage offered in it, both in relation to Christ and, as a deduction therefrom, in relation to themselves. Once the Messianic question became a point of controversy, the Christians had to deal with a primary Jewish objection that a man crucified could not be the Messiah, for the Law said explicitly ' he that is hanged on a tree is accursed of God '[5]. So far as we know, the manner of the Crucifixion excited no controversy in apostolic times. There is only one reference to it in the Pauline correspondence[6], and then it does not appear as a subject needing defence. But in the second century Christians had to think out an answer to the reproach that a man cursed by the Law could not possibly be the Messiah. Trypho puts the question directly to Justin, and Justin's answer is at first evasive[7]. But later Trypho returns

[1] *Divine Institutions*, Bk. IV, x; P.L., VI, p. 470.

[2] Chs. xxxi and xxxvi-xl; P.G., VI, p. 868.

[3] Bk. II, xxxiii; P.G., VI, p. 1105.

[4] *Ibid.* III, iv, p. 1125.

[5] Deut. xxi, 23, in the translation of the Septuagint.

[6] Gal. iii, 13.

[7] *Trypho*, lxxxix.

to the charge, and then Justin replies by the parallel of the brazen serpent[1]. This was the answer generally accepted in the Church, and it is still conventional to represent as symbols of the Old and New Dispensations the brazen serpent and the Cross. It is to be seen in innumerable stained-glass windows. Tertullian and Hippolytus both admit that the question as to whether the Messiah has come is the only issue between them and the Jews[2]. The question was vital for the obvious reason that it was not commonly held possible that there should be two Messiahs. If, therefore, Jesus was the Messiah, the only person for whom the Jews could be waiting would be, by their own method of arguing also, the Antichrist[3]. Moreover, a prophecy could not be fulfilled twice, and Jacob of Serug, a writer of the fifth century, rubs in the implication of this by stating, after he has proved that Christ fulfilled all prophecies, that even if the Jews did obtain a Messiah, he could not claim any of the Old Testament prophecies on his behalf, for ' Our Lord, when He came, fulfilled the totality of prophecy. And He gave no opportunity for another to come '[4].

As a result of this necessity to prove the reality of the Messianic claims of Jesus from prophecy, the Church turned the whole of the Old Testament into a vast quarry with no other function than to provide, by any exegesis however far-fetched, arguments for His claims. A large portion of the Dialogue with Trypho turns on this point. Trypho and Justin pit text against text, and differ only in the interpretation which they give to them. It is probable that by this time various collections of texts were already in existence in order to give Christians a handy compendium of arguments for possible controversies. One such collection has survived, compiled by Cyprian[5], but many others were probably in existence[6]. In Cyprian's collection over seven hundred

[1] *Trypho*, xcii and xciv.

[2] Tertullian, *Apologet.*, xxi; P.L., I, p. 391; and Hippolytus, *Refutation of all Heresies*, Bk. IV, xiii-xxv; P.G., VII, p. 1006 ff.

[3] Cf. Pseudo Hippolytus, *Discourse on Last Things*, xxviii; P.G., X, p. 932.

[4] *First Homily against the Jews*, line 283. Cf. Ch. VIII, Section III.

[5] *The Testimonies against the Jews*, P.L., IV.

[6] On the use of such collections see Rendell Harris in *The Expositor* for Nov. 1906 and June 1910. He considers that they were already in use by the time the present gospels were written (*Expositor*, Sept. 1905). See also Glover, *The Conflict of Religions in the Roman Empire*, Ch. VI.

texts are collected, dealing with every possible subject of controversy.

The Messianic question once settled, there was an inevitable deduction to be made by the Christian writers. If Jesus was the Messiah promised to Israel, then they were the true Israel[1]. It is here that we see how inevitable was the defamation of the actual history of the Jews, for if the Gentiles were the true Israel, then the Jews had all the time been sailing under false colours. That they were the true Israel they proved by innumerable passages from the prophets, in which God speaks of His rejection of His own people and His acceptance of the Gentiles[2]. Little by little the Church was read back into the whole of Old Testament history, and Christian history was shown to be older than Jewish history in that it dated from the creation[3], and not from Sinai, or even Abraham. Continual references to Christ were found in the Old Testament, and it was 'the Christ of God' who 'appeared to Abraham, gave divine instructions to Isaac, and held converse with Moses and the later prophets '[4].

In order to justify this reading of history, they were compelled to challenge the Jewish conception of the Law. The Pauline doctrine that it was good in itself, and divine, was not universally respected. The Old Testament as the embodiment of a complete conception of a community, and of the place of religion in common life, which is to the modern scholar the fascination of the Law and the prophets, had no meaning for the writers of the early Church. Gentiles themselves, they missed entirely the moral and corporate significance of the Mosaic legislation. Unconscious that they themselves were creating a ritual and a rule almost as complicated as the priestly code, they saw in the observances of Judaism something comic and contemptible. Their descriptions of Judaism, though probably perfectly sincere, read to us like a deliberate parody. Justin puts into the mouth of Trypho the following summary of his religion: 'first be circumcised, and then observe what ordinances have been

[1] Bonwetsch, *op. cit.*, passim.

[2] *Trypho*, cxxiii.

[3] Eusebius, *Ecc. Hist.*, I, iv; P.G., XX, p. 76.

[4] *Ibid.*

enacted for the Sabbath and the feasts, and the new moons of God, and in a word do all the things which have been written in the Law, and then, perhaps, you may obtain mercy from God '[1]. A little later Justin draws attention to the collapse of all the sacrificial ritual with the destruction of the Temple, and asks Trypho what he considers now to be valid of the Law. Trypho replies that it remains ' to keep the Sabbath, to be circumcised, to observe months, to be washed if you touch anything prohibited by Moses, and after sexual intercourse '[2]. The writer of the epistle to Diognetus, while admitting that ' in so far as they are monotheists, they are better than the heathen ', adds that ' their sacrifices are absurd . . . their scruples about the Sabbath ridiculous, their vaunting of circumcision nonsense, and their festivals folly '[3]. Such attacks might be legitimate criticisms of one side of Judaism in those who showed also a knowledge of its positive moral content. As an inclusive summary it was an inexcusable absurdity. Those who had such a strange ignorance of Judaism had no difficulty in considering the Law to be an unimportant portion of the Scriptures, a temporary addition to a book otherwise universal and eternal, added because of the special wickedness of the Jews[4].

Those who still clung to the Pauline conception of its dignity had two other courses open to them. They could claim that the Jews never observed it, or they could claim to interpret it allegorically. The latter method is that adopted by the epistle of Barnabas in a detailed review of many of its enactments. It was also followed by Hippolytus[5], and comes to its full flower in later centuries in works such as the amazing commentary of Gregory the Great on the book of Job. Those who wished to claim that the Jews had never observed the Law had only to refer to the Golden Calf,

[1] *Trypho*, Ch. viii.

[2] *Ibid.* xlvi.

[3] Chs. iii and iv (abridged); P.G., II, p. 1174.

[4] *Trypho*, xix-xxii. Jerome (Ep. CXXI) in the fourth century goes so far as to say that it was a deliberate deception of them by God to lead them to their destruction.

[5] See especially his interpretation of the Blessings of Jacob in Gen. xlix, in *Fragmenta Exegetica in Genesim*, P.G., X, p. 588 ff., and *Adversus Judaeos*, *ibid.* p. 788.

to the murmuring in the wilderness, and to the many other passages in the historical and prophetic books in which the difference between the real and the ideal is expressed. In later writers it is generally this line which is followed, for it made it easier to map out a consistent history of the Church in the Old Testament by contrasting it with every lapse from the ideal, while the sum of these lapses made up the whole of the history of the Jews. This method of rewriting history led later to the conclusion that the Jews were heretics, or apostates. 'For it is clear that they have deserted the Law, who have not believed in Him whom the Law proclaims to be alone sufficient for salvation. They should be considered apostates, for denial of Christ is essentially a violation of the Law.'[1] All the writers who wrote catalogues of heresies included under that heading many Jewish sects. While in pre-Christian Judaism they only include divagations from orthodox Judaism, for contemporary times they include all Jews. This is but another instance of their claim to possess whatever is honourable in Old Testament history[2]. In fact, it is occasionally denied that the Jews had ever known God at all, 'for they who suppose that they know God, do not know Him, serving angels and archangels, the month and the moon'[3].

The tendency to treat Jews as heretics, who knew the truth and refused it, is very evident in the apocryphal gospels which began to appear about the middle of the second century. Naturally, the critical period which needed to be rewritten was that immediately following the miracle of the Resurrection, though a later group also attach great importance to the incidents which are alleged to have accompanied the burial and assumption of the Virgin. In its earliest form the story is found in the *Gospel of Peter*. After the Crucifixion the Jews are filled with terror and remorse, beating their breasts and saying 'if these very great signs have come to pass at His death, behold how righteous He was'. They therefore ask Pilate to put a guard on His tomb. In spite of the guard many are witnesses of the Resurrection,

[1] Pseudo-Ambrose, *On Romans*, ix, 27; P.L., XVII, p. 139.

[2] Cf. Epiphanius and Philastrius.

[3] Fragments of the *Preaching of Peter*, collected in *Apocryphal New Testament*, p. 17.

and would believe it if they were not afraid of being stoned by ' the Jews '[1].

The next development is that the High Priest, also impressed by the events of the Crucifixion, calls a meeting to examine carefully whether the prophecies really prove that Jesus was the Messiah. The meeting finds that He was; and their decision comes to the ears of Pilate, who sends to them to adjure them to tell him the truth. They admit that He was the Messiah, but say that they have decided to conceal the fact, ' lest there should be a schism in our synagogues '. They implore Pilate to keep silence. Pilate, however, writes to the emperor Tiberius that ' the Jews through envy have punished themselves and their posterity with fearful judgments of their own fault; for their fathers had promises that God would send them His Holy One, and when He came, and performed marvellous works, the priests through envy delivered Him to me, and I, believing them, crucified Him '[2]. In the Acts of Philip the scene of the conversion of the Jews is laid at Athens, and all are convinced except the High Priest himself, who is swallowed up by the earth for his unbelief. The various Assumptions of the Virgin carry on the tradition for several more centuries. In one of the many versions of it[3], the ' Prince of the Priests ', struck blind on trying to overthrow the bier, exclaims: ' Do we not believe in Christ, but what shall we do? The enemy of mankind hath blinded our hearts and shame has covered our faces that we should not confess the mighty works of God, especially when we did curse ourselves, crying out against Christ "His blood be on us and on our children" '. The same suggestion that the Jews secretly believe is to be found in the Arabic History of the Patriarchs[4].

[1] *Gospel of Peter*, vii, 25, and viii.

[2] *Acts of Pilate*, Latin version. It is a short step from this to make Tiberius, and ultimately Pilate himself, believe in Jesus, and the emperor propose His acceptance by the Senate as a God. All these stages seem to have been gone through before the time of Constantine. Cf. also *Gospel of Nicodemus*.

[3] *Apocryphal New Testament*, pp. 196, 201, 214. Cf. also P.O., II, the *Coptic Gospel of Twelve Apostles*, in which Pilate wishes Jesus to be made King, and on the death of the Virgin the High Priest is openly converted.

[4] P.O., Vol. I, p. 122; see Ch. VIII.

The bitterness which infects these attacks can be seen from the remark of Justin on circumcision, quoted above, or from the even bitterer sarcasm of Tertullian on the same subject[1], in which he identifies it with the Roman prohibition against Jews entering Jerusalem, and suggests that God ordained it to the end that they might be more easily identified. It would be a mistake to imply that such unworthy bitterness is to be found continually in patristic literature, but it is to be found unhappily frequently, and it is not confined to one or two authors. The attack upon the Jews which is included in the works of Hippolytus begins with the exhortation:

> ' Hear my words, and give heed thou Jew. Many a time dost thou boast thyself that thou didst condemn Jesus of Nazareth to death, and thou didst give him vinegar and gall to drink, and thou dost boast thyself because of this. Come therefore and let us consider together whether perchance thou dost not boast unrighteously, O Israel, whether that small portion of vinegar and gall has not brought down this fearful threatening upon thee, and whether this is not the cause of thy present condition, involving thee in these myriad troubles. . . . Listen with understanding, O Jew, to what Christ says: " they gave me gall to eat, and in my thirst vinegar to drink ". And these things he did endure from you. Hear the Holy Spirit tell you also what return he made to you for that little portion of vinegar. For the prophet says as in the person of God: " Let their table become a snare and a retribution ". Of what retribution does he speak? Manifestly of the misery which has now got hold of thee.'[2]

One would never gather from this passage that the giving of vinegar and gall was a service organised by the charitable women of Jerusalem to dull the pain of the punishment!

The final seal was set upon the Church's adoption of the Scriptures of the Jews by the assimilation into Christian hagiology of all the heroes and religious leaders of the Old Testament. The mother and her seven sons who braved the

[1] Tertullian, *Answers to the Jews*, Ch. iii; P.L., II, p. 642.

[2] *Adversus Judaeos*, Chs. i and v; P.G., X, p. 789.

wrath of Antiochus[1] were already celebrated by a feast in the fourth century[2]. The story formed the basis of Origen's great *Exhortation to Martyrdom.* Later on at different periods the others were added, until the memory of every reputable character in the Old Testament was associated with the past of the Church rather than with the ancestors of contemporary Jews. Abraham, Lot, Moses, Miriam, Aaron, Job, Shemaiah, Elijah, Elisha, Tobit, and all the prophets were included. The intention of the Church in thus adopting these figures is well expressed in the commentary which accompanied the account of the Maccabean martyrs, and was read on their feast day in the Jacobite Church:

> ' It is right that thou shouldst know, O listener, that our Christian fathers have established the rule to hold a feast in memory of the just of the Law of Torah, that we may know that we have not abandoned the work of the Law of Torah by rejecting it, but by passing to a better Law. We admit the just of the old Law in their rank: we do not honour them more than the fathers of the New who have done much more than they.'[3]

The great characters of the Old Testament having been thus removed, this is the final résumé of Jewish history as the Church presented it to her congregations:

' Moses they cursed because he proclaimed Christ,
Dathan they loved because he did not proclaim Him;
Aaron they rejected because he offered the image of Christ,
Abiron they set up because he opposed Him;
David they hated, because he sang of Christ,
Saul they magnified, because he did not speak of Him;
Samuel they cast out because he spoke of Christ,
Cham (?Egypt) they served, because he said nothing of
 Christ;
Jeremiah they stoned while he was hymning Christ,

[1] II Macc. vii.

[2] Both Chrysostom and Gregory of Nazianzen preached sermons in their honour, and the latter refers to their feast as not yet very widely observed, so that we may presume it to be a fourth century innovation.

[3] S.A.J. in P.O., Vol. XVII, p. 712.

Ananias they loved while he was opposing Him;
Isaiah they sawed asunder shouting His glories,
Manasseh they glorified persecuting Him;
John they slew revealing Christ,
Zechariah they slaughtered loving Christ,
Judas they loved betraying Him.'[1]

No people has ever paid so high a price for the greatness of its own religious leaders, and for the outspoken courage with which they held up an ideal and denounced whatever seemed to them to come short of it. If they had known the use that was to be made of their writings, then, indeed, many of the prophets might have obeyed literally the sarcasm of Irenaeus when he says that 'the Jews, had they been cognisant of our future existence, and that we should use these proofs from the Scriptures which declare that all other nations will inherit eternal life, but that they who boast themselves as being the house of Jacob are disinherited from the grace of God, would never have hesitated themselves to burn their own Scriptures'[2].

IX. THE CREATION OF AN OFFICIAL ATTITUDE TO CHRISTIANITY

It might be thought, and it is claimed by certain writers, that the fact that Christianity now stood out as a Gentile religion would have led to a change in the Jewish attitude[3], and apparently it did lead to a certain softening of their attitude to the Jewish Christians[4]. The strongest argument for this ignoring of Gentile Christianity is the paucity of reference to it in the Talmud[5] during the second and third centuries, the centuries during which the Church com-

[1] Pseudo-Cyprian, *Adversus Judaeos*, C.S.E.L., III, iii, p. 135.

[2] Irenaeus, *Contra Haereses*, III, xxi; P.G., VII, p. 946.

[3] *E.g.* Israel Abrahams in *Studies in Pharisaism and the Gospels*, Vol. II, p. 57: 'The synagogue had far less quarrel with Gentile Christianity, . . . and Christianity as such was not the object of much attention, still less of attack'.

[4] Travers Herford, *op. cit.*, Div. 2, Ch. II.

[5] The only reference found by Travers Herford is the one which refers to the time of the triumph of the Church in the fourth century, *op. cit.*, p. 210.

plained bitterly of the attitude of the Synagogue to Christianity. But in spite of this silence it is impossible to believe that the Jewish authorities, at least in the diaspora, were uninterested in the progress of Gentile Christianity. No organised group could be expected to pass over in silence such perpetual libels on their history as were being produced by Gentile theologians. But there was a still more serious reason. The Synagogue had by no means ceased from its missionary activity. Even in turning to the Gentiles, the Church was competing for influence over the same personalities. In the second century it is possible that a much smaller proportion of its converts came from the ranks of the 'metuentes Deum', for the Christian no longer had easy access to the synagogue; but the type of pagan likely to be attracted by either religion was the same. Though the terms upon which they offered it were different, both offered a life of discipline and of hope, and the promise of future happiness. Both emphasised morality, and fought against the corruption of the surrounding world.

The extent to which proselytism was encouraged by the authorities of the Talmudic period has been much discussed, and the remark of Rabbi Helbo, a Babylonian who taught in Palestine in the third century, has frequently been quoted as though it were final—'a proselyte is as harmful to Israel as a scab to the skin'. A detailed study of the evidence, however, suggests that the quotation of this remark four times in the Talmud, and the stories of Shammai's hostility to prospective converts, are inserted because general opinion was against them, and that throughout the period in which the Babylonian Talmud was being composed, the main Jewish opinion was in favour of proselytism. In a detailed survey, M. Israel Levi, the chief Rabbi of France, comes to this conclusion. 'There is no doubt that in its attitude towards proselytes there are two tendencies in Judaism. Nor is it questionable that those in favour of proselytism were more powerful outside Palestine, in the diaspora. It is also probable that the missionary volunteers in the diaspora were not recruited from among the rabbis. It is therefore not surprising that in rabbinic literature there are unquestionable traces of the tendency hostile to these conversions. What is surprising is to find so much evidence of the opposite view. Was the favourable tendency the stronger of the two? Yes; unquestionably. But in a particular milieu, that of the Hagadists, or preachers. Among them the note is almost always consistent. In preaching, the tendencies are not opposed to each other as they are in the legislation. One note alone dominates the Palestinian Midrashim, that shapeless collection of popular sermons spread over several centuries. It is the attitude of those who proclaim the example of Abraham, the father of proselytes. Now, where does one find the ideal of a religious body, in its *corpus juris* or in its preaching, in its canon law or in its literature? Is the spirit of Christianity to be found in the gospels or in the Leges Visigothorum?'[1] There were throughout the first centuries many half-way houses from Christianity to Judaism, and it is fair to suppose that something in them was due to the activity of contemporary Jews, and not only to the written word of the Bible.

If the Jews were still interested in making converts in the Roman world, it is obvious that they must have been ready with detailed answers to the Christian approach to the same individuals. These answers would be of two kinds, a statement of the Jewish interpretation of passages in the Old Testament used by the Christians, and comments upon the New Testament from a Jewish standpoint. There is evidence in the Talmud for both of these answers, and traces of them can also be found in Christian literature. The Messianic belief having passed into a definition of the doctrine of the Trinity, most of the Talmudic texts deal rather with the assertion of the unity of God, than explicitly with the claims of the Christians about Jesus. For in this way the denial of the claim to divinity of Jesus was involved without direct reference to it[2]. In the Church of the fourth and later centuries the Hebraic interpretations of disputed passages of prophecy were well known, and the commentaries of Jerome are full of them. The interpretation of a passage accepted as genuine by both sides was not the only issue. Jews and Christians disputed as to what the actual text contained. The Jews did not accept the Christian translations,

[1] *R.E.J.*, Vols. L and LI.

[2] Travers Herford, *op. cit.*, pp. 239 and 291 ff., and the homilies against the Jews of Jacob of Serug, *passim*.

and few Christians could read Hebrew. The interpretation of the passage of Isaiah referring to the Virgin Birth was, naturally, the most hotly disputed of these passages, but even as early as Justin others existed[1].

Just as Christians show a knowledge of post-Christian Judaism, so also the rabbis show a knowledge of the New Testament and of the details of the life of Jesus. The gospels are known as ' Aven-gillayon ' by Rabbis Meir of Jabne and Jochanan. The word is an offensive pun meaning ' revelation of sin ' or ' falsehood of blank paper '[2]. There is a discussion reported as to what shall be done with ' external books ', which would doubtless include primarily Christian books. Rabbi Meir says that they are not to be saved from the fire, but to be burned at once, even with the names of God in them. Rabbi Jose says that on a week-day the name of God ought to be cut out and hidden away. Rabbi Tarphon invoked a curse on himself if he did not burn the books, names of God and all[3].

While the references to the life of Christ are few in the Talmud, they are inevitably insulting. Jesus was the illegitimate child of a soldier called Panthera. He performed His miracles by magic, which He had learnt in Egypt. After His death, which was a legal condemnation in which He was given every chance to prove His innocence, His body was stolen by His disciples in order to invent the story of the Resurrection[4]. He was a ' deceiver of Israel ' and His teaching was evil. The Talmud and Midrash have little more than this, but it is evident that common Jewish stories went far further, and that all the main elements of the ' Sepher Toldoth Jeshu ' were in existence from a very early date. There are explicit references in Origen to some of the stories. Jesus collected a band of malefactors around Himself, and with these He lived the life of a bandit up and down Palestine[5]. More references are to be found in Tertullian, who speaks of the libels on Jesus as the ' son of a carpenter or

[1] *Trypho*, xliii and lxxi-lxxiii. Cf. H. A. Hart in the *Expositor*, Nov. 1905.

[2] *T. B. Sabb.*, 116, a, foot.

[3] W. M. Christie in *J.T.S.*, Vol. XXVI, p. 361.

[4] Travers Herford, pp. 35 and 51. Strack, pp. 18-46.

[5] Origen, *contra Celsum*, I, xxxii, xxxviii, and lxii; P.G., XI.

furniture maker, the destroyer of the Sabbath, the Samaritan possessed of a devil '[1]. Eusebius expresses his disgust that 'when a writer belonging to the Hebrews themselves [Josephus] has transmitted from primitive times in a work of his own, this record concerning John the Baptist and our Saviour, the Jews should proceed to forge such memoirs against them '[2]. The passage he is referring to is that alluding to Christianity which many now think to be original and not an interpolation. In any case, it existed in the copies of Josephus in the fourth century.

There are also many references in the Talmud to the Judeo-Christians under the name of 'Minim '[3]. As the word 'Minim' is often found associated with the word 'Mosarim', which means traitors or betrayers, it is probable that most of the bitterness against them is to be associated with the war under Hadrian, when the Jews were forbidden to study the Law and the Judeo-Christians were accused of betraying those who did to the Romans. In the Gentile Christian the Talmud shows practically no interest. It is, however, one of the most serious charges made by Tertullian and Origen that the Jews stirred up the pagans against the Christians. The former makes the general statement that the synagogues were 'the seed-plot of all the calumny against us '[4]. Origen is much more explicit and says that Celsus has acted 'like the Jews, who when Christianity first began to be preached, scattered abroad false reports of the Gospel, such as that Christians offered up an infant in sacrifice, and partook of its flesh, and again that the professors of Christianity wishing to do the works of darkness used to extinguish the lights, and each one to have sexual intercourse with any woman he chanced to meet'. These calumnies, says Origen, 'have long exercised, although unreasonably, an influence over the minds of many, leading those who are alien to the Gospel to believe that Christians are men of such character, and even at the present time they mislead some, and prevent them from entering into the simple intercourse of conversation

[1] Tertullian, *de Spectaculis*, xxx; P.L., I, p. 662.

[2] *Ecc. Hist.*, I, ix, 9; P.G., XX, p. 105.

[3] Travers Herford, *op. cit.*, and Strack, pp. 47-80.

[4] *To the Nations*, I, xiv; P.L., I, p. 579.

with those who are Christians '[1]. It is, of course, impossible to deny that individual Jews may have taken a share in spreading such calumnies against Christians. But before accepting this picture given by Origen and Tertullian as *generally* reliable, it is necessary to consider the evidence on the other side. Although this is negative it is extensive. We possess no less than eight complete 'Apologies' addressed to the pagan world during the second century[2]; in other words, the century of the greatest Jewish unpopularity, and in which it would have been a telling argument to say: 'Why do you believe the Jews of all people?' Two of the authors who wrote Apologies also wrote against the Jews. All of them mention the unpleasant accusations made against the Christians. But none of them ascribe the accusation to Jewish sources. Yet these apologists come from all parts of the Christian world—Asia, Rome and Africa—and all wrote in the second century.

But in addition there is positive evidence that the libel did not come from Jewish sources. Justin speaks of it to Trypho, and asks him if he has believed it; and Trypho replies: 'These things about which the multitude speak are not worthy of belief. Moreover, I am aware that your precepts are so wonderful and great that I suspect that no one can keep them '[3]. Athenagoras, in his *Plea for the Christians*, is still more definite. When he says that 'it is not wonderful that they should get up tales about us such as they tell about their own gods', he is clearly implying a heathen source of the statement[4]. It is also significant that these statements have almost always to be searched for in odd corners in writings which have nothing to do with the Jews. They are not to be found in the many writings addressed to them. While, then, no man can prove that *no* Jew ever repeated them, it is clear that the evidence is against the accuracy of the statement of Origen that the *main* source of the more unpleasant accusations against the Christians was Jewish. On the other hand, it is not to be expected that when a Jew

[1] *Contra Celsum*, VI, xxvii; P.G., XI, p. 1334.

[2] By Aristides, Justin (2), Minucius Felix, Theophilus of Antioch, Athenagoras, Tatian and Tertullian.

[3] *Trypho*, Ch. x.

[4] *Op. cit.*, Ch. xxxii. Cf. Ch. ii ff.; P.G., VI, pp. 894 and 964.

was asked his opinion on the Christian Church he should load it with praises; and if we possessed copies of addresses given by local Jewish preachers, it is probable that we should find in them plenty of uncomplimentary references to Christianity.

The written 'Altercations' yield astonishingly little precise information upon the discussions which must have frequently taken place. They are arranged to give the victory to the Christian or to the Jew, and the arguments of the other side are given little weight. Only in one Christian Altercation does the Jew make a really good stand, and that is the seventh century Altercation of Gregentius and Herbanus[1]. But that the Jew was not without ammunition is shown *en passant* in two stories in the Acts of the Martyrs. From these it appears that one Jewish defence was to claim a superiority of their miracles over those of the Christians. After Donatus, bishop of Istria, who was martyred in Egypt, had made a great apologetic speech which had led to the conversion of seven philosophers, eleven lawyers, and two hundred and eighty-two others, the Jews began to make trouble. When Donatus spoke of the miracle of the raising of Lazarus, they admitted it was a miracle, but claimed it was inferior to one reported in the Old Testament. Christ had been alive when He raised Lazarus, but the very bones of Elisha had performed a similar miracle[2]. In the same strain, when the martyr Romanus at Antioch is about to be burnt, the Lord sends a miraculous storm to quench the fire in case there are any Jews standing about who might compare the event contemptuously with the safety in the flames of the Three Holy Children[3].

It would appear that the latter event was a strong point in Jewish apologetic, for there are many other references to rival miracles as evidently designed to put it in the shade. Saint Maris, who converted Persia, where the original miracle took place, had a special furnace constructed, through which he walked *twice*, and then began to *extinguish the fire*[4].

[1] See Ch. VIII, Section V.

[2] II Kings xiii, 21.

[3] *A.S.*, May, Vol. V, p. 145.

[4] *An. Boll.*, Vol. IV, p. 99.

It is a disputed question whether there are relics of long discussions between Jews and Christians in the Talmud. Naturally, when a discussion is referred to, the Jew wins, but according to Dr. Marmorstein, a full discussion is to be found in *Sifre*, which bears out the evidence of Christian writers as to the method followed. 'One day the community of Israel will say: Master of the universe, my witnesses are still living (and can testify in my favour), as it is said: This day I take the heaven and earth to witness. (Deut. xxx, 19.) To which he (the Christian) replies: I will create a new heaven and a new earth. (Is. lxv, 17.) Master of the universe, I look with repentance on the places where I have sinned, and I am ashamed, as it is said: Consider thy conduct in the valley, and recognise what thou hast done. (Jer. ii, 20.) But he replies: every valley shall be exalted, and every hill shall be brought low. (Is. xl, 4.) Master of the universe, my name still survives. But he: I will change it, as it is said: They shall call thee by another name. Master of the universe, Thy name is spoken of with those of idols. But he: I will make to disappear the names of Baals from their mouth. (Hos. ii, 19.) Master of the universe, hast thou not written: If a man repudiates his wife and she leaves him to marry another. And he replies: I have written "if a man", but of me it is said: I am God and not man. (Hos. xi, 9.) Are you separated from me, Israelites? Is it not written: Where is your mother's bill of divorcement, by which I have sent her away? Where is the creditor to whom I have sold you?' By the last sentence of this somewhat confused battle of texts, the victory of Israel in the encounter is evident[1].

There is also evidence of discussions with Christians held by Rabbi Hoshaye of Caesarea, a contemporary of Origen[2], and by Rabbis Simlai and Tanhouma at Antioch. But more complete than any references in the Talmud is a Genizah fragment[3], which gives the anti-Christian polemic with a directness which no censor of the Talmud itself would

[1] *Sifre*, ed. Friedmann, fol. 130b, quoted from A. Marmorstein in R.E.J., Vol. LX. It should be added that other Jewish scholars see in this passage only a discussion between a saddened Israelite and his God. Even so it may have been the memory of Christian propaganda which saddened him and framed his questioning.

[2] J.Q.R., Vol. III, p. 357.

[3] Article by Dr. Krauss in R.E.J., Vol. LXIII, p. 63.

have allowed to survive. The actual fragment is late, for it includes a reference to the dishonour of riding on an ass which must belong to either the Mahomedan or Byzantine periods, when Jews were not allowed to ride on horses. But the material it contains is likely to go back to the beginning. Various items in the life of Jesus are discussed. His attitude to His parents and their disbelief in Him are contrasted with the commandment to love father and mother. Moreover, it is absurd to say that God could have a mother. Jesus Himself says that He was a man, and He was known in Nazareth as an ordinary individual. His pure humanity is proved by His sufferings upon the Cross, by the fact that He fasted, and that He was tempted by the devil. Somewhat irrelevantly it is then pointed out that a young ass would not be strong enough to bear a man—Christian tradition insisted that the ass had never been ridden before—apart from the dishonour of riding an ass at all. As to His divinity, the author insists passionately on the unity of God, and asks how it is possible that if the heavens could not contain His glory, He could be contained in the womb of a woman?

The two lines of argument, that the miracles of the Old Testament are superior to those of the New, and that the personality of Jesus was inferior to that of the prophets, are joined together in a speech of the Jewish High Priest in one of the apocryphal gospels[1]. There it is pointed out that whereas the prophets worked more wonderful miracles than Jesus, they did not preach a new law, they did not speak in their own name, and they did not call themselves God. Jesus, on the other hand, did everything for ostentation, abused everyone else indiscriminately, and showed throughout a character inferior to the best of the prophets.

If we compare the situation of the Jews and the Christians, we can see that it is probable that the Jewish attack on Christianity would be less violent than that of the Christians on Judaism. The Christians were claiming the promises in a book which was composed of promises and denunciations. The denunciations, therefore, must belong to the Jews. But they, on their part, were only compelled to adopt a negative attitude, the refusal to accept the Christian claim as to the person of Jesus, and though this naturally involved

[1] Hebrew Gospel of Matthew, A.S., Feb. 24.

disputing His perfection and the two miraculous events concerned with His life, the Virgin Birth, and the Resurrection, there is not much evidence in these first centuries that their attack went further. The stories contained in the Sepher were in existence, but apparently not widely known. For one reference to it (in Origen) we have a dozen or more to the purely negative approach, that Jesus was *not* what the Christians claimed Him to be.

X. INFLUENCES OF CHRISTIANITY ON JUDAISM

It may well be that there was a subdued note in Jewish apologetic during the second century, the century of the triumphant Christian apologists, and that even if we had as much material from the Jewish as we have from the Christian side, we should still find fewer violent insults to the opposing faith. For Judaism had been more severely shaken by the tragic events from 70 onwards than is generally realised. Though in the end rabbinical teaching not only survived, but succeeded in doing more than salving a wreck, yet inevitably the terrible failures of those years tried severely the faith of the simple and unlearned. Doubtless, too, the growing arrogance of the Christian Church and its obvious successes would not only nerve the Jew to greater efforts on his own behalf, but would also cause him to cast wistful eyes at those doctrines which seemed to enshrine the rival power of Christianity. The doctrine of forgiveness and the mediatorial power of Christ, so potently preached by the Church, must have caused anxious searchings in many Jewish hearts. Origen tells us that in his day Jews told him that ' as they had no altar, no temple, no priest, and therefore no offerings of sacrifices, they felt that their sins remained with them, and that they had no means of obtaining pardon'[1]. Dr. Marmorstein, in a close examination of numerous rabbinic texts of the third century[2], has found ample evidence of this preoccupation with the question of how to achieve forgiveness apart from sacrifices. Innumerable solutions of varying spiritual value were proposed. Some

[1] *Hom. on Num.*, x, 2; P.G., XII, p. 638.
[2] R.E.J., LXXI, p. 190.

said that the blood of circumcision was itself a sacrifice, others that Elijah offered continual sacrifices in heaven; yet others offered more deeply spiritual explanations to comfort the faithful, and stressed the redemptive value of suffering—a natural development in a century so full of suffering for the Jews. Others took the line that prayer and repentance were in themselves creative of forgiveness, which is the teaching which Judaism has retained.

Still more interesting was the attempt to provide an alternative mediator to Christ. Rabbis of the second and third centuries found a parallel to the Cross in the sacrifice of Isaac. In the book of Jubilees, which is pre-Christian, the sacrifice of Isaac is said to take place on the fourteenth day of Nissan, the day of the Passover, and to be a type of the paschal lamb[1]. Post-Christian Jewish writers associate his sacrifice with the ceremonies of forgiveness of Rosh Hashanah; and the horn that is blown is symbolically connected with the horns of the ram caught in the bush. In one of the prayers of that day Israel demands that the merits of the sacrifice of Isaac cover it and save it from the consequence of its faults. As Abraham suppressed his feelings as a father, so they appeal to God to forgo His righteous anger. Rabbi Jochanan (Palestine, third century) makes Abraham say 'when the descendants of Isaac are guilty of transgressions and evil actions, remember the sacrifice of Isaac and have pity'[2]. In another version Abraham says, 'when the descendants of Isaac are in danger, and there is none to intercede for them, be Thou their defender, remember the sacrifice of Isaac and have pity'[3]. Isaac is called the 'expiator of the sins of Israel'[4], and emphasis is laid on his willingness to be offered up—a detail which is not explicit in the Biblical narrative[5]. Rabbi Isaac says that at the moment all the angels marvelled at his acquiescence and interceded with God that he might be spared[6].

[1] Chs. xvii and xviii.

[2] *Ber. Rabba*, 56. *Ps. Rabb.*, XXIX, 1.

[3] *Taanit*, 65d.

[4] *Cant. Rabba*, I, 14.

[5] *Ber. Rabba*, 56.

[6] I. Levi, in R.E.J., Vol. LXIV. The Talmudic quotations are all taken from the same source.

Although no doctrine of the vicarious sacrifice of Isaac has ever been an official part of Judaism, it appears that it is still a favourite subject for sermons in the synagogue. The parallel between Isaac and Jesus is, on the other hand, one which is rarely used by the Fathers. It is used by Origen, and his use of it suggests that he knew it was quoted in the synagogue[1]. Irenaeus, Clement and Tertullian, who belong to the second century, also make use of the parallel[2]. But, considering how apposite the parallel is, it is surprising that it is not used more frequently. It may be that this silence is due to the fact that they were aware that it was used by the Jews, and that therefore they were unwilling to emphasise the similarity.

XI. RELATIONS OF CHRISTIAN SCHOLARS WITH JEWISH SCHOLARS

Inevitably the borrowings of Christianity from Judaism were of a different kind. The main transference took place in the first century. What Christianity required from its parent religion it had taken at that time. Its spirit in the second century was scarcely such that it would be prepared to admit that contemporary Judaism had anything to teach it. Yet it had to go to Hebrew masters for help in interpreting the Scriptures, and there is much evidence in fathers such as Justin, Clement of Alexandria, Origen, Aphraates, Ephraim the Syrian, and above all Jerome, of knowledge which must have been the result of hours of patient discussion. It is impossible to believe that these were never carried on in the tranquil spirit of the student. Many of the writings which are left to us show extensive knowledge of Jewish legend and story which are not included in the Old Testament. Many interpretations given in the endless homilies on the Scriptures of the period show considerable acquaintance with the work going on, side by side with that of Christian scholars,

[1] *Hom. on Gen.*, viii; P.G., Vol. XII, p. 203.

[2] Irenaeus, *Contra Haereses*, IV, 5; P.G., VII, p. 893. Clement, *Stromata*, II, 5; P.G., VIII, p. 952. *Paedagogi*, I, 5; P.G., VIII, p. 277. *Tertullian adv. Judaeos*, x; P.L., II, 626. Cf. also Paulinus of Nola, Ep. XXIX, 9; P.L., LXI, p. 317. Some of these passages are discussed in the article of Levi.

in the rabbinical schools[1]. The accusation made that the Jews falsified texts, and the contrary determination to get accurate texts from the Jews, inevitably imply contacts and discussions of the passages concerned.

Christians also needed Jewish teachers for learning Hebrew—and Jerome complains that they charged a great deal for their lessons. But if all relations were such as a first reading of the literature which remains would suggest, it is doubtful if any Jew would have consented to teach a Christian at all. Eusebius[2] refers to the Jewish teachers of his time as 'people gifted with an uncommon strength of intellect, and whose faculties have been trained to penetrate to the very heart of scripture'. Doubtless in many of the discussions which took place the Jew gave as good as he received, and even won the victory. There is an air of reality about the remark of 'Zacchaeus' in discussion with 'Athanasius', who has taunted him with the loss of Jerusalem, that 'insults are not a serious form of argument'[3]. It is reasonable to assume that, since human nature is generally better than it appears to be, this was a protest which did not need constant repetition from either side.

XII. JEWS AND CHRISTIANS

So far it has been mainly polemic and apologetic literature which has been discussed, but it is obvious that there must have been many day to day contacts between Jews and both Jewish and Gentile Christians when they did other things than hurl abusive texts at each other's heads. In daily practice their common attitude to the surrounding paganism must often have drawn them together, and their common interests must often have been more important to ordinary folk than the disputes of the theologians. Even in those days every man did not live with a book of proof texts in his pocket.

[1] See articles of S. Krauss in J.Q.R. for Oct. 1892, Oct. 1893, and Jan. 1894.

[2] *Prep. Evan.*, XII, i; P.G., XXI, p. 952.

[3] *Dispute of Athanasius, Archbishop of Alexandria, and Zacchaeus, a teacher of the Jews,* edited by F. Connybeare, Oxford, 1898. The dialogue is probably a re-edition of the second-century dialogue of Papiscus and Jason.

Though there is no evidence of Christianity adopting any practices of post-Christian Judaism, yet relations with contemporary Jews were continual, and are shown by the number of centuries which it took to separate the Jewish Passover from the Christian Easter. It was not until the time of Constantine that a formal decision was taken, and even in later centuries councils had frequently to prohibit Gentile Christians from celebrating Easter on the same day as the Jews celebrated the Passover. In other matters also it is evident that many, apart from Christians of Jewish birth, were powerfully influenced by the teaching and practice of the Synagogue. Though this provoked the furious denunciation of such bishops as Chrysostom[1], it is significant that he has no definite moral charges to bring against the Christians who were involved, and it seems to have been fear of Jewish influence which caused his violence more than anything else. Jerome refers to Christian women using phylacteries for covering religious objects as a mark of special reverence[2]. The importance attached by many Christians to observing Jewish dates[3] is a frequent cause of abuse and of differences between heretics such as Novatian and the Catholics.

Of Jewish life at this period comparatively little is known, and what is known suggests that there was nothing special to distinguish it[4]. It was in no way specialised as it was in the mediaeval ghetto. Various professions are referred to casually, but there is no suggestion of special importance attaching to the reference. Jerome refers to the wealth of the Jews of Palestine, but as he also says that it is legitimate to relieve the wants of poor Jews from Christian alms if there is anything over, they were obviously not all rich. Christianity and Judaism, viewed from outside, probably appeared very much alike: they were distinguished in their doctrines, but neither in their social status nor in their attitude to the

[1] *Adversus Judaeos*, eight sermons preached at Antioch in 387.

[2] In Matt. xxiii, 6; P.G., XXVI, p. 174.

[3] There is frequent conciliar legislation at much later dates than this to prevent Jews and Christians from celebrating their religious feasts together.

[4] Cf. Justin, *Trypho*, xvi: 'You are not recognised among the rest of men by any other mark than your fleshly circumcision'.

heathen world. There is no evidence of any emperor or governor being favourable to one and hostile to the other. He might persecute the Christians for the crime of atheism, which was not a crime allowing of persecution for the Jews. But that implied no special affection for the Jews. Even Julian, though to begin with he liked the Jews because they offered sacrifices, ended by disliking them as heartily as he did the Christians.

To each other they were still rivals for the conversion of the pagan world around them, but there the scales were heavily weighted for ritual and later for political reasons in favour of the Christians. Judaism was still making proselytes in the second and third centuries, but there were difficulties which more than compensated for its doctrinal simplicity. The confused and quarrelsome theology of the early Church must have been a great moral hindrance, but the link between Judaism and the nation of the Jews was a greater one. Christianity at least made no distinction between clean and unclean, and had not yet rites which were an unlearnable complication to those who were not born in them. There was probably also a real difference in their attitude to their missionary task. Judaism proclaimed, indeed, that God forgave sin, but Christianity proclaimed that God redeemed sinners.

Yet even so the Church never really ceased to fear the rival influence of Judaism, and the contact of Christians with Jews. As late as the thirteenth century in Poland the Charter of Boleslav of Kalish provoked violent protestations from the clergy because of the danger of settling Jews among the newly converted Poles. It is significant that the first law which the Church imposed upon the newly Christian empire was the prohibition to the Jews to make converts, and from this time onwards Judaism became more and more a closed faith until proselytes came to be considered more a danger than a blessing.

CHAPTER FOUR

THE PART PLAYED BY THE JEWS IN THE PERSECUTIONS

BIBLIOGRAPHICAL INTRODUCTION

The material for a study of the part played by the Jews in the various persecutions which Christians endured during the early centuries is to be found in the lives of the martyrs. ' Acta ', ' Vitae ' and ' Passiones ' of her heroes were early collected by the Church, and from the fourth century to the Middle Ages they formed one of the most popular elements of Christian literature. Every church possessed its collection, and many national and local churches had their own special group of saints, and wrote and rewrote their lives 'with advantages'. The collection of these different lives was undertaken by many writers from the eighth and ninth century onwards, and their scientific study began in the seventeenth century with the work of two savants, Ruinart, who published a collection of Acta which he considered worthy to be counted historical, and Bollandus, who undertook the much greater task of collating all the material which existed in the different collections and individual narratives, and of producing a critical study of the lives of all those who were commemorated in the calendars of the Roman and Greek Churches. This work has been going on ever since, and the *Acta Sanctorum* of the Bollandists is the main repository for the study of the lives of the martyrs. It has now reached the saints commemorated in the middle of November.

The *Acta Sanctorum* may be taken to contain the traditions of the western churches and of the Greek Orthodox Church. In the eighteenth century the study of the collections in Syrian and other western Asiatic languages was undertaken, and the Syriac Acts of the Persian martyrs and Syriac versions of the lives of western martyrs were published by Assemani. Since then much has been published in those languages, but there will only be quoted in this chapter those oriental Acta which are accessible in European languages and in Latin, through the publications of the Bollandists and of the Patrologia Orientalis. The former have published a number of separate documents and the latter have published the complete Synaxaria of the Armenian Church and the Jacobite Church, and are in process of completing the Synaxaria also of the Ethiopian and Georgian Churches.

In addition to this collection of sources, certain modern studies are of great assistance. Hagiology is a special science of its own, and in order to know what to expect and how to understand the different Acta, whose historical value differ considerably, the two books of Hippolyte Delehaye are indispensable. The five volumes of P. Allard on the persecutions in the Roman empire give the general framework for the study of the individual Acta, and the works of Labourt, Uhlmann and Funk do the same for the persecutions in Persia.

In addition there are certain works professing to deal with the Jewish responsibility for the persecutions, which are cited rather as a warning than for any objective value they possess. There are generalisations on Jewish malignancy in the introductions to the Acta of most of the saints referred to in this chapter (*e.g.* A.S., Nov., I, p. 33, para. 63, Austremonius), and a long introduction on the same lines in the volume quoted of Leclercq. In addition there is a very one-sided and at times inaccurate study by Rösel. Otherwise the references are to be found scattered through the general works on Church history.

LIST OF BOOKS

Ancient Sources

ACTA SANCTORUM — Vol. I, Antwerp, 1643—continuing.

ASSEMANI, S. E. — *Acta Martyrum Orientalium et Occidentalium*. Rome, 1748.

ANALECTA BOLLANDIANA — A periodical publication of the Bollandists.

EUSEBIUS — *The Martyrs of Palestine*. P.G., XX.

DELEHAYE, H. — *Greek Acts of the Persian Martyrs under Shapur II*. In P.O., Vol. II.

LE SYNAXAIRE ARABE JACOBITE — Ed. René Bassett, in P.O.

Aug. 29—Oct. 27	In Vol. I.
Oct. 28—Dec. 26	In Vol. III.
Dec. 27—Feb. 24	In Vol. XI.
Feb. 25—May 25	In Vol. XVI.
May 26—Aug. 28	In Vol. XVII.
Indices	In Vol. XX.

LE SYNAXAIRE ARMENIEN DE TER ISRAEL — Ed. G. Bayan and Prince Max of Saxony, in P.O.

Aug. 11—Sept. 9	In Vol. V.
Sept. 10—Oct. 9	In Vol. VI.
Oct. 10—Nov. 8	In Vol. XV.
Nov. 8—Dec. 8	In Vol. XVI.
Dec. 9—Jan. 7	In Vol. XVIII.
Jan. 8—Feb. 6	In Vol. XIX.
Feb. 7—Aug. 10	In Vol. XXI.

SYNAXARIUM ECCLESIAE CONSTANTINOPOLITANAE — In *Acta Sanctorum*. November, Propylaeum.

Le Synaxaire Ethiopien — Ed. I. Guidi, in P.O.

May 26—June 24	In Vol. I.
July 8—Aug. 6	In Vol. VII.
Aug. 7—Sept. 12	In Vol. IX.
Nov. 27—Dec. 11	In Vol. XV.

Le Synaxaire Georgien — Ed. N. Marr, in P.O., Vol. XIX.

Modern Studies

Allard, P. — *Histoire des Persécutions des premiers Siècles*. 5. vols. Paris, various dates.

Delehaye, H. — *Les Passions des Martyrs et les Genres Litteraires*. Brussels, 1921.
Les Legendes Hagiographiques. Brussels, 1903.

Funk, S. — *Die Juden in Babylon* 200-500. Berlin, 1902 and 1908.

Labourt, M. J. — *Le Christianisme dans l'empire Perse sous la Dynastie Sassanide*. Paris, 1904.

Leclercq, H. — *Les Martyrs*. Tom. IV. Paris, 1905.

Rösel, G. — *Juden und Christenverfolgungen in den ersten Jahrhunderten*. Münster-i-W., 1893.

Uhlmann, F. — *Die Christenverfolgungen in Persien unter der Herrschaft der Sassaniden*. Zeitschrift für die Historische Theologie, 1861.

I. THE VIEW OF MODERN SCHOLARS AND THEIR AUTHORITY IN PATRISTIC LITERATURE

The statement that the Jews were directly or indirectly responsible for the persecutions which the Church endured in the early centuries is a commonplace among nearly all modern historians. Even where no such specific accusation is made they are described as perpetually inspired by the most violent hatred for the Church and the individual Christian, waiting only for an opportunity to do them some harm. Harnack boldly asserts that ' the hostility of the Jews appears on every page of Acts from chapter thirteen onwards. They tried to hamper every step of the Apostle's work among the Gentiles; they stirred up the masses and authorities in every country against him; systematically and officially they scattered broadcast horrible charges against the Christians which played an important part in the persecutions as early as the reign of Trajan; they started calumnies against Jesus; they provided heathen opponents of Christianity with literary ammunition; unless the evidence is misleading they instigated the Neronic outburst against the Christians, and as a rule wherever bloody persecutions are afoot in later days, the Jews are either in the background or the foreground '[1]. The Bollandist Joseph Corluy, in an introduction to the life of Abdul Masih—a saint whom another Bollandist, Paul Peeters, explains as of very doubtful authenticity—writes in his polished Latin: ' Judaeis ad Christianos persequendos nullum imperatorum decretum necesse est; sed debacchante persecutionis procella ipsi saepe maiore quam ethnici furore in Christianos ferebantur. Cuius furoris in Perside, tempore Saporis regis, plurima exempla fuerunt '[2]. Dom H. Leclercq, in his voluminous history of Martyrs, devotes the entire introduction to one volume to a description of the implacable violence of Jewish hostility[3]. M. Allard, in his five-volume history of the persecutions, whenever he has the

[1] *The Mission and Expansion of Christianity*, English Ed., Vol. I, p. 58 ff. For a Jewish criticism of Harnack, see R.E.J., Vols. LI and LII, *L'Esprit du Christianisme et du Judaisme*.

[2] *An. Boll.*, Vol. V and Vol. XLIV. On the persecution under Shapur, see below, Section VII.

[3] *Les Martyrs*, Vol. IV.

possibility, attributes the active rôle to the Jews and the passive to the pagans[1].

If the accuracy of this estimate of the rôle played by the Jews in the first three centuries of the life of Christianity were challenged, its defence would be found in the allusions to Jewish hostility which are scattered throughout patristic literature. Justin, Tertullian, Origen, Eusebius and others all imply that such was indeed the situation. ' You have not now the power to lay hands upon us on account of those who have the mastery ', says Justin to Trypho, ' but as often as you could, you did so.' And again in his Apology to Antoninus Pius, he says that 'the Jews count us foes and enemies, and like yourselves they kill and punish us whenever they have the power, as you may well believe. For in the Jewish war which lately raged Barcochebas, the leader of the revolt, gave orders that Christians alone should be led to cruel punishments '[2]. Tertullian's famous remark: ' the synagogues, the sources of the persecutions ', is equally clear[3]. A reference which is even more impressive, because it is an aside, lies in the attack of an anonymous author upon the Montanists. When he disallows their right to be called Christians, because they and their women prophets have neither been scourged in the synagogues of the Jews nor stoned by them, he is clearly implying that such treatment was, to some extent at least, the lot of the orthodox Christians[4]. Finally, Origen, in commenting upon the thirty-seventh psalm, remarks that ' the Jews do not vent their wrath on the Gentiles who worship idols and blaspheme God, and they neither hate them nor rage against them. But against the Christians they rage with an insatiable fury '[5]. It would be possible to collect further references, but these are sufficient to express the point of view of the writers of the third and fourth centuries.

[1] *Histoire des Persecutions*, Vol. I, p. 308; Vol. II, p. 374 and p. 353; Vol. IV, p. 256.

[2] *Trypho*, xvi; and *First Apology*, xxxi; P.G., VI, p. 375.

[3] *On the Scorpion's Bite*, x; P.L., II, p. 143.

[4] Quoted by Eusebius, *Eccl. Hist.*, V, xvi, 2; P.G., XX, p. 469.

[5] Origen, *On Ps. xxxvi*; P.G., XII, p. 1322.

II. THE NATURE OF THE AVAILABLE EVIDENCE

If we knew of the persecutions of the Church only from such literary sources we should certainly be justified in accepting such quotations as proof of a steady and malicious hatred on the part of the Jews, even though they are all, as it were, statements of the prosecution, and we are ignorant as to the other side. But, in fact, we possess thousands of documents of varying value dealing with the sufferings of individual martyrs and several histories of particular persecutions. These have on the whole been neglected by modern historians, with the exception of the contemporary story of the martyrdom of Polycarp, and the three martyrdoms of Pionius, Pontius and Philip[1]. It is therefore essential, before examining the basis of the charge made by Justin, Tertullian and the others, to see what evidence these documents offer us on the subject.

It was a very early custom for Churches to keep a record of their local heroes, and to commemorate them upon a particular day of the year. At first such commemorations were local, but soon Churches began to acquire names from their neighbours, and to communicate to them their own lists. In some cases letters relating the storms through which they had passed were sent out by the Churches themselves to a considerable number of others. A famous example of this is the letter describing the persecution at Lyons and Vienne recorded by Eusebius[2]. The next stage was for the great metropolitan churches to make general collections, and to introduce some uniformity into the different local celebrations[3]. At first such lists contained little more than names. But monastic writers began to embroider them with all kinds of wonders and miracles, so that it is possible for many different versions to exist of the fate of the same martyr.

[1] There must be some common source from which Juster, Frey and others quote these three cases. It is evident that it is not the coincidence of original study of the Acta, for two of them are of doubtful authenticity, and none of them prove any Jewish initiative in the martyrdom of the saints concerned!

[2] *Eccl. Hist.*, V, i; P.G., XX, p. 409 ff.

[3] On the history of martyrologies see the two books of Delehaye in the bibliography to this chapter.

When this rested upon a basis of a contemporary written document, the main traits can be followed through all the embroideries, but where no such document existed, all was left to the fancy of the scribe, and to popular imagination. Even these, however, are not entirely without value for our purpose, for in inventing what he imagined to have happened, the scribe was bound to some extent by popular memory of what was likely to have occurred.

To-day we have any number of such collections. The main local and general western collections and the Greek menologies have been collected together in the huge volumes of the Bollandists, the *Acta Sanctorum*, a work which was begun in the seventeenth century and, working by months, has now reached the middle of November. But it is not the first of its kind. It is itself based upon collections made in the early and late Middle Ages as well as upon small local collections and individual acts. More recently this collection has been supplemented by the discovery and gradual publication of the lists and stories of eastern Churches which in many cases enshrine quite an independent tradition.

III. JEWS IN THE ACTA OF THE FIRST CENTURY

Embodied in these collections as they now exist are many stories which to-day are recognised to be entirely fabulous, to be nothing more than novelettes produced in some monastic centre, based upon a local legend possibly of pagan origin, or due simply to the ingenuity of the writer. A group of persons around whom such legends were especially likely to cluster are those characters mentioned in the New Testament about whom the earliest Church, with its lack of interest in history, preserved no authentic details. It is this last class which contains by far the largest number of references to Jewish malice and to Jewish initiative[1].

The Acts of the Apostles provides the starting point for these legends. They recall a time of frequent and, at times, violent hostility to the preaching of the Gospel. They record, in the person of Stephen, one act of summary execution, and in that of James, the brother of John, an

[1] See Appendix Five.

official, if capricious, death sentence. It was not an unreasonable presumption that other persons of the period suffered the same fate as these two. But the stories are not entirely confined to the compass of the experience of the Acts of the Apostles. It was a tradition that the Apostles themselves and their earliest followers had evangelised the whole of the ancient world, and had visited regions in which Jews and Greeks were not the natural actors. These two traditions can occasionally be seen in the stories of the same person. In most of the western accounts the apostle Andrew was killed by Herod at Bethlehem[1]. But according to the Ethiopian Church he was murdered by a heathen priest at Patras[2]. Aristobulus, the brother of Barnabas, was supposed to have preached to Jews and Greeks, to have been persecuted by them, and finally to have met his death by stoning at their hands[3]. The Armenian Church, while agreeing as to his career, states that he died in peace[4]. But western traditions make him the first bishop of Britain, where he died peacefully[5].

While thus the two tendencies, the tendency to copy actual events of the Acts of the Apostles and the tendency to illustrate the breadth of the missionary work of the first generation of Christians, are at times found concentrated in the same person, there are others of whom the tradition is consistent throughout, and can even be traced back to fairly early sources. The death of James the Just, the first bishop of Jerusalem, is mentioned by Eusebius[6], and the story is substantially the same in the records of all the Churches. In view of the important position which he occupied, the accuracy of the story may be accepted. The same is possibly true of the death of Barnabas, whom all agree to have been killed in Cyprus by, or at the instigation of, the Jews[7]. But unanimity does not necessarily mean historicity, any more

[1] A.S., Feb. 10.

[2] P.O., Vol. XV, p. 583.

[3] S.A.J., March 15.

[4] S.A., March 15.

[5] A.S., March 15.

[6] *Eccl. Hist.*, II, xxiii; P.G., XX, p. 196 ff.

[7] A.S., June 11; S.A.J., Dec. 17; S.A., June 11.

than diversity denies it. One would expect all the martyrologies to agree with the straightforward account in the Acts of the Apostles of the death of James, the brother of John. But they do not do so. In one account he was accused to the Roman governor of preaching 'another king', and was stoned at his order[1]. The name of the scribe who accused him and was afterwards converted by him and shared his death is given in another martyrology[2]. A third ascribes his death entirely to the Jews[3]. But none of these stories cast any real doubt on the original narrative of the Acts of the Apostles. That unanimity is also not necessarily convincing is illustrated by the stories clustering round Longinus, the centurion who pierced the side of Christ, and was impressed by His death. The gospels do not identify these two soldiers, and in any case give neither a name. The name Longinus cannot be traced to within centuries of the occurrence, and if the soldier had actually been a prominent convert it is surprising that he does not figure in any of the second century apologies to the Roman authorities as an objective and Roman proof of the story which they had to tell. But he is a familiar figure to the hagiologist, and his story with a wealth of detail is given in almost every collection[4] with surprisingly little variation, if we accept the fact that the accounts derive from two versions of the same original, in one of which the malice of the Jews is shown in their bribing him to make sure of the death of Jesus, and in the other in their bribing Pilate to ensure the death of Longinus[5]. Yet all these accounts do not end by creating a conviction that such a Longinus ever existed.

With all this confusion it would seem at first sight a hopeless task to seek for a historical basis for any of these stories, and a dangerous assumption to claim them as an adequate foundation for any conclusion. But if we pass from the consideration of individual cases to an examination of them as a group of stories we find certain traits which are

[1] S.A.J., Feb. 4.

[2] S.A., April 30.

[3] S.C., Oct. 9.

[4] A.S., March 15; S.A., Oct. 16; S.A.J., July 18 and Nov. 1; S.E., July 30.

[5] Cf. S.A.J., July 18, with S.A., Oct. 16.

inherently probable, and which may well portray an accurate historical tradition as to the period which followed the original preaching of Paul to the Gentiles. If they were based on the Acts of the Apostles only we might expect the preaching of the next generation to have been exclusively directed to the Gentiles. But all the Acts which record preaching to Greeks record also preaching to Jews. We have seen that it is historically probable that the Church continued to exist within the Synagogue for some thirty years after the death of Paul, but this is not a natural deduction from the Acts of the Apostles. There is also more variety in the stories than there is in the mythical acts of later martyrdoms. In the latter case the routine of torture and miracle follows through with a monotony of accumulated horror. The same replies, the same events, succeed each other again and again. It would be simple if we could explain this variety by attributing to all the stories a single author who sought variety for artistic effect. But this solution is ruled out by the contradictions of the stories which have been already discussed. What we have is a number of stories alike in general line and differing in detail. One man was killed by the Jews; another was killed by the pagans; one suffered much persecution but finally died in peace; and another encountered little opposition during his ministry. One travelled from place to place. Another worked all his life in a single spot. Here it was at the hands of the mob that he met his death, there it was at the hands of the officials. If we leave out the names the stories are inherently probable.

It is a well known tendency of popular tradition to become more and more precise, to give the exact spot where each event occurred, and to give a name to every actor. This is what seems to have happened in this case. There was an authentic tradition that the first preacher of Christianity was stoned by the Jews. Who was he? It was natural to seek a name among the unallotted personalities of the New Testament. Two local Churches selected the same name. Hence the different lives attributed to the same man. If such an explanation be accepted, then it can be said that the first period of the expansion of Christianity was marked by many and violent conflicts between the new preachers and the Jews in whose synagogues and under whose auspices they preached. The remarks of the patristic authors find confirmation in numberless local traditions. To say more is difficult until a scientific study of the earlier Acta of the different Churches has been undertaken. But one detail may be pointed out. Even a superficial reading of the hagiologies reveals the superiority of the historical sense of the western and Greek Churches over the imagination of the eastern groups. Even where they invented they gave a sufficiently probable account for it to be possible to debate whether an event did or did not take place. The eastern Acta pay no attention to historical—or even moral—probability. In the cases under consideration it is to be noticed that nearly all the descriptions of official action by governors and prefects are in the eastern narratives. The western speak of mob action, and it is just what we should expect at this stage.

So far it has been suggested that these stories as attached to the names of particular persons have no historical value, but that as a group they embody an authentic, if anonymous, tradition. This view finds strong confirmation if we consider them as a particular group within the wider frame of the Acta as a whole. We are then faced at once with a most illuminating fact. These stories cease entirely at the beginning of the second century. Acta attributed to the first century number at most a few hundred among the thousands of individual records. In them we find a very high proportion of stories ascribing definite hostility to the Jews, culminating sometimes in the death of the saint. From the beginning of the second century onwards there is almost complete silence as to any Jewish responsibility for, or even interest in, the fate of the heroes of the Church. Apart from a genuine historical tradition, it is difficult to explain so precise a fact. Its accuracy is, however, confirmed by the form in which Justin speaks of the persecution which the Church endured at Jewish hands. ' You cannot harm us now, but as often as you could you did ', describes exactly the situation presented by the Acta[1]. Before considering the reliability of the later statements, of Tertullian and Origen, it will be well to consider other references to Jewish action in the persecution of Christians as recorded in the lives of the martyrs.

[1] Cf. Gaudentius, *Sermo*, IV; P.L., XX, p. 868; and Jerome, *On Amos*, i, 22; P.L., XXV, p. 1001.

IV. STORIES SHOWING JEWISH INITIATIVE IN THE PERIOD FROM HADRIAN TO CONSTANTINE

By far the greater mass of Acta refer to the period between that already considered and the peace of the Church under Constantine, the period covered by the great general Roman persecutions culminating in the ten years' reign of terror under Diocletian. Responsibility passes completely from the Jews to the Romans. Such stories as there are of Jewish action belong, in character, to the earlier and unsystematic violence of the individual and the mob. This is well illustrated by the fate of the first missionary bishop of the Chersonese, Basil. He was consecrated at the beginning of the fourth century by Hermon, patriarch of Jerusalem, together with some others, to preach among the heathen of that region. The success of his preaching earned him the hostility of the adherents of the older worship, and of the Jews who were numerous in the region. Stirred up by the latter, a mob of pagans seized the bishop and dragged him through the streets until he expired[1]. His successor, Antherius, is said to have applied to Constantine to obtain soldiers to drive out his murderers[2]. On the death of Antherius, the inhabitants sent for a new bishop. When he arrived the unbelievers demanded a miracle to prove his claims. The bishop walked through fire in full canonicals, and the Jews and unbelievers were thereupon converted, 'the soldiers with the other Christians receiving them at the font'. This last detail suggests that the narrative covers a forced conversion, exacted as the penalty for the murder of Basil.

A story of a somewhat similar character comes from Clermont in Auvergne. Bishop Austremonius, who is said to have been of the first century, but was more probably of the beginning of the fourth, was particularly successful in preaching to the Jews of Clermont, and among his converts was Lucius, the son of one of the Jewish elders. The father, enraged at the disloyalty of his son, seized a knife, and killed both the bishop and his own child[3]. Ubricius, the successor

[1] A.S., March 7; S.C. Sel., March 6; S.A.J., March 6; S.A., March 7.
[2] S.A., April 20.
[3] A.S., April 3.

of Austremonius, convened the authorities, and secured a decree that all the Jews should either accept baptism or, if they remained in Clermont, be sentenced to death[1]. The actual narrative contains various miracles which are clearly embroideries. The most serious difficulty is, however, the action of the Roman authorities. Ubricius is said to have so acted in 312, when Judaism was a lawful religion, and Christianity was not only unrecognised but actually being persecuted. Either the incident occurred after the peace of the Church, or it is a memory of the similar action of Avitus in Clermont in the sixth century[2]. Even if this be the case, the original story remains probable enough. The action of Ubricius may be only what a scribe thought ought to have happened for so great a crime. But a family tragedy of such a character is not an unknown occurrence in the history of religious differences.

Two other cases are of particular interest in view of the continual legislation of the Church against the possession of Christian slaves by Jews. Matrona, the slave of a Jewish mistress at Salonica, was found by her to be a Christian, who refused to enter the synagogue. In a rage she beat her, and locked her up in a room without food or water. Finding her still recalcitrant, she beat her so severely that she died. The story was an exceedingly popular one, and the versions of it are manifold[3]. A similar case, though less well attested, is reported from Portugal. No time is given, and it may belong to the fifth or sixth century. But in its essence the story is the same as that of Matrona. A slave, Mancius, is found by his Jewish master to be a Christian. He is severely beaten, but refuses to alter his religion. Finally, he dies under the punishment[4].

Indignation at the conversion of a Jewish family to Christianity is said to have been responsible for the death of a group of Jews at Leontini in Sicily. A Christian, Alphius, was being with some companions led to prison by the Roman soldiers, when he was observed by a Jew ' who

[1] A.S., Nov. 1.

[2] See Chap. IX, Section VIII.

[3] A.S., March 15; S.C., March 27; S.A.J., Sept. 7; S.A., March 21. (A.S. gives more than one version.)

[4] A.S., May 21.

was possessed of a devil'. The Jew implored Alphius to cure him. Alphius did so, whereon all his family became converted, and were stoned by the other Jews for their apostasy[1]. Here again there is nothing improbable in the story. The action of the epileptic—or otherwise spiritually diseased—Jew in throwing himself at the feet of Alphius is not incredible. The glamour which must have attached itself to a Christian going to his fate is exactly the kind of power to exercise an influence over any one in such a condition. The conversion of his family in gratitude, and the indignation of the other members of the Jewish community are equally within the bounds of probability.

The final case which can be quoted rests upon much less certain evidence. Paul, Valentina, and Thea were Egyptian Christians who were taken for sentence to Diocaesarea, a predominantly Jewish town. There they were tried by Fermilian and sentenced to death. In his last prayer, Paul prayed for the Jews and pagans. This is the account given by Eusebius in the *Martyrs of Palestine*[2]. There are two other accounts of the incident. What we may call the 'Constantinople tradition' adds that when they were brought before Fermilian, a mob of Jews stirred him up against them, and secured their conviction. The 'Armenian tradition' goes further. The accused lived in Diocaesarea, and did not come to the notice of Fermilian until the Jews denounced them[3]. It is reasonable to take these three versions as an admirable example of the growth of legend. If we take the account of Eusebius as the authentic narrative, which we are justified in doing, we can explain the reference to the Jews in the prayer of Paul by the fact that their presence must have been apparent to him. But the Constantinopolitan scribe felt that there must have been some special nobility in this prayer. It became, therefore, the reply of Paul to the Jewish clamour at the judgment seat for his death. The Armenian goes one further. It was still nobler, for it was by the Jews that he was originally denounced as a Christian.

[1] S.A., April 9.

[2] Ch. viii. P.G., XX, p. 1489.

[3] S.C. Sel., July 16, and S.A., Aug. 5.

V. CASES OF JEWISH HOSTILITY IN THE CROWD

In addition to these cases showing definite Jewish initiative in securing the death of the martyr, there are also a few cases in which the special hostility of the Jewish members of the crowd which watched the different stages of the trial and execution are commented upon by the narrator. It is important to distinguish them from the cases already quoted. It is indeed reprehensible to gloat over the condemnation of a fellow man for his religious convictions. But it is much more revolting to be the actual betrayer of him to the authorities, or the direct cause of his death.

The most familiar, and the earliest of these cases, is the martyrdom of Polycarp, bishop of Smyrna[1], in 155. In this story there is no Jewish responsibility for any of the events. Polycarp is betrayed by a Christian, a member of his own household, who confesses his whereabouts under torture. The Roman authorities make every effort to persuade him to sacrifice, but when Polycarp refuses, he is taken to the stadium to be examined by the pro-consul. The latter again urges every argument upon him, without success, and finally Polycarp is condemned to be burnt. When the proclamation is made, 'the whole multitude, both of the heathen and Jews who live in Smyrna, cried out with uncontrollable fury: "This is the teacher of Asia, the father of the Christians, and the overthrower of our gods, he who has been teaching many not to sacrifice, or to worship the gods" '. The Jews can hardly be considered to have taken the active part in that cry, but the decision having been taken, it appears that there are no materials prepared, and the crowd begin to collect wood from the neighbouring shops and baths, 'the Jews especially, according to custom, eagerly assisting them in it'. Polycarp is then placed among the faggots, and bound, but the fire refuses to touch him. (Some writers think that this miraculous element is a later interpolation.) As he is not burned, a soldier kills him by stabbing him. The Christians wish to take his body, but the Jews persuade the father of

[1] A.S., Jan. 26. The letter of the Church of Smyrna describing the death of Polycarp is to be found among the writings of the Apostolic Fathers.

the Roman official in charge to refuse to give it up. The centurion, 'seeing the strife created by the Jews', places the body on the pyre and it is consumed.

The whole event is said to have taken place upon 'the great Sabbath', whatever the author may mean by the phrase, and this is used as an argument by Dr. Abrahams to discredit the whole story, for, he argues, if it were such a day, Jews would neither be found frequenting the theatre nor carrying wood[1]. If it could be presumed that all the Jews of Smyrna were orthodox, the objection would be valid. But it has this value, to show that it was in no way an official Jewish manifestation against Polycarp. It was the action of Jewish 'lewd fellows of the baser sort', such as once persecuted Paul. Such as it was, the Jewish action was not responsible for any of the events of the actual martyrdom. The betrayer was a Christian. The condemner was a Roman, the actual executioner a soldier. At most, Jewish initiative appears in the disposal of his dead body. Everything would have happened, had no Jews been there. Their presence accentuated but did not cause the tragedy.

A hundred years later Smyrna was again the scene of a martyrdom in which the Jews were said to have taken part. In the persecution in 251, under Decius, one of the victims is Pionius. He has been warned of his approaching martyrdom in a dream, and is performing a last act of worship with his fellow Christians when Polemon, who is the official charged with seeing that every citizen offers sacrifice, comes and arrests him and his companions. They are marched to the forum, where, as it is again the Sabbath, there is an immense crowd and many Jewesses. Polemon invites Pionius to sacrifice, and he refuses. It is to be imagined that the crowd make a hostile manifestation at this refusal, for Pionius turns and addresses them in these words:

> 'You who rejoice in the beauty of the buildings of Smyrna, and delight in its adornment, you who are proud of your poet Homer, and you Jews also, if any of you are present, listen to these few words. For I hear that you laugh at those who have sacrificed, whether they have done it voluntarily, or yielded to compulsion, and in both cases

[1] *Studies in Pharisaism*, Vol. II, p. 67.

you condemn what is weakness as deliberate infidelity. You should obey rather the words of your teacher and master Homer, who says that it is a sin to insult the dead, and that none should war against the blind or the dead. And you who are Jews should obey the precepts of Moses, who tells you that if the animal of your enemy fall, you should help it and not pass by. And Solomon likewise says that you should not rejoice over the fall of your enemy or the misfortune of others. Wherefore I would rather die and suffer any torment, however awful, than renounce either what I have learnt or what I have taught. I say this to you Jews who dissolve in laughter and mockery at those who voluntarily or involuntarily sacrifice, and who laugh at us also and shout insultingly that we have been given too much licence, I say to you that if we are enemies, we are also men. Have any suffered loss through us? Have we caused any to be tortured? Whom have we unjustly persecuted? Whom have we harmed in speech? Whom have we cruelly dragged to torture? Such crimes are very different from those of men who have acted in fear of the lions. There is an immense difference between voluntary and involuntary sin. There is this difference between him who is forced, and him who of his own free will does wrong. There it is the will, here it is the occasion which is responsible. And who compelled the Jews to foul themselves with the worship of Belphegor, with heathen rites and sacrifices? Who forced them into fornication with strange women, or into sensual pleasures? At whose compulsion did they make burnt offerings of their own sons, murmur against God, and secretly speak ill of Moses? At whose behest did they forget so many benefits? Who made them ungrateful? Who compelled them to return in heart to Egypt, or, when Moses had ascended the Mount to receive the Law, to say to Aaron: "Make us Gods, and a calf to go before us"; and to commit all their other sins? You pagans, perhaps, they may deceive, but they will never impose upon us.'

In the whole collection of hagiological literature there are few utterances more moving than this defence of the weaker brethren by one who, though he confessed that he loved life, was yet prepared to die for his faith; and it is one of the most amazing abortions of the religious mentality that with models before them of such exquisite and poignant beauty as the story of Pionius, they produced the thousands of morally repulsive Grand Guignol travesties of heroism which deface the whole of this literature.

After his speech, Pionius is examined by the pro-consul, who does all he can to save him. But Pionius will not compromise, and is led away to be burnt[1]. There is a later, and much inferior, version by Simeon Metaphrastes, who composed martyrologies at the beginning of the tenth century. It contains one detail which is interesting, if it can be considered authentic. The Jews are said to have offered the Christians the shelter of Judaism during the persecution. Naturally, such a solution was unacceptable to Pionius, but one would like to believe that it was some attempt at reparation for the conduct for which Pionius reproached them in words which must have touched the hearts of many, Jews and pagans, who stood in the forum that day.

There are in the Acta a few other and briefer references to Jewish hostility among the crowd of bystanders. At the martyrdom of Leo at Patara in Lycia, in the third century, when Leo begins a defence of Christianity, 'a crowd of irreverent Jews and pagans began to clamour that he should not be allowed to speak'[2]. On the appearance of Philip, bishop of Heraclea, in the forum of that town, there is a hostile demonstration on the part of the Jews, 'for, as is usual, some when they see the martyrs pity them, but others grow more furious at the actual sight of them, especially the Jews, according to the scripture. For the Holy Spirit says through the prophet, "they have sacrificed to demons and not to God"'[3]. There is one more story, dealing with an incident of the Diocletian persecution. At Caesarea a martyr, Carterius, is sentenced to be burnt, and is thrown into the fire. But he remains unharmed in the midst of it. A Jew in the crowd, in a frenzy, seizes a spear and kills him with it. This story is on the border-line of history and myth.

[1] A.S., Feb. 1. Cf. *Les Passions des Martyrs*, p. 28 ff.

[2] A.S., Feb. 18. The Acta are a late compilation.

[3] *Ibid.*, Oct. 22. The Acta are late and their reliability is questioned by some. But they are defended by Delehaye, A.B., Vol. XXXI, p. 243.

It is only recorded in one martyrology, and the main defence for it is the originality of the action and the poverty of invention of the monastic novelists[1].

VI. JEWS IN THE PERSECUTION UNDER JULIAN

Such is the record of the Jews in the persecutions which preceded the peace of the Church. There are two other periods during which their active malevolence is most frequently alleged. During the reign of Julian there was a brief moment of violent attack upon the Christians. The Acta offer three stories of Jewish participation. There was at Toul in northern France a preacher, Eliphius, who was always attacking the Jews in his sermons. For this they hated him, and when the opportunity offered, under Julian, they seized him and his companions, and threw them into prison to please the emperor. They then, apparently, forgot them, for they came out of prison again and were arrested by the Romans and put to death. At Lyons there was a Christian woman, Benedicta, who was brought before a judge, who was also a Jew, who condemned her with gusto because of his hatred of Christ[2]. Both these stories are of exceedingly doubtful authenticity, and only merit mention because of the coincidence that both come from France, and might, perhaps, be considered to gather mutual support thereby. More probable is the story of the soldiers Bonosus and Maximilianus who refused to remove the cross from their standards at Antioch. All that is alleged of the Jews in their story is that when they resisted the effects of torture in the arena, ' Jews and Gentiles who had come to mock at their deaths cried out " Sorcerers, criminals " '[3].

VII. JEWS IN THE PERSECUTION UNDER SHAPUR II

The second case in which generalisations on Jewish malignity are frequent is that of the persecutions under Shapur II in the fourth century in Persia. The situation of Jews and Christians in Persia changed radically at the beginning of the

[1] A.S., Jan. 8, from the *Synaxarium Constantinopolitanum*.

[2] *Ibid.*, Oct. 16, and Oct. 8.

[3] *Ibid.*. Aug. 21.

fourth century. Before the peace of the Church the Jews were on the whole unmolested within the Roman empire, and the Christians were similarly unmolested in Persia. But the peace of the Church, and the consequent legislation against the Jews, caused a considerable influx of Jews into Persia, and at the same time caused the Persian Christians to look with more friendship towards Rome, no longer a persecutor but a great Christian state. Two events in Persia itself helped to bring about the attacks upon the Church. The Sassanid dynasty was more fanatically Zoroastrian than its predecessor, and abandoned complete religious toleration for a policy of active proselytisation. The Jews were able to make a *modus vivendi* with the Magi which allowed them to retain their religious freedom by minor concessions which did not involve principles. The Christians were not disposed to be so tolerant. More serious was the resumption in 338 of the traditional war with Rome. This increased the friendliness between the Persians and the Jews who were naturally hostile to Rome, and similarly increased the hostility towards the Christians who were with equal reason friendly towards Christian Rome.

Religious intolerance and political bitterness led to a persecution which lasted intermittently for several decades. But authentic references to Jewish participation are limited to a particular moment, and a particular person, Simeon Bar Sabbae, the Archbishop of Ctesiphon, who was executed in 339. The incidents connected with his arrest are frequently and fully recounted. The Archbishop, who was supposed to be a personal friend of the king, Shapur, was ordered to provide double taxation from his community for the purpose of the war. The Jews had also been compelled to pay this tax, and had accepted it. But Simeon refused in a haughty letter to the king. The Jews are said to have prejudiced the king against him by telling him that the Roman emperor would despise any gifts which the king might send him, however costly, and would venerate with exaggerated humility the tiniest scrap of paper which came from Simeon. There is much obscurity and some contradiction in the exact part allotted to the Jews in this incident, and the natural deduction is that in fact Simeon was engaged in a treasonable correspondence with Rome, and the Jews, or Jews and Magi, betrayed this fact to the king[1]. The death of the Archbishop and the general persecution which followed was as much a political measure as a religious oppression. When Tarbula, the sister of Simeon, was also arrested, the Jews were again accused of responsibility. Sozomen gives the reason that she was trying to poison the queen, who had Jewish sympathies[2]. But other accounts make the queen a Christian[3]. In any case, there appears to be a widespread tradition that the Jews were concerned in the deaths of these two victims, and in view of their loyalty to Persia, and the probability that Simeon was overtly friendly with Rome, it is not unlikely that the tradition is correct. But apart from these two, the only mention of the Jews is casual. They were present at the stoning of Mar Kadagh[4], and they provided a prison for Sira, a victim of the hostility of the Magi, and used her cruelly while she was under their charge[5]. Neither of the stories are particularly trustworthy. No other participation in the persecution which lasted, with intermissions, throughout the long reign of Shapur is mentioned.

Two documents which might be expected to contain a reference to general Jewish responsibility, if such existed, are silent on the point. Aphraates, who wrote his *Twenty First Demonstration* in reply to the Jewish taunt that the Christians ought to be able to work a miracle to prevent their being persecuted, might legitimately be expected to attack the Jews for their responsibility if he was aware of it. But he says nothing about it[6]. The other document is the 'treatise on the martyrs celebrated on the Friday after the Crucifixion' of Iŝai the Doctor, which contains the words, 'we pass from the passion of our Redeemer *whom the wicked Jews killed*, because of the truth of His teaching, to the commemoration of the confessors *whom the pagans killed* for preaching the

[1] For references to Simeon, see Sozomen, *Hist. Eccl.*, II, ix; P.G., LXVII, p. 956; *Martyrium Simeonis* in P.S., II, p. 737; *Nestorian History* in P.O., IV, p. 297; and Assemani, p. 20. Jewish responsibility is not mentioned in the Armenian story (April 13) or the Jacobite (April 14).

[2] Sozomen, *Hist. Eccl.*, II, xii; P.G., LXVII, p. 964. Cf. P.O., II, p. 439.

[3] A.S., Nov. 2.

[4] A.B., Vol. IX, p. 101.

[5] A.S., May 18.

[6] P.S., Vol. I. It was written before the arrest of Simeon, so that his silence on that point is natural.

hope of the Resurrection. *The Jews* crucified Christ because they could not receive His teaching: *the pagans* tortured the martyrs because they could not bear the outrage done to their idols '[1]. It would be difficult to find a case where negative evidence is more illuminating, for the feast was established not for the general commemoration of the martyrs, but to commemorate the Persian martyrs in particular.

VIII. JEWS IN THE MYTHICAL ACTS

It is also interesting to consider the rôle allotted to the Jews in the frankly mythical acts. Mention of them is very rare. In some cases there is clearly a reminiscence of biblical events. In the *Acta Pontii*, which abound in the form of miracle which has no moral value, first the crowd are moved to demand the release of the martyr on observing his immunity from torture, and cry that the God of the Christians is the only God; then the judge himself quails before such supernatural insensitiveness to pain, and finally the execution only proceeds because the Jews cry ' Kill him, kill the malefactor '. Pontius thanks the Lord for allowing his passion to be like that of his Master, in that the Jews have shouted the same condemnation at him as they once did to Pilate, and gracefully expires[2]. At the martyrdom of Isbozetas by Chosroes, the saint is impaled on a cross with a Magus on his right side and a Jew on his left. The Magus desires to become a Christian, and, being accepted, expires. The Jew expresses his willingness to do anything to save his life, but is ignored and expires with the others[3]. At Nicomedia, during the persecution under Aurelian, the Christians retire from the city. The governor offers the command of his guard to anyone who will reveal where they are concealed. A Jew, Simeon, exposes the place and goes by night with a band of soldiers to arrest them[4].

[1] *Is̑ai the Doctor*, P.O., Vol. VII, p. 27.

[2] A.S., May 3. And this is one of the cases always quoted.

[3] *Ibid.*, Nov. 9.

[4] A.B., Vol. XXXI. The story is told with the comment, ' on n'oserait s'appuyer sur un pareil document pour ajouter à la liste des martyrs de Byzance '.

Myth, bordering on farce, accompanies the mention of the Jews in the stories of Marciana at Caesarea in Mauretania, and Demetrius at Thessalonica. In the first case the whole house of the Jew who mocked at her in the arena falls upon his head; and in the second, Gentiles came from Athens, Jews from Jerusalem, Manicheans from Mesopotamia, and Arians from Alexandria to slaughter the unhappy victim. But their voyage was fruitless, for a rascally Greek caught him with a spear on the way to his bath, before their arrival[1]. Myth without the burlesque marks the charming and pathetic story of the little Jewish martyr Abdul Masih. He was a shepherd boy in Persia, who fed his flocks in the company of little Christians and little Magi. But he was the only Jew, and at his meals he was lonely, for neither of the other groups would allow him to feed with them. He begs the Christian boys to let him share their meal, but they will only do so if he is baptised. This he is ready to accept, and after a discussion marked by the earnestness of childhood, the little Christians themselves baptise him, and give him a gold earring as a symbol, for a free Jew will never pierce his ear. On his return his mother and ultimately his father observe the symbol of his apostasy, and in spite of the pleadings of the other Jews who are present, the father pursues the boy and kills him by the very pool where he was baptised[2].

IX. CASES OF JEWISH KINDNESS TO THE MARTYRS

To form a true estimate of the place of the Jew in the minds of those who composed the different histories and myths of the Martyrologies, it is essential to consider also references which do not show hostility. For the Jews are not always monsters in these stories. It has already been mentioned that in one account of the martyrdom of Pionius the Jews offer the shelter of the Synagogue to those who wish to avoid martyrdom. It is usually assumed that this was an invitation to complete apostasy. But if a Christian wished to apostasise, he had only to offer sacrifice. If it be genuine, it can only be a real offer of protection, for the Romans had no authority

[1] A.S., Jan. 9 and Oct. 8.
[2] A.B., Vols. V and XLIV.

to ask a member of the Jewish community about his religious opinions, and the Jews could cover with their name any one they liked. We know from other sources that there were Christians who adopted this expedient, both in Rome and Persia[1]. If it is sometimes related that Jews were among the most hostile elements of the crowd, it is also sometimes mentioned that they showed pity. The tortures to which Theodore of Cyrene was subjected were such that 'all the people, Jews and infidels as well as Christians, wept at the sight '[2]. After the martyrdom of Habib at Edessa, 'even some Jews and pagans took part with the Christian brethren in shrouding and burying his body '[3]. The life of Venantius of Arles was 'so beautiful that he was loved alike by Hebrews, Greeks and Latins '[4]. Such was the memory of Agatha of Catania that 'Jews and Gentiles as much as Christians venerated her grave '[5]. There are also three cases in which Christian martyrs are said to have been buried in Jewish cemeteries[6], either with or without the knowledge of the Christians. At the least this does not suggest the hostility of the Jewish community concerned. In the mythical acts, while there is almost complete silence as to Jewish hostility, there are constant references to their miraculous conversions by the Saint concerned.

X. ABSENCE OF ANY RECORDS OF JEWISH RESPONSIBILITY FOR THE PERSECUTIONS

Finally, we have to consider not only the evidence of their presence, but also that of their absence, the evidence from silence. Naturally it is not possible to claim that there are no other cases in which the Jews are mentioned in the accounts of martyrdoms. Many texts are not yet published or are inaccessible. But it can legitimately be claimed that

[1] Cf. Eusebius, *Eccl. Hist.*, VI, xii; P.G., XX, p. 545; Vogelstein, *Geschichte der Juden in Rom*, Vol. I, p. 35; Funk, *Juden in Babylon*, Vol. II, pp. 52, 53.

[2] S.A., July 6.

[3] Martyrs of Edessa in *Euphemia the Goth*, by F. C. Burkitt.

[4] A.S., May 30.

[5] *Ibid.*, Feb. 1.

[6] Agricola and Vitalis at Milan, Nov. 4; Hermes, Aggaeus, and Caius in Dacia, Jan. 4; Vincent and Orantius in Spain, Jan. 22.

it is improbable that even if they add to the amount of evidence we possess, they would substantially alter its character. It is also evident that we cannot expect that every time Jews were present the writer thought of mentioning it. But again, we have sufficient positive evidence to make it improbable that any such general hostility as modern writers assume would have been passed over, not only by those who were accurately recording a single incident, but also by those whose imagination allowed them to embody in their fiction the main elements of popular ecclesiastical tradition.

In view of the number of documents preserved the argument from silence is, in fact, a very strong one, and it is strongest at the starting point, the persecutions of the first century. Here we have seen that there are a large number of statements involving Jewish hostility and even initiative. But there is complete silence as to Jewish participation in any part of the persecution which is supposed to have occurred in the reign of Nero. It is usually worthless to quote examples to prove a negative, but in this case, as the number of documents concerned is slight, it may be permitted to refer to the martyrdoms of Hermagoras, Paulinus, Severus, Justus, Orontius, Priscus, the Martyrs of Aquileia, and Hedistus[1]. They are at least sufficient to prove that no general Jewish responsibility for this persecution was believed to exist. In view of this silence, the argument that the Jews were responsible for the arrest of Christians for burning Rome loses much of its force. It is not an accusation made by any early writer, and it rests upon the assumption that the choice of a victim must have lain between the Jews and the Christians, and that the Jews would have inevitably been selected if they had not had powerful protection at court in the person of Poppaea and others. But so far as we know it is a gratuitous assumption that the Jews or Christians were the only possible alternatives. Nero might equally well have chosen the worshippers of Isis or Astarte for all that Suetonius or Tacitus tell us to the contrary.

When we come to the great persecutions of the second and third centuries, we are confronted with the same silence. The cases which reveal Jewish initiative do not enter into

[1] A.S., July 12 and 28, Aug. 26, Sept. 1 and 3, and Oct. 12 (in the Auctarium).

the category of general persecution. Nor is it that the narratives only begin with the trial of the victim. The method by which he is discovered is usually given. Sometimes he declares himself; sometimes his refusal to sacrifice reveals him; sometimes he is betrayed by heathen priests. But he is not betrayed by the Jews. The same holds good for persecutions outside these centuries. The Jews are supposed to have been particularly friendly with the Arians. They are not recorded as taking any part in the Arian persecutions under the Vandals in Africa, or in any of the Arian persecutions in Europe. They are supposed to have been very friendly with the Arab conquerors of Spain. But they are not mentioned in the stories of the martyrdoms of the eighth and ninth centuries in Mahomedan Spain. They are represented as being permanently and violently hostile to the orthodox Christians in Alexandria, and their participation in the Arian riots in the time of Athanasius and his successor is quoted as evidence of this. But in two long narratives in which it is specifically mentioned that all the inhabitants of Alexandria took part, they are passed over in silence[1]. Finally, it is clear that in the narratives in which they are mentioned their presence is not considered to be an essential or even important part of the narrative. The martyrdoms of Polycarp and Pionius are found in many collections. That of the Armenian Church is a lengthy account which has clearly used the letter of the Church of Smyrna. But while it states that Polycarp disputed much with Jews, and brought many to the faith, it is completely silent as to the presence of Jews at his death, and actually ascribes to the influence of 'idolators' the destruction of his body[2]. The same Church gives a long account of the martyrdom of Pionius, without referring to the Jews.

[1] The Martyrdom of Theodorus, A.S., Sept. 12, and Philip, A.S., Sept. 13.

[2] S.A., Feb. 23. Cf. S.A.J., same date.

XI. SUMMARY OF THE EVIDENCE

On the basis of this examination of the martyrs we can turn back to the generalisations of the theologians which appear to contradict it. Justin has already been discussed, and the evidence which justifies his statement can to a considerable extent also be used as an explanation of the statements of Tertullian and Origen. But the key to the explanation lies in the quotation from the latter. The statement of Jewish hostility in general terms is based on theological exegesis and not on historical memory. It has already been shown how the Christian use of the Old Testament made of the Jews an historical impossibility. The accusation now under consideration is a specific example of this general rule. Origen remarks that the 'Jews do not vent their wrath on the Gentiles who worship idols and blaspheme God, and they neither hate them nor rage against them. But against the Christians they rage with an insatiable fury'. He is commenting upon a passage of Deuteronomy[1]. 'They have moved me to jealousy with that which is not God; and they have provoked me to anger with their vanities (idols).' As the Jews were no longer themselves idolators, Origen interprets this by making them exceedingly friendly with idolators —a statement allegorically necessary, but historically inaccurate. The passage then goes on to say: 'I will move them to jealousy with those which are not a people; I will provoke them to anger with a foolish nation'. The 'not a people' are Christians, for they are not a separate people. The interpretation requires, therefore, that the Jews shall be very hostile to the Christians. The events of the first century give ample historical justification for the statement. To claim that Origen must be implying immediate hostility at the moment is unnecessary[2]. Such an interpretation is confirmed by the speech of Pionius, who without any feeling of irrelevance justifies his charges against the Jews by relating events which had happened in a previous millennium, and which bore no relation to Jewish conduct in his time. One would expect him to mention their action towards

[1] *I.e.*, *On Deut.*, xxxii, 21.

[2] Compare his superb *Exhortation to Martyrdom*, in which no mention of Jews occurs; P.G., XI, p. 564 ff.

Polycarp, only a century earlier in the same city, but neither he nor the author of his Acta think of the parallel. A reference to the index of almost any volume of the Patrologia will give numbers of accusations of Jewish hostility based upon quotations from their pre-Christian history and their prophets. It was the natural result of their belief in the verbal inspiration and eternal validity of the scriptures, coupled with their own method of allegorical interpretation. To take these texts out of their context, and use them to justify generalisations in the modern sense, is to ignore the actual evidence provided by the lives of the martyrs and to produce a distorted picture.

The material which these offer allows us to reconstruct with considerable accuracy the sequence of events. The period which immediately followed the Apostolic age and the fall of Jerusalem was marked on the Jewish side by the official determination to oust the Christians from the shelter of the Synagogue. On the Christian side it was a period in which a doctrine of the position of the Jews in the scheme of salvation was being evolved which was so offensive to Jewish feelings that violent hostility inevitably marked its proclamation. The offence was the greater for the bitter and unsympathetic attitude adopted towards the national tragedies in Palestine, and because of the determination of the Christians to rob the Jews of the one hope left to them, the promises made to them in the Old Testament. In this period we find in the documents considerable evidence of the bloodshed which such a situation provoked. A true picture of the situation is a humiliating one for both religions. The charity they showed to others they did not show to each other. It is obvious that the blame lies on both sides. But while the attitude of each side is regrettable, the attitude of neither side is abnormal. The history of religion offers many unhappy parallels, and the internal divisions of Christians themselves in later centuries have produced far more victims than their first conflict with Judaism.

In the second century the situation changed. The Jews were themselves involved in an exhausting struggle with Rome which ended disastrously for them, and the Church was a definitely Gentile institution. It is a period in which ' incidents ' took place occasionally. But if there is anything abnormal in them, it is their rarity and not their frequency. Of a steady, deliberate, and unsleeping hostility there is no trace. The time has not yet come when it is a reasonable presumption that Jews will only be motivated by hatred in their attitude towards Christians. Sometimes there was intense local hostility of the kind of which Tertullian speaks when he tells the story of the Jew who paraded through the streets of Carthage with a placard bearing an offensive caricature[1]. At other times relations were friendly. Much, doubtless, depended on the behaviour of the local clergy and rabbis. The theologians of both sides were either hostile or contemptuous towards each other, and in later centuries their persistence prevailed. But in these centuries, for the rank and file, special provocation was necessary for any overt or secret act of hostility.

The universal, tenacious, and malicious hatred referred to by Harnack, Corluy, Allard and others, has no existence in historical fact. The generalisations of patristic writers quoted in support of the accusation have been wrongly interpreted. The evidence that the Jews took no part in the great persecutions of the second, third and fourth centuries comes not from Jewish sources, nor from inference, nor from later generalisations, but from the masses of contemporary lives of those very martyrs themselves whose deaths are in question.

[1] Tertullian, *To the Nations*, I, xiv; P.L., I, p. 579.

CHAPTER FIVE

THE FOURTH CENTURY

BIBLIOGRAPHICAL INTRODUCTION

There is extremely little to say by way of bibliographical introduction to this chapter. Its material is almost exclusively taken from the great patristic writers of the century, and from the Theodosian Code. Special studies on this period are few. The books of Lenz and Murawski form a striking contrast, the former with his rabid antisemitism, collecting only the most virulent passages of patristic literature to serve as a guide for his unfortunate contemporaries, the latter, a Roman Catholic Bishop, writing an objective and scholarly study of his subject. The work of Lucas contains much valuable material, including special studies of Basil, Athanasius, Jerome, Ambrose and Augustine. He perhaps emphasises unduly the ascetic side of Christianity, but his insistence on the importance of Jewish propaganda during this century is certainly justified, and the material thereon is excellently presented.

LIST OF BOOKS

BERARD, P. — *S. Augustin et les Juifs.* Besançon, 1913.

DOUAIS, G. — *S. Augustin et le Judaisme.* L'Université Catholique, Lyon, 1894.

LENZ, H. K. — *Der Kirchenväter Ansichten und Lehren über die Juden, den Christen in Erinnerung gebracht.* Münster-i-W., 1894.

LUCAS, L. — *Zur Geschichte der Juden im IV. Jahrhundert.* Berlin, 1910.

MURAWSKI, BP. — *Die Juden bei den Kirchenvätern und Skolastikern.* Berlin, 1925.

RAHMER, M. — *Die Hebraischer Traditionen in den Werken des Hieronymus.* M.G.W.J., Vols. XIV, XVI and XVII.

I. THE PROBLEM FACING THE LEADERS OF JUDAISM AND CHRISTIANITY

The fourth century marks a decisive moment in the history of both Judaism and Christianity. Though neither were born in this century, yet both owe more to its outstanding leaders than to any other similar group of contemporaries, and both are to this day, in many ways, fourth century religions. The councils of Nicaea and Constantinople, the schools of Pumbeditha and Sura have left an indelible mark on their respective faiths. Augustine, Chrysostom, Jerome and Ambrose were contemporaries, and they are not the only names of note in a period which counted also Athanasius, Cyril and Basil. It was also a century of great Talmudic teachers. Rabbah bar Nachmani, who died in 330; Joseph bar Hama, who died in 333; and Abaye, the pupil of both, taught at Pumbeditha. Raba (bar Joseph bar Hama), who died in 352, founded the school at Mahuza on the Tigris. In the next generation Nahmani bar Isaac, who died in 356, taught at Pumbeditha, and Papa, who died in 375, founded the school of Neres near Sura. After their deaths Sura again became prominent through the presence of Ashi, who died in 427. The sayings and controversies of Joseph and Rabbah, and those of Abaye and Raba occupy a considerable portion of the Babylonian Talmud. Though less distinguished, the Palestinian scholars were also busy. The patriarchate of Jerusalem was not suppressed until about 425, and during this period the Jerusalem Talmud was also receiving its main contributions.

In spite of this intense contemporary activity there was practically no interchange of theological discussion between Jew and Christian, though most of their work was based upon the same books. As far as we know Jerome was the only Christian father who both knew Hebrew and was acquainted with the Talmudic schools and the rabbinical method of argument. He lived in Palestine in close contact with Jews, but it would be difficult to detect in his writings any trace of an attitude to the Jews other than that held by his contemporaries. Sharing the conventional view, he saw only material for ridicule or disgust in their behaviour and beliefs. 'The Jews', he sneers, 'run to the synagogue every day to study the Law, in their desire to know what Abraham, Isaac and Jacob and the rest of the holy men did, and to learn by heart the books of Moses and the prophets'[1]. 'I could not tell you how many Pharisaic traditions there are to-day, told by the Talmudists, and I do not know their old wives' tales. Many of them are so disgusting that I blush to mention them'[2]. His idea in learning Hebrew was not to acquire Jewish wisdom, but to be able to confute them with an authority which most Christian scholars, by their ignorance of the language, lacked[3]. Though he shows much knowledge of Hebrew exegesis, and often quotes Jewish interpretations, yet he shows very little sign of having ever discussed theological points with his expensive Jewish teachers. While, on the other hand, some Talmudists doubtless knew Greek, and some even Latin, it is not to be expected that they would follow with any detail the interminable controversies as to the relation between the divine and the human in One whom they did not consider to be divine at all. Nor could they follow these controversies except at a distance, for neither in Persia nor in Palestine existed great intellectual centres of Christian thought. The orthodoxy of Aphraates would, as we shall see, have horrified Arians and Athanasians alike.

It has already been said that the Judeo-Christians, though they still existed, had lost all influence. Jerome has as much contempt for them as the Jews themselves[4]. Hellenistic Jews of the type of Philo had disappeared even more completely. Proselytes who chose Judaism in the third and fourth centuries did so on the ground of a conscious rejection of the alternative, Christianity, and would not form a bridge between the two. Even in the second century Justin refers to their hostility to Christianity, and later it would certainly have been still greater. So far as the future was concerned Christianity was a Gentile religion, and Judaism was rabbinic Judaism.

[1] *On Isaiah*, lviii; P.L., XXIV, p. 582.
[2] Ep. CXXI; P.L., XXII, p. 1006.
[3] *Contra Rufinum*, III, xxv; P.L., XXII, p. 497.
[4] *On Ezekiel* xxxviii; P.L., XXV, p. 370; *Isaiah* xi, 6; P.L., XXIV, p. 150, and *Ep. to Augustine*, 112; and the reply of Augustine, *Ep.* 116 in P.L., XXII.

The problems facing the leaders of the two religions were also entirely different. Christianity was faced with the immense task of imposing moral and intellectual standards on the happy-go-lucky pagan Roman world. Judaism was attempting to find a new basis for survival for its own community without either land, central authority or Temple. The solutions found or attempted thrust them still further apart. The Christian authorities, presented by Constantine with the empire as their playground, were in no easy position. The laws whose passage they secured may seem to us unduly harsh. Their attitude towards virtuous heretics —for Origen had explained that a virtuous heretic is worse than any other[1]—may appear to-day to be very remote from the Christian ideal. The extravagances of the ascetic, the interminable lucubrations on the advantages of virginity, may seem to us repulsive. But before condemning the men who proposed these actions we need to understand what they were attempting to do. Had Judaism had to fight the same battle, she would almost inevitably have used the same weapons. Judaism no less than Christianity insisted on a definite theological belief in God, even if she expressed it for her own purposes in much less theological terms. The early, and primarily Jewish, Christian Church was content with a simple expression of her belief. The Christological discussions of the fourth century were forced upon her not by the inherent complications of her own faith, but by the acuteness and confusion of philosophic speculation among the Greek and Roman intellectuals with whom she came into contact. Yahweh, in such surroundings, would have fared no better than the Trinity. For in spite of much mediaeval Jewish accusation, the cause of all the trouble was the insistence of the Christians that the Church should retain uncontaminated her belief in the unity of God.

The same transformation would also have taken place had Judaism, with its quiet and dignified personal morality, attempted to clear out the Augean stables of Roman sexual and stomachic standards. Already the slight contact with Greek and Roman civilisation in Judaea and Syria had produced ascetic movements. The healthiest-minded

[1] Jerome's translation of Origen *On Ezek.*, Homily VII; P.L., XXV, p. 742 ff.

Pharisee would have found it hard not to approve of the teaching of Jerome before circumcising an average batch of infants in Rome or Antioch. The extraordinary prohibitions as to episcopal conduct to be found in the decrees of Church councils have no counterpart in Talmudic discussions with all their splitting of hairs. But neither did Judaism ever see a man elevated to the rank of Gaon a month after his circumcision. The Jewish community passed with little change from generation to generation. With its insistence on the importance of the family, it had little difficulty in handing on its healthy traditional sex morality and its high principles of conduct. The Christian Church had a mass of nominal adherents, often in high official or ecclesiastical positions, who were entirely unacquainted either by environment or tradition with her standards. The effort made by the Fathers compares very favourably with the compromise attempted by the Herodians, and, after all, the morality which the Church was attempting to teach was Jewish morality, as often supported by Old Testament quotation as by quotations from the Gospels[1].

A period of extravagant denunciation of what was not in itself immoral may have been necessary as a counterblast to contemporary laxity. Like enforced Prohibition in America, it may have done as much harm as good. But it was a state of affairs created by circumstances, and not the expression of something inevitably inherent in Christianity. Its persistence has less justification than its original emergence. But its emergence not unnaturally profoundly alienated Jewish opinion, which, having never faced the same dangers since its earliest days, saw no justification for its adoption. Fortunately or unfortunately the Christian Fathers of the fourth century could not attempt to apply the solution of Samuel or Elijah and settle the question by wholesale massacre, a method which was entirely forgotten by the Jews themselves at the time of the rabbinical schools of Babylon.

The problems confronting these schools, if different, were no less grave. To find a foundation for survival, with the

[1] This comes out in the battle which the Church waged against 'usury' among Christian laity and clergy, and which was based entirely on the Mosaic Law. Cf. p. 192, n. 4.

loss of any national centre, was not easy. The bitterness of the Jew against the Christian was based on his adoption of the promises of the Scriptures, which were all that the Jew had left for his own comfort. To centre a people's life around a book was a tremendous task. The method adopted by the rabbis, to incorporate it into every act of daily life, even at the cost of far-fetched interpretation, was a reasonable and natural one. But the result was unhappily as repulsive to the Christian as was Christian theological quibbling and ascetic exaggeration to the Jew. The followers of the councils, and the followers of the Talmud were inevitably poles apart.

II. THE CHRISTIAN VIEW OF THE JEWS

The battle between the two had so far been a battle of words, varied with the occasional violence of exasperation. But the victory of the Church brought a new element into the struggle. One party to the dispute now became possessed not only of official recognition—which the other enjoyed already—but, increasingly, of power over the whole executive machinery of the empire. The claim for equal toleration with others which was advanced by the apologists in the days of their suffering[1], the Church did not grant to others in the days of her triumph. Though argument ceased to be her only weapon, yet the words of Justin or Tertullian are moderate in tone compared with the denunciations from the pulpit of Chrystosom or Cyril of Jerusalem.

A second change was the widespread adoption of a superficial Christianity by the upper classes of Roman society. This brought into the Church a large membership which was probably already hostile towards the Jews. The wars of the period from Vespasian to Hadrian had destroyed the popularity which they had previously possessed, and they had, at most, regained a silent toleration, accompanied by a certain watchfulness on both sides. For the Jews had not lost their turbulence, and were still ready to break into open rebellion at a threat to their privileges. Even the presence of their rival, Christianity, at the court of the emperor did not

[1] *E.g.* Athenagoras, *Plea for the Christians*, Ch. i; P.G., VI, p. 889.

overawe them, and in the fourth and succeeding centuries there were revolts which needed considerable military force to suppress. This was soil on which the hostility of the Church Fathers found it easy to sow seed.

The Jew as he is encountered in the pages of fourth-century writers is not a human being at all. He is a ' monster ', a theological abstraction, of superhuman cunning and malice, and more than superhuman blindness. He is rarely charged with human crime, and little evidence against him is drawn from contemporary behaviour, or his action in contemporary events. He is as unreal as the ' Boche ' created by the Allied press during the war from 1914 to 1918, and far more abstract. The colourful imaginations of later antisemites, such as Drumont or Chamberlain, at least tried to show the Jew as a menace to contemporary society as they saw it. The Fathers of the fourth century saw no such necessity. In view of the close relations which obviously existed between local Jewish and Christian communities, it is amazing how this myth of Jewish character could so long have passed muster. But certain considerations help to explain, if they do nothing to excuse, its survival. The most important factor was the universal attitude of the time, shared alike by Jew and Christian, to the written word of the Bible. To the modern critic the fact that the Jews reached so high a standard in their conception of the mutual obligations of the community as is shown in the Mosaic Law, and so lofty an idea of God and His relation to the world as is shown in the prophets, would argue for considerable moral progress on the part of the nation producing these phenomena. But to the student of that time the whole of the Bible was written by God, and human hands had little and human hearts and brains nothing to do with it. This idea did little harm to the Jew, for he still preserved the unity of the Scriptures, with its combination of denunciation and encouragement, of threat and promise. But the moment these were separated and all the promises applied to one group, and all the curses to an entirely separate one, an appalling falsification took place.

The Fathers obtained the perspective of a distorting mirror and drew faithfully what they saw. The monstrosity of Israel was evident to them. There was not one single virtuous action in her history. She had been a perpetual disappointment to God, in spite of all the wonderful things He had done for her. For it was impossible to separate these from the main strain of the history of the people. The Church might claim all the virtuous actions in the Old Testament for a kind of pre-existent Church, but she could not deny that *all* the people had been led out of Egypt, guided by day and night across the desert, and into the Promised Land. But their record was one of nothing but disobedience, and their ultimate rejection was almost inevitable from the very beginning. The one mystery which the Fathers never attempted to solve was why, if they were really like that, God had either chosen them, or having done so, had expected them, after a career of unchanging and unrepentant malice and vice, to accept His final revelation in Christ.

This picture of the Jew was still further coloured and confirmed by their eschatological conceptions. For, if they looked for any change of heart in the Jews as a whole, they expected it only at the second coming of Christ. Even of this they were not quite sure, and Jerome, who gives more attention to Jewish matters than any of his contemporaries, hesitates between three opinions. At times he proclaims with gusto their final and absolute rejection[1]. At other times he holds that a remnant of them will be saved[2]. Sometimes he holds a third view, that all will ultimately be saved, and that after the gathering of the Gentiles 'all Israel shall be gathered in'[3]. Even if this latter was the more commonly accepted version, it inevitably created an artificial relationship, for it expected no *immediate* response from the Jews to any appeal that might be made to them[4].

[1] *E.g.*, *On Isaiah*, vi, 9, 14; xxvi, 11; and lxv, 13; P.L., XXIV, pp. 100, 307 and 665 ff.

[2] *On Isaiah*, xlviii, 22; xlix, 1; and lix, 19; P.L., XXIV, pp. 480, 482, 608.

[3] *On Jeremiah*, xviii; P.L., XXIV, p. 829.

[4] It is not surprising that in this uncertainty Jerome at one place pathetically remarks: 'Haec pie quidem dicuntur, sed quomodo cum ceteris congruant, et consummationis mundi temporibus coaptentur, difficilis interpretatio est'. For a collection of passages from different authors dealing with the ultimate destination of the Jews, see P.L., CCXX, p. 1004.

III. EUSEBIUS OF CAESAREA AND HILARY OF POITIERS AND JEWISH HISTORY

The endless repetition of the same epithets, the same charges, and the same crimes can only be explained by this theological and exegetical necessity. The phrase ' a Jew ', or ' some Jews ', is almost unknown in patristic literature. On the rare occasions when an action of contemporary Jews is mentioned it is always ' the Jews ', and more often than not, when a specific accusation seems to be made, it is proved only by a reference to past history. If error be an excuse, then this must be the excuse for those who first framed Christian legislation against the Jews, and for those who by their continual preaching and writing ultimately persuaded the ordinary people that their picture of the Jew was permanently true, and that any contact with him was a defilement. It is related of Hilary of Poitiers that his orthodoxy was such that he would not even answer the salutation of a Jew in the street[1], a fact which amazed his biographer. But we can understand it if we realise that he really believed that ' before the Law was given the Jews were possessed of an unclean devil, which the Law for a time drove out, but which returned immediately after their rejection of Christ '[2]. In another passage commenting on Psalm 52, he says that the strong man who scoffs at the righteous is to be applied to ' that people which has always persisted in iniquity, and out of its abundance of evil has gloried in wickedness. For it was mighty when it was, as a slave, visited by God; when on its account Egypt was struck by so many plagues; when in the three days' darkness it did not feel the dark, for the light was with it; when it left Egypt to its fate despoiled of its silver and ornaments; when it was accompanied day and night by a column of smoke and fire; when it crossed the Red Sea on foot; when it lived on the bread of angels; when it saw the majesty of God descending on the mountain; when it heard His voice speaking from the fire; when it overturned many kingdoms in terrible wars; when it saw Jordan flow back for its own passage; when it possessed prophets,

[1] *Life of Hilary*, P.L., IX, p. 187.

[2] Hilary, *Commentary on Matthew*, xiii, 22; P.L., IX, p. 993 ff.

when it enjoyed priests for cleansing it from sin and for redeeming its soul; when it deserved to obtain its kingdom. In all these things it was mighty. But ever it was mighty in wickedness; when it longed for the flesh-pots of Egypt; when through its addiction to wickedness it preferred an unholy slavery to a holy liberty; when it worshipped the calf; when it cursed Moses; when it hated God; when it vowed its sons as offerings to demons; when it killed the prophets, and finally when it betrayed to the Praetor and crucified our God Himself and Lord, who for its sake became man. And so glorying throughout all its existence in iniquity, when it was mighty, it was persistently in iniquity that it showed its might '[1]. It is upon this background of Jewish history, which was prepared by the previous centuries, that the Church was to act for many centuries to come.

While a more or less violent form of this attitude is to be found in most of the commentaries and writings of the period, scattered here and there in the exegesis of suitable verses from the Old Testament, its classic expression is to be found in two immense volumes of Eusebius, the *Preparatio Evangelica* and the *Demonstratio Evangelica*[2]. These two works, the first in fifteen books which have been completely preserved, and the second in twenty, of which only the first ten remain, were written just before the peace of the Church, and completed in 311. They are of great importance to us, because they constitute the most complete example of the instruction given at this critical epoch in Church history to the pagan world. In the first book Eusebius proves the superiority and greater antiquity of Christianity in comparison with all other religions; in the second he proves the superiority of Christianity over Judaism and the uniqueness of the person of Christ.

In so far as the relations between Jews and Christians are concerned, the fundamental hypothesis from which he starts in both books is a sharp distinction between ' Hebrews ' and ' Jews '[3]. The Hebrews are the most ancient people in the world, and their religion is the basis of Greek philosophy[4].

[1] *Commentary on Psalm li*, 6; P.L., IX, p. 312.

[2] P.G., Vols. XXI and XXII.

[3] *E.g.*, *Prep. Evan.*, VII and X; *Dem. Evan.*, I.

[4] *Prep. Evan.*, X and XI.

But they themselves, though not 'Jews', were not 'Gentiles' either. Rather they were from the beginning 'Christians, and led a Christian way of life'. The Patriarchs pleased God by their lives, and Abraham, 'in that he lived by virtue', lived as a Christian and not as a Jew[1]. Into this primitive and 'Christian' life of the Patriarchs, for reasons which Eusebius leaves obscure, came Moses, with his special law for the Jews. This law which he introduced was never meant to have any meaning for the Gentiles[2], and he himself bears witness to the independent righteousness of the 'Hebrews'[3]. Even for the Jews who lived outside Palestine the law was impossible, since its provisions could not be carried out without a temple[4]. In his insistence on these points it is possible that Eusebius is implicitly opposing himself to the efforts among the pagans of Jewish missionaries.

While Eusebius is thus careful to insist on the partial character of the law, he is equally careful to insist that it was only a temporary expedient even for the Jews. Throughout the period of 'Jewish' history, that is from Moses to the Incarnation, 'Hebrew' prophets[5] were continually pointing to the period of its supersession by a new and superior law. Eusebius realises that this attitude might well cause pagans to ask why Christians should bother themselves at all with Jewish literature. He replies by copious quotations from the prophets, which command the abandonment of the Jewish law, and foretell the utter reprobation of the Jews themselves. It is for these prophecies alone and for the historical conceptions based on them that they are valuable[6].

Eusebius thus gives a picture of the Jew as negligible rather than contemptible, as a relatively unimportant companion to the older 'Hebrew' who foretold and anticipated Christianity[7]. But, equally with Hilary, he was presenting the pagan world with a complete caricature of the history of the Jews.

[1] *Dem. Evan.*, I, vi.

[2] *Prep. Evan.*, VIII; *Dem. Evan.*, II.

[3] *Dem. Evan.*, I, ii.

[4] *Ibid.*, I, iii.

[5] The prophets are never called Jews. Only the law is Jewish. Cf. *Dem. Evan.*, II, III and IV *passim.*

[6] *Dem. Evan.*, I, i.

[7] Cf. *e.g. Prep. Evan.*, VII, vi, viii and xi.

IV. CHRYSOSTOM AND THE JEWS OF ANTIOCH

While in their writings Hilary and Eusebius introduced the pagan world to this strange version of Jewish history, Chrysostom expressed similar theories with much greater violence from his pulpit at Antioch. In eight sermons which he delivered in 387 he speaks with a bitterness and lack of restraint unusual even in that place and century[1]. If it were not for the exegetical background which has already been shown, it would be impossible to explain, let alone excuse, his tone. Christianity was no longer in any danger. He himself had not, like Athanasius, ever known any persecution from the Jews, and the period of trial under Julian had been very short. Even had they been a menace in old times, the rich and powerful Jewish community of Antioch was now hemmed in, like every other, by numerous imperial edicts issued under Christian inspiration. Moreover, Chrysostom was a man whose character excited the admiration of his contemporaries. If he was hated by politicians for his unswerving firmness, he was loved by the multitudes, and his commentaries on the gospels are still read and studied in the Orthodox Church because of their deep spiritual beauty.

Such was the man who in eight sermons covering more than a hundred pages of closely printed text, has left us the most complete monument of the public expression of the Christian attitude to the Jews in the century of the victory of the Church. In these discourses there is no sneer too mean, no gibe too bitter for him to fling at the Jewish people. No text is too remote to be able to be twisted to their confusion, no argument is too casuistical, no blasphemy too startling for him to employ; and, most astonishing of all, at the end he turns to the Christians, and in words full of sympathy and toleration he urges them not to be too hard on those who have erred in following Jewish practices or in visiting Jewish synagogues. Dealing with the Christians, no text which urges forgiveness is forgotten: dealing with the Jews only one verse of the New Testament is omitted: ‘ Father, forgive them, for they know not what they do ’.

[1] P.G., Vol. XLVIII.

The only explanation of his bitterness contained in the sermons themselves is the too close fellowship between Jews and Christians in Antioch. There is no single suggestion that the Jews were immoral or vicious; no suggestion that Christians were actually corrupted by the contact, either in their morals or their orthodoxy. Only one contemporary event is referred to at all, apart from general denunciations of the visiting of the synagogue at times of Jewish feast or fast. This was the case of a Christian woman who was taken into a Jewish house to take an oath in a business affair, because the Christian with whom she had to deal believed that an oath taken in the Jewish manner was more binding than any other. What the actual affair was we are not told. To Chrysostom's eyes the crime was that a Christian woman had been taken into a Jewish house, not that she had been seduced or taught heretical doctrine or anything else. It was enough that she had been made to enter the house[1].

There is no material in these sermons for a study of contemporary Jewish life. Events and beliefs of centuries earlier are quoted as though still accepted. On the strength of Psalm xcvi, 37, he states that they 'sacrificed their sons and daughters to devils: they outraged nature; and overthrew from their foundations the laws of relationship. They are become worse than the wild beasts, and for no reason at all, with their own hands they murder their own offspring, to worship the avenging devils who are the foes of our life'[2]. It seems almost as if his hearers in Antioch objected to so monstrous a statement, for in his sixth sermon he returns to the charge, and says that even if they no longer murder their own children, they have murdered the Christ, which is worse[3]. The synagogues of the Jews are the homes of idolatry and devils, even though they have no images in them[4]. They are worse even than heathen circuses[5]. The very idea of going from a church to a synagogue is blasphemous[6]; and to attend the Jewish Passover is to insult

[1] Sermon, I, 3.
[2] I, 6.
[3] VI, 2 and 3.
[4] I, 3; II, 3; based on Jer. vii, 11, etc.
[5] I, 3.
[6] II, 3.

Christ. To be with the Jews on the very day they murdered Jesus is to ensure that on the Day of Judgment He will say 'Depart from Me: for you have had intercourse with my murderers'[1]. Some say that the synagogue is hallowed by the fact that the Holy Books of the Law are to be found in it. One might just as well say that the temple of Dagon was hallowed by the Ark being in it, even though the Ark destroyed the idol to prove the opposite[2]. It is truer to say that the fact that these Books are to be found in the synagogues makes them more detestable, for the Jews have simply introduced these Books, 'not to honour them, but to insult them, and to dishonour them'[3]. The Jews do not worship God but devils[4], so that all their feasts are unclean[5]. God hates them, and indeed has always hated them. But since their murder of Jesus He allows them no time for repentance[6]. It was of set purpose that He concentrated all their worship in Jerusalem that He might more easily destroy it[7]. The Jewish pretence that their misfortunes are due to Rome are not worthy of attention. 'It was not by their own power that the Caesars did what they did to you: it was done by the wrath of God, and His absolute rejection of you.'[8] It is childish in the face of this absolute rejection to imagine that God will ever allow the Jews to rebuild their Temple or to return to Jerusalem. Their experience under Julian should convince them of that[9]. When it is clear that God hates them, it is the duty of Christians to hate them too; and he begins his sixth sermon with a revolting analogy of a beast in the arena, who has tasted blood, and longs for it again. So he, Chrysostom, having once begun to denounce the Jews, cannot leave off[10], for he who has no limits in his

[1] III, 5, and VI, 8.
[2] I, 5, referring to I Sam. v.
[3] I, 5, and VI, 6.
[4] I, 3, based on John viii, 19.
[5] I, 6.
[6] VI, 1.
[7] IV, 6.
[8] VI, 3.
[9] V, *passim*. The whole sermon is an insulting sneer at their misfortunes and exile, and a gloating over the certainty of their damnation. Cf. the sermon 'That Christ is God: addressed to Jews and Pagans' in the same volume.
[10] VI, 1.

love of Christ must have no limits in his battle with those who hate Him[1]. 'I hate the Jews' he exclaims roundly, 'for they have the Law and they insult it'.

But when in the last sermon he comes to address those miserable sinners who had been frequenting Jewish celebrations his tone is unrecognisable. He insists that they must be dealt with gently, for the true attitude to a sinner is 'whenever we hear any good of him, to tell it to all; but when we hear any evil or wicked thing, to keep it to ourselves, and do all in our power to change it'[2]. It is evident that Chrysostom's Jew was a theological necessity rather than a living person. If he looked different from the actual Jews living in Antioch it was part of the malice of the Jew, one of the snares of the devil, set to catch the unwary Christian. The comment of a Catholic theologian on these sermons is worth quoting[3]: 'Das Gebot der Nächstensliebe wird man in diesen Reden nicht wiederfinden, und ebensowenig werden solche Reden fähig gewesen sein die Juden mit Sympathie für das Christentum zu erfüllen'.

V. AMBROSE AND THE BURNING OF A SYNAGOGUE

Midway between the theologian of Gaul and the preacher of Antioch, stands Ambrose, the Christian statesman and bishop of Milan. His attitude to the Jews is also known in full detail from his two letters on the subject of the burning of the synagogue of Callinicum in Asia by a Christian rabble led by the bishop in person[4]. The details of the incident, and possible provocation by the Jews, are not known. The offenders were punished by the Roman governor, and the bishop was ordered to rebuild the synagogue out of his own resources. This decision was confirmed by the Emperor Theodosius, and came to the ears of Ambrose. The latter at once wrote a long letter to the emperor, in which he denounced this condemnation. After claiming that the accusation is false, or at least unproved, he changes his

[1] VII, 1.

[2] VIII, 3.

[3] Murawski, *op. cit.*, Chrysostom.

[4] Ambrose, *Epistles*, Bk. I. Nos. 40 and 41; P.L., XVI, p. 1101 ff. The event took place in 388.

ground. The emperor is forcing the bishop either to become an apostate, if he accepts the sentence, or a martyr if he has the courage to refuse to obey. He then roundly denies that it was a crime at all, and asks the emperor to punish him instead, for though it is true that he has not burnt down the synagogue of Milan, it is only by laziness on his part, and the fact that God had already destroyed it Himself. But it would be a glorious act to do so, 'that there might be no place where Christ is denied'. It may be that someone will come forward and pay for the rebuilding of the synagogue in place of the bishop. If the governor allows this, then he, the governor, becomes an apostate. In any case, police obedience must give way to religion, and the synagogue was probably a miserable hovel, and it is ridiculous to make a fuss about 'a place of unbelief, a home of insanity, which God Himself has condemned'. The Jews paid no compensation for the many churches they destroyed under Julian, and now Christians are going to give them a new festival to gloat over, a festival of triumph over Christ, and they will inscribe over their synagogue the words:

THE TEMPLE OF IMPIETY
BUILT FROM THE SPOILS OF CHRISTIANS

Maximius lost the empire through ordering the people of Rome to rebuild the synagogue they had burnt, and it is monstrous that Jews who despise Roman law should look to it to avenge themselves. 'Why should we fear their vengeance in any case? Who will avenge them? God whom they have insulted, or Christ whom they Crucified?'

Such is the tone in which Ambrose addresses the emperor, and the following Sunday, in his cathedral, in the presence of the emperor, he preaches on the Church and the Synagogue, picturing the richness of the one and the poverty of the other. The emperor asks him if the sermon is preached against him, and Ambrose replies that it is to save him. The emperor states that the action was perhaps severe. The bishop refuses to continue the service until the sentence is annulled. The emperor says that he will do so. The bishop replies that he relies on the emperor's promise. 'Age fide mea' responds the emperor, and at last the service is allowed to continue. The extraordinary arguments of Ambrose are thrown into higher relief by his own pre-episcopal career. He had himself been a governor. How in those unregenerate days he would have received such arguments as those which he advanced to the emperor, it is difficult to imagine.

VI. EPIPHANIUS AND JEWISH BELIEF

A fourth writer who is entitled to separate consideration is Epiphanius, bishop of Salamis in Cyprus from 357 to 403.

He was of Palestinian Jewish origin, and is supposed to have been converted about the age of sixteen[1]. Though his reputation has not survived the test of time, as have those of his three great contemporaries already considered, and though, indeed, he has left no reason why posterity should honour him, in his own day he enjoyed a reputation for holiness and learning second to none of his contemporaries. He was a friend of Jerome and a great patron of the monastic movement, and an enemy of Chrysostom, on the somewhat inadequate grounds that Chrysostom had not condemned certain holders of Origenistic beliefs prior to the meeting of the synod called to hear their defence. To posterity he appears narrow-minded and quarrelsome. His type of piety explains something of the bitterness of fourth-century controversies and the need for the continual disciplinary measures passed by the councils. For him anathema and excommunications were expressions of faint disagreement—or even of the fear that there would be disagreement if he knew what the opinions were of the man he anathematised. He never hesitated to meddle in the dioceses of other bishops, and even ordained presbyters in their dioceses to contradict their teaching[2]. For our present purpose his main interest is that he was a Jew until adolescence, and that he wrote about Jewish beliefs.

Epiphanius was regarded as the great authority on heresy, including therein all false belief, even Greek philosophy. And he wrote a work in which he contentedly confutes no

[1] It is typical that later ages considered his conversion to have been due to a miracle. On the many versions of the fate of his donkey, see the *Acta Sanctorum* and *Eastern Acta*.

[2] See his life by Lipsius in the *Dictionary of Christian Biography*.

less than eighty varieties. While he used earlier writers, especially Irenaeus and Hippolytus, much of it is his own observation. In his work he includes four Samaritan and seven Jewish heresies, in addition to three Judeo-Christian sects. The seven Jewish sects are the Sadducees, the Scribes, the Pharisees, the Hemerobaptists, the Nazareans, the Ossenes, and the Herodians; and the three Judeo-Christian sects are the Nazarenes, the Ebionites, and the Sampseans[1]. The heresy of Paul of Samosata can really be considered also as coming under this heading. ' His communications regarding the Jewish sects are for the most part worthless, and what he says of the Nazareans and Ossenes is derived purely from misunderstood narratives concerning the Ebionites and Elkasites. The accounts he gives of the Judeo-Christian and Gnostic sects of the second and third centuries exhibit a marvellous mixture of valuable tradition with misunderstandings and fancies of his own.'[2] In spite of this lack of permanent value they are of importance in that they show the complete ignorance of Judaism of fourth-century Christians—even of Jewish origin. Though we have no evidence that Epiphanius was as profound a Hebrew scholar as Jerome, yet he clearly knew some Hebrew, and if he was born of Palestinian Jewish parents, he had some opportunities of knowing something at first hand about Jewish opinion. But this fact is deduced more clearly from his biographer's statement than from anything in his own writings.

To the New Testament account of the Sadducees he adds nothing. The scribes, whom he explains next, are said to add in their interpretation of the Law ' a certain grammatical knowledge '—a deduction one imagines from the name scribe. They are completely legalistic, and admit four interpreters, Moses, Akiba, Annanus or Judas, and the four sons of Assamoneus[3]. The Pharisees agree with the scribes, but are much more severe in their discipline, of which he

[1] *Epiphanius Adversos Haereses.* P.G., XLI. The Samaritan Heresies are Nos. IX-XIII, the Jewish Nos. XIV-XX, the Nazarenes No. XXIX, the Ebionites No. XXX, and the Sampseans No. LIII.

[2] Lipsius in D.C.B.

[3] A mixture of the Mishnah of Judah and the earlier one ascribed to Akiba. No Mishnah is ascribed to Hananyia. The ' four sons ' is unintelligible.

writes with monastic approval. They are ascetics, and believe in the resurrection, and in angels, but not in the Son. Their failing is that they are astrologers, and too interested in reading the stars[1]. This Epiphanius considers acutely to be in contradiction to their belief in a judgment following the resurrection, since if all is determined by fate, there is no such thing as free will and therefore no sin to form the basis for judgment. The fourth sect are the Hemerobaptists, who apparently have no doctrine of their own, but agree with the Sadducees, scribes and Pharisees. In addition, they insist on a daily bath of purification. The fifth are the Nazareans, who come from the north of the country, and Trans-Jordania. They keep the Law, but do not believe in fate or in astrology. They do not believe in animal sacrifices and they eat no living thing. They do not accept as genuine the parts of the Bible referring to such practices. The sixth sect are the Ossenes, who are ' spiritually disingenuous and intellectually ingenious '. They come from Nabatea and Perea, and are gnostics, ' detesting virginity, damning continence, and insisting on marriage '. They teach that apostasy is allowable in times of persecution, for it is possible to agree with the tongue and disagree in the heart. They accept Christ and call Him ' the great king ', recognising Him as a power. The Holy Spirit is also a power, but female. They pray, not towards the east, but towards Jerusalem, and they accept neither sacrifices, meat, nor the use of fire. Their only points of contact with other Jews are circumcision and the Sabbath. In a word, ' their wickedness is blindness, and their aberrations are senseless '. The last sect are the Herodians, who are ' real Jews, being lazy and dishonest '. They believe that Herod was the Christ. Epiphanius concludes by saying that in his time there were still some traces of Essenes, but otherwise only ' Jews ', by which he presumably means Pharisees and Nazareans. The Ossenes have adopted the Sampsean heresy and are neither Jews nor Christians.

[1] This is a confusion with the Essenes described in Josephus, *Ant.*, XIII, v, 9.

VII. CONVERTS, CATECHUMENS AND CHURCH SERVICES

From the rest of the literature of the fourth century there is nothing new to learn. Indeed there was little which could be added to the body of belief built up by previous centuries. The main interest was Christological in the philosophical and not in the historico-prophetic sense. There was no change in the attitude to the Jews, but there was no addition to it. Neither Athanasius nor Augustine showed any special interest in them; Augustine's remarks on them are quite conventional, and those of Athanasius can even be considered to be moderate in tone—when contrasted with the epithets he applies to Arians. The Talmud has as little to say about Gentile Christians[1]. It is generally believed that the Synagogue was making few proselytes in countries under the domination of Christianity, though Lucas considers that the attacks upon synagogue buildings, which were as much schools as places of worship, indicate that this was not so[2].

It is certain that the Church was still making a certain number of converts among the Jews themselves, for one of the first laws passed under her inspiration forbade Jews to insult or molest such persons. It is fairly frequently mentioned of illustrious ecclesiastics that they had converted many Jews. It is said of Philastrius, bishop of Brescia, that among his other good works,

> Barbaras gentes idolis recurvis
> Atque Judaeos, homines iniquos
> Perfidos contra monitis supernis
> Restitit ipse
> Regis aeterni amabilis minister[3].

That the Jews should use every argument possible to prevent such apostasy is natural, and it is also true that, if they wished either to annoy the Church or to divert pagans from her to

[1] Dr. Marmorstein sees a reference to Gentile Christians in some of the passages dealing with the 'nations of the world'. Cf. *Religionsgeschichtliche Studien*, p. 11 ff.

[2] *Op. cit., passim*, but especially in the latter half of the book. On the other side is the fact that to circumcise a non-Jew was now a crime.

[3] *In laudem Filastrii*, by Gaudentius; P.L., XX, p. 1003.

the Synagogue, the newly converted were admirable material for attack. During the period of the catechumenate a pagan was being for the first time introduced to the doctrines of the Church, and perhaps also was making his first acquaintance with the Scriptures common to both Jews and Christians. It was an obvious opportunity for Jews to put forward rival interpretations, and in actual fact we find considerable evidence that they did so in the frequent warnings against Jewish interpretations contained in the catechetical addresses of different preachers. There is nothing particularly original in the subjects at issue[1]. They are inherent in the situation.

The Jew of the time probably regarded the Trinitarian doctrine of the Church as an aberration rather than as deliberate tritheism. He could, however, easily challenge the Church interpretation of various passages in the Old Testament in which the Fathers affected to find allusions to the division of personality within the Godhead. A second subject for challenge was, naturally, the foretelling of Christ in the prophets. A third was the possibility of the ultimate restoration of the Jewish people to Palestine. A fourth was the observation of Circumcision and the Jewish ritual Law, which was commanded by God to Moses in passages which the Christians accepted as inspired. The Jews might well reproach the average Christian interpreter with getting exactly what he wanted out of these passages ἀναιδῶς και ἀναισχύντως [2]. Even after their acceptance of Christianity converts were still troubled by Jewish objections. This is revealed not only by the passages already quoted, but even more by various letters in which new Christians are warned of the danger of conversation with Jews, or are given the answers to objections raised by the Jews to which they had been unable to reply[3]. Jews were naturally acute critics and quick to catch the Christians out

[1] See, for example, Augustine, *De Catechizandis*, Chs. vii, xx, xxv, xxvii; P.L., Vol. XL; Gregory of Nyssa, *Catechetical Address*, P.G., XLV, p. 9; Cyril of Jerusalem, *Catechetical Addresses*, IV, 2, and X, 2; P.G., XXXIII, pp. 456 and 661; Nicetas of Aquileia, *Explanatio Symboli*, V, ix; P.L., LII, p. 869.

[2] Eusebius, *Dem. Evan.*, I, ii; P.G., XXII.

[3] *E.g.* Nilus, *Ep.*, 57; P.G., LXIX, p. 108; and Isidore of Pelusium, I, 141; III, 94; IV, 17; P.G., LXXVIII, pp. 276, 797 and 1064.

if they had a chance. And the fact that most Christians had to use a not too perfect Greek or Latin translation of the Bible gave them endless opportunities for detecting errors of translation or interpretation[1]. In fact, it was to arm the Christian against such attacks that Jerome learnt Hebrew and undertook to translate the Scriptures into Latin[2].

It must also be remembered that Jews and pagans were permitted to be present at the services of the Church up to the moment of the ' missa catechumenorum '[3], and availed themselves of this permission. In fact, their presence so seriously annoyed the Church of Jerusalem that the synod complained bitterly of ' Jewish serpents and Samaritan imbeciles listening to sermons in Church like wolves surrounding the flock of Christ '[4].

In the early liturgical uses themselves there is little anti-Jewish material. That was left for the sermon. The liturgical explanation of the Creed which was always given to the catechumens contains no reference to the Jews under the clause ' was crucified under Pontius Pilate '[5], and Christian worship itself retained many Jewish forms. ' Our early second-century information justifies us in believing that the influence of the Palestinian Jewish community on Gentile Christianity had been sufficiently strong to induce the latter not only to adopt from the former the main elements of the Synagogal worship, but also, after the final severance of the Jewish and Christian Churches, and the consequent cessation of attendance at the synagogue, to transfer much of the Sabbath Synagogue worship to the specific Eucharistic service on the first day of the week.'[6] Apart from the special Jewish form of abjuration, and a special form for the dedication of synagogues, which is to be found in the Gelasian

[1] Jer., *On Ezek.*, xxxvii, 1; P.L., XXV, p. 363.

[2] Jer., *contra Rufinum*, III, 25; P.L., XXIII, p. 497.

[3] Council of Carthage, IV, can. 89.

[4] Letter of the synod of Jerusalem in P.L., XXII, p. 769.

[5] See Assemani, *Codex Liturgicus*, Vol. I *passim*. On references to the Jews in patristic writings for catechumens, see Juster, *op. cit.*, I, 297 ff.

[6] *The Jewish Background of the Christian Liturgy*, Oesterley, Oxford, 1925. See also *The Jewish Antecedents of the Christian Sacraments*, Gavin, S.P.C.K., 1928, and Juster, *op. cit.*, I, 304.

and other early Sacramentaries[1], it is only in the services of Holy Week, and especially Good Friday, that there are any references to Jews at all. At that season there were always special prayers for their conversion.

VIII. THE COUNCILS OF THE FOURTH CENTURY

The significant contribution of the fourth century to Jewish Christian relationships is not, however, to be found in the theologians, but in the enactments of the ecclesiastical and secular authorities. The earliest Council whose canons survive was actually held before the time of Constantine, but the multiplication of councils was possible only when Christians were able openly to travel and meet on ecclesiastical business. Their main task was to introduce uniformity and discipline into the different Christian communities. They were only incidentally interested in the Jews. There is at first no attempt to use conciliar action for actual restrictions upon the internal life of the Jewish communities. The interest of the councils is only in Jewish Christian relationships, and they thereby reveal how close those relationships were.

The pre-Constantinian council is a Spanish meeting at Elvira, and its decisions were of only local importance. Four of its canons deal with the Jews. Intermarriage between Jews and Christian girls is prohibited, unless the Jew is willing to be converted[2]. The reason given is that girls should not be given to Jews or heretics ' because there can be no fellowship between a believer and an unbeliever '. The penalty for disobedience is five years' abstinence from communion. A second canon prohibits adultery with pagan or Jewish women, and is probably a reference to concubinage. The penalty for disobedience is the same[3]. The other two canons emphasise still further the intimacy between the Jewish and Christian communities. Neither cleric nor layman is to accept Jewish hospitality[4]. Both are to be excluded from communion as long as they persist in doing

[1] Assemani, Vol. IV, pt. ii, p. 90. See Appendix Four.

[2] Elvira, Canon 16.

[3] *Ibid.* Canon 78.

[4] *Ibid.* Canon 50.

so. Finally, Christians are forbidden to have their fields blessed by Jews. Excommunication is the penalty for disobedience. The strange reason given is that such profanation would be likely to render fruitless the subsequent benediction of the fields by a priest[1]. This canon is of special interest in that it reveals that agriculture must have been largely practised by the Spanish Jews. It is difficult to see what would lead Christians to ask the Jews to perform this action unless they had seen some ceremony which impressed them in Jewish fields. What they saw was probably a sort of invigilation connected with the preservation of a vineyard from possible pollution. A Jewish vineyard would become unclean if drops of wine taken from it were used for pagan sacrifices.

From the western churches of the fourth century there is no further conciliar legislation on the Jews, but the situation is substantially the same in Africa and the east. The eastern councils suggest even closer relations than the canons of Elvira, and presuppose very definite 'judaising' tendencies among those who, because they were amenable to orthodox conciliar jurisdiction, cannot have been definitely heretics. The council of Antioch excommunicates any cleric who celebrates Easter with the Jews[2], and in view of the canons of Laodicea some twenty years later, and the practices referred to by Chrysostom, it is possible that this refers not merely to the adoption of the same date for Easter as for the Passover, but to actual participation in the latter. Such a practice is certainly implied by Chrysostom, and the council of Laodicea dealt with kindred questions. It is laid down that the gospels are to be read on the Sabbath as well as the rest of the Scriptures[3]. Christians are not to 'Judaise' but work on the Sabbath, and rest upon the Lord's day[4]. They are not to receive gifts from the festivals of Jews and heretics[5]. And finally they are not to accept unleavened bread from them nor take part in their 'impieties'[6]. These regulations taken

[1] Elvira, Canon 49.
[2] Antioch, Canon 1.
[3] Laodicea, Canon 16.
[4] *Ibid.* Canon 29.
[5] *Ibid.* Canon 37.
[6] *Ibid.* Canon 38.

together certainly leave a strong impression that even in the fourth century there were not only Judaic practices in the Church in Asia, but that there was actual religious fellowship with the Jewish inhabitants. The *Apostolic Canons*, which are a Syrian compilation of the fourth century, strengthen this interpretation. They deal in still further detail with religious fellowship between the clergy and the Jews. ' No bishop, presbyter or deacon, or any other member of the clergy is to share in Jewish fast or feast, or to receive from them unleavened bread or other material for a feast.'[1] No cleric or layman is to go into the synagogue of Jews or heretics to pray[2]. No Christian is to tend the lamps of heathen temples or of Jewish synagogues on the feast days[3]. This is clearly a reference to Christian servants, who performed acts on the Sabbath which were prohibited to orthodox Jews. A final canon seems to date part of the collection at least to the time of Julian. ' If any cleric through fear of Jews, pagans or heretics denies the name of Christ he is to be expelled: if it be his own rank which he denies and he repents, he is to be received back as a layman[4].

Of the African canons it is more difficult to speak, since their dates are by no means clear, and the collection was made in Gaul some centuries later. The adoption of Jewish superstitions and festivals is prohibited in general terms[5]. Two other canons are peculiar to Africa, and somewhat contradictory in tone. One reminds bishops that they are by no means to prohibit Jews from attending the services of the Church up to the ' missa catechumenorum '[6]; and the other, which is twice repeated, reminds judicial authorities that Jews, being in the category of ' infamous ' persons, are not to be allowed to give evidence in court, except against each other[7]. The inclusion of this reminder in an ecclesiastical collection is curious, but it is probably the copy of an

[1] Can. Apost., 69.

[2] *Ibid.* Canon 63.

[3] *Ibid.* Canon 70.

[4] *Ibid.* Canon 61.

[5] Carthage, IV, Canon 84.

[6] *Ibid.* Canon 84. Cf. the invitation at the beginning of the second part of the Mass, ' si quis catechumen procedat, si quis Judaeus procedat '.

[7] *Ibid.* Canon 196; and VI, Canon 2.

imperial edict which has become accidentally included in the collection. Actually, no such edict is known at so early a period[1], but its existence is not improbable.

IX. LEGISLATION AFFECTING THE JEWS UP TO THE DEATH OF THEODOSIUS THE GREAT

With the exception of the last canon, the councils dealt only with religious and social contact between Jews and Christians, but the influence of ecclesiastical authority was equally visible in the imperial legislation of the century, which dealt with the actual rights and privileges of the Jewish community itself. The *Codex Theodosianus*, which was put together in the middle of the fifth century, does not contain all the legislation previously passed. But it contains all that was in force, or not explicitly withdrawn, at the time of its composition. As it gives the date of each law, the place at which it was issued (an important consideration when the unity of the empire was only nominal, and the legislation of east and west reflect very different conditions), and the name of the recipient, it allows us to reconstruct with a fair degree of certainty the progressive decline in the privileges and ultimately in the security of the Jewish communities of the empire.

The fourth century witnessed the gradual breakdown of the immense machine of imperial central government. This was due to a number of causes, social, economic and political, into which it is not necessary to enter[2]. It was a period in which the rich became richer, or at least more powerful, and the poor became poorer. The middle class was crushed by the burden of imperial taxation which the great proprietors avoided, and this burden, added to the barbarian invasions, ruined commerce. The frequent suggestion that the Jews were extremely wealthy because they numbered both merchants and slave-owners rests on no foundation of fact.

[1] See C.J., 1.5.21, which implies the existence of previous but confused legislation.

[2] See S. Dill, *Roman Society in the last century of the Western Empire*, Macmillan, 1905, and F. Lot, *La Fin du Monde Antique*, Part I, Chs. 4 and 7. Dill underestimates the moral collapse by ignoring the evidence of the many councils of the period, with their monotonous prohibition of ecclesiastical immorality.

Doubtless there were wealthy individuals, but there is no direct evidence for wealth in these two facts themselves.

The legislation of Constantine affects the Jews at three points, their treatment of proselytes from Judaism, their treatment of their non-Jewish slaves, and their share of the burdens of the decurionate. That Jews should share in the burdens of the decurionate was just. Their ancient immunity had rested on their inability in pagan days to hold an office which involved offering sacrifice. This was no longer the case in the Christian empire. At the same time the ' curiales ' were the unhappiest class in the empire. They were responsible for the collection of taxation, and compelled to make good the deficit from their own fortunes. The evasions of the wealthy, and the increasing poverty of the time, made the burden an increasingly impossible one to bear, and huge penalties had to be imposed on any attempt to evade the responsibility. No member of the class was allowed to leave his town or sell his property, without the most stringent safeguards for the imperial treasury. The class was hereditary, and as the caste system of the empire became more rigid, to be born into the ' curiales ' became an ever greater misfortune. Many were prepared to become serfs or monks rather than retain its imaginary honour[1].

While it was not unjust that the Jews should be compelled to enter with Christians of equal wealth into this unfortunate class, it is not surprising that they made continual efforts to evade it, and throughout the whole period of Roman legislation there is continual repetition of this obligation. It was customary to exempt from this burden those who occupied religious positions. The Catholic clergy possessed this exemption, and the same was accorded first to ' two or three ' in each Jewish community[2], and then, more explicitly, to all who were entirely occupied with such functions[3]. There was thus no intention to be more severe towards Jews than to the rest of the population, and this is borne out by the terms of the law which grants Jewish curials the immunities from other official duties which the rest of their class enjoyed,

[1] Cf. Dill, *op. cit.*, p. 250 ff.

[2] C.T., 16.8.3.

[3] *Ibid.*, 16.8.2.

and forbids in perpetuity the imposition of curial responsibility on those who are not of the class. It would seem that in the first flush of victory Christian officials were disposed to stretch a point against the Jews, for not only did the freedom of religious functionaries need to be twice repeated, but it was reaffirmed in a special charter addressed to those persons themselves[1].

If the Christians were behaving insolently in the hour of victory, the Jews were evidently not yet cowed. The dramatic change in the status of Christianity seems to have led many Jews to desert the Synagogue for their now triumphant rival. Within two years of the transformation it was necessary to attach the severest penalties to those who molested converts from the ' baleful ' religion of the Synagogue to the light of the Church. Addressing the Jewish authorities themselves, Constantine informs them that he is well aware that it is ' their present habit to pursue with stones and other violence ' such persons, and he sentences all such offenders to death at the stake. This was more justifiable than the second part of the same law which makes it a crime to become a Jew[2]. The first part of the law had to be repeated towards the end of his reign[3]. The same law marks the beginning of the long struggle to prevent the Jews acquiring other than Jewish slaves. Any Jew who circumcised a slave who was either a Christian or a member of any other non-Jewish religion, forfeited the slave. The latter acquired his freedom. No extra penalty was suffered by the Jew, and he was apparently not prohibited from owning such slaves provided he did not circumcise them[4].

It is sometimes stated that Constantius, because he was an Arian, was more favourable to the Jews than was Constantine. If this was so, he did not show it in his legislation, which goes considerably further than that of his father. In the year following his accession he considerably strengthened the restrictions upon the Jewish possession of slaves. If a Jew bought a pagan slave he forfeited him. If he bought a

[1] C.T., 16.8.4.

[2] *Ibid.*, 16.8.1.

[3] *Ibid.*, 16.8.5, and *Const. Sirm.*, 4. In both the penalty is reduced to a sentence commensurate with the particular offence.

[4] *Const. Sirm.*, 4, and C.T., 16.9.1.

Christian slave he forfeited also all his property. If, in either case, he circumcised the slave, he was sentenced to death. The slave, however, did not become free, but the property of the fisc[1]. This insistence on the rights of Christian slaves at the very beginning of the law-making power of the Church is probably due to two causes. For a Jew to circumcise his slave was a natural action, and one intended for the slave's benefit, since in that way he became in some sort a member of the owner's family, and shared in its religious observances. It would, however, be easily interpreted by the Church, if the slave had previously been a Christian, as a hostile action, and doubtless the average Jew, with the attitude to official Christianity which he was likely to have at the time, would get a not entirely religious satisfaction out of the action. The second reason was the extent to which Christianity had penetrated into the lower strata of society. If the Jews were, as is supposed, an important section of the slave traders of the time, it would give them a considerable power of harming the Church if they were allowed to convert their slaves to Judaism. The law was also the natural sequel to the law already quoted which makes it a criminal act to join the Jewish faith. The slave could only be included in the intentions of this law by an attack upon his master. The two other laws of Constantius exhibit the same tendency. Any Christian who became a Jew was to forfeit the whole of his property to the fisc[2]. Any Jew who married a Christian woman employed in the imperial factories (*gynaecea*) was to be put to death, and the woman returned to the factory[3].

No laws of Julian are extant, but his letter to the Jews implies that he had in some way lightened their lot[4], and a law of Gratian reimposing the burdens of curial office suggests that he had actually again released them from it[5].

[1] C.T., 16.9.2. In the Justinian edition of this law (C.J., 1.9.2) other methods of acquisition are included.

[2] C.T., 16.8.7.

[3] *Ibid.*, 16.8.6.

[4] Julian, Ep. 51.

[5] It is usually held that Julian abolished only the 'fiscus Judaicus', but the terms of the law of Gratian, 'Iussio quae sibi Judaeae legis homines blandiuntur per quem eis curialium munerum datur immunitas rescindatur', imply that he abolished the law of Constantine also.

The reign of Julian, short though it was, was long enough to remind each side of the past, persecution on the one side and real toleration on the other. It was well that his successor was not a fanatic, for had he been disposed to yield to it, the temper of the Church would have sanctioned any measure of revenge which he might have proposed. Though Jovian only reigned for some months, he gave time for spirits to cool, and his successors, Valentinian and Valens, continued a policy of toleration, though the former was an adherent of Nicaea, and the latter an Arian who from time to time showed his dislike of the Nicaeans by repressive measures. But the toleration he extended to Jews was complete, and the only incident of his rule which was remembered by later chroniclers was that ' he gave gardens to the pagans for their sacrifices, and the same to the Jews at Antioch for their worship '[1]. The immunities which the Jews secured from Julian they seem to have kept undisturbed for twenty years.

It is not until 383, under Gratian, the successor in the west of Valentinian, that they were again compelled to shoulder the burden of the decurionate. But the new law was more severe than the old had been. The clergy also were included in it, and either had to postpone their religious duties until their public functions had been performed, or pay for a substitute out of their own pocket[2]. This is the first real infringement of the rights of Judaism as a lawful religion, for it placed it on a definitely inferior plane to orthodox Christianity. Having thus returned to the policy of Constantine, with additional severity, in the matter of public duty, Gratian followed up with the re-enactment, also with additional stringency, of the prohibition of conversion from Christianity to Judaism. The convert and the missionary responsible were both to be punished, the former with intestacy, the latter at the discretion of the court. A charge might even be preferred under certain limitations against one who was dead, and his descendants robbed of their inheritance[3]. In this return to previous conditions it was natural that the slaves of Jews should also be considered, and in a spirit similar to that animating his other legislation

[1] *Michael the Syrian*, Bk. VII, Ch. vii.

[2] C.T., 12.1.99.

[3] *Ibid*. 16.7.3.

Gratian enacts that no Jew is to buy a Christian slave, or convert him, when bought, to Judaism. Circumcision is not explicitly mentioned. The masters are to be punished in addition to forfeiting their slaves. But a new clause is added. Christian slaves, or slaves who had been converted from Christianity to Judaism, already in the possession of Jewish masters, are to be compulsorily sold at a fixed price to Christian masters[1]. This second phase of Jewish legislation was completed by Theodosius I, who enacted, first that any marriage between Jew and Christian (man or woman) was to be considered adultery, and that anyone might make the accusation[2], secondly that Jews might only marry among themselves according to Christian practices. They had to observe the Christian tables of affinity, and might not contract two marriages at the same time[3].

It is possible, and indeed probable, that we should add yet another restriction to those in force at the death, in 395, of Theodosius the Great. One of the crimes of the patriarch Gamaliel, referred to in a law of 415, is that he had built new synagogues[4], whereas the first surviving law prohibiting such building is of 423[5]. It is evident, therefore, that an earlier law has been lost, and a reference in a work of Zeno, bishop of Verona, who died in 380, makes it probable that this law was anterior to this date[6]. On the other hand, the reference of Zeno (' if Jews or pagans were allowed, or if they wished, they might build more beautifully their synagogues and temples . . .') may only refer to a prohibition to alter the existing buildings. The Church was always jealous of especial beauty in a synagogue, and this may have been the first step in the attack. But some legislation was clearly in existence by the time at which Zeno wrote, and has now been lost, having been replaced by the later laws.

[1] C.T., 3.1.5.

[2] *Ibid.* 3.7.2 and 9.7.5.

[3] C.J., 1.9.7; the copy of the law in C.T. is lost.

[4] C.T., 16.8.22.

[5] *Ibid.* 16.8.25.

[6] Zeno, *Tract.*, xiv; P.L., XI, p. 354. For a discussion of the passage see Juster, Vol. I, p. 469, n. 2.

X. THE TREATMENT OF HERETICS

We should have a very false picture of the place of this legislation in the life of the times if we imagined it to be the attack of an otherwise homogeneous population upon an alien minority. That became the situation in the Middle Ages, but the fourth century was otherwise constituted. If the Jews were one thorn in the flesh of the Christian emperors, heretics (that is, Christians from whom they disagreed) were another. During two reigns, that of Constantius and Valens, the 'Catholics' were themselves 'heretics', though neither emperor seriously attacked them. It was a period of many different groupings, whose rival powers might change almost overnight, each occupied in using what secular power it possessed to oppress the other, and each indulging in anathema and excommunication when legislation failed.

While this was but cold comfort to the Jew, and is but a poor justification for the Christian apologist, it enables us, looking at the century from a distance, to avoid seeing more definitely anti-Jewish tendencies in the legislation than actually existed. So far as abuse was concerned, Jews and heretics may be said to have fared equally badly. So far as the underlying implications of the abuse were concerned the heretic had the advantage. For it was more likely that he would bow to ecclesiastical anathema than that the Jew would accept baptism. In the matter of conciliar legislation, which was designed to preserve the purity of the Catholic fold, they were on an equal footing, for contact with a heretic was as polluting as contact with a Jew, and was punished with the same penalties. But in the secular legislation of the empire, the Jew had an advantage. For if the law took cognisance of the existence of a heresy, it could imperially forbid it to continue. But the Jewish community, so long as it avoided contact with Christians, was a lawful community, and had even to be protected.

Certainly, so far as the fourth century is concerned, it was better to be a Jew than a heretic. Constantine passed a general law reserving the privileges extended to Christianity to Catholics, that is, adherents of Nicaea. Heretics were 'diversis muneribus constringi et subici'[1], an instruction

[1] C.T., 16.5.1.

which allowed an infinity of torments to be applied by local spite or enthusiasm. Otherwise little was done to them until the time of Gratian, who simply forbade them to exist[1]. Theodosius, more practically, forbade them to hold any meetings, confiscated all their property, ordered their expulsion from any city in which they tried to teach, forbade them to enter any church of the orthodox, and insisted on their restoring to the latter any sees which they held. Further, they were not to call themselves Christians, or to pretend that their views were true[2]. There are fourteen other laws affecting heretics which were issued by Theodosius the Great, varying in severity from the comparative mildness with which he treated, for example, the Eunomians, to his application of the death sentence to certain groups of Manichees[3]. At times the method of wholesale expulsion was applied to them, either from the capital cities of Constantinople or Rome, or from all the cities of the empire[4]. At other times a complete system of graduated fines was substituted[5]. The repetition of these laws proves their almost complete futility, but at any rate they show the anti-Jewish laws in their true perspective. They were dictated as much by general conceptions as by specific hatred of the Jews, and even showed the Jew to be less hated than the heretic. For the heretic was forbidden to hold meetings or to possess property. The Jew enjoyed the right to both. The heretic was frequently exiled. He was forbidden to make a will or to receive a legacy. These were penalties which could only affect the apostate to Judaism. The heretic could be put to death for being a heretic. The Jew could only be executed for some crime in relation to the non-Jewish community. The books of the heretics were burnt. The Torah of the Jew was a sacred book of the Church. In a word, the heretic could be forbidden to exist. The Jew could not.

[1] C.T., 16.5.4 and 5.

[2] *Ibid*. 16.5.6.

[3] *Ibid*. 16.5.8.

[4] *Ibid*. 16.5.13 and 14.

[5] *Ibid*. 16.5.21.

XI. EVENTS IN FOURTH CENTURY HISTORY

But if the Jew could not be forbidden to exist, and if the main purpose of both conciliar and secular legislation was to shut the Jews within the limits of their own community so far as religious matters were affected, and to remove their privileged position in so far as their civic rights and responsibilities were concerned, it was difficult to stop at this point. Inferiority and equality cannot be permanently combined. The equilibrium is bound to change in one direction or the other. Either it returns to equality, or it becomes increasingly inferior. Already the descriptions of the Jewish community in the laws betray the desire to punish and humiliate them. They are a 'feralis secta'; the law speaks of 'turpitudo sua', and 'sua flagitia'; their meetings are 'sacrilegi coetus'; to be converted is 'Judaicis semet polluere contagiis'. To marry a Jew is equivalent to adultery, and to serve them an 'indigna servitudo'. Moreover, the very inefficacity of the laws compelled the emperors to ever stricter rules and more violent threats. For the Jews did not easily accept this separation and confine themselves within their own community. Nor did the local Christian churches readily break off either social relations with Jews, or theological connections with Judaism.

And, on the other hand, the authorities found that it was not easy to persuade minor officials and enthusiastic bishops that these laws did not cover a tacit permission to go a good deal further. At the time of the death of Theodosius it is doubtful if the emperors intended to do more than had already been done. Ambrose might bully Theodosius into an illegal action. For it was an illegal action to deny to the Jews, a recognised religion of the empire, compensation for the attack made upon them. But in his legislation the emperor correctly protected them. Had the Jews shown any sign of accepting Christianity legislation might well have stopped at this point. But this was not even expected by the ecclesiastical leaders, who, in their continual denunciation of Jewish blindness, clearly expected the Jews to continue their flagitious path to destruction. It was, indeed, a theological necessity that they should do so. While, therefore, it is convenient to make a break at the death of Theodosius, in 395, because the unity of the empire comes to an effective end at that point, and from then onwards legislation in east and west needs separate consideration, actually the path from Constantine to Justinian is a continuous one, and one marked by ever-increasing severity.

This was inevitable, because the combination of pulpit rhetoric with official disapproval was bound gradually to produce an open hostility which could only be repressed by further legislation, now trying ineffectively to protect the Jews from the violence of the local clergy and officials, now designed to protect the local Christians from the resentment of the Jews.

It is not possible to say of the fourth century that hostility was general. Rather the reverse is the case. But an added political or religious opposition might quickly bring it into existence. Later legend describes incidents in the reign of Constantine himself. A council is supposed to have been held before Constantine and Helena between Christian bishops and Jewish scribes and Pharisees from Palestine, which resulted in the discomfiture and condemnation of the latter by Pope Sylvester[1]. Constantine himself is said to have expelled all the Jews from the empire as a preliminary to the building of Constantinople[2]. Actually the first incidents date from the middle of the century, if we exclude the Jewish participation in the riots at Alexandria of the Arians against Athanasius[3], which was really a political conflict where religion only played an incidental rôle. Athanasius, as Patriarch, was almost a sovereign prince, and was in addition an Egyptian Nationalist. The Egyptian party in Alexandria was always in opposition to the Jews and Greeks. Hence the sympathy of the latter with the Arians. Political also was the Jewish share in the persecution under Shapur II which led to the death of Simeon, Archbishop of Ctesiphon, and the trouble in Edessa in the time of Julian[4]. These two

[1] *Ep. of Pope Hadrian to Charlemagne*, see Mansi, Vol. II, p. 551.

[2] *Nestorian History*, Ch. xix in P.O., IV, p. 281.

[3] See the vivid account in Athanasius, *Ep. Encyc.*, para. 3 in P.G., XXV, p. 228. Similar events accompanied the installation of his successor, Theodoret, *Eccl. Hist.*, IV, xviii, xix; P.G., LXXXII, pp. 1163 and 1175.

[4] *Chron. of Michael the Syrian*, Bk. VII, Ch. v.

are the first of many incidents which were the natural consequence of the repressive legislation of the Roman empire. The Jews lived at peace under the Sassanids, and the Jews living on the eastern frontiers of the empire were naturally and inevitably pro-Persian. At Edessa, trusting in the favour of Julian, they planned to rise and kill the Christians. But the latter, being informed of the plan, rose first and massacred the Jews. There was also a serious rising of the Jews of Diocaesarea in Palestine in 355. It came at a period following the repressive legislation of Constantine and Constantius, and may have been intensified by it, but its main cause was a series of local incidents due to the oppressive rule of the Roman governor[1]. It ended as unfortunately for the Jews as did the events at Edessa. Diocaesarea was destroyed, and according to the *Chronicle of Eusebius* other cities also[2].

Of more sinister import for the future were the attacks made upon the synagogues. The first recorded was made by Innocentius, bishop of Dertona in northern Italy, who died in 355. Under his rule ' the Christians together with their bishop destroyed the synagogue, and erected a church on the site '[3]. They seem also to have confiscated all the property of the Jews in the town. At a somewhat similar period the Christians also seized the Jewish synagogue at Tipasa in North Africa, and consecrated it as a church[4]. Thirty years later they did the same at Rome, and Ambrose considers it to have been the cause of the downfall of the usurper Maximius that he compelled the Christians to rebuild it, and thereby forfeited all the sympathy of the Christian inhabitants[5]. His own action when a synagogue at Callinicum on the eastern frontier was destroyed has already been discussed. There is, thus, evidence from Italy, Africa and Asia of these destructions. In addition, Innocentius, who seems to have been exceptionally thorough, after destroying

[1] Graetz, *Geschichte*, Vol. II, p. 575.

[2] Socrates, *Hist. Eccl.*, II, xxxiii, in P.G., LXVII; and Jerome, *Chron. Euseb.*, A.D. 356; P.L., XXVII, p. 501.

[3] *Vita*, edited from fragments of the life written by his deacon Celsus, in A.S., April, Vol. II, 483.

[4] *Passio S. Salsae*, in R.E.J., Vol. XLIV, p. 8.

[5] Ambrose, *Ep.*, Bk. I, xl, para. 23; P.L., XVI, p. 1109.

their synagogue, offered the Jews living in Dertona baptism or expulsion[1].

The Jews had a short period in which to take their revenge under Julian. It is difficult to say to what extent they availed themselves of it. That they play little part in the martyrdoms which took place during this time has been already shown. But Ambrose accuses them of having burnt down churches innumerable, two at Damascus, and others at Gaza, Ascalon, Beirut, and elsewhere; and also to have aided the pagans to burn the great church at Alexandria. But other writers do not confirm this accusation. Gregory of Nazianzen, who wrote two lengthy Orations over the heinous offences of the deceased emperor, mentions the church at Gaza, but not the Jewish share in its destruction. He only mentions the taunt flung at the Christians by Julian's encouragement of the rebuilding of the Temple[2]. He ascribes to the Jews 'inveterate hostility' but does not specify its expression other than in this effort at rebuilding[3]. Theodoret of Cyr is also silent upon the point as are Socrates and Sozomen[4]. If Ambrose was not so obviously arguing an extremely bad, and indeed patently illegal cause, his affirmation would outweigh the silence of the others, but it is quite inadequate to stand alone, and while it is probable, indeed certain, that the Jews would *share in* the attacks of the pagans upon the Christians, it is difficult to assert that they took the initiative in such attacks.

That the violence of the century was mostly on the Christian side is rendered more probable by the contrast between the protective legislation issued by Valentinian and Theodosius, and that issued by their successors in the fifth century. The earlier legislation is direct, and contains no counter charges of Jewish unrighteousness. In fact, none of the laws of the century can be said to refer to actual Jewish misdoings. The law prohibits that which was, up to the time of its passing, legal. It does not repress existing criminal behaviour. Until the end of the reign of Theodosius it would seem all to be directed towards the protection of the

[1] See note 3, page 187.

[2] *Oratio*, iv and v; P.G., XXXV. See especially Chs. lxxxvi ff., p. 616.

[3] *Ibid.* p. 668.

[4] Theodoret, *Eccl. Hist.*, Bk. III; P.G., LXXXII. Socrates, Bk. III; P.G., LXVII; and Sozomen, Bk. V; P.G., LXVII.

Jews from the officiousness of particular officials, rather than from the general violence of the Christian population. Valentinian forbids the billeting of troops in the synagogue[1]. Theodosius forbids the Prefect of Egypt to impose special burdens upon the Jews and Samaritans in connection with the duties of ' navicularii ', who fulfilled the onerous and not very remunerative function of supplying the capitals with grain[2]. On another occasion he has to insist upon the internal liberty of the Jewish community against officials who were cancelling its excommunications[3]. His final law, addressed to the governor of the eastern provinces, implies a more general malaise, and is a presage of the continual trouble in the following century which arose especially from the turbulent Syrian monks. ' It is sufficiently evident ', writes the emperor, ' that the Jewish sect is not prohibited by any law. We are therefore seriously disquieted to learn that in certain places Jewish meetings have been prohibited. Your Excellency will, on the receipt of this order, restrain with suitable severity the excesses of those who under the name of the Christian religion are committing illegal actions, or attempting to destroy or ruin synagogues '[4].

XII. RELATIONSHIPS BETWEEN JEWS AND CHRISTIANS

Though His Excellency and His Excellency's successors were to find this particular task an impossible one, and though so far this chapter has dealt almost exclusively with official or unofficial manifestations of hostility, it would be a mistake to assume that during this period all Christians and Jews hated each other. The canons of the councils and the violence of such as Chrysostom both have their origin in the friendly relations between local Jewish and Christian communities. Trouble, when it comes, comes clearly from the ecclesiastical or imperial authorities, and not from the

[1] C.T., 7.8.2.

[2] *Ibid.* 13.5.18. The whole of this section deals with the difficulties encountered in the maintenance of this essential service.

[3] *Ibid.* 16.8.8.

[4] *Ibid.* 16.8.9.

populace. Jewish attacks are due to the particular and general political situation and not to any immediate hatred of their Christian neighbours.

Happily, all Christians were not theologians, and in daily life Christianity was a different affair from a theological controversy. From this point of view the short reign of Julian has an interest beyond the number of churches which were burnt by Jews during the period. Though he was violently prejudiced against the Christians, and in the end disliked the Jews almost as much, yet he pays an involuntary tribute to both religions by his attitude towards paganism. The picture of fourth century Christianity given us in the polemic writings of the fathers and in their sermons, in the ecclesiastical historians, and in the canons of the councils is a singularly unattractive one. The posts of the empire continually disturbed by travelling bishops, the peace of the cities disturbed by perpetual wars between their rival partisans, mutual intolerance and extreme vindictiveness against individuals, such are the impressions gained by reading the lives of Athanasius, John Chrysostom and others. That Christianity did not so strike an outsider is shown by the form taken by Julian's effort to revive paganism. He is naturally sarcastic about these excesses, and he has no use for Christian theology, but he was obviously impressed by the moral force of Christianity in the life of the empire, by the charity of the Christians, by their religious devotion, by their orderly services, and by the faithful lives of their priests[1]. For it was just these virtues which he tried vainly to introduce into the dead bones of temple worship in order to make it more attractive than Christianity to the man in the street. As a theological force he could ignore it, as a moral and social force he found it invincible. Some aspects of Jewish theology also raised his anger, and he disliked their exclusiveness. But the straightforward morality of the Jewish idea of God caused him to ask the Jews to pray for his reign, and in Judaism as much as in Christianity he admired their care for the poor[2].

Julian, unintentionally, allows us to see what the ordinary Christianity of the time was like, and we cannot be too

[1] See his letters to the different high priests whom he created.

[2] *Letters*. Ed. Loeb Classics, Vol. I, p. 391, and Ep. 22.

grateful to him for the picture. Unfortunately we have little detail for filling in a similar picture of Judaism in the Roman empire. The Talmud reflects such different conditions that it is difficult to quote. And the Talmudists themselves were more like the Christian theologians than the Christian laity. Their field of action might be different, but their method within the field was very similar to that of the Christians. To draw out of a text a meaning its author never meant to put into it, to allegorise, to split hairs and to hang interminable arguments from the slenderest thread was as common to the one as to the other[1]. But the problems facing the leaders were different from those facing the ' man in the street ', Jew or Christian, and in daily life the two monotheists must still have found much in common in the face of a not-yet-dead pagan world. At this period it is doubtful if the stories of the Sepher Toldoth Jeshu were more believed than the fantasies of the Christian pulpit.

Naturally the pictures we get in Christian writings of contemporary Jewish life are not complimentary. Jerome denounces them several times for their love of money[2] and for their immoderate love of food[3]. Chromatius, bishop of Aquileia[4], and others denounce them for their ' pessima licentia '. But as with the sermons of Chrysostom, so here it is dangerous to take these accusations at their face value. There is too often an apposite quotation from the prophets to prove it. Jerome's denunciations rest indeed on considerable knowledge of living Jews, but we need to know what he, with his extreme views of asceticism, would consider immoderate eating. He couples together the Jews and Romans as the two most avaricious peoples in the world, whereas the accusation against the Romans is more often lavish spending than avarice. In any case, none of his accusations against either equal his attack on the Syrians[5].

Ambrose warns his people that they must ' avoid contacts with Gentiles and also with Jews, conversation with whom is

[1] Cf. the description of the principles of eastern monasticism, Ch. VIII, Section II, *infra*.

[2] Jerome, *On Isaiah*, ii, 8. Preface to Hosea, P.L., XXIV, p. 49; XXV, p. 855.

[3] *Ibid.*, also Ep. CXXI; P.L., XXII, p. 1006.

[4] Chromatius, *In Evan. S. Matt.*, Tract X; P.L., XX, 351.

[5] Jerome, *On Ezekiel*, XXVII, 16; P.L., XXV, p. 266 ff.

an extreme pollution. For they insinuate themselves among people, penetrate houses, get into the courts, disturb the ears of judges and others, and get on all the better for their impudence. Nor is this a recent failing of theirs, but an inveterate and original evil. For of old they persecuted the Lord and Saviour in the Roman Court '[1].

As to Jewish occupations, we hear casually that Hilarion in his wanderings was recognised by a Jewish hawker of old clothes[2]. We hear of Jewish sorcery[3]. There is in Pusey House, Oxford, the tombstone of a Jewish sausage-seller. References such as these, and the occasional expressions of dislike, would be impressive if they were all we heard of the Jews at this time. They would at least be straws showing the direction of the current, and we might be justified in describing the Jews as a people of hawkers, wandering magicians, and sausage sellers, with the unpleasant personal habits of gluttony, avarice and pushfulness.

But they are not the only references. There is no single writer of the century who did not devote much of his time to the Jews and their misdeeds, and in this mass of literature references to living examples are so few, and often so contradictory, as to suggest that there was nothing abnormal in the people referred to. The apt illustration from daily life is too frequently missing. Jerome refers to their avarice, but there is complete silence about the Jews in the many sermons on usury[4]. A striking example is a sermon of Gaudentius on avarice and the neglect of the poor[5]. He takes as his text Judas Iscariot: the Jews are frequently compared to Judas Iscariot. It is a commonplace[6], to be made still more common in the era of popular religious drama. But in the whole sermon he never connects Judas in this capacity with contemporary Jews. Arguments could be multiplied in this sense to show that it is only by special

[1] Ambrose, *Sermo VII*; P.L., XVII, p. 618. The allusion would be more impressive without the additional text.

[2] Jerome, *Vita Hilarionis*, xxxviii; P.L., XXIII, p. 48.

[3] Cf. the article in R.E.J., Vol. XLIV, on the Jews in Africa.

[4] *E.g.* Basil, *Homily on Ps. xiv*; Ambrose, *De Tobia*; Gregory of Nyssa, *Contra Usurarios*; Salvianus of Marseilles, *De Avaritia*, Libri IV; etc.

[5] *Sermo xiii*, P.L., XX, 933.

[6] *E.g.* Jerome *On Ps. cviii*; P.L., XXVI, p. 1224.

pleading that a case can be made out for any abnormal characteristics in the Jews of the fourth century.

Accusations frequently made in generalisations are singularly lacking when precise conditions are being described, and, on the other hand, the Jews would be an abnormal people if they showed no sign of contemporary vices whatever. They burned down churches during the reign of Julian, according to Ambrose, and were not punished for it. Christians burned down synagogues and went equally unpunished. They were riotous in Alexandria. The Christians, led by Cyril, in the next century paid them back in their own coin with usurious rates of interest. They were exclusive, and did not mix with people outside their own group. This was abnormal in pagan Rome, but in Christian Rome everyone did the same. Contacts with Jews are not more violently forbidden than contacts with heretics, and it may be added that the crimes alleged against Jews are no greater than those alleged against heretics. So far as the common people are concerned, it is indeed questionable whether any of these prohibitions succeeded in securing their objects. Their frequent repetition in the next century suggests their ineffectiveness.

In fact, it may well be suggested that in this century alone the Jew lived in natural contact with his surroundings, neither the abnormal monotheist of pagan days, nor yet the outcast of later generations. A picture of continuous local hostility, such as the historians or Church Fathers might suggest, is not borne out by any facts that we know of the lives of ordinary men. Alexander the sausage seller, the unknown rag merchant, Theodosius the local rabbi[1], probably lived on excellent terms throughout their uneventful lives with Philip the orthodox silversmith, Callistus the Arian, and the rest of their different communities in just the same way as Augustine, Ambrose, and the leaders of Christian orthodoxy seem to have maintained friendly relations with the leaders of pagan Rome, in spite of their religious conviction that the latter would ultimately be damned[2].

It is easier to realise that such must have been the situation when we remember that the victories of Rabbinism and

[1] *Arabic History of the Patriarchs of Alexandria*, P.O., I, 122.

[2] See *Roman Society in the Last Century of the Western Empire*, Dill, Bk. II, Ch. iv.

Catholicism were not at that time assured. In the light of subsequent history we can accurately state that the events of the fourth century made these victories inevitable. But, if these two stood over against each other in sharp contrast, they were not the only respectable faiths of their time. Practising believers were to be found along the whole of the line from the one to the other, fading into each other by such subtleties of metaphysic or similarities of practice that it would really have been difficult to tell with assurance the dividing lines. There were observing Jews who believed that the Messiah had come in the person of Jesus of Nazareth. There were Gentiles who called themselves not merely 'Israelites', but who adopted the title 'Jew'. There were Christians who observed the Law, even circumcision, and others whose interpretation of the person of Christ was consistent with the current Gentile interpretation of what the Jew meant by the unity of God. When Theodosius imperially forbade heresy to exist, he had to address the 'Arians, Macedonians, Pneumatomachi, Apollinarians, Novatians, Sabbatians, Eunomians, Tetradites or Tessarescaedecatites, Valentinians, Papianists, Montanists, Priscillianists, Phrygians, Pepuzites, Marcianists, Borborians, Messalians, Eutychites, Enthusiasts, Donatists, Audians, Hydroparastates, Batrachites, Tascodrogites, Hermeiecians, Photinians, Paulians, Marcellians, Ophites, Encratites, Apotactites, Saccophorians, and the perfectly appalling Manichees'[1]. And even so he left out the Sampseans, the Ebionites, and the Nazarenes. Conformity did not come about in a single century, and the heretics of the fourth century were probably as respectable as those of the twentieth. In spite of the collapse of the empire, which every decade made more evident, human life must have gone on for most people in its daily relations. And it is to be questioned whether the excommunications of individuals or councils really always affected the local respect in which the excommunicated person was held. It was a quick-tempered period, but not necessarily a period in which personal worth, whether in Jew, Christian or heretic, counted for nothing.

Literature leaves us only the lives and works of those who were proclaimed right, or those whom it took centuries to

[1] *Cod. Just.*, I, 5, 5.

discover wrong—such as Origen. It gives us a picture of disputing rabbis, travelling bishops, and rabid monks. But not every man, in the words of Basil, ' folded up his stomach for want of use ', and in the provinces at least the empire could not afford to forgo the public service of Jews and heretics, and make orthodoxy the condition of tax-paying. When that period did come, it is to be presumed that the number of heretics was much fewer, and the standard of statesmanship equally lower. Until then, in all the normal contacts of life, all kinds of opinion lived, ate, paid taxes, and worked together.

CHAPTER SIX

THE THEODOSIAN CODE IN THE WEST

BIBLIOGRAPHICAL INTRODUCTION

Most of the source material for this chapter is adequately given in the footnotes. This is not the place for a general bibliography of the conditions which attended the collapse of the western empire. A very extensive bibliography will be found in the work of Lot. Special studies of this period are few. The early chapters of Vogelstein and Rieger naturally contain detailed studies of the letters of Gregory and the attitude of the papacy. For the somewhat lengthy letters of Cassiodorus the work of Hodgkin, half translation and half résumé, is valuable. For the letters of Gregory the edition of Ewald and Hartmann in M.G.H. is much better than that of Migne, but the numbering of both are given in the notes.

LIST OF BOOKS

DOPSCH, ALFONSO — *Wirtschaftliche und Soziale Grundlagen der Europäischen Kulturentwicklung aus der Zeit von Cäser bis auf Karl den Grossen.* Wien, 1920-1924.

EWALD, P., and HARTMANN, L. M. — *The Letters of Gregory the Great.* M.G.H. 4°. Ep. I, i, 1891.

HODGKIN, T. — *The Letters of Cassiodorus.* Frowde, 1886.

HOMES-DUDDEN, F. — *Gregory the Great.* Longmans, 1905.

LOT, FERDINAND — *La Fin du Monde Antique et les Debuts du Moyen Age.* Paris, 1927.

VOGELSTEIN, H., and RIEGER, P. — *Geschichte der Juden in Rom.* Berlin, 1896.

I. THE PROGRESS OF LEGISLATION

With the death of Theodosius the Great the division of the empire became permanent, although there are cases in which laws passed at Constantinople are applied in the west. As time went on the situation in the west clearly differentiated itself from that in the east. The condition of the Jews was sometimes better in the one, and sometimes in the other. But, strangely enough, the great event of the fifth century left them almost entirely untouched. The invasion of Italy, and the overrunning of western Europe by various barbarian peoples did not affect their legal status. They continued to be Roman citizens, and the edicts of the emperors, as embodied in the Theodosian Code, were carried out by the barbarian kings and the episcopal and ecclesiastical authorities. Such was the case when Italy was ruled by the Ostrogoth Theodoric, and it had not altered later in the days of Gregory the Great. For both, the Jews were Roman citizens. In the last shreds of the Theodosian Code, contained in the *Lex Romana Raetica Curiensis*, they are still included.

The period is marked throughout by one consistent characteristic. In so far as popular feelings were concerned there might be ups and downs. In so far as legislation was concerned, a right once lost was never permanently regained. The restrictions were continually reinforced. The path towards their mediaeval position and the mediaeval ghetto was followed relentlessly and without deviation. The Theodosian Code embodied the maximum of their rights. Lawlessness and ecclesiastical enthusiasm from time to time encroached thereon, but it never cancelled any provision in a manner favourable to them. In the end all the different systems under which they lived ' finished under the influence of the Church by considering the Jews ethnically as strangers, and religiously as unbelievers, and in this capacity persons deprived of civil rights, and subject to special restrictions '[1].

The same situation existed in the kingdoms of the Franks and Visigoths. Beginning with the Theodosian Code in a shortened adaptation, they added further restrictions of their own. And side by side with the law-makers of Church and

[1] Juster, *op. cit.*, II, 27.

State, the theologians continued their conventional utterances on Jewish obliquity, supported still by references to Moses and the prophets rather than to any actual malignity of contemporary Jews.

II. HONORIUS AND VALENTINIAN III

The successors of Theodosius were his two sons. Arcadius ruled the eastern portion of the empire from Constantinople, and Honorius the western from different centres of northern Italy. At first the main problem of the former was the preservation of the Jews against over-zealous officials, and of the latter the securing of curial service from the Jews. It is clear that Honorius was in need of money, for he complains bitterly that 'Jewish citizens of various ranks are wandering about in southern Italy', and are 'under the delusion that by some law or other of the eastern provinces they are freed from the obligation of their public charges'. So far as the western provinces were concerned this law did not exist, for, says Honorius, if it did exist it would be ruinous to public finances[1]. This class was not allowed freedom of movement, and the Jews were consequently ordered to return forthwith to their own cities and to resume their duties. Not content with this, in the following year, 399, he boldly appropriated the whole of the money which was normally sent by the Jews to Jerusalem, and addressed the Patriarch in opprobrious terms as the 'ravager of the Jews'. This action, coming from the west, marks clearly the division of the empire. Honorius felt that such sums were being paid to a foreign province, and he expected the Jews of Italy to feel the same, for he announced that he had 'preserved them from this exaction'[2]. In this latter feeling he was disillusioned, for we find him, five years later, in 404, again allowing the sums to be sent[3].

In this same year appears for the first time a prohibition which extends down to the nineteenth century, and has reappeared in National Socialist Germany in 1933. A natural

[1] C.T., 12.1.157 and 158.

[2] *Ibid.* 16.8.14.

[3] *Ibid.* 16.8.17.

consequence of the abolition of sacrifice on the part of public officials was the entry of Jews into public functions. During the fourth century no objection had been made to this, but the more rigid orthodoxy of the fifth saw in such action on the part of either Jews or heretics an insult to the majesty of the empire. Honorius began with a simple prohibition: ' Jews and Samaritans who are deluding themselves with the privileges of imperial executive officers are to be deprived of all military and court rank '[1]. This prohibition proving both inadequate and unjust, a more comprehensive edict was issued some years later. Those who were already occupied with official functions were to be allowed to complete their term of service and to retire with the usual pension—this concession to be considered a special privilege, and not to be repeated. Nor was it to be applicable to military service. Any Jew in the army was to be immediately degraded. On the other hand, they might practise as lawyers and enjoy the doubtful privilege of the ' honour ' of curial responsibility. In words reminiscent of the utterances of modern antisemitic polemists, he added ' these things ought to be enough for them, and they ought not to take their exclusion from government service as a slur '[2].

Though, then as now, it is difficult to see in what other way such an exclusion can be taken, it appears from the general tenor of the legislation of Honorius that, for his time, he can only be considered friendly towards the Jews. One of his motives may well have been his desire to leave his hands free to deal with the barbarians whose invasions of Italy culminated during his reign in the capture of Rome. Another may have been the economic collapse of Italy which was proceeding apace, and his unwillingness to forego any possible advantages from Jewish industry. But, whatever the causes, there is considerably less virulence in his attitude to the Jews than in that of his eastern contemporary Arcadius, and in view of the fact that the western empire was at this time suffering even more than the eastern, it should be counted to him for righteousness.

The attitude which he took is made particularly clear by the legislation on the question of sanctuary, which was

[1] C.T., 16.8.16.

[2] *Ibid.* 16.8.24.

passed in both sections of the empire in the beginning of the fifth century. In normal conditions the violation of sanctuary was considered as the crime of *lese majesté*[1]. But the reigns of Honorius and Arcadius were not normal. The economic distress of the empire forced Arcadius to permit the violation of sanctuary in the case of Jews who fled thither for the purpose of avoiding their debts or charges[2]. For a short period even Christians taking sanctuary from the same motives might meet similar treatment[3]. Honorius, while recognising the influence of economic distress on the flight of Jews to sanctuary and to Christianity, allowed them, even when converted, to return without any penalty to Judaism[4], an attitude in extraordinary contrast to the prevailing views of the period, as seen in conciliar and secular legislation.

The flight of the Jews to sanctuary and to Christianity is not the only evidence of the difficult economic situation at this period[5]. Honorius also took the unique step of revoking the consistent policy of Christian imperial legislation in the matter of slaves. He allowed them Christian slaves provided that the master did not interfere with the slave's religion. This the master was simply forbidden to do, no penalty being attached. Any interference in their possession of such slaves, however, was to be severely punished[6].

Of more interest for this study are the three laws which were promulgated in Africa in the years 408 and 409. At this period Augustine was engaged in his long battle with the Donatists, a group which, for violence, rivalled the eastern monks. The Jews are only incidental to the imperial attempt to suppress them, but it appears that Jews had taken part in their attacks upon Catholic churches and their services. That this was not a large part is probable. For Augustine devotes a considerable number of his works to his defence against the Donatists, and remains silent on a Jewish

[1] Cf. C.J., 1.12.2.

[2] C.T., 9.45.2.

[3] *Ibid.* 9.45.4.

[4] *Ibid.* 16.8.23.

[5] An interesting study of the economic collapse of Rome is to be found in *Genseric, Roi des Vandales*, by E.-F. Gautier, Paris, 1932.

[6] C.T., 16.9.3.

share in their outrages. But this silence, while it may temper, cannot contradict the positive evidence of a twice repeated law[1]. Together with the Donatists there appeared at this time in Africa other heretics who involved the Jews, the ' Caelicoli '. Beyond the references to them in the law of Honorius, we are entirely ignorant of the nature and beliefs of this group. They were clearly a ' Judaising ' group, for they ' tried to force certain Christians to adopt the foul and degrading name of Jew '[2]. Possibly they should be connected with two other references. A council of Carthage, possibly the fourth, expelled from the Church ' those using auguries and incantations, and those clinging to Jewish superstitions and festivals '. The law mentions the second of these crimes, and the name of the sect, ' Caelicoli ', suggests the first[3]. The other reference is to be found in a letter of Augustine[4], where he refers to Christians who call themselves ' Jews ', and says that though Christians are the ' true Israel ', they should not use this name. Whatever their tenets, the sect is given one year to cease to exist—and apparently it took the unique course of doing so, for it is never heard of again, except as part of the title of the chapter of the Theodosian Code dealing with ' Jews, Samaritans and Caelicoli '[5].

There is thus certain evidence that the Jews were a social and religious danger to the Christians in Africa. There is even clearer evidence that the Christians were a danger to the Jews. Though the lawlessness of the eastern provinces was not equalled, so far as we know, by anything happening in the west, Honorius issued edicts to protect both the sanctity of the Sabbath[6] and the security of the synagogues[7]; a clear sign that both had been violated.

We possess a lengthy narrative from Severus, bishop of Majorca, describing just such events in the island of Minorca

[1] C.T., 16.5.44 and 46.

[2] *Ibid.* 16.8.19.

[3] Carthage IV, Can. 89, in Mansi, III, p. 958.

[4] Augustine, *Ep.*, 196; P.L., XXXIII, iii, p. 894.

[5] For an ingenious theory as to their beliefs see the discussion of Gothofredus on this law in his edition of the Code.

[6] C.T., 8.8.8 and 2.8.26.

[7] *Ibid.* 16.8.20.

in 418[1]. The narrative is contained in a letter addressed to 'their most holy and blessed lordships the bishops, presbyters and deacons of the whole world'. The narrative has always been taken as a genuine but coloured account of the actual events by the bishop himself, but it would seem possible that the 'colouring' is more extensive than is usually admitted. The chief convert among the Jews was Theodorus, who occupied the position of 'defensor' or mayor of Magona in Minorca. The event is supposed to take place in 418, but in 409 an edict was issued in Ravenna ordering that 'defensores' should be chosen by the clergy, and only from the orthodox[2]. It is, of course, possible that the law had not reached so obscure a city in nine years, but it is also a feature of apocryphal documents to give lofty titles to their actors. The narrative also contains a considerable amount of that kind of miracle which has neither a psychological nor a moral probability. The other town of the island, for example, had a miraculous divine privilege, by which it was immune from the presence of snakes, wolves, foxes and Jews, and though it had scorpions, these were of a heavenly variety which did not sting. If any Jews entered the town and were removed neither by mysterious sickness nor by the inhabitants, their elimination was undertaken by divine thunderbolts.

The first cause of the events which the bishop narrates was the arrival in the island of a deacon from Jerusalem who came with the relics of Saint Stephen which were to be transported to Spain. But his voyage was interrupted by the invasion of the Vandals into that country. According to the usual accounts, the first translation of Saint Stephen took place in the fourth century, to Byzantium, and there is no record other than this letter of a subsequent translation to Spain, an event in itself exceedingly unlikely in view of the political situation.

The presence, however, of these relics stirs up the population to a solution of the Jewish question. The Jews, alarmed, recall Theodore from Majorca, whither affairs had called him. He tries in vain to quiet matters down. The Christians insist on a disputation, but when the time comes only accuse

[1] *Epistola de Judaeis*, P.L., XX, p. 731.

[2] C.J., 1.55.8.

the Jews of piling up weapons in the synagogue. This the Jews deny, and Severus demands ocular proof. Leading his followers to the synagogue, he is the object of a hostile demonstration from some Jewish women. Introducing, perhaps unnecessarily, the miraculous, he explains that no one was hit. The Christians retaliated with similar results, for the Jewish women had, presumably, retired. Arriving at the synagogue, and forgetting the motive which had led him there, he sets fire to it and destroys everything in it except the silver, which he returns to the Jews, and the books which he keeps to ' preserve from Jewish defilement '.

The despair and confusion of the Jewish population are painted with considerable power, but consisting as it does largely of dreams and visions, internal feelings and private conversations, it is clearly of the romantic rather than of the eye-witness school of writing. In the end all the Jews are baptised, and the letter is written to appraise the world of this example of grace. The victory is due to a combination of miracle with the tactics of the Ephesians, continuous shouting, and is not apparently due to the power of either the oratory or the lives of the Christians. While thus the narrative is clearly unreliable, it is probable that the two main facts, the burning of the synagogue and the forced(?) baptism of the Jews, really took place. For both of these events are in the spirit of the times—as also is the inaccurate reporting of them.

Valentinian III repeated the law by which Jews could not hold office, and added the reason that he did not wish Christians to serve such persons, ' lest by their office they found occasion to corrupt the venerable Christian faith '[1]. In addition he enacted one further law which is of considerable importance[2]:

> If the son or daughter or grandchild, singly or together, of a Jew or Samaritan, shall on better thoughts leave the shadows of his own superstition for the light of the Christian religion, it shall not be lawful for his parents or grandparents to disinherit him or to pass him over in their will or to leave him less than he would have received if

[1] *Const. Sirm.*, vi fin.

[2] C.T., 16.8.28. Cf. Juster, Vol. II, pp. 90-91.

> they had died intestate. If they do so, we order that he shall succeed to the inheritance as though it was a case of intestacy, and the will shall be null, except for the manumissions (up to the legal maximum) which it may contain, and which shall retain their validity.
>
> If it shall be proved that such children or grandchildren have committed serious offences against their parents or grandparents, while the latter have legal means of taking revenge if the accusation shall have in the meantime been brought to trial, yet they shall in their will both attach credible and clear documentary evidence (of these crimes) and shall leave them only the Falcidian quarter of the succession which should have been theirs. This seems to be due to the children or grandchildren in honour of the religion which they have chosen though, as we have said, they will also be punished if any charge against them be proved.

Such a law is evidence that even when a purely political or social right is in question the influence affecting it is religious. Neither in this case nor in the case of Jewish officials do we possess any evidence which would otherwise justify such extraordinary action.

III. THEODORIC THE OSTROGOTH

The fact that by the time of the passage of these laws the effective rule in Italy had passed to the barbarians did not affect the situation, and in 438 the whole of the Theodosian Code became valid for the west, and introduced into these provinces the laws of Arcadius and Theodosius II, both of whom had passed more anti-Jewish legislation than their western colleagues[1]. The barbarians themselves, and the shadow emperors still ruling at Ravenna, had little time to introduce new laws; no councils dealt with them; and we know little of how the Jews fared during the rest of the fifth century. But in 493 Theodoric the Ostrogoth, an Arian, conquered Italy and extended his dominion over the Visigoths of Provence and Northern Spain.

[1] For this legislation see Ch. VII.

Theodoric has left a consistent record behind him of justice in his treatment of all his Roman subjects. Though he was himself an Arian, he would not allow the Jews to encroach on the Catholics. If he never ceased to remind them (though the inspiration may come rather from his minister Cassiodorus than himself) that they had erred from the true religion, yet his real attitude is summed up in his determination to preserve the ancient usages: 'As to the Jews, let the privileges they enjoy be preserved and let them preserve their own judges'[1]. That this was no theoretical or unnecessary statement is shown by the actual cases with which he had to deal, which were all connected with violence of some kind between Jews and Christians. Both in Ravenna and Rome synagogues had been burnt, and complaints made to the king, who ordered justice to be done. In Ravenna the trouble had apparently started from some forced baptisms, which had led the Jews into ridiculing Christianity[2]. The Christians then rose and burnt the synagogue, and the Jews rapidly complained to the king at Verona. Theodoric ordered

[1] *Edictum*, Cap. 143.

[2] *Anonymus Valesianus*, XVI, 80; M.G.H., 4to, Vol. IX, i; *Chron. Min.*, p. 326. The possibilities of the growth of legend even in modern scholarship are well illustrated by this story. Dr Homes Dudden in *Gregory the Great*, Vol. II, p. 152, by a happy transposition says that the Jews of Ravenna were in the habit of throwing baptised persons into the river, and making a mockery of the Eucharist. M. Demoulin in the *Cambridge Modern History*, says that it was the Jews who were flung in the river by the Christians (Vol. I, 453). The next stage of the legend should be a complaint from the Congested Rivers Board. The sentence in question runs: 'quare Judaei baptizatos nolentes dum ludunt frequenter oblatam in acquam fluminis jactaverunt'. The phrase 'baptizatos nolentes' for 'baptizatos esse nolentes' or 'baptizati (os) contra suam voluntatem' is almost impossible even in late Latin. Moreover, 'oblatam' did not then mean the Eucharist, but the bread which has been blessed but not used for the Eucharist. It would seem necessary to suppose a corruption, either of 'baptizari nolentes' or 'baptizati violenter'. The latter is more probable, for it provides the only explanation of how the Jews obtained access to the 'oblata'. It is impossible to consider this a 'profanation of the Host', an accusation which does not occur until centuries later, and if this is excluded, there seems no reason for making a special point of stealing so unimportant a piece of Christian ritual as the 'oblata'. The most probable sequence would then be this. The Jews had been baptised against their will. After the ceremony they had received pieces of blessed bread. To show their contempt for the whole proceeding, they marched together ('frequenter') to the river and threw it in. As against the translation of Dr Dudden, it may be added that not only does 'oblata' not mean Eucharist, but 'baptizatos' is never used for ordinary Christians, but only for people like the Jews, who were normally not baptised.

the Roman population of Ravenna to rebuild the synagogue, and those who were too poor to be flogged instead. The affair at Rome, which also led to the burning of a synagogue, was more complicated. Cassiodorus is not easy to interpret, but slaves had murdered their master, and somehow a riot followed their condemnation. Presumably, in defiance of the law, the slaves were Christian ; otherwise it is difficult to see how the crowd came into the matter. Something, however, roused them, and the mob burnt the synagogue. Theodoric reproved the Senate that in Rome of all places such ' levitas' should take place, and ordered them to make a careful enquiry into both the burning and the alleged malpractices of the Jews, and to do justice[1]. Theodoric also wrote to Rome on a question affecting a Samaritan synagogue. It was alleged that Pope Simplicius had bought a property on which a synagogue had stood, and had thereby deprived them of it. Theodoric again ordered an impartial enquiry to be made, with a view, presumably, to its restoration to the Samaritans, if it had contained one of their religious buildings[2]. Here Theodoric was showing himself milder than the Theodosian Code, which neither made reciprocal allowance for the return of buildings of other religions bought by Catholics, nor allowed any toleration to the Samaritans in particular.

The Jews of Genoa and Milan also turned to him for protection against the violation of their rights, and again his attitude reveals his veneration for the Romans whose rule he had replaced. To the Jews of Milan he writes that for the preservation of ' Civilitas ' the benefits of justice are not to be denied even to those ' who are erring from the right way in matters of faith '. He forbids any ecclesiastic to meddle with their rights and, at the same time, forbids them to do anything ' incivile ' against the Church. Then, lest the spirit of Ambrose should rise and haunt him, this Arian monarch adds: ' But why, O Jew, do you seek in your petition for earthly quiet, when you are not able to find eternal quiet? '[3]

To the Jews of Genoa he writes: ' we gladly accede to your request that all the privileges which the foresight of antiquity conferred upon the Jewish customs shall be renewed to you;

[1] *Cassiodorus Varia*, IV, 43; P.L., LXIX, p. 636.

[2] *Ibid.* III, 46; p. 600.

[3] *Ibid.* V, 37; p. 669.

for in truth it is our great desire that the laws of the ancients shall be kept in force, to secure the reverence due to ourselves '[1]. But that he did not wish to go beyond the law is shown by the fact that he would not allow this same community to do more than roof in the ruins of their old synagogue, and that he expressly forbade them to enlarge it[2]. It is in this letter that, after protesting against their errors of faith, he adds the famous sentence that he grants the permission because ' we are not able to command religion, for no one is compelled unwillingly to believe '—a sentiment not always shared by his Catholic contemporaries. Though this reflects truly enough the attitude of the Gothic sovereigns, yet it is possible, even probable, that this mildness is due to the influence of his Catholic secretary Cassiodorus, for it is very similar to that shown in the commentaries of which he was the author[3]. Not unnaturally the Jews were loyal to the Ostrogoths, and when Belisarius besieged Naples in 536 the Jews were amongst the firmest opponents to the idea of surrender, and, when the city was taken, the last to resist[4].

IV. THE LOMBARDS

Of the Jews under the Lombards, who invaded Italy in the second half of the sixth century, little is known. It is probably a case of ' happy the people that has no history ', though once the Lombards became Catholics, matters may have changed, for there is one record of forced conversion or execution at the end of the seventh century[5]. In general they still lived under a rough version of the Theodosian Code, for another edition of that Code was produced at the end of the eighth century, and contains in barbaric Latin a summary of their status. ' Those who were accustomed to consider themselves Romans ' were to keep their internal autonomy,

[1] *Cass. Var.*, IV, 33; PL., LXIX., p. 630.

[2] *Ibid.* II, 27; *ibid.* p. 561.

[3] See Cass., *Expositio in Psalterium*, Pss. 49 and 81, in each case the *conclusio*. P.L., LXX, pp. 357 and 595.

[4] Procopius, *History of the Wars*, V, 8, 9, 10.

[5] *Carmen de Synodo Ticinensi*, M.G.H., 4to, *Scrip. Rerum Langobard.*, 190.

though they were to use Christian judges in mixed cases[1]. The old prohibitions with regard to intermarriage and the owning or purchase of Christian slaves were naturally retained[2].

V. THE PAPACY: GREGORY THE GREAT

The Lombards formed no united kingdom in Italy, and left the ‘ patrimony of Saint Peter ’, the nucleus of the papal States, independent. The Popes thus became important Italian princes. During the earlier centuries it is not possible to ascribe to them any particular attitude to the Jews. If a Pope was a writer, nothing in particular distinguished his views from those of others. In conciliar and imperial legislation it is not possible to attribute to them any special rôle. But a different situation arises once the Popes become secular potentates ruling in Rome over a more or less defined territory. They also stand in a very different position of authority towards the new kingdoms of the west from that which they were able to occupy towards the old empire. As long as the empire lasted they were occupied with purely religious questions, and, when legislation was necessary, it was the emperor who legislated. But when ecclesiastical councils began to assume the function of legislator, when bishops, by their education and understanding, or by their influence over princelings, came to exercise authority in their dioceses, it was natural that the papacy also should play a part in the political life of the west where it touched the interests of the Church.

In the period in which most of the barbarians were still Arians, it is often said that the Catholics were always intolerant, but just as mediaeval history shows us many examples of Popes far in advance of their clergy in toleration and humanity, so the first Pope of whose attitude to the Jews we have full information, Gregory the Great, shows an attitude of firmness and, at the same time, justice which, in view of the age in which he lived, is far removed from intolerance. More than eight hundred letters of this Pope still exist, and over twenty deal with matters affecting the

[1] *Lex Romana Raetica Curiensis*, 2.1.8. M.G.H., folio, Leg. V, 313.

[2] *Ibid.* 3.1.5 and 3.7.2.

Jews. At that time (the end of the sixth century) his authority over all the churches of western Christendom was but vaguely established, but his patriarchal authority over the region which corresponded to the jurisdiction of the former Vicarius Urbis was quite definite. Outside this territory, which included large portions of central and southern Italy, and the islands of Sicily, Corsica and Sardinia, it depended largely on the moral influence of the individual Pope. With Gregory it was naturally considerable. Within his patrimony we find him dealing with every kind of question, not merely ecclesiastical, but economic and military. He lived at a time when Italy was going through a period of acute distress. The Lombards were in possession of large sections of the country, and Gregory will break off another subject in a letter to advise a bishop to look well to the fortifications and provisioning of his town in case there is an attack from these enemies. He negotiates himself for peace with the Lombard kings, and advises the Exarch of Ravenna on the policy to adopt towards them.

Gregory was ever ready to listen to just complaints brought to him, and many of his letters on Jewish questions begin by telling the recipient that Roman Jews or Jews coming to Rome have brought him a complaint of their treatment in the recipient's city. His main interest on the Papal patrimony was their conversion, and he sends several letters of instruction to his Sicilian representative laying down his views on the subject. Of forced conversion he expresses his strongest disapproval, and he writes to the bishops of Marseilles and Arles, telling them of the complaints he has received from Jewish merchants coming from Marseilles to Rome, that Jews in these cities are being brought to the font more by force than by persuasion. While Gregory approves of the motive of love for the Lord which had led the bishops to this action, he disapproves of the action itself, and fears that its result is likely to bring more evil than good, for such converts cannot be sincere. It is only by preaching that a sincere conversion can be effected[1]. He writes in a somewhat similar strain to the bishop of Terracina, approving of the bishop's effort to preach to the Jews, but disapproving of his use of threats. The terror of the future judgment should be

[1] Ep. I, 47, Migne; I, 45, Ewald and Hartmann.

enough, and they are more likely to be won by kindness[1]. The bishop may well have offered them conversion or expulsion, as had several of his contemporaries under Frankish rule.

His own attitude is shown by his letters to the rectors of his patrimony in Sicily. When he hears that there are many Jews on the estates of the Church, he begs them to use every effort to win them to Christ. They are to be offered a reduction of their rent if they will accept baptism, an offer which is in interesting contrast to his instructions to increase the rent for pagans who refuse to be converted. By this means Gregory hopes that others may be led to follow their example[2]. Gregory shows an equal solicitude for the welfare of those who have already accepted conversion. His rector is instructed to make an annual grant out of the Papal funds to a converted widow and her three children[3]. On another occasion he directs that converts too poor to provide their own baptismal robe shall be given one from the Papal funds[4]. In spite of the advantages he offers, a few years later Gregory finds that many on his estates are still refusing conversion. He therefore offers them explicitly a reduction in rent of one-third, unless the rector decides upon another figure. He was under no illusion as to the effect of his offer, but he balances the loss on Church revenue, and the possible insincerity of the actual converts, by the fact that their children will be baptised and receive Christian teaching. Thus the Church will win either one generation or the other[5]. Gregory was also disposed to give privileges of a more spiritual kind to possible converts. Hearing from the Abbess of Saint Stephen's in Agrigentum that there are many Jews on her estates who wish to be baptised, he writes at once to Fantinus, the guardian of the Papal estates in Sicily, to make a visit to Agrigentum himself and to give instruction to those Jews seeking baptism. If they wish to be baptised at once, they are to be given forty days' abstinence, and then baptised at the nearest convenient

[1] Ep. I, 35, M.; I, 34, E. and H.

[2] Ep. II, 32, M.; II, 38, E. and H.

[3] Ep. IV, 33, M.; IV, 31, E. and H.

[4] Ep. V, 8, M.; V, 7, E. and H.

[5] Ep. V, 8, M.; V, 7, E. and H.

feast. If they wish to wait for the usual time, which in that century was Easter, they are to be made catechumens at once (the letter was written in May), and the bishop is to pay special attention to them in the intervening period. As has been already said, the poor are to have their robes provided for them[1]. Some of Gregory's converts turned out unsatisfactory, for in one case he had to write to his rector to protect the bearer of his letter, a certain Paula, from the evil intentions of a converted Jew Theodorus[2]; and in another he speaks of a certain Peter who, the day after his conversion, proceeded to desecrate his old synagogue[3]. That the enmity of the Jews was aroused by this policy is possibly hinted at in a letter of commendation of a convert and his wife, who are to be guarded from all molestation. This would presumably be from unconverted Jews[4].

While thus anxious for their conversion, and prepared to accept possible insincerity in the parents for the sake of the children, Gregory was firm in allowing them exactly the privileges which they enjoyed under Theodosian Law. In four different places he is told of oppression, Terracina and Palermo in Sicily, Caglieri in Sardinia, and Naples. In Terracina the Jews possess a synagogue in such close proximity to the church that the singing is said to disturb Christians at worship. If on a careful inspection this disturbance is found to exist, they are to be given another site, where ' they can live under the protection of Roman Law, and enjoy their observances without hindrance '[5]. The complaint was apparently found justified, for a few months later there is a protest from the Jews that they have been given another site and then turned out of it. Gregory orders the bishop to abstain from giving them cause of complaint of this kind[6].

In Palermo the trouble comes from an enthusiastic bishop, Victor, to whom Gregory writes that the Jews in Rome complain that he has without any cause confiscated some of their

[1] Ep. VIII, 23, M.; and E. and H.
[2] Ep. VII, 44, M.; VII, 41, E. and H.
[3] Ep. IX, 6, M.; IX, 195, E. and H.
[4] Ep. I, 71, M.; I, 69, E. and H.
[5] Ep. I, 10, M.; II, 6, E. and H.
[6] Ep. I, 35, M.; I, 34, E. and H.

synagogues with their attached guest chambers. Gregory is anxious to do no injustice to the bishop, and expresses his unwillingness to believe that his action was unprovoked[1]. But finding there is no excuse for it, he writes to his representative to see that the bishop is made to pay for the buildings, which cannot be returned as they have been consecrated, at a price fixed by reputable persons. He must return any ornaments which he has taken. ' If the Jew may not exceed the law, he ought to be allowed peaceably to enjoy what the law permits.'[2]

The aged bishop of Caglieri was a perpetual thorn in the side of the Pope. He was violent and incompetent, and, as a result, there was always some trouble in Sardinia. This time a converted Jew, with rash enthusiasm, had immediately after his baptism collected disorderly persons and seized the synagogue, putting there a cross, an image of the Virgin, and his own baptismal robe. This fact had been confirmed by letters from the secular authorities—and Gregory tempers the implied rebuke by adding that they stated that the bishop had attempted to restrain him. Gregory, therefore, orders the bishop to restore their synagogue to the Jews, since they may not build a new one, and to attempt also to restore peace in the city[3]. In Naples the bishop had been interfering with internal Jewish affairs and prohibiting certain lawful practices. Gregory forbids this on the grounds that he cannot see that such conduct is in the least likely to lead to their conversion, and that, on the other hand, the prohibited practices were in themselves legal. He recommends the bishop to try kindness[4].

Even in secular matters he is prepared to intervene to protect Jewish rights. A Jamnian Jew complained to him that the Papal Guardian had wrongfully, with other creditors, seized his ship and property. Gregory orders an immediate full enquiry into the matter, that justice may be done[5].

While he was determined that justice should be done to them, and every effort be made to win them to Christianity,

[1] Had they, for example, been new buildings, this would have justified their confiscation.

[2] Eps. VIII, 25, and IX, 55, M.; VIII, 25, and IX, 38, E. and H.

[3] Ep. IX, 6, M.; IX, 195, E. and H.

[4] Ep. XIII, 12, M.; XIII, 15, E. and H.

[5] Ep. IX, 56, M.; IX, 40, E. and H.

the Pope was quite firm on the question of the limits of their rights. Just as he had refused to allow them to build new synagogues, so also he would not allow them to exceed the Theodosian Code in the matter of Christian slaves. No less than ten letters deal with this question, and he is concerned with the matter outside his own direct jurisdiction as much as within it. His letters cover the possession, the circumcision, and the buying and selling of slaves. He writes to the Frankish sovereigns, Theodoric, Theodobert, and Brunichild, expressing his astonishment that they tolerate this insult to Christ, the Head of the Church, that they allow His members to be 'trampled on by His enemies'[1]. At the beginning of his reign he even finds this abuse on his own estates in Sicily[2]. Other cases are a little more complicated. In Syracuse a Christian boy had served a Samaritan master for eighteen years, and then become free. His master had followed him to the font, and then reclaimed him. This Gregory correctly refuses to allow[3]. In another case he hears that a Samaritan owner has actually circumcised a pagan slave. Gregory orders the slave to be set free without compensation to his owner, and adds that the latter ought legally to be punished into the bargain[4]. The old bishop of Caglieri causes Gregory trouble also in the matter of slaves. Acting on an obsolete statute of Valentinian, he allowed purchase money to be paid to Jews for slaves who had fled to the Church, and announced their desire to become Christians. In some cases he had even returned them to their Jewish masters[5]. In a letter to the bishop of Luna in Etruria, Gregory makes the distinction made by Honorius[6] allowing Jews to retain Christian slaves engaged in agriculture, provided they permit them undisturbed possession of their religion. All others are to be liberated at once[7].

[1] Ep. IX, 109 and 110, M.; IX, 213 and 215, E. and H.

[2] Ep. I, 10, M.; II, 6, E. and H.

[3] Ep. VIII, 21, M.; and E. and H. Gregory was acting on *Cod. Just.*, 1, 3, 54.

[4] Ep. VI, 33, M.; VI, 30, E. and H. The legal position is given in C.T., 16.9.4.

[5] Ep. IV, 9, M.; and E. and H.

[6] C.T., 16.9.3.

[7] Ep. IV, 21, M.; and E. and H.

More complicated were questions of the slave trade, in which, it is obvious, the Jews took a considerable part. Gregory had at first desired to make the hard-and-fast rule that Jews were not to buy Christian slaves, and that any found in their possession were to be removed without compensation. He shows his essential reasonableness of spirit by listening to a Jewish delegation on the subject. In a letter to the bishop of Naples, which was apparently the great port at which slaves arrived from Gaul, he explains the argument of the Jews, and propounds his solution, which he considers fair alike to the Jewish merchants and the Christian captives. The Jewish traffic in slaves received official recognition in Gaul, and it was at the request of the Gallic authorities that the Jews were buying them. In making such purchases they could not distinguish which were pagans and which Christians. Gregory therefore lays down that once they have discovered any to be Christians, they are either to be handed over at once to those who ordered the purchase (it is not quite clear who these are) or sold to Christian masters within forty days. If the slave is sick a delay is allowed. He is then to be sold as soon as he is well. If the Jew retains a Christian slave more than forty days, this is to be considered evidence that he intends to keep him for his own use. In this case he should be set free and no compensation paid. They are to be given a fair time to dispose of slaves at present in their possession, since it is not fair to penalise them for actions committed in ignorance[1]. In a postscript he raises the question of the slaves of a particular Jew, Basilius, who had come with the delegation to Rome. Basilius had sons who were Christians. He wished permission to give some of his slaves to his sons and retain the use of them himself. Gregory provides an ingenious solution. They may not remain in his house, but his sons may offer them to him for the services which it is fitting for sons to render to a father. This postscript is interesting from other points of view than that of the question of the slaves. It is a pity we do not know the motives with which the sons became Christians. At first sight it suggests a business deal and a clever way of keeping the slaves in the family, parallel to that by which in later centuries Jews possessed property

[1] Ep. IX, 36, M.; IX, 104, E. and H.

under the name of Christians. But it is doubtful if Gregory, with all his practical acuteness, would have tolerated such a collusion between the works of light and darkness. It is more likely that he accepted the conversion of the sons as sincere, and that the incident shows that perfectly good relations could exist between a converted son and an unconverted father.

There is a puzzling letter to 'Candidus our Presbyter in Gaul' about four Christian captives in the possession of a Jew in Narbonne. Gregory orders them to be redeemed, and to be provided with adequate funds from the papal chest if they have not enough money to pay for their own redemption. As this letter is dated May 597[1], and the letter just discussed is of February 599, it seems as if there was no excuse for his not ordering them to be immediately set free without compensation paid to their owner. We have not adequate data for deciding the actual circumstances of the case. That they were not as simple as they sound is shown by the fact that the Presbyter is ordered to make a careful enquiry. The consistency of Gregory's action throughout makes it difficult to accept the story simply on the evidence given[2].

Finally, there was the question of slaves who were pagans when they were bought, and who declared their desire to become Christians while in the possession of the Jewish slaver. The Jews tried to pretend that the law allowing the pagan slave of a Jew to become free on expressing his desire to become a Christian did not apply to slaves acquired for the purpose of sale. Gregory will not accept this. Any slave has at any time the right to freedom on expressing this desire. But he recognises that this would be unfair to the slaver, if stated without qualification. He therefore gives him the opportunity of selling him within forty days to a Christian. If he is still in the Jew's possession after three months, he is to receive his freedom[3]. This decision, addressed to Naples two years before the general issue had

[1] Ep. VII, 24, M.; VII, 21, E. and H.

[2] Neither the kings nor the councils in France had accepted the idea that a Jew might not own a Christian slave, but Gregory's letter to the sovereigns clearly shows that he did not accept this situation. On the councils see below, Ch. IX, Section VI.

[3] Ep. VI, 32, M.; VI, 29, E. and H.

to be decided, probably provided the basis from which the Pope evolved his later solution.

There are three other letters dealing with Jewish questions which throw some light both on Gregory and on contemporary conditions. Two priests at Venafro had sold church plate to the Jews. Gregory orders it to be immediately restored[1]. More interesting is the case of an enterprising but 'most wicked' Jew who had set up an altar to Elijah, and had persuaded many Christians to worship at it. It is a pity we do not know more of this case, for it is impossible to tell whether this was a new Judaistic heresy—the Jew being sincere but in error—or whether he was an ingenious charlatan producing a miracle-working shrine for the deception of the faithful. The odds are in favour of the former, for if he had been a humbug he was unwise in neglecting the preliminary of a miraculous conversion. Accepting his action as sincere, the most probable explanation seems to be that the Jew saw the reconciliation of Judaism and Christianity in the second coming of the Messiah, and had therefore erected an altar to Elijah who was due to precede Him, and that he had found Christians to share his belief. The fact that he had Christian slaves supports his sincerity, for again, if he were a humbug, he was behaving so foolishly that it is unlikely that his activities would have survived long enough to come to the ears of the Pope. In any case Gregory did not sympathise with his efforts, and he ordered the Prefect of Sicily to confiscate his slaves and destroy his altar[2]. The last letter is one which it is probable Gregory would never have written had he seen what was to follow the conversion of the Arian Visigothic kings of Spain to Catholicism. It is a letter congratulating Reccared on his conversion, and particularly on refusing the offer of a large sum of money from the Jews offered him on condition that he did not put into force the new laws against them[3].

As can easily be seen, the letters of Gregory give us a unique picture of Jewish life at the end of the sixth century, and of the relations between Christians and Jews. While

[1] Ep. I, 68, M.; I, 66, E. and H.

[2] Ep. III, 38, M.; III, 37, E. and H.

[3] Ep. IX, 122, M.; IX, 228, E. and H.

it is evident that the slave trade formed an important Jewish activity, the number of letters devoted to that question is due as much to the complicated issues involved, and the difficulty of ensuring that Jews did not possess Christian slaves, as it is to the number of Jews possessing slaves or indulging in the traffic. We see also Jewish peasants on the papal estates and Jewish slaves engaged in agriculture in North Italy. We see poor Jews who cannot afford their baptismal robe. We see Jews and Jewish converts to Christianity apparently living in amity, and we see also the reverse, Jewish converts in danger of molestation by Jews. There is the riotousness and oppression of a lawless age, and there is life going on quietly through it all with its manifold practical and missionary tasks.

Before turning from the picture to the painter it is worth looking at the attitude to the Jews of Gregory as theologian, to see if in it is reflected the practical and sympathetic administrator whom we know from the letters. His writings are voluminous, and as they are mainly biblical commentaries, they offer good ground for the study of his attitude to this question. If we had not his letters we would have absolutely no idea that he had ever had any contacts with Jews, or that he regarded them with anything but the deepest horror and loathing. There is no word of either sympathy or understanding, nor any desire to convert them. As his commentaries present an extreme case of the allegorical method, condemnatory references to the Jews are inevitable. When the Scriptures are divided into black and white in this way, the Jew must perforce be black. It will suffice to give one instance. Job's camels are stolen from him by Chaldeans descending in three hordes from the desert. Who are the three hordes? They are the Sadducees, the Pharisees, and the Scribes. Who are the camels? They are the Jews, whom these three hordes led away. How do we know that they are the Jews? Because the camel chews the cud, but has an undivided hoof. To chew the cud is clean, and the Law of God on which the Jews ruminate is clean. But the camel has an undivided hoof, and this shows that the Jews do not know how to discriminate what they read. It is a method by which the Jews become in turn wild asses, unicorns, basilisks and serpents. Even Saint Paul is found foreshadowed in a rhinoceros. At the same time he holds firmly that the Jews will ultimately be saved[1].

It is extremely difficult for the modern mind, accustomed to an entirely different method in the treatment of historical documents, to understand the way in which patristic writers remained entirely uninfluenced by contemporary relationships in their treatment of the Jews in biblical literature. The burning of a synagogue by a mob is a direct outcome of the intellectual gymnastics of the learned, who themselves would rarely have dreamed of committing such violence. The case of Gregory, the wise, sympathetic and practical administrator, is perhaps the most striking example of the situation, and accepting as we are bound to do the deep sincerity of his piety and charity, we cannot but ask ourselves how he could have tolerated anything so diametrically opposed to the rest of his personality, both as a Christian and as a practical statesman. While we cannot hope really to understand a man of the sixth century as one of his contemporaries might have understood him, we have already seen some of the reasons. The acceptance of the verbal inspiration of the Scriptures was undoubtedly a reason of extreme importance. The allegorical method of interpreting them, the belief that every verse had by divine action a secret meaning, was a second. But in this particular instance, we can probably add a third. The career of the Jews in its main lines was laid down by Paul. They were to remain unfaithful until the Gentiles were gathered in. Then all Israel was to be saved. This latter fact, as it were, took the edge off the violence of the denunciation of their past and present existence. A writer could let himself go to the full in his denunciation, because it only added to the miracle of their ultimate salvation. But even so it is a curious picture to think of Gregory turning from the dictation of one of his more flowery denunciations of their diabolical perversity and detestable characteristics to deal with his correspondence, and writing to a bishop who has only been carrying these denunciations into logical

[1] *On Job*, iii, 1; P.L., LXXV, p. 636; cf. xlii, 11; P.L., LXXV, p. 756. *On Ezekiel*, Bk. I, Homily 12; P.L., LXXV, p. 921, etc.

action, to remind him that it is by love and charity alone that we can hope to win them, and that even when they do not wish to be converted they must be treated with justice and allowed the undisturbed use of the rights which the Law allows them.

VI. THE PAPACY: HONORIUS, GREGORY III, STEPHEN AND HADRIAN

The next Pope of whom we have information is Honorius, who occupied the papal chair in 637. The sixth council of Toledo was informed that he had allowed baptised Jews to return to Judaism, and it expresses its horror at this permission[1]. In fact, the Pope was only carrying out the Roman law on the subject[2]. Whether the information received by the Visigothic bishops was true or not we do not know, nor have we the answer they received from the Pope, but the incident illustrates both the independence of the Pope and the independence of the local churches. For it is evident that Honorius no more succeeded in making the authorities of Spain conform to this wise toleration than Gregory himself was able to impose his will on the Frankish sovereigns.

Among the judgments of Gregory III (731) are two referring to Jews. In one, dealing with the adultery of a Christian with a Jewess, Gregory refers to the decision of the council of Elvira[3]. The other case is concerned with the date of Easter, and its celebration 'cum Judaeis'. Here also Gregory simply conforms to the usual canonical prohibition.

A letter from Stephen VI (768-772) to Aribert, Archbishop of Narbonne[4], shows that the Jews in that region still possessed far more rights over Christians than was permitted by either code or council. Both within and without the city they had Christians, both men and women, to cultivate their fields, and these slaves and servants were

[1] R.E.J., Vol. II, 137.

[2] C.T., 16.8.23.

[3] *Mansi*, XII, 294, referring to Elvira, Canon 78.

[4] P.L., CXXIX, 857, Aronius 67.

compelled to live with them and to share 'all their abominations'. According to Stephen the Jews based their position on 'some decree or other of the kings of France'. Septimania had only just returned to French rule. Under the Visigoths, a hundred years earlier, such a situation would certainly have been legally impossible. But apparently the rules against which Gregory had protested were still in force in France, and we have no information as to whether they were abolished on the protest of Stephen. Alternatively it is possible that the Franks were merely continuing in the newly acquired territory the favourable treatment which the Jews had received from the Arabs, and that by this time in the rest of the kingdom their privileges were reduced.

Hadrian, the successor of Stephen, was requested by Charlemagne to send him an abstract of conciliar law, and in this epitome the laws against the Jews are naturally represented. In particular Hadrian includes the law forbidding the celebration of Easter on the same date as the Jewish Passover, the acceptance of any gift from the Jews from their feasts, the giving of evidence by Jews against the clergy, and Judaising by resting on the Sabbath[1]. Of these laws Charlemagne only included two in the collection which he issued in the beginning of his reign. He forbade Jews to give evidence against Christians, and Christians to rest on the Sabbath[2]. Later he superseded the first law by composing a special Jewish oath.

Hadrian also corresponded with the Catholic bishops in Spain, where, after the Arab conquest, all sorts of heresies broke out, and where there was apparently some fraternising between Jews and Christians. This was natural, for both were minorities. His letters to them show the attitude typical of the Papacy: 'surely you are not ignorant of the canons'. He rebukes them for eating, drinking and living with Jews and unbaptised persons. And he reminds them that it is forbidden to do so. He supports his different arguments with patristic quotations, and throughout adopts an air of calmness and authority. His tone is one of surprise rather than abuse. He cannot understand

[1] *Mansi,* XII, pp. 867, 909 and 914.

[2] M.G.H.. folio, Leg. I, 57 and 61

how they do that which is forbidden by the canons and by all the Fathers of the Church[1].

That this was their attitude is also supported by the fact that the only conciliar legislation emanating from Rome during this period is a canon amplifying the ancient imperial prohibition either of intermarriage between Jews and Christians, or of selling Christian slaves to Jews[2].

Apart from Gregory the Great we have no information as to the conduct of the Popes within the papal patrimony, but from the fact that such information as we have shows the Popes carrying out the measures of the Theodosian Code and the earlier councils, we can assume that such was their general policy, and that they did not indulge either in the spasmodic cruelties of sudden expulsions, or in the determined severity of the Visigothic councils. Their power was not adequate to control their national clergy, but they themselves continued the equable tenor of their ways, showing no special favour to the Jews, but allowing them the rights which were theirs by law.

[1] *Mansi*, XII, 807 ff.

Conc. Romanum, Can. 10; *Mansi*, XII, 384.

CHAPTER SEVEN

LAW AND HISTORY IN THE BYZANTINE EMPIRE

BIBLIOGRAPHICAL INTRODUCTION

Apart from the inevitable treatment of this period in general terms in Jewish histories, the only special study of the subject is the valuable work by Dr. Krauss, which includes a section on the period covered by this chapter.

The main material for the study of the legal status of the Jews is naturally provided by the Codices of Theodosius and Justinian, together with, for the later centuries, the two editions of the Eclogues of Leo. The other Byzantine law books, in particular the Basilica, fall outside the period treated.

For historical material it is necessary to turn to the host of more or less inaccurate chroniclers. A list of the main works is given below; others are quoted in the relevant footnotes. Further material is from time to time being edited, especially in the *Revue de l'Orient chrétien*, and in the different journals of Byzantine history. In addition special material is occasionally to be found in the *Analecta Bollandiana.* To these sources must also be added the Syriac and Oriental Patrologies, and the Corpus Scriptorum Christianorum Orientalium, collections which are still in process of completion.

Apart from Michael the Syrian the later chroniclers are rarely quoted. Works such as those of Cedrenus add little to the information afforded by their predecessors, and the little needs to be viewed with suspicion. References to the later Byzantine chroniclers need always to be verified by comparison with earlier works: various modern histories quote such sources with unfortunate results. John of Nikious, Joshua the Stylite, or Sebeôs, who are almost or quite contemporary with the events which they describe, are themselves often inaccurate, but they are preferable to chroniclers such as Cedrenus.

Though the actual subject with which he deals is different, yet for a study of the mind and purpose of chroniclers, the introduction to Molinier's *Sources de l'Histoire de France* (Vol. V) is of considerable interest. A discussion of most of the writers will also be found in the relevant sections of Vasilief's *Histoire de l'empire Byzantin*.

LIST OF BOOKS

A. GENERAL

KRAUSS, S. *Studien zur Byzantinisch-Judischen Geschichte.* Wien, 1914.

B. LEGAL

CODEX THEODOSIANUS Ed. Mommsen and Meyer. Berlin, 1905.

CODEX JUSTINIANUS *Corpus Juris Civilis.* Ed. Krueger and Mommsen. Berlin, 1886.

SYRISCH-ROMISCHES RECHTSBUCH Ed. Bruns und Sachau. Leipzig, 1880.

ECLOGA LEONIS ET CONSTANTINI Ed. A. Monferratus. Athens, 1889.

ECLOGA LEONIS ET CONSTANTINI Collectio Librorum Iuris Graeco-Romani. Ed. Zachariae a Lingenthal. Leipzig, 1852.

ECLOGA LEONIS ET CONSTANTINI Rendered into English with an introduction by E. H. Freshfield. Cambridge, 1926.

ECLOGA PRIVATA AUCTA A revised Manual of Roman Law, Ed. Freshfield. Cambridge, 1926.

C. HISTORICAL

AGAPIUS *Universal History.* P.O., Vols. V, VII and VIII.

BARHADBESABBA 'ARBAIA *Ecclesiastical History.* P.O., IV and IX.

BARHEBRAEUS *Chronography.* Ed. Abbeloos et Lanuy. Louvain, 1872.

Barhebraeus	*Chronography*. A. W. Budge. Oxford, 1932.
Barhebraeus	*Chronography*. C.S.C.O. Scrp. Syr., Series 3, Tom. IV, xiii-xv.
Chron. Anon. II	C.S.C.O. Scrp. Syr., Series 3, Tom. IV, ii.
Chron. Edessenum	C.S.C.O. Scrp. Syr., Series 3, Tom. IV, i.
Chron. Pascale	P.G., Vol. XCII.
Dionysius of Tel Mahre	*Chronicle*, R.O.C., Vol. II, and Ed. J. B. Chabot. Paris, 1895.
Eutychius	*Annals*. Palestine Pilgrims Text Society, tr. A. Stewart, 1893, and P.G., CXI.
Evagrius	*Ecclesiastical History*. P.G., LXXXVI.
George Hamartolus	*Chronicles*. P.G., CX.
History of the Nestorian Church	P.O., IV, V and VII.
John of Ephesus	*History*. Ed. R. Payne Smith. Oxford, 1860.
John of Ephesus	*Lives of the Eastern Saints*. P.O. XVII, i; XVIII, iv; and XIX, ii.
John of Nikious	*Chronicle*. Ed. Zotenberg in *Notices et Extraits*, Vol. XXIV.
John of Nikious	*Chronicle*. Ed. R. H. Charles, Text and Translation Society, 1916.
Joshua Stylites	*Chronicle*. Ed. W. Wright, Cambridge, 1882.

MALALAS	*Chronography*. P.G., Vol. XCVII.
MICHAEL THE SYRIAN	*Chronicle*. Ed. J. B. Chabot. Paris, Leroux, 1899.
SEBEÔS	*History of Heraclius*. Ed. Fr. Macler. Paris, 1904.
SEVERUS OF ANTIOCH	*Letters*. Ed. E. W. Brooks, Text and Translation Society, 1904.
SOCRATES	*Ecclesiastical History*. P.G., Vol. LXVII. Tr. in Post Nicene Fathers.
SOZOMEN	*Ecclesiastical History*. P.G., Vol. LXVIII. Tr. in Post Nicene Fathers.
THEOPHANES	*Chronicle*. P.G., Vol. CVIII.
ZACHARIAH OF MITYLENE	*Chronicle*. Ed. Hamilton and Brooks. Methuen, 1899.

I. THE REIGN OF ARCADIUS

While there are few incidents to relate of Jewish history in the west during the fifth century, and while the legislation affecting them is not conspicuous for violence, the situation in the eastern provinces was very different. Arcadius, who succeeded to the eastern portion of the dominions of Theodosius the Great, was an inexperienced boy of seventeen. Power lay with a succession of favourites. Such a situation was unfortunate at a time when the empire was passing through a period of grave internal conflict and external invasion. It is on a troubled background that the legislation affecting the Jews was passed, and the disorders of the time had their natural repercussions on their situation.

Apart from the evidence provided by the laws themselves we know little of the relations between Jews and Christians during the reign of Arcadius. But that is enough to reveal that the fiery teaching of such men as Chrysostom at Antioch and Cyril at Jerusalem was bearing its inevitable fruit. The Jews had to suffer the attacks of both officials and ecclesiastics. A petty vexation which was forbidden by a law of 396 was the interference with the Jewish slave markets[1]. This cannot be a question of the sale of Christian slaves, for the emperor gives complete protection to the Jews. It was, apparently, mere officiousness. A more direct consequence of the attitude of the preachers is to be seen in the attacks upon the character and dignity of the Patriarch, despite his very high rank in the official nobility[2]. He was not only insulted, but his rights were questioned and his officials challenged. Nor was this all, for Christians were not confining themselves merely to petty vexations and verbal insults. As in the west, they were attacking and destroying synagogues and assaulting their Jewish occupants[3]. The edict which refers to these outrages is addressed specifically to the governor of Illyricum and may imply that the idea came from the west, but it is more probable

[1] C.T., 16.8.10.

[2] *Ibid.* 16.8.11 and 15.

[3] *Ibid.* 16.8.12; cf. 16.8.21 addressed to the same governor.

that it was due to the disorder in the province which accompanied the raids of Alaric and the Visigoths into that region. This province was still in disorder fifteen years later.

The economic situation of the Jews, which led them in the west to seek sanctuary and conversion to avoid their debts, declared itself twenty years earlier in the east, and such conversions were viewed with the same suspicion. But instead of allowing them to return to Judaism Arcadius permitted the violation of sanctuary, and ordered their expulsion therefrom until their debts were paid[1]. His policy with regard to curial responsibilities vacillated. At first he gave them a very broad immunity[2]. It was probably this law which so troubled Honorius, and which he prophesied would lead to the economic ruin of his provinces. Arcadius soon made the same discovery, for this liberal policy only lasted two and a half years, at the end of which time Jews, in the east as in the west, were all compelled to take their share in this office[3].

The extent to which Arcadius actually increased the restrictions from which they suffered is uncertain, for the laws of his reign, or of the years immediately following it, are not complete. He reduced their judicial autonomy[4]: so much is certain; but he also, apparently, took away from them the right of giving evidence in a Christian court. A law to this effect and of this date is to be found included in the Canons of the African Church[5], and it would hardly be incorporated into an ecclesiastical collection unless it were supported by imperial approval, and therefore by the existence of a parallel imperial prohibition. It would also appear that either he or Theodosius II prohibited the building of further synagogues, for such a law was in force in 415 at the time of the degradation of the Patriarch[6]. The sermons of Chrysostom at Antioch would lead one to suspect that these two laws were passed during the period (398-404) of his Patriarchate.

[1] C.T., 9.45.2; cf. 16.8.23.

[2] *Ibid.* 16.8.13.

[3] *Ibid.* 12.1.165. Cf. Ch. VI, Section II.

[4] C.T., 2.1.10.

[5] Canon 196, in P.L., LXVII, p. 959.

[6] Cf. 16.8.22.

The only evidence which we possess of Jewish retaliation for this increasing oppression is to be found in a life of the brigand monk Barsauma, who, when a young man, visited Palestine (about 400), and was much persecuted by Jews and Samaritans during his visit, ' for there were few Christians in Palestine, and the Jews and Samaritans who dominated the country persecuted them '[1]. Jerome, who was living at Bethlehem at that time, and who was certainly no friend of the Jews, relates nothing which could be called persecution. In view of the character and subsequent life of Barsauma it would be unwise to state that dislike of that individual was evidence of any general condition of affairs.

The reaction of the Jews to the century through which they had passed was more likely bewilderment and fear. We hear nothing as yet of revenge apart from the single rising in Samaria in the time of Constantius. But this was the rebellion of a compact population, an easier action than reprisals on the part of isolated communities. Their increasing subjection seems to have inclined them rather to a revival of Messianic speculation, for at this period a Messiah, calling himself Moses, appeared in Crete, and persuaded thousands that he would lead them across the sea to Palestine. In this belief they leapt from the cliffs, and would all have been drowned had not a considerable number been rescued by Christians whose curiosity or charity had led them to watch the affair from boats. Not unnaturally the reaction from the failure led to a number of conversions[2].

II. THEODOSIUS II AND THE THEODOSIAN CODE

The reign of Theodosius II introduces a new note into legislation, a note of petulance and undisguised dislike, showing itself in blustering and insulting language, and betraying the weakness and incompetence of parts at least of the imperial administration. The causes for this intensification of the hostility to the Jews are manifold.

[1] *Life of Barsauma*, by F. Nau in R.O.C., 1913.

[2] Socrates, *Hist. Eccl.*, VII, xxxviii, in P.G., LXVII, p. 825.

The breakdown of society through the presence of the barbarians and the economic collapse were general causes. A more specific cause was the emergence of a lawless monasticism, especially in Syria. As the Jewish communities of the eastern half of the Mediterranean were larger and more aggressive than in the west the results are unhappily easy to foresee.

The legislation of Theodosius opens with a complaint about the Jewish method of celebrating Purim, the feast which commemorates the deliverance of the Jews from Haman, and at which riotous behaviour was common. The Jews were forbidden to burn the image of Haman or to use the feast for the purpose of mocking the cross. If they continued to commit such unlawful acts they would 'lose what had so far been lawful privileges '[1]. This was no vague complaint, for ten years later an actual case is recorded from Inmestar. There the Jews took a Christian boy and, in drunken revelry, proceeded to hang him on a cross and so used him that he died. There was naturally an outcry at such an action, and the authorities heavily punished the guilty parties[2]. The authenticity of the narrative is vouched for by the fact that no miracles were worked through the body of the boy victim. A similar example of drunken riotousness in Alexandria is reported only by a late chronicler. There some Jews who had been forcibly baptised took a statue of Christ and crucified it, mocking the Christians and crying 'that is your Messiah'. A riot naturally followed, and many Jews and Christians were killed[3].

Alexandria is the scene of much more serious trouble a few years later. As a result of real or fancied provocation

[1] C.T., 16.8.18.

[2] Socrates, *Hist. Eccl.*, VII, xvi; P.G., LXVII, p. 769. It is a mistake to call this a case of ' ritual murder ' though there is no reason to suspect the authenticity of the narrative, as does Juster (Vol. II, p. 204).

[3] Agapius, in the section covering the third to sixth year of Theodosius; P.O., VIII, p. 408.

Zotenburg, in *Notices et Extraits*, Vol. XXIV, p. 467, n. 1, refers to another Arab chronicler (whom I have not been able to trace) who recounts an event similar to that at Inmestar as having happened at Alexandria. It is probably the incident referred to by Agapius, and both may be a confused memory of the miraculous image of Beirut referred to below, Chap. VIII, Section VI.

in the theatre, the Jews entice the Christians into the streets at night on a false alarm that the great church is burning, and proceed to massacre many of them. The following day, led by Cyril himself, the Christians fall on the Jews, completely pillage the Jewish quarter and expel the Jews from the city, killing many of them in the process[1]. It is a waste of time to attempt to allot blame to one side or the other for events occurring in that city, but it is probable that the events of Inmestar and Alexandria were responsible for the most serious blow the Jews had yet suffered from Roman legislation, the degradation of the Patriarch Gamaliel. It would appear that he himself was also to blame for this step, for he had been assuming powers which the law did not allow him. He had been building new synagogues. He had been arrogating to himself the right to judge cases in which Christians were involved. He had been circumcising slaves and possessing Christian slaves[2]. His degradation was equivalent to the abolition of his office, but the funds which the Patriarch had received were still paid by the Jews to their leaders in Palestine, until this also was abolished by Theodosius some years later, and the sums were ordered to be paid to the charities section of the privy purse[3].

Gamaliel was not the only offender against the law relative to slaves, for it was necessary to re-enact it with fresh severity and precision. A Jew was not to buy, or acquire as a gift, a Christian slave. If he acquired him as trustee or by inheritance, or if he was a heretical Christian, he might keep him on condition that he did not convert him to Judaism. For the infringement of the law the excessive penalty of capital punishment and complete confiscation was enacted[4].

Official hostility was more than equalled by mob violence. In 418 (or 412) the emperor has to refer to 'the widespread burning of synagogues and houses, and the assaults on individuals' and to remind the populace that there are law courts in which Jews who commit crimes will be

[1] Socrates, *Hist. Eccl.*, VII, xiii; P.G., LXVII, p. 760.

[2] C.T., 16.8.22.

[3] *Ibid.* 16.8.29.

[4] *Ibid.* 16.9.4.

punished. He adds that 'just as we wish to make provision for the benefit of the Jews, so we consider also that a warning should be addressed to them that they must not presume upon their security to commit outrages against the Christian faith '[1]. There is no reason to doubt that this double rebuke was necessary. How much effect it had on either side we cannot judge. We do not hear much of further Jewish rowdiness, and no law refers to it. In view of their tone and of the venomous language which is used towards the Jews, it is reasonable to assume that fear or prudence secured the respect of this law on the Jewish side. It had not the same effect on the Christians. The very year following its promulgation the sinister figure of Barsauma again appears in Palestine, accompanied by forty monks. For three years he destroys temples and synagogues in Palestine, unchecked[2]. The activity of Barsauma was purely destructive, but in other cases the synagogue buildings were seized and consecrated as churches. This happened at Edessa under Rabbulas, who became bishop in 411[3].

In 423 there was a change in policy, which is attributed by Dr. Nau to the marriage of the emperor, in the January of that year, to Eudoxia, who had been a pagan and whose uncle was Prefect of the Eastern Provinces[4]. The result is a law which lacks all the offensive language and attempts to deal firmly with the evil. The emperor orders that in future no synagogue in any district is to be pulled down or burnt. If any synagogue has been confiscated it is to be returned. If it has been consecrated as a church, a site of equivalent value is to be given in exchange. If furniture has been taken the same is to happen. The Jews, on the other hand, are not to build new synagogues (except presumably where the old one has been destroyed?) or to enlarge the existing buildings[5].

The law had no effect. Within two months the Jews are complaining to the emperor and demanding more

[1] C.T., 16.8.21.

[2] F. Nau in R.E.J., Vol. LXXXIII, p. 184.

[3] *Chron. Edess.* in C.S.C.O., S.S. III, iv, pt. 1; and Michael the Syrian, Bk. VI, x.

[4] R.E.J., LXXXIII.

[5] C.T., 16.8.25.

effective protection. This the emperor grants, but with a full return to the old offensive language and only the mildest reprobation of the offenders. 'Jews must know that to their wretched pleading we grant only this much, that those who are constantly acting illegally under the cloak of Christianity should abstain from outrages and assaults against them. Both now, and for the future, no one is to seize or burn down their synagogues.' It is noticeable that no penalty is attached if they do so, whereas at the tail end of the law Jews are threatened with perpetual exile and confiscation if they circumcise Christian slaves[1]—a matter entirely beside the point in a law dealing with the lawlessness of Christians, however serious it might be as a Jewish crime. It was in fact the most difficult of all the enactments against the Jews to enforce, and there was some reason for his indignation, for, a week later, the matter requires a separate law against the 'disgrace of servants of strong religious convictions being subjected to infidel owners'[2].

Laws which indulge in futile abuse of those whom they are meant to protect are not likely to be successful. The obvious reluctance with which they are granted is evidence to the lawless that their infringement will not be taken seriously. Yet it was the only protection which the Jews could obtain. The same method is again repeated two months later. 'Jews are not to build new synagogues, but they need not fear the confiscation of their old ones.' On the same day, in an edict which begins by denouncing with all kinds of threats Manichees, Pepyzites, and Quatuordecimans—matters irrelevant to the protection of Jewish property—he 'earnestly requests' Christians, 'whether real or pretended', not to defy religious authority and attack Jews or pagans who are living quietly and not offending against the laws. If they seize the goods of such people, they are to pay compensation to the extent of three or four times the value of the stolen article[3].

All these laws belonged to the same year, 423, and thereafter he gave up the attempt to protect the Jews. As a result

[1] C.T., 16.8.26.

[2] *Ibid.* 16.9.5.

[3] *Ibid.* 16.8.27, and 16.10.24.

the violation of synagogues continued, and when the emperor made an attempt to restore to the Jewish community at Antioch the synagogues which the Christians had stolen from them, the intervention of Simeon Stylites was enough to make him humbly apologise to the orthodox for his action and leave them their stolen property[1]. He himself authorised the confiscation of the Jewish synagogue in the Copper Market in Constantinople in 442[2]. At the same period Barsauma made a final appearance on the stage of Palestine. Infuriated by the permission which the empress had granted to the Jews to lament at the Wailing Wall, he instituted a general massacre of them in Jerusalem.

In the publication of his third novella Theodosius reverts to the more familiar method of denunciation and contempt. In a long theological exordium he makes a happy confusion between orthodoxy and monotheism, and expresses his wonder that heretics, Jews and Samaritans who contemplate the works of nature 'have wits so ensnared and souls so damned by the monstrosities of their beastliness' that they fail to seek an Author for mysteries so great. But, since they are in this condition, 'if we take the law as doctor to recall them to sanity, they themselves are answerable for our harshness, for their obstinacy leaves no room for forgiveness'. Therefore, 'whoever builds a synagogue shall know that he has laboured for the Catholic Church; whoever has wormed himself into office shall be degraded even if he has received decorations; whoever repairs a synagogue shall be fined fifty pounds; whoever corrupts the faith of a Christian shall be put to death'. However, imperial permission may be obtained for the repair of synagogues in imminent danger of collapse, but they must not be decorated; Jewish courts may deal with private cases between Jews; Jews may bear all the burdensome offices of the public administration[3]. Here the exclusion of Jews from all the privileges of public office is made much more definite than it is in any previous legislation

[1] Evagrius, *Hist. Eccl.*, I, xiii; P.G., LXXXVI, pt. 2, p. 2456; Metaphrastes, *Life of Simeon Stylites*; P.G., CXIV, p. 381.

[2] Theophanes, anno 442; P.G., CVIII, p. 265. Cf. Juster, Vol. I, p. 470, n. 2.

[3] Novella 3.

that we possess. But it is probable that previous legislation existed, and has been lost. In the anonymous Altercation between the Church and the Synagogue, which is to be found incorrectly included in the works of Augustine, we find this taunt addressed to the Synagogue: 'you pay me tribute and cannot obtain authority; you may not possess the Prefecture; a Jew may not be a Count; you may not enter the public services; you may not attain to the tables of the rich; you have lost the right to the title of *Clarissimus* '[1]. The dates of these restrictions, and their application to the eastern or western provinces, are unknown, but they apparently precede the publication of the third novella.

In all this novella any pretence that these laws are made necessary by Jewish rowdiness or lawlessness is abandoned; and, indeed, we know of only one case of such violence in the last thirty years of Theodosius. It is said that the Jews of Laodicea took the saintly archdeacon and 'punished' him in the theatre[2]. This incident is related in one of a collection of letters dealing with the Nestorian controversy, and it is possible that it has nothing at all to do with real Jews, but with Nestorians, who are frequently referred to by their adversaries simply as 'Jews'. This would make the narrative more comprehensible, for while it does not conform to any known Jewish outrages, it has a dozen parallels in the theological controversies of the fifth century.

III. THE TREATMENT OF HERETICS IN THE FIFTH CENTURY

In this century it is even more necessary than in the fourth to study the treatment of heretics and the battles between groups of different theological opinion, if a true perspective of the Jewish situation is to be obtained. In the fourth century the two groups had to bear the burden

[1] *Altercatio Synagogae et Ecclesiae*; P.L., XLII, p. 1133. This dialogue is considered to be a prototype of the mediaeval mystery play. Cf. Juster, Vol. II, p. 245, n. 4.

[2] Ep. of John of Antioch to Proclus of Constantinople in *Variorum Episcoporum Ep.*, ed. Chr. Lupus, Louvain, 1682.

of legal restrictions upon their civic and religious liberty. In this century riots and massacres must be added to the picture. The legislation against heretics shows the same petulance and narrowness as the legislation against the Jews, but even more weakness and instability. In 395 Arcadius deprived the Eunomians of all testamentary rights and expelled them from Constantinople. A few months later these disabilities were removed and they were allowed all their civil rights. But they were still refused permission to hold meetings. This mildness lasted a few months, and then they were again expelled[1], this time for three years, after which the order was again cancelled. In 395 all heretics were dismissed from the public services, an expulsion from which the Jews did not suffer until ten years later[2]. In 396 all their buildings, public and private, were confiscated to the Catholic Church[3]. At different periods either all heretics or particular groups, such as the Eunomians, Montanists or Manichees, were expelled either from Constantinople or from all the cities of the empire[4]. Individual heretics, such as the unhappy Jovianus who was to be sent into exile ' contusum plumbo,[5]' were also pursued by the secular as well as the ecclesiastical arm. Such a policy was extremely unprofitable both to the imperial finances and to the public services, and it is not surprising that such laws alternated with others in which they were either restored to their rights or at least driven to their duties[6].

These laws were less effective than those against the Jews, for they were continued after the Jewish community was apparently left in peace. Marcian in 455 issued a law in thirteen paragraphs against the Eutychians and Apollinarians in Constantinople and Alexandria which is worth quoting for its completeness[7]:

[1] C.T., 16.5.25, 27, 33 and 36.

[2] *Ibid.* 16.5.29.

[3] *Ibid.* 16.5.30.

[4] *Ibid.* 16.5.34 and 66.

[5] *Ibid.* 16.5.53.

[6] *E.g.* Nov. Th., 3, 6.

[7] C.J., 1.5.8.

All existing penalties for heresy are to be enforced against them.

They are to have no clergy, and any man found acting as a cleric is to be exiled and his property confiscated.

They are to have no right of meeting by day or night.

The property of any individual who has allowed them to meet on his estate is to be confiscated to the Catholics.

If the owner was not responsible for the invitation his agent is to be fined and beaten.

They are to be expelled entirely from the army and all public office.

They are to be allowed no opportunity for explaining their doctrines.

They are not to write or publish anything against the Council of Chalcedon.

They are to possess no books.

Any one who listens to them is to be fined.

The books of the Apollinarians are to be publicly burnt.

Any official who fails to carry out these rules is to be fined.

Such was the success of the famous utterance of Theodosius the Great: 'omnibus vetitae legibus et divinis et imperialibus haereses perpetuo quiescant'[1]. But Marcian was not the first to discover that the great emperor's prohibition had exceeded his power. Theodosius II had pathetically forbidden the Nestorians to call themselves Christians, in the same spirit as his grandfather had forbidden all heretics to believe that their views were true[2]. Marcian was more prosaic, but more practical.

His law allows of an interesting comparison with the Jewish legislation up to the same period. The heretics were to have no clergy: this could not be done to the Jew, but the Jewish clergy had been deprived of their immunities from curial service. They were to have no meeting place: as we have seen, anti-Jewish legislation went as near this as possible in forbidding new synagogues to be built or old ones to be repaired. Any property on which they were allowed to meet was to be confiscated to the Catholic

[1] C.T., 16.5.5.

[2] *Ibid.* 16.5.37.

Church: any new synagogues which the Jews built were confiscated to the same body. If any agent allowed their meeting without the knowledge of the owner, he was to be beaten or fined: here the owner fared better than the Jew who allowed his slaves to be circumcised, for he shared the same punishment as if he had circumcised them himself. They were to be expelled from the army and public life: so was the Jew. They were to have no opportunity of explaining their doctrines: the efforts of the Church were continually directed to preventing the Jews from explaining their doctrines to Christians, but the Codes only recognised the crime of actual secession to Judaism. Heretics were not to write, speak or publish anything against the Chalcedon formula: it was centuries before so direct a prohibition was addressed to Jews, but the thin end of the wedge is the prohibition to the Jews to celebrate Purim in a manner offensive to Christians; and Gregory the Great acts on a lost law by which they could be prohibited from disturbing a church with the noise of their singing. They were to possess no books: Justinian will forbid the Jews to use their interpretations (deuterosis) in the synagogue. Any who listened to them were to be punished: an apostate to Judaism was always liable to severe punishment.

Another set of laws offer a contrast rather than a comparison. It has already been said that the violence of the monks was one of the most unhappy features of the time. Arcadius was compelled on several occasions to forbid them to enter any city, or to leave their deserts[1]. Twice also he had to forbid them to interfere with the course of justice[2], and to complain that 'their insolence is such that they behave as if it were a battle in question and not a lawsuit'. These laws were no more effective than those against heretics. Theodosius in 445 was compelled to take steps to keep them out of Constantinople[3]. Leo in 459 found them occupying public buildings, and, by introducing into them some sacred object, claiming that they could no longer be used for their original purpose, whether

[1] C.T., 16.3.1 and 2.

[2] *Ibid.* 9.40.16 and 11.30.57 of July 398.

[3] C.J., 1.3.32.

pleasure or business[1]. During the period laws had also to be passed to prevent the 'tumultuosa conventicula' of religious discussion[2]. It particularly distressed Marcian that these disorderly meetings allowed an opportunity for Jews to mock at Christianity[3]. The reality of the disgraceful violence against which the emperors legislated in vain is to be seen not merely in the accounts of the writers of the time but in official documents. In the attempt to make peace between the warring theologians the emperor Zeno issued his ill-fated 'Henoticon', in which he speaks of the 'thousands who have perished in massacres, so that not only the earth but even the air is contaminated with blood'[4]. The histories and chronicles are full of bloody battles and murderous riots between Orthodox, Monophysite and Nestorian; and often it was not even a theological difference but personal jealousy that resulted in such horrors. Michael the Syrian says that 'when the Chalcedonians stopped persecuting the "orthodox", they began to attack each other with a violence such as a savage would not use to a pagan, a Jew, or a heretic'[5]. Against such a background the Jews seem an absolutely peaceful and favoured people, and if we may legitimately say that this is only one side of the life of the fifth-century Christians, and that there was a more attractive side, then we must in justice say the same of such incidents of Jewish violence as are reported.

IV. THE JEWS OF ANTIOCH

In actual fact we only know of one anti-Christian outbreak during the fifth century, apart from the more individual incidents already mentioned. This was a Samaritan rising which took place during the reign of Zeno, and led to con-

[1] C.J., 1.3.26.

[2] C.T., 16.4.4, 5 and 6.

[3] C.J., 1.1.4.

[4] Evagrius, *Hist. Eccl.*, III, xiv. P.G., LXXXVI, pt. 2, p. 2621. Michael the Syrian, IX, vi. Cf. Zachariah of Mitylene, III, vi, and Acts of Council of Constantinople in P.O., II, pp. 341 and 353.

[5] *Op. cit.*, X, xiii.

siderable bloodshed on both sides before it was suppressed[1]. On the other hand the Jews of Antioch, who had already lost their synagogues in the time of Theodosius, lost the synagogue of Daphne also, in a riot of the circus faction of the 'Greens' in 489 or 490. This is the first occasion on which the faction of the 'Greens' appears in Jewish history[2]. On hearing that they had also burnt the bones of many Jews, the emperor is said to have remarked that it was a waste of time to burn dead Jews when many were still alive whom they could have better burned. The Jews appear to have been allowed to rebuild the synagogue, for it was again destroyed twenty years later in another riot. This time they lost it permanently, for the Christians immediately built and consecrated a church upon the ruins, dedicated to the Martyr Leontius[3]. Antioch at this time seems to have possessed much of the turbulence which was a permanent feature of Alexandria, for order was only restored with great difficulty and a considerable force of soldiers.

We should be better informed of the situation if we possessed a larger number of the letters of the monophysite Patriarch Severus. He is said to have published nearly four thousand letters of which only a few hundred have survived. Had we the whole collection we should probably have as good a picture of Antioch in the beginning of the sixth century as we have of Italy at the end of it in the letters of Gregory. For in the little that is left we see several references to Jews. Writing to Theodosius of Alexandria, he ends by saying that the letter has been written 'under the domination of the fear of the Jews'[4]. Two letters to the bishop of Berrhoea, a city fifty miles east of Antioch, also refer to Jewish outrages of some kind, which Severus wishes the bishop to repress with severity. The Patriarch has discussed the matter with the governor, who will support the bishop's action[5]. In another letter he refers to some

[1] Malalas, XV; P.G., XCVII, p. 568; Michael the Syrian, IX, vi; *Chron. Pascale*, *sub anno* 484.

[2] Dionysius of Tel Mahre in R.O.C., II, p. 462; Malalas, XVI; P.G., XCVII, p. 585.

[3] John of Nikious, Ch. lxxxix.

[4] Zachariah of Mitylene, IX, xxiv.

[5] *Letters*, ed. Brooks, Bk. I, Nos. 15 and 16.

question affecting slaves[1]. Unhappily all the references are incomplete, and refer to incidents of which we have no other information; but they show that Antioch was a centre of tension liable at any moment to break into violent hostility. A century later it is again the scene of trouble. In reaction against the order for their compulsory baptism in the reign of Phocas, the Jews broke into a riot, and seizing the Patriarch Anastasius murdered him with every brutality and dragged his body through the streets. Many other prominent Christians were murdered, and troops had again to be called in to quell the disturbance[2].

It is not entirely fanciful to connect the long story of disturbance at Antioch with the inflammatory addresses of Chrysostom given half a century before. It may well be that the Jews of Antioch were both powerful and aggressive. If they were so, they shared these characteristics with the Christians of that city. In such a situation it would have better become a priest to have tried to calm tempers rather than to inflame them with as complete an absence of interest in veracity as is shown by Chrysostom. In view of the affection of the people of Antioch for the later Patriarch of Constantinople, and the halo of persecution which surrounds his death in exile, it is to be expected that the Antiochians guarded jealously the copies of the sermons which he had delivered from their pulpits, and among them his long series directed against the Jews.

V. THE LEGISLATION OF JUSTINIAN

These disturbances at Antioch, and the still graver disturbances of the following centuries, are also largely the consequence of repressive legislation. Though the unity which Justinian restored to the empire proved but transitory, and though his ceaseless wars only resulted in permanently weakening the eastern provinces, on which the power of Byzantium relied, yet in his legislation he left an enduring mark upon the history of the Jews. The eighth century

[1] *Letters*, Bk. I, No. 52.

[2] Theophanes, sub anno 601; P.G., CVIII, p. 624. Ephraem Mon. *Lib. Imp. et Pat.* in Cor. Scrip. Byz., XI, p. 62; Michael the Syrian, X, xxv.

Eclogues of Leo, and the Basilica of Basil a century later, are both entirely based upon his work. In western Europe the Theodosian Code and its barbarian recensions were to hold the field for many centuries to come, but in the Middle Ages the influence of Justinian was to be felt in the west also.

Justinian found in the Codex of Theodosius over fifty laws dealing with the Jews. Of these he retained a little less than half, discarding the others as superfluous or as no longer applicable. In some cases these omissions, however, meant the abolition of real Jewish privileges. Not only were the laws issued at the beginning of the fifth century for the protection of Jews and Judaism omitted[1], but the formal statement of the legality of Judaism itself, issued by Theodosius the Great[2], found no place in the new statute book. All statements of immunities to be granted to synagogue officials were also dropped, especially the law of Arcadius putting them on the same basis as the clergy of the Christian Church[3]. Neither the Patriarchate nor the Aurum Coronarium were revived, but this was not to be expected. But there seems no reason why he should have dropped the laws allowing them their right of excommunication[4], or their right to try with their own judges cases affecting their own law[5].

In retaining laws of earlier emperors the legal experts of Justinian used a perfect freedom in altering the texts, and in adding, or more usually omitting, paragraphs. The versions in the two texts are very rarely word for word parallel. In some cases these omissions concerned simply the hysterical verbiage with which emperors such as Theodosius II had emphasised their orthodoxy. In other cases parts of a law contradicted other legislation on the same subject. In yet others penalties were made more or less severe.

The laws exercising the most important influence on the economic status of the Jews were those which gave or refused

[1] C.T., 16.8.2 and 20.

[2] *Ibid.* 16.8.9.

[3] *Ibid.* 16.8.13.

[4] *Ibid.* 16.8.8.

[5] *Ibid.* 2.1.10, which Justinian repeats with the omission of the one word which excepts these cases from Roman jurisdiction. Cf. C.J., 1.9.15.

permission for the unrestricted ownership of slaves. Justinian showed himself more severe than his predecessors in this matter. Christian, that is Catholic, slaves were to be released according to previous legislation[1], but in addition if an heretical slave wished to become Catholic he was also to be released and his master could not regain possession of him by following him to the font[2]. For some reason this law was addressed in the first instance to Africa, where the problem was found to be acute, but its main interest is that for the first time it entrusts the ecclesiastical authorities as well as the civil magistrates with its enforcement. What penalty Justinian attached to the possession of a Christian slave is not clear. According to the law just quoted the offender was sentenced to death; but a further law, which may or may not precede it in date, fixes the penalty at a fine of thirty pounds[3]. Justinian also restricted their right to acquire property, by forbidding them to lease land either from a church or religious order, or from any other owner, if a religious building happened to stand upon some part of it[4]. Not only the Jew but also the owner suffered severely if he offended against the law. The only cases in which these laws were not valid were those arising out of trusteeship. A Jew was compelled to accept trusteeship for a Christian minor, for trusteeship gave him possession of the property only and not the person of the ward[5].

In the Theodosian Code there are two laws affecting Jews who, to avoid their debts, take refuge in the churches. An earlier law of Arcadius ordered them to be refused admission. A later law of Honorius allowed them to return to Judaism unmolested if they had fled to the church for economic and not spiritual reasons. Justinian retained the former, but omitted the latter[6]. What testamentary rights the Jew retained is not quite clear. Converts to Judaism were deprived of these rights by a law of Theodosius the Great, and though Justinian omits the greater part of

[1] C.T., 16.9.1, 2 and 4.

[2] C.J., 1.3.54, paras. viii to xi.

[3] *Ibid.* 1.10.2.

[4] Nov. 131.

[5] Digest, 27.1.15. vi. Buckland, *Text Book of Roman Law*, p. 154.

[6] C.T., 9.45.2=C.J., 1.12.1. The law omitted is C.T., 16.8.23.

this law, such cases are probably covered by the general denial of such rights to all non-Catholics in Novella 118. If the alleged convert was dead his will could be set aside on his conversion being proved[1]. If the heirs of a Jew became Catholics, then they were still to be entitled to special privileges in inheritance[2]. Otherwise it would seem that the Jews retained normal testamentary rights and were not affected by the general prohibition of the Novella[3]. The main economic privilege which they retained unchanged was the right to fix their own market prices[4].

The hostile influences visible in the regulation of their economic status are also evident in the attitude taken towards their civic rights. Not only were all the laws granting certain officials immunity from curial service omitted, but the exclusion from the honours of office was strengthened. If any Jew was found in a position of authority over Christians he was not merely to be degraded, as previously, but also to be fined[5]. Moreover, the most elementary privileges of rank were to be denied him: immunity from arrest, immunity from transference to other provinces, and all similar immunities. Equally serious was the inclusion of the legal profession among the prohibited honours. As in the laws controlling the possession of slaves, here also the ecclesiastical authorities were given permission to watch over and enforce obedience. The curtailment of their jurisdiction has already been mentioned. But Justinian also curtailed their right to give evidence. So far a Jew, not otherwise disqualified as a criminal, was entitled to give evidence on any question and in any suit. But now, in two separate laws, this right was restricted[6]. In the first place no Jew could give evidence in a suit in which either party was a Catholic Christian. He could give evidence only where it was a matter exclusively affecting Jews or heretics. Even so

[1] C.J., 1.7.2.
[2] *Ibid.* 1.5.13.
[3] Juster, Vol. II, p. 92.
[4] C.J., 1.9.9.
[5] *Ibid.* 1.9.18. and 1.5.12.
[6] *Ibid.* 1.5.21 and Nov. 45.

he was better off than Samaritans and members of certain heretical sects who were not allowed to give evidence in any case whatever. But this rigidity soon proved to be unworkable, and in a Novella certain exceptions are made. A Jew is entitled to act as witness to a will or contract by the earlier law. By the Novella he is also allowed to give evidence *for* the Catholic in a suit between a Catholic and a heretic, and, if one party to the suit be the State, he is allowed to give evidence for the State against a Catholic. This was especially to be allowed when the State was proceeding against a defaulter from curial duties. There is vague evidence that the Jews also suffered another disability, exclusion from the protection afforded by the law limiting the right to bring an action to within thirty years of the event. In certain editions of the Syrian Roman Law book of the fifth century the phrase is used ' if a man who is a Christian . . .', thereby apparently excluding Jews[1]. In the Code of Justinian the law, which was issued by Theodosius II, makes no mention of ' Christian '[2]. It is possible, therefore, that either he abolished the restriction, or that it only existed in Syria. For the Jews to recover a privilege which they had lost would have been an unusual, almost an unprecedented, event, and the latter alternative is the more probable one. The different versions of the Eclogues of Leo show that there were often variants in practice within the empire.

It was not to be expected that an emperor who dealt thus hardly with their economic and civic status would leave their religious position unchallenged. The dropping of the Law which expressly states the right of Judaism to exist left the Jews at the mercy of the sovereign. He could either tolerate or control them as he willed. In theory they were, with all other heretics including pagans, without any rights whatever. This is laid down in one of the earliest laws of Justinian extant, passed while he was still co-emperor with his father[3]. He was therefore within

[1] *Syrisch-Römisches Rechtsbuch,* ed. Bruns und Sacher, paragraph 45 in the Arabic and 53 in the Armenian text. Some texts, however, read only ' if a man . . . '.

[2] C.T., 4.14.1; C.J., 7.39.3.

[3] C.J., 1.5.12.

his legal rights when he confiscated all their synagogues in Africa, and handed them over to the Catholic Church[1]. Nor could the Jews of Borion make any legal protest when he forced them, according to Procopius, to accept baptism[2]. But these excesses were exceptional. Normally, so long as they remained inoffensive, they were left undisturbed, and he retained on the statute book laws ordering their synagogues to be respected, and protecting them against vexations on the Sabbath[3]. But the penalty for stealing their goods was reduced from a triple or quadruple to a double restitution.

In the main Justinian left in force the restrictions imposed by previous emperors. The death penalty was imposed on those who attacked Jewish converts to Christianity[4]. But the convert to Judaism was only punished by exile and the confiscation of his goods[5]. The accusation could be made after the death of the apostate. Jewish polygamy and intermarriage with Christians remained prohibited[6]. But a Jew could marry a Christian on accepting Christianity. The prohibition of uproarious behaviour at the feast of Purim naturally remained in force, but the privilege of attending Christian services up to the ' missa Catechumenorum ' was withdrawn, at least for Africa[7]. This reverses a previous ecclesiastical canon of the African Church[8]. The prohibition against building synagogues and the restrictions on repairs remained unchanged[9]. In fact, it is evident that they were strictly enforced, for the chroniclers have several references to the collapse of synagogues in succeeding centuries. Already before the time of Justinian there is record of the collapse of the synagogue of Beirut in an earthquake[10]. During his reign all the

[1] Nov. 37. See Juster, Vol. I, p. 251, on the text of this law.

[2] Procopius, *De Aedif.*, VI, ii.

[3] C.J., 1.9.4 (C.T., 7.8.2.); C.J., 1.9.13 (C.T., 2.8.26); C.J., 1.9.14 (C.T., 16.8.21); C.J., 1.11.6 (C.T., 16.10.24); see also C.J., 1.9.2.

[4] C.J., 1.9.3=C.T., 16.8.1.

[5] C.J., 1.7.1 and 2=C.T., 16.8.7 and 16.7.3.

[6] C.J., 1.9.6 and 7.

[7] Nov. 37.

[8] Carthage, IV, Can. 84; *Mansi*, III, p. 958.

[9] C.J., 1.9.18.

[10] Joshua Stylites, Ch. xlvii.

synagogues of Laodicea collapsed under similar circumstances, but the earthquake did not touch a single church[1]. In another earthquake of the eighth century thirty synagogues of Tiberias collapsed[2]. It is also possible that by local legislation which has perished, or by the chicanery of local officials, the Jews of Borion were not the only community to lose their synagogue altogether, for when during the Monophysite controversy Justinian confiscated all the Monophysite churches of Alexandria, 'they took counsel together to build themselves another church, lest they should be like the Jews'[3]. The last phrase certainly suggests that there were Jewish communities with no place of worship.

But the most surprising innovation of Justinian is the attempt in Novella 146 to regulate Jewish beliefs and services. All such questions as synagogue procedure and Jewish belief had been considered to be matters entirely within Jewish jurisdiction. The Jews were wrong in what they held, but, that admitted, how they held it was a matter of little account. Even the writers who included Jewish beliefs in their heresies, such as Epiphanius and Philastrius, showed extremely little accurate knowledge of the positive content of those beliefs. Mostly—like later antisemites—they seized on a single point to ridicule, as does Epiphanius when he describes the main doctrine of the Pharisees as astrology. To their minds the denunciations of the prophets provided adequate material for a complete knowledge of what the Jews of the third or fourth century A.D. actually believed. But in these regulations Justinian or his advisers show that much more accurate knowledge was available, and when needed could be put to use—to the only use conceivable to the Church authorities, which was to bring the Jews out of their darkness to a true belief in the Incarnation.

The occasion of the law was a conflict within the synagogue as to the language in which the Scriptures should be read. An appeal was made to the emperor by the party which did not understand Hebrew, demanding that the

[1] Malalas, XVIII; P.G., XCVII, p. 652.

[2] Michael the Syrian, XI, xxii.

[3] *History of the Patriarchs of Alexandria*, P.O., I, p. 467.

Law should be officially read in a language which they could understand. The reply of Justinian goes far beyond the request made to him. Not only does he side with the party making the petition, but he demands the excommunication of certain Jewish sects and forbids certain usual portions of the synagogue service.

As to the reading of the Scriptures, he orders that they shall be read in Greek, Latin, or any other language which is understood by the congregation. He then goes on to forbid the explanation which was always given after the reading—the technical question as to what is actually implied in this prohibition is of great importance from the point of view of synagogue worship, but is a side issue for the present study[1]. Finally he orders the excommunication of those who deny that angels are part of the creation, or who disbelieve in the resurrection and the judgment. Such persons are to be expelled from the synagogue and handed over to execution. Those who contravene the other portions of the law are to be beaten, exiled and their property confiscated.

To introduce punishable heretical categories into the already heretical beliefs of Judaism was an extraordinary innovation. For the study of Jewish sects the information which this law affords is of special interest, since it shows the survival of Sadducaic doctrine into the sixth century. But Judaism itself has always been extraordinarily tolerant of differences of belief, and it is difficult to believe that the inspiration of this section of the law was Jewish in origin. Its purpose must be sought not in an attempt of one Jewish party to move the imperial power against the other, but in the Christian intention obvious behind the whole law, and clearly visible in the comments with which it is interspersed.

For the law is obviously intended to undermine from within the powers of resistance of Talmudic Judaism to Christian missionary activity. Whatever may be exactly implied in the interpretations which he prohibits, he clearly has in mind the Talmudic method of biblical comment. He is referring to what later develops into 'pilpul', but

[1] For a discussion of this question see Krauss, *op. cit.*, p. 57 ff., and Juster, Vol. I, p. 369 ff.

which was not a specifically Jewish characteristic at this time. Had he demanded that the Christian theologians also abandon interpretations which stray a long way from their text, the body of patristic literature would find itself reduced to a far more manageable size. It is, however, the content of the teaching which he has in mind. He is embodying in legislation the complaint frequently made by Jerome and others that the Jewish teachers *consciously* and *deliberately* gave teaching which falsified the meaning of the original text, and therefore prevented the congregation, which could not itself understand Hebrew, from seeing the continual allusions to the coming of the Messiah in Jesus, and to the passing of the Promises to the Christian Church. From the standpoint of sixth-century orthodoxy his action is logical and right. To them the conventional Christian interpretation of the Scriptures was the only possible and sensible one. It leapt to the eye from every text. Therefore the Jew must be allowed an unrestricted view of the text.

To make assurance doubly sure, he not only forbids the giving of rival interpretations, but he lays down which translations are to be used. They must choose between the Septuagint and the version of Aquila, for these two were felt to give the translations which most clearly vindicated the claims of Christian exegesis.

These two prohibitions are a logical result of his whole attitude. For the entire law is not only unwarrantable, but also inexplicable, except upon the basis that the Church accepted as absolutely true the Scriptures which were read by the Synagogue. Preachers might and did affirm that the Jews neither understood nor appreciated them, but the fact remained that they still possessed them, and could not legally be deprived of their use. Justinian decided to go to the root of the matter. His law is not 'antisemitic'. It is 'grandmotherly'. It is far removed from the violent but conventional strictures of the pulpit, or even from other laws contained in the Code of Justinian himself, where the Jews are described in far from flattering terms. It is a serious attempt to make the Jews convert themselves. The method is that adopted by the Protestants at the Reformation, in their belief that the corrupt power of the mediaeval Church would be best destroyed by putting into people's hands the actual words of the Bible in the language which they could best understand. So Justinian, instead of the ' handiwork of man speaking only of earthly things, and having nothing of the divine in it ', offers them the chance ' to start afresh to learn the better way, and to cease to stray vainly in error upon the fundamental point of hope in God '.

Though the effort was a failure, and mistaken in its hopes, it remains the most interesting attempt of the time to solve the Jewish question. There is a more truly Christian spirit behind it than there is behind most of the contemporary legislation. Toleration could not in that age be expected to go further. As a precedent it was unfortunate, for it opened the door to obvious abuses. That such an effort, made by an outsider in a moment of tension and repression, could succeed was impossible. But in a conglomerate of restrictions, denunciations and sneers, it stands out as the only measure dictated by a sincere attempt to understand why Jew and Christian had drifted so far apart. Its diagnosis of the cause was a mistaken one. But it is surprising that in that age so serious an attempt at diagnosis should have been made.

The work of Justinian is the last Roman attempt at unified Christian legislation affecting the Jews. From time to time in future centuries the papacy will attempt to recreate this unity, but without success. Already in the west the Jews are suffering in one quarter while they are at peace in another. Their treatment depends on the power of clergy or of kings, on the religious ideas of the age in question, or on the economic importance of the particular Jewish community.

At the same time the seeds of all later legislation are contained in that of Justinian and his predecessors. No fundamentally new step will be taken until France has the courage to proclaim and put into practice their total equality with other citizens. The right to interfere with their political, their economic, their juridical status is already conceded. The novella just discussed is the precedent for the burning of the Talmuds by the Sorbonne in the thirteenth century. The temporary actions of Justinian in Africa are precedents for the forced baptisms operated again and again in Spain and elsewhere. The destruction of synagogues finds its first legal authority in him. Finally, he first invites the ecclesiastical arm to carry out laws affecting the civil rights and civil status of the Jews. The extension of these restrictions ultimately produces the complete exclusion of the Jew from normal life, concentrates him into a few professions in which he may become, or be thought to become, a menace to the community, and creates the Jewish type, in so far as such a type exists, which is the basis and problem of modern antisemitism. And it is clear from all that has been described that the motive which set going this chain of events was a religious motive, that the Jewish problem to the Christian Roman world was a religious problem, and that so far the Jews were in no way distinguished from their neighbours by any economic or other characteristic, but only by a religious difference.

VI. THE TREATMENT OF HERETICS BY JUSTINIAN

As before, the essentially religious character of the treatment of the Jews is confirmed by the similarities which it shows with the treatment of heretics.

Justinian retains the generalisations of earlier legislation, the principle that privileges are for Catholics only, and that heretics should rather be given burdens[1]; he repeats the optimistic gesture of Theodosius the Great by which they were ordered in all places and at all times to cease to exist[2]; and the prohibition of all their services and the confiscation of all their buildings ordered by Arcadius[3]. In addition he retains some of the legislation affecting individual heresies, especially those of the Manichees, Donatists[4], Eutychians and Apollinarians[5].

Justinian also retained the law of Leo by which heretics were forbidden under any pretext to acquire Catholic

[1] C.J., 1.5.1.

[2] *Ibid.* 1.5.2.

[3] *Ibid.* 1.5.3.

[4] *Ibid.* 1.5.4 and 5.

[5] *Ibid.* 1.5.6 and 8.

property. He himself enacted the same against the Jews[1]. In many of his laws—that on the holding of office is an example—he classed heretics and Jews together under the same disabilities[2]. By two laws heretics were punished with complete intestability[3]. Their exclusion from office was enforced in great detail, and they were also forbidden to seek employment in any capacity as teachers, or to receive their share in the distribution of grain[4]. From these latter privileges the Jews were not excluded. The parallel to Novella 146 is the complete prohibition of all heretical services whatever[5].

In general it may still be stated that the Jew fared somewhat better than the heretic, though his disabilities were of the same kind. There is no striking privilege allowed the one and denied the other; and as it would be difficult to distinguish the economic significance of the rejection of the Apollinarian heresy, so with the Jews, other evidence failing, we must accept the legislation affecting them as coming from religious motives.

VII. THE COUNCIL OF CHALCEDON

The activity of imperial legislation made it unnecessary for the councils to take action on Jewish questions, and the only canon of an eastern council which mentions them between the beginning of the fifth and the end of the seventh century is the fourteenth canon of Chalcedon. This prohibits intermarriage between those degrees of the clergy who were still permitted to marry, and heretics, pagans or Jews. They were only to be allowed to contract such marriages if the non-Catholic in question accepted the Catholic faith.

[1] C.J., 1.5.10, and Nov. 131.

[2] *Ibid.* 1.5.12; cf. *ibid.* 21.

[3] *Ibid.* 1.5.18 and 22.

[4] *Ibid.* 1.5.18. Juster gives convincing reasons for believing that this law, though professedly dealing with all who are not Catholics, does not apply to Jews. See Vol. I, p. 177, n. 3; and Vol. II, pp. 236 and 255.

[5] C.J., 1.5.20.

VIII. THE JEWS AND THE PERSIAN WARS

It has already been said that the violence in Antioch and the still more serious troubles which followed in the eastern provinces should be closely linked with the repressive legislation of Justinian. As long as Rome oppressed the Jews under her sway, and the Persians allowed their Jewish population full liberty, both religious and political, so long were Jewish eyes in the eastern provinces of the empire likely to be turned with longing towards the frontier. We have already had evidence of this in the events of the fourth century, during the reign of Julian and the persecution under Shapur II. Succeeding centuries which saw Jewish disabilities multiplied by the emperors saw the Jewish sympathy with Persia breaking out into rebellion against Rome and violent attacks upon the Roman population whenever opportunity offered. In the time from Anastasius to Leo the Isaurian, whenever there was war with Persia there was a danger of a Jewish rising. The same was to some extent true, *mutatis mutandis*, the other side of the frontier. Christians, when persecuted in Persia, looked with longing eyes westward. But the provocation was less, for in general the Persian authorities tolerated Christianity on the same terms as they tolerated Judaism, and there was consequently less temptation for the Christians to betray Persia to Rome when opportunities occurred.

The Persian war lasted from the beginning of the fifth century with occasional intermissions until well into the seventh. It was largely a war of small campaigns, guerilla operations and frontier engagements. It was fought over the area in which the Jews were settled in the largest numbers, and in which, consequently, their actions had the most importance. In the early years of the fifth century the Persians attacked the frontier town of Tella, or Constantia, near Edessa. The Jews were naturally made by the Romans to take part in the defence of the town, and were allotted the section of the wall on which their synagogue was built. They plot to surrender the town by digging under the wall, in the synagogue, and communicate this plan to the Persians. It is accidentally overheard by a prisoner, who manages to communicate it to the defenders. They search and find the tunnel. In spite of the appeals of the governor and bishop, a terrible massacre of the Jewish population follows[1]. Similar betrayals will be discussed at later periods also.

The next report of trouble comes from the other end of the frontier. In the south of Arabia there had been for some centuries a Himyarite kingdom whose rulers were either Jews or under Jewish influence. They retaliated for the persecutions which the Jews had to endure under the Byzantines by massacring the Byzantine merchants who passed through on their way to India[2]. In addition to this, there was a period of violent persecution of the resident Christians of the area. Either on their appeal, or through the influence of Justinian, the Ethiopians, who were Christians, undertook to avenge them, and the Jewish sovereign was defeated and either was killed or committed suicide[3]. While there is no doubt that some incident of this kind occurred, the details and extent of the massacre of the Christians are extremely obscure, and the narratives we possess are not very reliable.

More serious was the renewed Samaritan outbreak which took place early in the reign of Justinian. It is one of the few incidents of Byzantine Jewish history to which reference is made in western chroniclers, and seems to have rivalled in savagery the earlier rebellions of Jews and Samaritans. They attempted to set up their own state, and crowned their own king. Christians were murdered and churches were destroyed throughout the country. The rebels hoped to obtain the aid of Persia, and were prepared to offer her a considerable body of troops. The rising was suppressed with considerable difficulty, and the Samaritans thereafter treated with ruthless severity by Justinian. Their synagogues were destroyed and they were forbidden to build others. They

[1] Joshua Stylites, Ch. lviii.

[2] John of Nikious, Ch. xc.

[3] A full discussion of this incident and of the letters of Simeon and Jacob of Serug will be found in R.E.J., Vols. XVIII and XX, and in the *Zeitschrift der d. Morgenländischen Gesellschaft*, Vol. XXXI, p. 360, and in *Atti della Acad. delle Lincei*, 3rd Series, Vol. VII.

could only leave their property to orthodox Christians. And in addition they were subject to all the disabilities from which the worst kind of heretic suffered; their direct punishment was also considerable[1]. The enduring hatred of the Samaritans for the Byzantines is reflected in the travel book of Antoninus Placentius. He relates that as they approached Samaria the inhabitants followed them and wiped out their foot-prints; and when they tried to buy anything, they had to throw the purchase money into water to prevent the sellers from feeling themselves polluted[2].

There were two further risings in the sixth century, one at Caesarea, in which the leaders were Jews, and one later, during the reign of Justin II, in which Jews and Samaritans took part. In both cases there were massacres of the Christian population, and churches were destroyed[3]. Even if these two risings are in reality a confusion of the same incident, yet it is evident that in Palestine, where the Jews felt themselves—at times at any rate—strong enough to resist the oppressive legislation and hostile government of Constantinople, they were prepared to do so.

The situation was no different in the seventh century, and the consequences of their policy were even more fatal to the Byzantines. In the reign of Phocas the Jews are said to have meditated a general massacre of the Christians of Mesopotamia and a destruction of the churches. The plot was betrayed, and the Christians fell upon the Jews instead and killed many of them[4]. For this they were punished by Phocas with a fine. The incident is only reported by a single chronicler, and it would be unjustifiable to take it at its face value. Even if the massacre happened, it would still not be proved that the Christian belief in a general plot against them on the part of the Jews was founded on fact. But, on the other hand, it cannot be ruled out in this century as impossible. For the Jews

[1] Agapius, in P.O., Vol. VIII, p. 427; Zachariah of Mitylene, IX, viii; Malalas, XVIII, p. 656; *Chron. Pasc.*, P.G., XCII, p. 871; Landolfus, Bk. XVIII, xvi, in M.G.H. 4^{0}, Auct. 11; C.J., 1.5.17.

[2] *Itinerarium*, ch. v; P.L., LXXII, p. 897.

[3] Theophanes, A.D. 548; P.G., CVIII, p. 504; Michael the Syrian, IX, xxxi; and John of Ephesus, III, xxvii.

[4] Agapius, P.O., Vol. VIII, p. 449.

possessed both the provocation and the power for such a reprisal. A similar unconfirmed incident at this period is the surrender by the Jews to the Persians of the town of Neocaesarea in Cappadocia during a Persian raid on the province[1].

These incidents appear more natural if we realise that the eastern Jews were accustomed to arms, and looked to Babylon as their spiritual centre. In the Persian forces they were sufficiently numerous for a Persian commander on one occasion to ask the Byzantine general Belisarius to postpone a battle because it would have taken place during the days of unleavened bread, when the 'Jews and Nazarenes' would not willingly fight[2].

While there is much confusion and contradiction in the accounts of the Persian invasion of Palestine and the capture of Jerusalem in 614, it is certain that the Jews of Galilee in some numbers joined the Persian army on its passage through the country and assisted in the attack and capture of the Holy City[3]. Of the scenes which followed the capture of the city many accounts exist. The popular story, which is repeated in most of the chroniclers, is that the Jews purchased 90,000 Christian prisoners from the Persians for the pleasure of putting them to death[4]. Theophanes, in reporting the incident, takes the precaution of adding the words 'some say' to this extravagant narrative[5]. That Jews took part in the attack upon Jerusalem and in the massacres and destruction of churches which followed, it would be difficult to disbelieve. They had every reason to hate the Christians and to exult in the destruction of the Christian buildings of the city. Whether they really expected to be allowed to set up an independent Jewish state under the protection of Persia, and were

[1] Sebeôs, xxiii, p. 63.

[2] Zachariah of Mitylene, IX, vi.

[3] Eutychius, P.G., CXI, p. 1083, supported by the *Ode of Sophronius* in R.O.C., Vol. II, and Sebeôs, xxiv, p. 68.

[4] Theophanes, sub anno 606, P.G., CVIII, p. 632; George Hamartolus, IV, ccxxvii, P.G., CX, p. 829; Michael the Syrian, XI, i (where it has the appearance of an interpolation).

[5] The English translation of Theophanes carelessly applies 'as some say' to the total of those slain. The Greek quite clearly relates the phrase to the Jews, and it is so understood in the translation in Migne.

therefore expelled from the city, is less certain[1]. As to the story of the purchase of the 90,000 captives, it would seem that its origin was an incident of a very different kind. A monk of the monastery of Mar Sabas, who claims to have been an eyewitness of the siege and capture, relates that when the more valuable prisoners had been set aside, the rest, including himself, were imprisoned in a dry cistern. Some Jews approached them while they were in the cistern and offered to pay the ransom of any who would accept Judaism. The Christians refused, and the Jews then bought them to massacre them[2]. While the narrative of the monk contains that amount of miracle and bias to which one is accustomed in documents of this period, it would appear to contain a central element of truth, and the story that the Jews offered to ransom those who would accept Judaism is not the kind of thing that would be invented. While it would have been, doubtless, more generous to have offered the ransom without the condition, some Jews at least can be given the credit for an action which was rare on either side at such a time. That they purchased 90,000, or any other number, for the purpose of slaughtering them, can be dismissed as myth. Had they desired, they could have massacred as many as they wished to a few days earlier in the attack and sack of the city, and could have done it without payment.

When, fifteen years later, Heraclius entered Palestine and recaptured Jerusalem, the Jews met him at Tiberias and begged from him a written guarantee of security, which he gave them. But when he entered the Holy City, and was told by the monks of the destruction which the Jews had wrought, he withdrew the promise and executed many of them[3].

Two other incidents are mentioned from the campaigns of Heraclius. While he was in Persia the Jews of Edessa either helped the Persians against him, or refused to admit him after the departure of the Persian army[4]. On another

[1] Michael the Syrian, XI, i. Cf. *Chron. Anon.* in C.S.C.O., S.S., Ser. III, T. iv, p. 23, and Sebeôs, xxiv, p. 69.

[2] See R.O.C., Vol. II.

[3] Theophanes, sub anno 620, P.G., CVIII, p. 675, and Eutychius, P.G., CXI, p. 1089.

[4] Agapius, P.O., VIII, p. 466, and Sebeôs, xxx, p. 94.

occasion, when all the Roman troops were withdrawn from Syria for the defence of Constantinople, the Jews of Tyre tried to secure the co-operation of the Jews of the surrounding region for an attack upon the Christians of the city. But again they were betrayed, and when their confederates arrived they found the gates barred against them. They began to devastate the surrounding region, but for every church they destroyed the Tyrians executed a number of Jews, until, discouraged, they retired[1]. This incident, like the projected massacre of the Christians of Mesopotamia, may not be historical. Eutychius is not a conspicuously accurate historian, and the narrative has somewhat the air of invention.

The Byzantines had but a short while in which to enjoy their possession of Palestine. When, within a few years, it fell before the Moslem invaders, the Jews took their revenge for the executions of Heraclius by taking the part of the Moslems against them[2]. At a later date various versions of an imaginary treaty of alliance between the Moslems and Christians against the Jews were invented by Christians living under Moslem rule, but they have no historical basis[3]. The Jews, however, seem to have had friendly relations with the Moslems both in Palestine and Alexandria[4], and are said to have surrendered Caesarea to them. But this may be a confusion with the earlier Persian raid upon Neocaesarea in Cappadocia[5]. At the surrender of Alexandria special provision was made for them[6]. Finally, they were employed to buy church plate by Abdelas, the Mahometan governor of Syria[7].

But the most mysterious Jew of the time is to be found in the simple statement of John of Nikious that ' a Jew accompanied the army of the Moslems to Egypt '. On this slender foundation a modern historian makes of him a spy, a guide,

[1] Eutychius, P.G., CXI, p. 1084.

[2] Michael the Syrian, XI, ix; Sebeôs, xxxi.

[3] Cf. the Nestorian History, cii, P.O., XIII, p. 602 ff.

[4] Maximus Confessor, Ep. xiv; P.G., XCI, p. 540.

[5] Dionysius of Tel Mahre, IV, xxiv.

[6] John of Nikious, cxx; the Arab chronicler Tabari, however, does not refer to any provision for the Jews.

[7] Theophanes, anno 749, P.G., CVIII, p. 863.

a general dealer in prisoners and booty, responsible for the fall of Alexandria, and a companion of those who betrayed Caesarea[1].

This long list of betrayals and treason, of hostility and massacre, is attributed by the ancient chroniclers, and at times by modern historians, to the innate malice and inveterate hostility of the Jew to all things Christian. A more scientific reason is to be found in the legislation of Justinian, the violence of the Christians themselves towards the Jews, and the general lawlessness of the times.

IX. THE DESTRUCTION OF SYNAGOGUES AND FORCED BAPTISMS

All the tales of violence recounted in the previous section can be definitely related to the political conditions of the time. Apart from the massacre of the Himyarite Christians, which was said to be retaliation for the actions of Justinian, they were all connected with the friendship felt for Persia. But on the Christian side there is also evidence of purely religious hostility and violence. John of Ephesus recounts proudly that on his own mission through Asia he had turned no less than seven synagogues into churches—an action which was definitely illegal, and could only be carried out with violence[2]. He also relates the pious actions of the monk Sergius at Amida. He had built himself a hut in a village where there were many Jews, in order to dispute with them. He used to ' gnash his teeth at them daily ', exclaiming that ' these crucifiers of the Son of God ought not to be allowed to live at all ', and he was particularly severe with Christians who had any business dealings with them. As these actions produced no effect, he gathered his disciples and burnt down the synagogue. This caused great annoyance to the Christians, who lost a considerable sum thereby[3]. The Jews went to the nearest town to

[1] J. Pargoire, *l'Eglise Byzantine de 527 à 847*, p. 172 ff., based on John of Nikious, cxviii.

[2] *Lives of Eastern Saints*, P.O., XVIII, p. 681. There is a service for the consecration of a synagogue in the Gelasian Sacramentary Assemani, Vol. IV, pt. 2, p. 90. See Appendix 4.

[3] This sum may have been a kind of blackmail paid by the Jews to be left in peace.

complain, and in their absence Sergius and his disciples extinguished the fire and rapidly built and consecrated a chapel on the site. This was completed in a week, and the Jews on their return did not know what to do, as Sergius was still urging his disciples against them. So they burnt down the huts of Sergius and his followers. But Sergius easily rebuilt them. Then the Jews built a new synagogue and Sergius pulled it down. Undismayed, they built a third, and his disciples burnt it. So the Jews gave up the struggle and, victory obtained, Sergius 'continued his habitual practice of love towards God and towards strangers for forty years'[1].

That it was the monks and not the local Christian clergy and population which manifested such hostility is clear from an incident at Nisibis, where the Jews had the support of the Christians of the town in a complaint to the bishop about the conduct of the monks and of the head of the monastery, Mar Abraham[2].

On the other hand we occasionally hear of Jews taking part in mob action against one political or ecclesiastical party or another, especially in Constantinople[3]. But we hear nothing of purely Jewish rioting, except for the story of a seventh-century Forerunner of the Messiah who appeared on the Euphrates and, after collecting some four hundred followers, sacked several churches and killed the local governor. He was taken prisoner and crucified[4]. Times of persecution have, as we have already seen, always produced Messianic effervescence, but the Jews have rarely suffered from so complete a scoundrel as the successor to the gentleman from the Euphrates. This was a Christian in Syria who, having seduced a Jewish girl and incurred the anger of the Jewish community thereby, took to flight and having studied magic returned and gave himself out as Moses. Having convinced many of his claims he took all their money and led them into the wilderness, where

[1] John of Ephesus, *Life of S. Sergius*, P.O., XVII, p. 90.

[2] Barhadbesabba 'Arbaia, *Ecc. Hist.*, II, xxxii, in P.O., IX, p. 626.

[3] John of Ephesus, *History*, III, xxxi, ed. Payne Smith, p. 216; Nicephorus of Constantinople, *De rebus p. Maur. gestis*; P.G., C, p. 925; *Doctrina Jacobi*, lxii.

[4] *Chron. Anon.* in C.S.C.O., Script. Syr., III, pt. iv, p. 27.

they died of starvation. But enough of them came to their senses in time to seize him and surrender him to the Emir, who allowed them to execute him themselves[1].

A graver attack upon their situation than from such a Messiah came from some of the emperors themselves. It is recorded of Maurice and of his two successors, Phocas and Heraclius, and of Leo the Isaurian, that they ordered the Jews of their dominions to be baptised. In addition to these precise references, Michael the Syrian records at about the date of A.D. 660 that 'at that time many Jews became converts to Christianity', without saying why[2]. Each of these forced baptisms is related by a different chronicler, and it is possible that they may be duplicates of each other. Of Maurice it is related that to show his orthodoxy at the beginning of his reign he instructed his cousin Domitian to cause all Jews and Samaritans to be compulsorily baptised. This was done, and though they turned out very bad Christians, Domitian compelled the clergy to admit them to ecclesiastical functions[3]. The story of Phocas is somewhat similar. The action takes place in Palestine, and the mention of Samaritans in the previous story also suggests Palestine. The Jews try to evade the issue by saying that the time for baptism is past, but the Prefect, infuriated by this ingenuity, orders and accomplishes their immediate immersion[4].

More frequently repeated is the story of Heraclius. This is to be found in western chroniclers also, since he persuaded Dagobert to follow his example in France. Warned in a dream that his power would be destroyed by 'the circumcised', he ordered the baptism of all the Jews in his dominions, and though many fled to Persia, many were constrained 'to cease to be circumcised by the waters of baptism'[5]. Actually, the warning applied to the Arabs.

[1] Dionysius of Tel Mahre, ed. Chabot, p. 25; Barhebraeus, ed. Budge, p. 109; Agapius, in P.O., VIII, p. 504; Michael the Syrian, XI, xix; Theophanes, anno 715, P.G., CVIII, p. 812.

[2] Michael the Syrian, XI, xii.

[3] John of Nikious, xcix.

[4] Dionysius of Tel Mahre, for the (Seleucid) year 928.

[5] Michael the Syrian, XI, iv; cf. *Gesta Dagoberti*, xxv, in P.L., XCVI, p. 1405.

The forced baptism ordered by Leo was no more effective; for while disagreeing in detail the chroniclers who relate the event agree that the Jews ' unbaptised themselves ', and then profaned the sacraments by partaking of them[1].

While it is possible that in reality there were only three or four instead of five cases of compulsory baptism in the period from Maurice to Leo, yet even these show the gravity of the dropping by Justinian of the fundamental law of Theodosius: ' Judaeorum sectam nulla lege prohibitam satis constat '[2]—a law which was itself, by a tragic coincidence, addressed to the eastern provinces of the empire.

X. THE LEGISLATION OF LEO AND LATER COUNCILS

Though the followers of Justinian and the ecclesiastics of the sixth century thus marked their attitude to the Jews by arbitrary acts rather than fresh law-making, neither were completely silent in legislation. It is not always easy to be quite sure when Jews are definitely envisaged, for the laws occasionally refer simply to ' Christians ', whereby it is uncertain whether they affect Jews or not. Thus in a local law book of Syria, which actually precedes the reign of Justinian, the statute of limitations is said in certain manuscripts to apply to ' Christians '. In some cases the copyists themselves were clearly uncertain. The law referred to contains the three versions: ' when a man . . .', ' when a Christian . . .', and finally ' when a man who is a Christian . . .'. In the last case it is fairly evident that the copyist meant to exclude Jews. In the second case he is possibly referring to a Byzantine subject, as opposed to his Islamic neighbours. The first text may be the original, for neither in Theodosius nor in Justinian is there any mention of religious distinction in the statute[3],

[1] Theophanes, *Chron.*, year 714; P.G., CVIII, p. 809; Ekkehard, *Chron. Univ.*, year 723, in M.G.H. folio, VI, p. 157; George Hamartolus, *Chron.*, IV, ccl; P.G., CX, p. 928.

[2] C.T., 16.8.9.

[3] *Syrisch-Römisches Rechtsbuch*, para. 45 in the Arabic text, and 53 in the Armenian. Two other texts do not mention religion (pp. 107 and 76). See also p. 249, n. 1.

and Theodoric, writing to the Jews of Milan, mentions specifically that the statute of limitations does apply to them[1]. Thus, without new law-making, but by simple copying, the Jews may have lost this right at some period subsequent to Justinian.

A full revision of the Code of Justinian was not attempted until the reign of the emperor Basil at the end of the ninth century, but in the meantime certain simplified handbooks known as the ' Eclogues ' were issued by Leo the Isaurian. We possess various versions of different dates of these laws, and on the whole they contain nothing fresh. But they illustrate again how one law led to another, and always in the sense of fresh restrictions. Thus a law of Leo allows either Jewish parent to decide that a child shall be brought up as a Christian[2]. An edition of the end of the eighth century only allows orthodox children to inherit property[3]. In this way ancient laws affecting inheritance on the one hand, and mixed marriages on the other, are interpreted in such a way as to go far beyond their original intention. Justinian ordered the children of mixed marriages to be brought up as Christian: Leo encouraged *Jewish* parents to have their children baptised. Justinian insisted that Christian children of Jews should *share* in an inheritance: Leo allowed no others any part in it.

Similarly the *Ecloga Privata Aucta* ordains that all witnesses shall swear on the gospel before giving evidence[4], and from this it is a natural step explicitly to refuse Jewish evidence altogether[5], or to invent strange and humiliating forms in which alone it could be allowed[6].

One problem still remains permanent with the legislators throughout, the problem of preventing Jews from owning Christian slaves, and from converting them to Judaism[7]. It was still necessary to maintain the death penalty for those

[1] Cassiodorus, *Varia*, V, 37.

[2] *Ecloga*, app. iv, 7.

[3] *Ecloga Privata Aucta*, vii, 18.

[4] *Ibid*. xv, 7.

[5] *Basilica*, 21.1.45.

[6] *Ecloga ad Procheiron Mutata* (12th cent.), xxviii (xxvi), 14.

[7] *Ecloga*, app. vi, 26, 27, 28, 29 and 30; *Epanagoge*, xl, 33 and 34, etc.

who effected the conversion, and the complete loss of his property for the converted[1].

The identification of the secular and religious power is shown in a curious form in the original *Ecloga*, in that it contains as a supplement Mosaic laws on forty-seven different subjects, simply extracted from the Pentateuch without any effort to cast them into Byzantine shape, or to adapt them to Byzantine penalties[2].

The councils of this period have little to say about the Jews, but they reflect the general state of affairs created both by the forced baptisms of various emperors, and by the legislation of the period from Justinian onwards. What is surprising is that they also reveal the existence of Judaising tendencies within the Church, and offer evidence that relations between Jews and Christians were just as close as they had been formerly, in spite of all the laws and canons which had been passed. The forced baptisms created a class of 'Marranos', and the various disabilities under which the Jews suffered must have tempted others to effect a superficial transference of their allegiance. With this class the second council of Nicaea in 787 tried to cope by prohibiting the admission to Christian rites of Hebrews who hypocritically pretended to be Christian. In particular, baptism was to be refused to their children—in which prohibition the fathers at Nicaea showed much less acumen than Gregory the Great[3].

The council 'in Trullo' refers both to the existence of Jewish superstitions in Armenia[4], and in general to close friendship between even the clergy and the Jews. In particular it is specified that they are not to eat unleavened bread with the Jews, accept their hospitality in any form, visit them in sickness, receive medicine from them, or visit the baths with them[5].

Some reflection of the position suggested by this canon is to be found in a pastoral letter of Gregory of Nyssa

[1] *Ecloga*, app. vi, 16 and 24.

[2] *Ecloga*, ed. Freshfield, pp. 142-144.

[3] Nicaea, II, Can. 8; different texts of this canon will be found in Harduin, IV, p. 491, and Mansi, XIII, p. 751.

[4] In Trullo, Canons 33 and 99; in Mansi, XI, p. 958.

[5] In Trullo, Canon 11; Mansi, XI, p. 946.

of the fifth century. He refers to Christians who have become Jews and on their death-bed repented, and instructs that they are to be received back into the Church[1]. If Gregory confirms the fact that there were Christians passing to Judaism, Severus of Antioch reveals in his Catechetical Addresses that there were Jews listening to Christian teaching. In a most interesting passage he explains that the Trinitarian doctrine contains nothing to offend Jews and Samaritans who may be listening to him[2].

While it will be necessary to postpone a discussion of the general relationships between Jews and Christians in the early Byzantine empire until other aspects of the situation have been considered, it can be suggested already that the laws and events related in this chapter have not yet had the effect of creating an absolute gulf between Jews and Christians, and that the evidence of passage from the one faith to the other is also evidence of the existence of some mutual respect and genuine friendship among ordinary folk. In fact, even the clergy were not unaffected by this feeling, for we find a canon of uncertain date not only forbidding worldly minded clerics to indulge in money-lending and similar occupations, but especially insisting that they shall not take Jews into partnership in such activities[3].

[1] Gregory of Nyssa, Ep. to the bishop of Melitene, P.G., XLV, p. 225.

[2] Severus of Antioch, Catechetical Address 70, in P.O., XII, pp. 19 and 28.

[3] Forged Canons of Nicaea, No. 52; Mansi, II, p. 969.

CHAPTER EIGHT

THE JEWS IN BYZANTINE LITERATURE

BIBLIOGRAPHICAL INTRODUCTION

The source material for this chapter is mainly taken from two collections, the Patrologia Orientalis and the Revue de l'Orient Chrétien. Other sources are indicated in the footnotes. While the Greek literature of the period has been known for a long time, and some of the works here quoted are to be found in western editions of the sixteenth and seventeenth centuries, the general atmosphere of the period can best be gauged from such collections as the eastern synaxaries, the lives of the eastern saints by John of Ephesus, or the history of the patriarchs of Alexandria. And all these are works which have only recently become available to scholars ignorant of the languages of the near east. It is from these sources that the new element in Byzantine literature is best appreciated.

Certain aspects of the subject have been treated in special detail, especially the stories of images; and a good study of the later disputations is to be found in the introduction of Bardy to the Trophies of Damascus.

LIST OF BOOKS

BARDY, G.	*Les Trophées de Damas*, in P. O., Vol. XV.
BONWETSCH, N.	*Doctrina Jacobi nuper Baptizati, Abhandlung der Kglch. Ges. Göttingen*, Band XII, 1909-1912.
BUDGE, E. A. W.	History of a Likeness of Christ which the accursed Jews in the city of Tiberias made a mock of, Luzac, *Semitic Texts and Translations*, Vol. V, 1899.
CHAINE, M.	A Sermon on Penitence ascribed to Cyril of Alexandria; in *Melanges de la Faculté Orientale*. Beyrouth, Vol. VI.
v. DOBSCHUTZ, E.	*Christus-Bilder; Texte und Untersuchungen*, XVIII, p. 281**.
KRUMBACHER, K.	*Byzantinische Literaturgeschichte*. Munich, 1897.
PARGOIRE, J.	*L'Eglise Byzantine de* 527 *à* 847. Paris, Lecoffre, 1905.
PARISOT, J.	*Aphraate*, P.S., Vol. I. (The Post Nicene Fathers, Vol. XIII, translates Demonstrations i, v, vi, viii, x, xvii, xxi, xxii.

I. THE NATURE OF BYZANTINE LITERATURE

The passage from the Graeco-Roman to the Byzantine-Oriental world was doubtless a gradual one. The intellectual activity of classical ecclesiastical scholarship did not disappear all at once, and it was preceded by the collapse of the economic and political stability of society. But when it disappeared it disappeared for centuries.

Byzantine literature presents a sorry spectacle to the modern Christian historian. The violence of ecclesiastical passions, the bloodshed of their controversies, found their counterpart in a literature marked by an almost complete indifference to ethical and moral values.

The fathers of the early centuries may have held many beliefs we would reject to-day. But within their conceptions they were intellectually honest. They were prepared to use the law against their opponents, but rarely the bludgeon and the sword. The writings and actions of their eastern successors would have shocked them profoundly. This change may be partly due to the general decline of society, but is still more the result of the increasing influence of an oriental civilisation which had never been deeply affected by the intellectual history of Greece or the political history of Rome.

The Greek literature of Byzantium is for some centuries merely a pale shadow of the past. The new developments are shown in the writings of Syrian, Coptic, Armenian, and Ethiopian ecclesiastics. In a few centuries these different groups split into different Churches at war with each other, but in their general conceptions and in the general quality of their literature they remained members of one family, owing, spiritually at least, allegiance to the most powerful of the eastern Christian communities, the empire of Byzantium.

The scholarship of recent years has enormously enriched our knowledge of the early literature of these different Churches. To-day we can study the lives of these communities not in a few chroniclers and theologians, but in a mass of hagiological literature, apocryphal gospels and acts, novels, historical romances, controversies, biographies and letters.

The creation of a theological picture of the Jews has already been traced in the literature of the first four centuries. Now we can see the second stage of the development, the creation of a popular religious picture of them, a picture such as the lower clergy, monks and laity would be likely to obtain in the literature which was meant for their consumption.

II. PHYSICAL, OCCUPATIONAL AND MENTAL CHARACTERISTICS OF THE EASTERN JEWS

There were many reasons why the Jews should present a special interest to the inhabitants of the eastern provinces. They were naturally more numerous and more widely scattered in the east than in the west. But also they were much less easily distinguishable from the rest of the population. If events caused them in the west to be concentrated geographically and occupationally, no such causes were operative in the east.

As an example of the ease with which they could be confounded with the rest of the population, both in appearance and in occupation, there is the story of S. Simeon the Mountaineer as related by John of Ephesus[1]. Simeon comes upon a large population living isolated in a mountainous region east of the Euphrates, where he expected to find no one. He asks them who they are, and how they are able in their isolation to maintain orthodox religious services. They profess complete ignorance as to what he is talking about, whereupon Simeon bursts into tears and begs them to tell him the truth: 'Tell me, my sons, are you Christians or Jews?' But the question made them indignant, and they replied: 'We are Christians; do not call us Jews'. Another example of the completeness with which they shared the lives of those surrounding them is the story of Abdul Masih told in chapter Four. The Jewish lad fed his flocks with Christian and Magian children.

Moreover, it must be recognised that the ways of thinking of Jew and Christian were very similar. Modern scholars are apt to hold up their hands in horror at the hair-splitting

[1] John of Ephesus, *Lives of the Eastern Saints*, xvi; P.O., XVII, p. 234.

discussions of the Talmud, but the eastern theologians, especially the defenders of monasticism, acted in very similar ways. The referring of all kinds of precepts back to the revelation given to Moses finds its counterpart in the tracing of the monastic rule back to Elijah, Elisha and the sons of the prophets. Their methods are thus described by Dom J. Besse: ' The whole of Holy Scripture became the real rule of the monks. They were accustomed to look for an allegorical meaning in all the passages of the Bible, and thus it was easy for them to find anywhere, even in most insignificant details, precepts or examples which revealed to them the nature and extent of their obligations '[1]. But such was exactly the task and method of the Jewish scholar of Babylon, and if the Jew went further than the Christian in the field of the invention of miracles and incidents in the lives of the respective founders of their faiths, the Christian went a long way beyond the Jew in the exhibition of a complete contempt for the morality and ethical significance of their inventions. Jewish stories were often puerile. Christian stories were still more often perverted and diseased. The revolting tortures of the martyrs, their senseless and repulsive miracles, as related in all the eastern Acta, surpass anything related in the Talmud.

This is not a study of the relative merits of Judaism and Christianity, and it is not necessary to examine in details these vagaries of the human mind, but it is at least important to realise that the eastern Jew had to do with the eastern Christian, and that the Talmud, if its strength and weakness are to be properly understood, has to be judged in its proper setting and not contrasted with western thought of the modern period.

But the Jews were not only physically indistinguishable from, and occupationally mingled with, the general population. They not only thought in ways similar to the rest of the population. There was another reason for the Christians to take a special interest in them. The Jews of the east were in a much more powerful position than their western brethren for influencing their neighbours. Europe at this period contained no great intellectual Jewish centres.

[1] *Les Regles Monastiques Orientales* in R.O.C., Vol. IV, p. 466.

Jewish scholars were largely concentrated in Palestine and Babylon. Hence ‘ disputations ’ were more frequent and more lively. Though the Spain of the Visigoths contained a considerable Jewish population, neither Julian of Toledo nor Isidore of Seville, both of whom wrote against the Jews, showed the slightest signs of ever having met a Jew. Throughout, Byzantine literature of the same class shows close acquaintance with actual Jewish arguments in defence of Judaism and against Christianity. The Greek and Latin ‘ Altercations ’ differ in nothing from the many discourses ‘ Contra Judaeos ’, except in that they are cast in dialogue form. The Jew has never a leg to stand on. But in the east even those writings which are not in dialogue form reproduce definite and plausible Jewish arguments, and are at times hard put to answer them. The steady increase of the miraculous element in the conversions recounted may well be the psychological compensation for actual defeats.

III. EARLY EASTERN CHRISTIAN WRITINGS AGAINST THE JEWS—EPHREM, APHRAATES AND JACOB OF SERUG

The earliest writing of this class which we possess is the *Rhythm against the Jews* of Ephrem the Syrian[1]. This is a poetical sermon delivered on Palm Sunday, and its subject is naturally the triumphant entry of Christ into Jerusalem and His subsequent rejection by the Jews. In itself the sermon is not very different from other works of the kind. By making the idea of the synagogue as a harlot the theme for his verse, he is able to indulge in many unpleasant allusions suitable to his text, but that is all.

His successor, Aphraates, ‘ the Persian Sage ’, shows much more familiarity with the points at issue. Though his theology would have appalled the Nicene fathers, he gives the impression of an honest shepherd doing his best to defend his flock against the dangers presented by the presence of many Jews among them; and on the whole

[1] In the ‘ Select Works ’ of Ephrem, translated by J. B. Morris. Oxford, 1847.

he speaks without bitterness[1]. Though he belongs to the fourth century, the century of Christological controversy, he is content to explain the nature of Christ by pointing out to the Jews that Moses is also called ' God ', and that Israel is called ' Son ' and ' Firstborn '[2]. To this a Jew might well reply, ' Have you ever heard of a homoousian controversy among the rabbis as to the nature of Moses? '

Aphraates is by no means ignorant of rabbinical Judaism. He can quote to the Jews their own interpretations, and is even ready to adopt them himself when he finds them useful[3]. He constantly refers to his ' learned Jewish opponent '[4], and it is quite evident that this man was a real figure, not a rhetorical creation. He frequently asks him to explain points which he evidently considers unanswerable, and though in his ' Demonstrations ' these are naturally rhetorical questions, it is likely that they represent real questions in some battle of texts which he had had with actual Jews. Thus he challenges him to show that Deuteronomy xxxii, 21, is not a reference to the Christians[5]. He quotes Jeremiah ii, 8, with its condemnation of the leaders of the Jews, and tells them that being blind themselves they are inviting him to be blind also[6]. He asks them to reconcile their distinctions of meats with Samson's eating honey from a lion[7].

He relates that, on their side, the Jews mocked at the monkish system with its abstinence from marriage. To this Aphraates retorts by a list of the unfortunate marriages of the Old Testament—Adam, whose sons were so wicked that the Flood was needed to cleanse the world of them,

[1] The article ' Aphraates ' in the *Jewish Encyclopaedia* is worth consulting.

[2] Aphraates, *Demonstration* xvii.

[3] See introduction to Aphraates by Fr. Parisot, p. xlix ff.

[4] *Dem.* x, 1; xii, 7; xv, 8, etc.

[5] ' They have moved me to jealousy with that which is not God; they have provoked me to anger with their vanities; and I will move them to jealousy with those which are not a people; I will provoke them to anger with a foolish nation ' (see *Dem.* xii, 3).

[6] ' The priests said not, " Where is the Lord? " and they that handle the law knew me not: the rulers also transgressed against me, and the prophets prophesied by Baal, and walked after things that do not profit ' (see *Dem.* xiv, 26).

[7] *Dem.* xv, 2.

Eli and his sons, Solomon and his wives—and complains that the Jews by their clever casuistry destroy the minds of the simple Christians[1]. They mocked at Christian poverty[2]. They mocked at the Christian refusal to fight, and their inability to stop persecution[3]. And they contrasted the miserable condition of the Christians under Shapur with their own glorious future[4]. To these last questions the reply of Aphraates is interesting. He shows how even in the Old Testament suffering was a cause of blessing, and he points them to Jacob, Joseph, Moses, Joshua, Jephthah, David, Elijah, Elisha, and other heroes of their own. One whole Demonstration is devoted to proving that the Christian belief in the divinity of Christ does not infringe the unity of God[5].

Aphraates has evidently to deal not only with the attacks of Jews upon Christian doctrine, but also with the attractive power of Judaism over his own flock. The Jews claimed to have something in the rite of circumcision that the Christians had not got. He replies with unusual calm and weight, and with an absence of invective. Abraham was not circumcised when he received the promises, and the sons of Ishmael, though circumcised, are outside the promises. It is therefore evident that circumcision cannot of itself be an essential[6]. In equally measured argument he deals with the case for the Sabbath, showing that the purpose of the Sabbath is not to impose a rule of life and death for its observance, or non-observance, but to secure mankind quiet and recreation[7]. In another Demonstration he explains the superiority of the Easter of the Christians over the Passover of the Jews[8].

In all these Demonstrations he gives the impression of dealing with an opponent whom he respects, and who demands all his wits—and sincerity. But his calm breaks

[1] *Dem.* xviii.
[2] *Ibid.* vi, 20.
[3] *Ibid.* v and xxi.
[4] *Ibid.* xxi.
[5] *Ibid.* xvii.
[6] *Ibid.* xi.
[7] *Ibid.* xiii.
[8] *Ibid.* xii.

down in dealing with the question of the restoration of the Jews, obviously a point which troubled his congregation. In one Demonstration, by the familiar method of text arrangement, he reaches the conclusion that there are two congregations, Israel and Judah, which are of fornication and adultery respectively, and one true congregation which is the Gentile Church[1]. All the prophecies which refer to the return of the Jews have been fulfilled in the return from Babylon. There is no further return possible, and he adds, ' I will now write and prove to you that neither God, nor Moses, nor the prophets were ever well disposed towards the Jews '[2].

In view of the fact that Aphraates was evidently facing real dangers, his tone with few exceptions is amazingly reasonable. He was not a great theologian, but he had a clear mind, and was a good reasoner. He is one of the best examples in antiquity, not of the great intellectual, but of the first-class parish priest, dealing steadily and to the best of his ability with the problems which confronted his flock, themselves probably relatively simple folk, in the presence of the Jewish intellects of the Talmudic schools.

A century later we have a third Christian apologist in the same region, Jacob of Serug. From his pen we possess three ' Homilies against the Jews ', in which he also appears to be dealing with real difficulties raised in the minds of his congregation by their Jewish neighbours[3]. He avoids the conventional abuse directed against the crucifiers of Christ, and reproaches them rather for not subsequently recognising the fulfilment of prophecy in Him. His strong point is that a prophecy cannot be fulfilled twice, and that therefore there is nothing left for which the Jews can wait. ' Our Lord when He came grasped the totality of prophecy ', and therefore gave no opportunity for another to come[4].

[1] *Dem.* xvi.

[2] *Ibid.* xix. Hillel had already stated that prophecy could not be fulfilled twice and that all the Messianic prophecies were fulfilled in the days of Hezekiah (T. B. Sanhedrin, 98b) but it is unlikely that Aphraates was aware of this.

[3] I am indebted to the Rev. Dr. I. K. Cosgrove for the texts of these homilies, and I hope that his commentary on them will have already appeared by the time this is in print.

[4] Hom. i, 283.

In very different tone is the Taunt Song of Jacob against the Himyarite Jews for the persecution of the Christians in southern Arabia[1]. This poem is merely a violent diatribe against the Jews as the permanent enemies of the Christians, and the lines of the attack are purely conventional. He adduces no special evidence from Persian or oriental history to support his statements.

IV. EASTERN DISPUTATIONS: ANASTASIUS OF SINAI

In many ways these eastern homilies tell us more of the arguments of Jews against Christianity than the dialogues which were composed in large numbers from the earliest times. The most famous of these, Justin's Dialogue with Trypho, has already been extensively quoted. To the same century probably belonged the lost Dialogue of Jason and Papiscus, which formed the foundation of two fourth-century dialogues, that of Zacchaeus and Athanasius, and that of Timothy and Aquila. In both, and presumably in the original form from which they are drawn, the Jew is little more than a dummy figure, unable to reply to the arguments on the Person of Christ and the reality of the Incarnation which the Christian advances, and in both he ultimately accepts conversion. The same description would also apply to the fifth-century Dialogue of Theophilus and Simon ascribed to a monk Evagrius. Thus though they are of considerable interest from other points of view they add little to the present study. It is significant that in the Disputation of the sixth-century abbot, Anastasius of Sinai, the Jew never appears at all, but is only the passive recipient of the dialectic of the Christian apologist[2].

[1] 'Totschreiten Jacobs v. Serug an die himyaritische Christen', by R. Schöter, in the *Zeitschrift der d. Morgenländischen Gesellschaft*, XXXI, p. 360.

[2] The authorship of this work is not certain. Though found among the writings of Anastasius it is ascribed by some to a later epoch because of certain affiliations with other controversial works of the same character. But the detailed study and publication of Jewish-Christian controversies is not yet far enough advanced to take definite decisions, and for our present purpose the question of authorship and even of date is not of great importance.

The arguments of Anastasius show a considerable amount of originality. While the questions of the Incarnation and the nature of Christ as proved by prophecy inevitably occupy a large part of the work, other portions are distinctly original. The author makes considerable use of the New Testament, especially of the epistles to the Romans and to the Hebrews[1], reproducing the Pauline arguments against the law, and the arguments of the author of the epistle to the Hebrews that it was necessary for Christ to share our nature.

There is a long section dealing with the history of Christianity, though the arguments which he there uses in favour of Christianity might with greater justice be repeated to-day in favour of Judaism. For he argues that no faith unless it were true and protected of God could possibly have survived so many centuries, have escaped so many persecutions, and have won so many followers[2]. Against the fidelity of the Christians he sets the historic infidelity of the Jews, mingling, as was the custom of the time, incidents from any century together, as though all equally applied to the Jews of the sixth century A.D., who certainly needed more courage to retain their Judaism than did Anastasius to retain his Christianity[3].

The earnestness of the eastern discussions as to whether the Messiah had truly come in the person of Jesus is shown by the arguments of which both Jacob of Serug and Anastasius make use in order to point out to the Jews the implications of their rejection of Him. Jacob had pointed out that a prophecy could not be fulfilled twice, so that a Jewish Messiah could not lay claim to any prophecy which Jesus had fulfilled. Anastasius takes another line. He says to the Jews: you will not believe in Jesus because you say He was accursed and a deceiver, who therefore could not be the Messiah. But prophecy clearly says that these statements will be made about the Messiah. Moses says that you will see your life hanging before your eyes, and will not believe[4]. Zechariah says that you will look upon Him

[1] *Disputatio contra Judaeos*, iii; P.G., LXXXIX, p. 1253 ff.

[2] *Ibid.* i, p. 1224 ff.

[3] *Ibid.* ii, p. 1236.

[4] Version of Deut. xxviii, 66.

whom you have pierced[1], and many other prophecies are clearly fulfilled in Jesus. If therefore you refuse to accept Him, you will be in exactly the same dilemma when your Messiah comes. He will be a man accursed, and you will not believe in Him[2].

Though, therefore, the Jew in the ' Disputation ' never appears or produces any arguments in his defence, the author gives every appearance of having real Jews in mind in writing. This impression is borne out by a short supplementary dialogue which follows the main work, and which would justify the author in claiming a reputation for wit. It turns on the single question: why do the Christians eat pork and the Jews refuse? After an ingenious explanation that pork was eaten by the Egyptians while beef and other meats were sacred, and that therefore Moses forbade pork to make them turn away from the temptations of Egypt, he adds that the real reason is laziness! It has nothing to do with cleanliness, for the Jews will eat chicken, and chickens are disgusting feeders. But they prefer animals from which they get several benefits, such as eggs from the chicken, wool, milk or cheese from other animals, and they even keep dogs to guard their houses. But the pig, which eats exactly the same food as the sheep or goat, they will not eat, for they would have all the trouble of providing it with food during its lifetime without any compensating benefit[3].

All the material so far considered has this feature in common. It is composed of serious intellectual argument, devoted either to converting the Jew, or at least to confirming the faith of the Christian. Where the actual form of disputation is used, it is as a discussion between an individual Jew and Christian, even if there is a certain audience. And if the Jew is converted it is by argument.

That they represent a genuine tradition is certain. In many of the lives of the saints, and in many remarks made by ecclesiastical writers themselves, we hear of their discussions with Jews. Isidore of Pelusium frequently refers

[1] Zech. xii, 10.

[2] Anastasius, *Disput.*, iii, p. 1241. Cf. *Trophies of Damascus*, P.O., XV, p. 257.

[3] Anastasius, *Parvus Dialogus*, P.G., LXXXIX, p. 1271.

to such discussions in his letters[1], and Theodoret of Cyr, in the middle of the fifth century, exclaims ' He who sees all things knows how many conflicts I have had in most of the cities of the east with pagans and Jews and every heresy '. Similar quotations could be taken from many other writers. But unfortunately we lack entirely the Jewish side of these discussions, except in so far as they are often implied, in the rejection of certain interpretations of texts, in the course of midrashic discussion. In Aphraates especially we may see the attacks which Jews made on Christianity, but nowhere can we find the real Jewish defences against Christian apologetic. Later writers, as we shall see, allowed the Jews to score points with astonishing freedom, and even went so far as to include in their compositions Jewish arguments which they found themselves unable to answer, or Jewish counter-interpretations of the essential texts of the Old Testament.

V. EASTERN DISPUTATIONS: GREGENTIUS AND HERBANUS; THE TEACHING OF JACOB; THE TROPHIES OF DAMASCUS; THE CONVERSION OF THE JEWS OF TOMEI; THE HISTORY OF THEODOSIUS AND PHILIP

A new period opens with the more completely oriental disputations of which some have only recently been made available to western readers. They are written much more picturesquely: they have become religious ' novels ' with a mass of stage setting, often quite artistically and realistically arranged: they deal with mass movements; and they make extensive use of miracle.

The earliest of the disputations of the new type is that between Herbanus a Jew, and Gregentius, Archbishop of Tephren in Ethiopia. Although the Jews have a single spokesman, all the Jews of the kingdom are summoned to be present at the disputation, and the fate of all of them is made to hang upon its issue. The discussion is lengthy and ranges over all the ground usually treated in such works. The proofs of the doctrine of the Trinity from the Old

[1] Ch. V, Section VII.

Testament are succeeded by a similar study of the Incarnation and the Cross. The debate then turns to the rejection of Israel, and Herbanus has a good deal to say on the subject, forcing the archbishop to stranger and stranger interpretations of the prophets, coupled with feeble terms of abuse. These subjects occupy the first two days of the Altercation, and at the end each side retires congratulating itself on its victory.

The third day opens with a statement by the archbishop that God detests all Jewish observances, and demands of the Jews only baptism, to which Herbanus replies 'What can I do to you, archbishop, for there is not a word whose meaning you do not pervert, or a prophecy which you do not twist '[1]. A little later, in a discussion on whether the Christ has really come, he remarks: 'I see that you have one understanding (gnosis), and we have another. Would it not be better therefore for each to obey his own understanding and to be silent?'[2] The archbishop becomes abusive again, and the day closes. The Jews gather round Herbanus and congratulate him on the way in which he has put their case, but Herbanus is depressed, and is certain that he will be unable to overcome the archbishop. But the reason is not the argumentive powers of the prelate, but 'in the night I saw a vision of Moses the Prophet, and the crucified Jesus . . . and Moses was adoring Jesus and lifting his hands to Him as to the Lord God, and doing Him reverence. And I, as a spectator, suddenly said frankly and openly, "My lord Moses, is this good what you are doing?" and he turned on me with great severity and said "Be silent, you impudent fellow, for this is no mistake. I do not belong to your party, but I know my maker and God. What have you got to do with this just archbishop whom you are rashly troubling? Wait until the morrow, and you will be overcome and will also worship Whom I worship "'.[3] In spite of this Herbanus fights bravely during the day's discussion, which turns largely on the sufferings of Christ, which he cannot accept. When it passes to the Resurrection, and the archbishop claims that

[1] *Disputatio*, P.G., LXXXVI, i, p. 728.

[2] *Ibid.* p. 740.

[3] *Ibid.* p. 749.

Jesus is still living, Herbanus and all the Jews with him clamour to be shown Him, and promise to believe if they see Him. The archbishop prays for a revelation. There is a clap of thunder, and the heavens are opened and the wish of the Jews is gratified. Confusion reigns in the Jewish camp, and they are all struck blind. But the head of Herbanus is ' bloody but unbowed '. Led in his blindness to the archbishop, he exclaims 'When a man beholds his God, he receives a blessing therefrom. But we, when we behold your God, receive evil. If such are the gifts He bestows on those who come to Him, certainly He does not share the goodness of His Father '. ' It is your blasphemies which have blinded you', replies the archbishop. ' If He renders evil for evil', replies the undaunted spokesman of the Jews, 'to whom are you committing us?'[1] ' At the font you will receive your sight.' ' And if we are baptised and remain blind? ' ' I will baptise one and he will see; if not, do not believe.' Herbanus accepts. The archbishop succeeds. Herbanus is baptised. The king acts as godfather to him, and presses upon him ecclesiastical and secular titles. All the Jews of the kingdom follow his example. The Church rejoices, and the devil repines. The reputation of Gregentius rises higher than ever. General festivities and good works fill the whole kingdom.

'The teaching of Jacob the new convert '[2] is also cast in novel form. The basis of the story is the forced baptism of the Jews by Heraclius. There was a Jew named Jacob, who, ' faithful to Jewish traditions ', spent all his youth doing harm to the Christians by one subterfuge after another[3]. Subsequently he became a merchant, and to avoid being compelled to be baptised he pretended to be a Christian. But falling down a staircase, he gave himself away by his exclamation, and was then taken and baptised. Having become a Christian he set out to examine his new faith, and found it true. He therefore assembled other

[1] *Disputatio*, P.G., LXXXVI, i, p. 780.

[2] *Doctrina Jacobi nuper baptizati*, or *Sargis of Aberga*, which is an Ethiopian version thereof.

[3] *Doctrina*, para. 53. The Ethiopian version contains fewer details, doubtless as the terms were incomprehensible to the Ethiopian translator.

Jews in like situation to himself, and expounded to them their common faith, and cleared up their difficulties.

The meetings are held in secret, and only copied down by a hidden scribe unknown to those present. The reason for this precaution is that the Christians are themselves so learned in their faith, and so severe with those who hold erroneous views, that it would not be safe for simple and ignorant Jews, only just learning it, to commit their views to writing[1].

During the first two assemblies Jacob exposes Christian doctrine, emphasising naturally the faults and condemnation of the Jews[2]. The Jews are much encouraged by these teachings, but their joy changes to grief when a Jew from the east arrives (this is supposed to pass in Africa) and tells them that they are in error for two reasons whose combination sound strange in the mouth of an orthodox Jew: the Messiah has not yet come, and they have let themselves be baptised at the wrong season[3]. Moreover, he knows Jacob of old as a notorious scoundrel and maker of trouble. The Jews beg him to meet Jacob, and after much persuasion he consents.

The first meeting is stormy and ends in his trying to strangle Jacob, after which he demands eight days for preparation to achieve the same end by more intellectual means[4]. The second meeting, a week later, ends in uproar. Thereafter he is not allowed to speak, and Jacob continues his exposition, proving that Christ has come and fulfilled all prophecy, that the heroes of the Old Testament are but prototypes of Him[5]. The eastern Jew is convinced, and admits that there are many among the Jews themselves who, holding that the Christ has come, believe the Jews have made a great mistake in not accepting Him[6]. He quotes three cases of learned rabbis who have confessed

[1] Para. 59.

[2] For the punishment of the Jews see paras. 21, 24, 31, 40, 41; for the uselessness of the Sabbath, 35, 36; for the abolition of Jewish sacrifices, 57; for their unbelief in Christ, 60-62.

[3] Para. 63.

[4] Paras. 66-69.

[5] Isaac, Joseph, Jeremiah and Daniel (paras. 111-114).

[6] Paras. 82, 91 and 117.

openly or secretly this belief[1], and tells, on the other hand, of an unhappy Christian deacon who, under torture, became a Jew and then committed suicide[2]. He asks Jacob for baptism, receives it, is instructed, and sets forth to win other Jews to Christianity. Jacob retires to a desert and dies in sanctity.

The date of the story is the middle of the seventh century, and it was probably written in Syria or Egypt, even though the scene is laid in Africa under the governor Sergius (hence the Ethiopian name Sargis of Aberga=Sergius Eparchus) and refers to some twenty years earlier.

Half a century later appears another work of similar character, the *Trophies of Damascus*, also an anonymous work, probably written towards the end of the seventh century in Syria. In this case the Jewish parties to the dispute are not already baptised, as in the last work, but neither are they definite opponents of Christianity, as is the case in all earlier controversies. A group of Jews are much troubled by words of Saint Paul[3]—it is already something unexpected that they are familiar with his works—and go to a Christian child secretly, asking him to find them someone capable of explaining the verse to them. The child leads them to a monk, who is the Christian spokesman throughout the work. The dialogue opens in an admirable atmosphere of intellectual honesty. The monk asks: 'On what points are your doubts? Speak without fear, but also without exaggeration or blasphemy. For those who express themselves with the fear of God before their eyes should use neither exaggeration nor blasphemy against opposing views, until the truth is revealed'[4].

The first discussion, which takes place in private, turns on the familiar theme of the nature and Incarnation of Christ. The Jews find themselves unable to answer the stream of texts quoted by the monk, and propose to bring

[1] Cf. *Arabic History of Patriarchs of Alexandria* in P.O., Vol. I, p. 122.

[2] Para. 90.

[3] Gal. iii, 13: 'Christ redeemed us from the curse of the law, having become a curse for us: for it is written, "Cursed is every one that hangeth on a tree" '.

[4] *Trophies*, P.O., XV, p. 22: the pages are those marked in square brackets.

their intellectual chiefs to continue the argument. The monk expresses his joy, and the rest of the discussion takes place in public ' before a large crowd of persons, Jews, Greeks, Samaritans, heretics and Christians '.

The new Jewish protagonists succeed in completely flooring the monk with their first question: ' Scripture tells us that Isaac engendered two nations and two peoples; to which do you belong? '[1] The monk takes refuge in a long declaration ' setting aside all vain subtilties ' and appealing for honest and humble search. He then draws a sad picture of the failure of all Jewish hopes, as a proof of their rejection. But the Jew has no difficulty in applying the *tu quoque* argument by painting the misery of the Byzantine empire, which itself also has been expelled from the Holy Places[2]. He cannot accept the fact that the Messiah has come. For the peace which should accompany His reign is evidently absent. The monk's reply is triple: (*a*) it may refer to inner peace; (*b*) the Byzantine empire enjoyed peace until fifty years ago; (*c*) God often says one thing and does another[3].

The discussion then returns to the Incarnation, and the monk, after asking various questions in the Socratic manner, succeeds in turning the tables on his adversaries by a skilful exposition of the suffering servant in Isaiah. He succeeds again with the brazen serpent, and the Jews admit defeat. The crowd—which now includes Moslems also—is delighted, and the Jews ask how they may be converted. The Christian gives a strange reply: ' I do not wish to, or rather I cannot, make you all Christians. But I do make you bad Jews. For in pursuing your own defeat, you are no longer pure Jews nor fully Christians, but hybrids, even if you do not admit it '[4]. It is difficult to understand what is meant by this reply, or why the monk does not wish, in the spirit of earlier controversialists, to reap the

[1] *Trophies*, P.O., XV, p. 46.

[2] *Ibid.*, p. 51.

[3] Bardy translates ' appears to say ', and thereby somewhat softens this astonishing statement. But the Greek is φάινεται εἰπών which is a strong positive expression, and not φαίνεται εἰπεῖν, which would remove the contradiction and give the translation of Bardy.

[4] *Trophies*, P.O., XV, p. 63.

fruit of his victory. In any case his original seekers do not accept this as the end, and ask him to discuss also with some Cappadocian Jews who are present, and who have a very high reputation. The monk agrees, and a fourth interview takes place.

They begin again on the point of the origin of the Christians, and this time a reply is found. God says in Isaiah that ' He shall call His servants by another name '[1]. This is clearly a reference to the Christians, and renders superfluous the question of their origin. The most interesting parts of this section are, however, those dealing with the question of images, and the lack of harmony in the Gospels[2]. The fourth assembly deals primarily with the prophecies of Daniel, at the end of which the Jews admit complete defeat. ' They blushed with shame, were silent and still, were troubled, were agitated, grew sombre and embarrassed, blushed, were astray, ran off without stopping, got up, fled as if a fire pursued them, fell about like drunkards; all their wisdom was consumed, and they all departed, some in silence, some grumbling, some groaning, some exclaiming "Adonai, the monk has won ", some shaking their heads and saying to each other, " By the Law, I believe we are wrong"; and some of the elder ones made ridiculous remarks such as " Dear! Dear! How much bacon have we been robbed of?" Some instead of enemies became friends of the Christians. Others waited for an opportunity to be baptised, and the dearest of them came to the church in all sincerity and truth and received the seal of baptism.'[3]

A fourth seventh-century discussion between Jews and Christians which is worthy of mention is the History of the conversion of the Jews of Tomei in Egypt[4]. Unfortunately it is not yet possible to follow in detail the controversy itself, for the Arabic manuscripts of the Bibliothèque Nationale have not yet been published, and it is only possible to learn the main lines of the discussion from

[1] Isaiah, lxv, 15.

[2] *Trophies*, p. 75 ff. and 87 ff.

[3] *Ibid.*, p. 105.

[4] Edited by P. Griveau in R.O.C., Vol. XIII, p. 198.

the summary of M. Griveau. It is therefore impossible to judge the extent to which the intellectual victory really lay with the Christian protagonists.

The town of Tomei was primarily populated by Jews, the descendants of a settlement of Vespasian. Near to it was a monastery, and the monks used to send two of their number regularly to buy provisions in the town. Arriving one day they find a Jewish festival in progress, and the leader of the Jews, Amran the Levite, is reading and expounding the Law to his companions. The monks want to know what he is reading, to discover ' whether the worship the Jews offer on this day to the Lord will find favour in His sight '. From this they easily involve the Jews in a discussion, and begin with the Trinity. The discussion has the interest that Amran is convinced step by step, and not, as usual, at the end. Convinced of the existence of the Word, he requires conviction as to His humanity. And by this method the discussion passes through the usual range with variations. Amran leads the town to follow his example, and finally the whole Jewish population, over three hundred souls, is baptised by the bishop, and the record of the discussion is committed to paper to be read three times a year in all the churches.

A story which, though it does not contain any formal disputation, is yet worthy to be classed with these narratives, is the history of Theodosius the priest of the Jews in Alexandria. He had a Christian friend, Philip, with whom he held long discussions. In the course of these he told him that he believed in his heart that Jesus was the Messiah, but felt too sinful to be baptised. Moreover, there were other reasons against baptism, for he would lose his honour and dignity among the Jews without being accepted by the Christians, who had a proverb ' when a Jew is baptised, it is as if one baptised an ass '. He goes on to say that most of the Jews believe, but are repelled by the sinfulness of the lives of the Christians, and finally he asserts that in His lifetime Jesus was accepted as one of the twenty-two elders of the Jews. In the end he, and many Jews with him, are baptised[1].

The advent of Islam introduced a new kind of controversy,

[1] *Arabic History of the Patriarchs of Alexandria*, P.O., Vol. I, p. 122.

in which the three religions took part, and the Christian scored equally off his Jewish and Mohammedan opponents[1], but such fall outside the scope of the present study.

VI. THE JEWS IN THE ICONOCLASTIC CONTROVERSY

Very comparable to these stories of Jewish conversions as a result of discussion are the collection of romances which accompanied the Iconoclastic controversy in the time of the Isaurian emperors. The reaction against images on the part of the eastern provinces owed something certainly to the abuses of Byzantine monasticism, but it also owed a good deal to the neighbouring influences of Judaism and Islam, both of which religions refuse absolutely all such aids to devotion.

Nearly all the chroniclers recount in different forms how the controversy originated in the deep-rooted hatred of the Jews for Christ and the Virgin Mary, and ascribe the Mohammedan prohibition of images to the same influence[2]. We have already seen that the question of images figures in some of the disputations between Jews and Christians. A particularly interesting case of this is the record of such a discussion at the fifth *actio* of the second council of Nicaea, where a Jew is quoted who believed in Christ but who could not accept the images in the Christian churches. The full discussion is read out to the council, together with the way in which he is convinced by the reference to similar worship in Judaism[3].

It being an accepted view—for propaganda purposes at any rate—of the ' iconodules ' that the Jews were responsible for the attacks of the Isaurian emperors upon images, it was an ingenious thought to evolve a series of stories in which Jews were represented as having been converted by the power of those images which the iconoclasts claimed

[1] E.g. *La vie de S. Michel le Sabaite* in A.B., Vol. XLVIII.

[2] *E.g.* Nicephorus, P. of Constantinople, *Antirrheticus*, III; P.G., C, p. 528, A.S. for July 8 (July, Vol. II, p. 637) and Aug. 9 (Aug., Vol. II, p. 435); George Hamartolus, IV, ccxlviii; P.G., CX; and in western chroniclers also *e.g.*, Sigbert, *Chron.* for 724 in M.G.H. folio, VI, p. 330.

[3] See Mansi, XIII, p. 166.

to be merely idols[1]. No better way of convincing the faithful could indeed be imagined, for as Theodoret of Cyr remarks on another occasion: 'When Jews bear witness to Christian miracles, who can remain sceptical?'[2]

The general line of these stories is usually the same[3]. To insult Christianity a Jew who has by some means or other become possessed of a Christian image or precious object decides to profane it. The object proves its sanctity and power, and the Jew is usually converted. In one case the Jew steals an image of Christ which he has often seen in a church (one wonders how) in order to destroy the picture 'of the deceiver who has humiliated our people'. He pulls it down from the wall but, unobserved, it bleeds, and when he reaches home he is covered with blood. His bloody footsteps next day guide Christians to his house: the picture is found, and he is stoned. With their love of picturesque and apparently convincing detail, the Byzantines embroider the story in various ways. In one story a poor Christian is indignant at being poor while a neighbour, who is a Jew, is rich. He tries to become a member of the Jew's household in order to rob him, but the Jew will only accept him if he is converted. To this he agrees, and, as part of the ritual, is made to stab a crucifix[4]. In another version Jews rent a house near the synagogue, and the previous Christian tenants have left an image of

[1] It is possible that such stories did not actually originate at this time. For in the *Glory of the Martyrs* of Gregory of Tours, written two centuries earlier, appears a somewhat similar narrative. See note 3, below.

[2] Theodoret, *Religiosa Historia*, vi; P.G., LXXXII, p. 1358.

[3] *De Gloria Martyrorum*, I, xxii. I have not been able to discover whether there are any grounds for considering this story to be a later addition. If it were a detached incident, it would certainly be natural to ascribe it to the 8th rather than the 6th century. It is noticeable that in the stories which can be traced to the eighth century, the incidents are often alleged to have taken place some centuries earlier. Thus the famous story of the crucifix of Tiberias is said to have taken place in the time of Zeno (475-491), *i.e.* before the time of Gregory, so that a later copyist would not think he was committing any anachronism in inserting it into a work of Gregory.

[4] Version of the *Syn. Ethiop.* in P.O., IX, p. 318 ff. The incident takes place in the time of Theophilus, uncle of Cyril of Alexandria, and in a Coptic version the incident is related in a Sermon on Penitence ascribed to Cyril himself. See *Mélanges de la Faculté Orientale de Beyruth*, Vol. VI, where an introduction discusses all the stories.

Christ there on vacating it[1]. In another version the image itself is one of particular beauty, which has been specially carved by the Christian who had lived in the house[2]. In yet a fourth variant, which places the scene at Tiberias, it is the Jews who have had the image made, pretending that they wished to worship it, when their only purpose was to insult it[3].

The image having once been stabbed, again various effects ensue. Blood or blood and water flow out, and the Jews are filled with horror at their action. They are struck with foul diseases (or they bring in those who are possessed of foul diseases), and are only cleansed by the water and blood, or by the water of baptism. They are all converted, and in one case, where the incident takes place in a synagogue, the building is converted into a church.

A distinct version is the story of the image in S. Sophia. A Jew who frequently passed through the church had always especially hated one particular image, and waiting for an occasion to be alone he stabbed it, but such quantities of blood and water flowed out that the whole pavement of the church was flooded, and the crime instantly discovered. The Jew and his family were converted[4].

A further variant is told by Agapius, a chronicler of the tenth century. This time the scene is laid at Antioch in the reign of Maurice, the image is one of the Virgin, which the Jews insult in repulsive fashion, and the result is not the conversion but the expulsion of the Jews from that city[5].

Such is one family of stories dealing with the miraculous conversion of Jews by images. A quite different narrative, leading to the same conclusion, is the eighth-century ancestor of the *Merchant of Venice*, the history of Theodore the Christian merchant, and Abraham the Jew of Constan-

[1] John Cassian in S.A., P.O. XXI, p. 104; cf. also Sigbert, *Chron.* year 765 in M.G.H. folio, VI, p. 333.

[2] The sermon of the pseudo-Athanasius in P.G., XXVIII, p. 797, which was read in the 4th Actio of Nicaea II, M., XIII, pp. 24 and 580. See Dobschutz, *op. cit.*, p. 281**.

[3] *History of the Likeness of Christ*, Budge.

[4] Combefis, De maximo miraculo, in *Historia Haeresis Monothelitarum*, Paris, 1648.

[5] Agapius in P.O., VIII, p. 439.

tinople. Details of the story are strangely reminiscent of Shakespeare—though the Jew has a different rôle to play.

Theodore, like Antonio, loses his fortune with the wreck of his fleet. He goes to his Christian friends to raise money. They refuse to lend it, and he remembers Abraham, a Jewish merchant who had frequently desired to share his ventures, and to whom he had consistently refused this participation. Abraham reminds him of this in much the same way as Shylock addresses Antonio and reproaches him for his past insolence, but consents to the loan if surety can be found. Theodore returns to his Christian friends, who reply: 'Away from me, man, I am so far from consenting to go and see that infamous and unbelieving Jew, that I would not even speak or say " good morning " to him '. Theodore, depressed, goes and weeps in a church—the ancient synagogue which Theodosius II had taken from the Jews in the Copper Market. There an image tells him that it will be guarantor. Abraham, amazed by his faith, accepts the guarantee of the image, and after initial failure his loan leads to the re-establishment of the fortunes of Theodore. Impressed thereby he is converted, and identified with a subsequent abbot[1].

Another story, tending to the same end, is related by John of Nikious. A Jew of Alexandria possesses a coffer which cannot be opened. One day, while making a special effort to open it, he hears heavenly voices praising Christ, and lightning plays around the box. Alarmed, he goes to the bishop, who opens it without difficulty. Inside are found the very towels which Christ used in washing the disciples' feet. The box is taken to the church, and the Jew is converted[2].

Further research will very likely lead to the discovery of more stories of the same kind, but these are sufficient to show that such inventions were not casual, but were definitely part of the armoury of the iconoclastic controversy, and that the varied periods to which they are assigned are merely versions of the opening ' once upon a time '.

[1] Combefis, *op. cit.*, De Salvatoris Imagine dicta Antiphonetes; see also A.S., Oct., Vol. XII, Auctarium, p. 760.

[2] John of Nikious, xci.

VII. THE MIRACULOUS CONVERSIONS OF THE JEWS

It was all the easier to gain credence for these stories, in that the lives of the saints and the histories of the time were full of the accounts of the miraculous conversions of Jews. These fall into several classes. At times there is merely a short reference that such a saint converted many Jews. At other times a full and circumstantial story is given.

The first kind need not detain us, for they present no particular interest, though they are sometimes amusing, as when it is accurately related that on the miraculous conversion of Entawos the Amorean, 10,798 Jews and pagans followed him to the font[1]. The others are worthy of some attention.

First there are the stories and miracles of those who were themselves converted Jews, such as Epiphanius[2]. It may be assumed that such stories were a bait to attract Jews to the fold by recording the eminence after conversion of their fellows, just as the leader of the Jews, converted at Tomei, succeeds ultimately the bishop who baptised him.

Then come the stories where Christian miracles are brought into play to prove the superiority of Christianity over Judaism. Such stories we have already encountered in studying the lives of the martyrs[3]. An example of the readiness with which the Byzantines allowed the Jews to score points off their Christian antagonists is the story of Donatus, bishop of Istria in Egypt, which has been already quoted. He was a great apologist, and after his defence of the Virgin Birth the Jews professed contempt for the claims of Christ, and when asked the reason pointed out that Christ had been living when He performed His miracles, whereas the dead bones of Elisha sufficed to bring a corpse back to life[4]. But their triumph was short lived, for they were ultimately confounded by the Resurrection[5]. An

[1] S.E., Aug. 23, in P.O., IX, p. 343.

[2] *E.g.* in S.A.J., P.O., XVI, p. 1031.

[3] Ch. IV, Section IX.

[4] II Kings xiii, 21.

[5] Greek Acta in A.S., May 22, Vol. V, p. 145.

extremely popular story of this kind is based on the incident of the three Holy Children in the fire. A Jewish boy in Constantinople partakes of Communion without anyone knowing that he is a Jew. He tells his father, who is a glass blower, and is thrown into the furnace. His mother finds him there later unharmed, and she and the boy are baptised[1].

A third variety is devoted to proving the efficacity of particular Christian symbols or sacraments. Thus, in the life of Basil of Caesarea, a Jew who comes secretly to Communion sees a child in the wafer and blood in the chalice and is converted[2]. Saint Constantine, who became a monk in Bithynia, was converted by observing the marvellous effect upon himself of signing himself with a cross[3]. Many are the stories in which Jews are cured of diseases by baptism[4]. Sometimes the miracle consists in an appeal to a Christian saint and precedes the baptism[5], and in one case a Jew, smearing his eyes with the blood of some monks murdered in the Monophysite controversy, immediately receives his sight[6].

Other stories reflect merely the love of story telling, and have no moral lesson at all. In fact, some of them exhibit rather the opposite characteristics. The many stories of Epiphanius and his donkey belong to this class. Another, told of at least two saints, is that of the two Jewish beggars, one of whom shammed dead that the other might ask the saint to bring him to life. The saint spreads his mantle over him—and he is dead[7]. A lengthy narrative

[1] The story is told of the time of S. Menas, P. of Constantinople (536-552), A.S., Aug. 25; and may for that reason have been inserted into the Miracula of Gregory of Tours (I, x), who was a contemporary. It is also related by Evagrius, IV, xxxvi; P.G., LXXXVI, 2, p. 2769; and by George Hamartolus, *Chron.*, IV, ccxxii; and Nicephorus Callistus, *Ec. Hist.*, XVII, xxv.

[2] *De Vitis Patrum*, Basil, ii, P.L., LXXIII, p. 301, repeated in S.A. for Jan. 1, P.O., XVIII, p. 153.

[3] A.S., Nov., Vol. IV, p. 627.

[4] *E.g.* S. Martyrianus in A.S., Nov., Vol. IV, p. 442; S. Atticus in A.S., Jan., p. 477; Aaron of Serug in P.O., Vol. V, p. 710 etc.

[5] *E.g.* A.S., April, Vol. III, p. 479, and July, Vol. II, p. 226.

[6] Zachariah of Mitylene, III, vi.

[7] Told of James of Nisibis in P.O., XVIII, p. 47; and of Gregory of Neocaesarea in the works of Barhadbesabba 'Arbaia, P.O., XXIII, p. 260.

relates how a Jew named Saktâr desires to dispute with S. Severianus, bishop of Philadelphus, but the saint has a better argument than words. He strikes his opponent dumb, and the dumbness is only removed by baptism[1]. But the palm of all such stories must be given to the Jew of Theodore of Mopsuestia. This patient soul listened for long to a daily sermon of the saint, but one day, being prevented from attendance, he fell dead. It was some time before the saint realised his absence, and when he did he was dismayed, for he had made sure of a conversion. He asked an attendant what had happened, and was told of his death. Without a moment's delay he made for the cemetery, dug up the now decaying gentleman, brought him back to life again and baptised him. He then asked him whether he would prefer to remain alive or return to the tomb, and when the Jew chose the latter alternative, he pushed him back into his coffin and reburied him—safely baptised[2].

VIII. JEWS IN APOCRYPHAL WRITINGS

So far we have been dealing primarily with stories terminating in the conversion of the Jews. There is, however, yet another series of Byzantine romances in which Jews figure prominently, but almost exclusively in an unfavourable light. If for conversional purposes the Byzantines invented stories such as that of Theodosius the Jewish priest of Alexandria, on the other hand, in their apocryphal gospels and in their lives of the saints of the apostolic and sub-apostolic ages, they generally represented the Jews as monsters of iniquity.

Apocryphal gospels in themselves are a very early invention, but the purpose of the early attempts of this kind was usually to give a particular turn to the teaching of Jesus, and they contained little in themselves that was remarkable. Later ages specialised in the lives of the saints, which offered freer scope for invention than the life of Christ Himself. Yet even here strange details were added to the gospel narrative. A Coptic text of the ' Gospel

[1] S.A.J. in P.O., I, p. 241.

[2] *Nestorian History*, P.O., V, p. 287.

of the Twelve Apostles' recounts that after the raising of Lazarus the Jews tried to kill Him, but 'Caius', the Roman governor, wished to make Him king in the place of the Tetrarch Philip. The Jews offered him large bribes not to do so, and produced evidence, which was denied by Joseph of Arimathea and Nicodemus, against His whole life. Caius accepted the bribes and did not make the suggestion to Tiberius. When Pilate appeared on the scene at the time of the trial, he also wanted to make Him king. The whole responsibility for His condemnation is made to lie with the jealousy of Herod[1]. In the Apocryphal Acts of Pilate, another Coptic version, Pilate throughout the trial treats Jesus as a king[2].

In inventing new miracles they naturally had a free hand—and used it. The first thing that strikes a modern reader in such collections as the Ethiopian Book of the Miracles of Jesus, is the entire moral worthlessness of most of the miracles recounted[3]. Even the good fairies of Grimm's *Fairy Tales* do not act with such a complete contempt for everything except their own power.

Parallel to the theological conception of the Jews as heretics, conscious of the truth and rejecting it, are the stories accompanying the Resurrection, or the death of the Virgin, already discussed[4]. A further set of stories deal with the trial of Peter and Paul at Rome. Pagans and Jews meet together romantically in a temple to discuss how to stop the mouths of the intrepid Apostles—in the interests of polytheism![5]

Having once begun to compose historical scenes, they did not stop at the Apostolic period. Agapius recounts at immense length a confession of the Jews to Constantine. They admit having falsified the dates in the Torah in order to make it appear that the Messiah had not come, knowing quite well that He had really come in the person of Jesus at the dates foretold[6]. Other narratives clustered round

[1] See P.O., II, pp. 140 and 152.

[2] See P.O., IX, p. 59.

[3] P.O., XII, XIV, XVII.

[4] See Ch. III, Section VIII.

[5] Cf. *Syrian Acts*, published in R.O.C., Vol. III.

[6] P.O., V, p. 645.

the reign of Julian. Four hundred Jews, all rabbis of Tiberias, are said to have gone to meet him at Constantinople at his accession, and to have offered him a crown of gold, which was fashioned with seven idols as decoration. Julian demanded of them that they should worship the idols and partake of a meal of pork. The Jews hastened to obey both commandments of the emperor, and to prove their delight repeated their obedience several times[1]. This unusual conception of the Jews is parallel to the astonishing statement in the *Arabic History of the Patriarchs* concerning the rebuilding of the Temple during the same reign. When the building collapses, some Jews of Jerusalem tell the builders that they will never succeed as long as the bones of ' the Christians ' still rest on the site. The Jews therefore dig up and throw out—the bones of Elijah and John the Baptist! [2]

IX. JEWS IN THE THEOLOGIANS

Of the theological views of the period there is little to add to what has already been developed. The theological picture of the Jew as fashioned in the first three centuries remains. Some of the great writers of the period, such as Theodoret of Cyr and Severus of Antioch, speak with great moderation of the Jews in their sermons[3].

Others, and especially the later ones, blend into their sermons the ideas of the Jews created by apocryphal writings. Eusebius of Emesa is fond of coupling together the devil and the Jews, and this trait is even more characteristic of his namesake of Alexandria. The devil refers casually from time to time to ' his old friends, the Jews '[4]. Eusebius of Alexandria, at least, had no doubt as to their ultimate destination. In his sermon on the Resurrection every paragraph of the first half begins with the words: ' Woe to

[1] *Nestorian History*, P.O., V, p. 238.

[2] *Arabic History of the Patriarchs*, P.O., I, p. 419.

[3] Cf. Severus of Antioch, *Catechetical Address*, No. 70, P.O., XII, pp. 19 and 28; and Theodoret *Quaestio in Genesim*, xlix, No. 110; P.G., LXXX, p. 216.

[4] See the works of these fathers in P.G., LXXXVI, *passim*, but especially Eusebius of Alexandria, sermo. xv.

you, wretches, for you follow evil counsels, for you were called sons and became dogs. Woe to you, stiff-necked and uncircumcised, for being the Elect of God you became wolves, and sharpened your teeth upon the Lamb of God. You are estranged from His Glory; woe to you, ungrateful wretches, who have loved Hell and its eternal fires. For when Hell yields up those entrusted to it, it shall receive you in their place. And Hell shall revenge itself upon you for the defeat it received from the Lord, and it shall imprison you with your father the devil '[1].

The theologians in their denunciations of the Jews go back again and again to the accusations contained in the Old Testament. Reflections of the tension in the eastern provinces are not to be found in their works, and if, on the one hand, this silence about facts which we know to have taken place warns us to be cautious in the use of the *argumentum e silentio*, on the other it shows that the incidents must be taken at their own value only, and not used as an argument of permanent and universal conflict between Jews and Christians.

X. ' JEW ' AS A TERM OF ABUSE IN THE NESTORIAN-CHALCEDONIAN-MONOPHYSITE CONTROVERSY

Loose thinking is more likely to lead to exaggeration than to mitigation, especially on such a subject, and what we have seen in the weaving of romances we find to be confirmed from a different field, that of heresy. Legislation had for some centuries been approximating the lot of the Jew and the heretic, and certain passages have been quoted to show that the Jew could himself be regarded as a Christian ' heretic '. But it is only in the Nestorian controversy that a heretic is for the first time simply called a ' Jew '.

The possible influence of the Jews in the formation of heretical doctrine has already been referred to at various times. There are few problems of the period more difficult to solve than that of the extent of Jewish influence over

[1] *Sermon on the Resurrection* ascribed to Eusebius of Alexandria, and included in the works of Chrysostom; P.G., LXI, p. 733.

their Christian contemporaries. But nowhere is the accusation more continuously and consistently flung from side to side than in the great Christological controversies of the fifth and sixth centuries, between the Nestorians, the Monophysites and the Chalcedonians. The Nestorians saw in Christ two natures mechanically joined together rather than an essential and personal union. This was condemned at the Council of Ephesus in 431 and again at Chalcedon in 451. This latter council established the still orthodox doctrine of the two natures 'unconfused and unchanged, indivisible and inseparable' united in the Person of Christ, 'the distinction of the natures being by no means taken away by the union, but rather the property of each nature being preserved'. This is the doctrine embodied in the 'Athanasian' Creed. This did not satisfy a large portion of the Church, the Monophysites, who professed to believe in one nature in composite form, so that the humanity becomes a mere accident of the divinity. This controversy raged for over a century, accompanied by appalling bloodshed, and ended in a schism still unhealed within the eastern Church.

It is evident that there is nothing 'Jewish' about the Monophysites, with their belief in one nature and their small emphasis on the humanity of Christ, but both of the other two were called 'Jewish' by their opponents. Thus in the controversy between Nestorians and Chalcedonians, the Nestorians are constantly called 'Jews'. The synod of Ephesus writes to Nestorius, and heads its letter: 'The Holy Synod to Nestorius the new Jew'[1]. The emperor Anastasius, in opening a council to discuss the theology of Macedonius the Nestorian Patriarch of Constantinople some seventy years later, begins his address with the words: 'Have you not seen what this Jew who is amongst us did?'[2]. Two hundred years later, at the Council *in Trullo*, a reference is made to those who follow the doctrine of Nestorius, separating the natures of Christ and 'reviving Jewish impiety'[3]. There is thus a consistent tradition that

[1] *Chron.* IV, in C.S.C.O. Scrip. Syr., III, iv, p. 161.

[2] Letters of Simeon the Presbyter in the *Chronicle* of Zachariah of Mitylene, VII, viii.

[3] Trullanum, Can. 1, M., XI, p. 938.

Nestorianism owed something to Jewish influence, and we can trace the working of this tradition in the belief which grew up that Nestorius had actually denied the existence of a divine nature in Christ, an erroneous idea, for Nestorianism was an attempt to interpret the decision of Nicaea. Nestorius never attempted to question the fact that in His divinity Christ was ' equal to the Father '. But Gregory the Great in a letter to the emperor Maurice simply accuses Nestorius of ' Judaica perfidia '[1], and other references speak of the Nestorian Christ as ' merus homo ', and speak of His fear of death[2].

That a belief which denied the divinity of Christ might owe something to contemporary Jewish influence is possible, and indeed probable, but it is a different thing to ascribe Jewish influence to a theological idea which its opponents chose to characterise as ' Jewish '. We can judge of the justice of the accusation only by estimating whether it is probable that Jewish controversialists would in reality be likely to influence Christians with whom they came into contact in the sense of the idea under discussion. And here we have to admit that there is nothing in Nestorian doctrine in the least likely to be due to Jewish influence. Its very point of departure, the Nicaean formula, was the exact antithesis of any possible Jewish conception of the Messiah, and the different interpretations which devolved from that idea were therefore without interest for the Jews.

This belief, that Nestorianism owed nothing to contemporary Jewish influence, and that the use of the word Jew is merely abusive, is borne out by the fact that the Monophysites, with equal fervour, called the Chalcedonians ' Jews '. We have already seen that at times it is impossible to tell whether incidents referred to Jews are really caused by them[3], but when it comes to calling the Chalcedonian formula of the nature of Christ ' Jewish ', we can be in no doubt.

A pleasant story circulated by the Monophysites was

[1] Gregory, Ep. V, xx; cf. XI, lxvii.

[2] Michael the Syrian, XI, xx; and M. Mercator, *Diss. I de Haeresi et libris Nestorii*; P.L., XLVIII, p. 1124.

[3] See Ch. VII, Section II.

that after the council of Chalcedon the Jews petitioned the emperor Marcian in these terms:

> 'For a long time we were regarded as descendants of those who crucified a God and not a man, but since the Synod of Chalcedon has decided that we crucified a man and not a God, we beg to be forgiven for this offence, and to have our synagogues restored to us.'[1]

To Severus of Antioch Nestorians, Chalcedonians and the Henoticon of Leo, are alike 'Jewish'[2]. The successors of Severus, who were Chalcedonians, are likewise called Jews by the Chroniclers[3].

The Jacobites in Egypt also used the term 'Jew' to cover all sects with whom they disagreed. Thus at the end of the seventh century the Emir of Egypt asked the Bishops of the Melkites (Chalcedonians), Gaianites (extreme Monophysites holding the body of Christ to be incorruptible), Barsanuphians (sect of Eutychians) and Jacobites which of the others they found nearest to their own teaching. The first three all replied that the nearest to themselves was Simon the bishop of the Jacobites, but he being asked as to his view of them, excommunicated them all and condemned them as Jews[4].

Whatever may have been the situation in earlier centuries, in these controversies we can conclude that the word 'Jew' is simply a term of abuse, and that to look for any real basis for it is futile. That there were many contacts and discussions with Jews we know, but that they exercised any influence over Christian doctrine, except in their disapproval of images, we cannot assert.

[1] Michael the Syrian, VIII, xii; and the *Ecclesiastical History* of John of Asia in R.O.C., Vol. II, p. 458.

[2] *The Conflict of Severus* in P.O., IV, pp. 629, 655, 680; *Homily* 56 in P.O., IV, p. 80; and *Letters*, No. 46 in P.O., XII, p. 321.

[3] Michael the Syrian, IX, xiv and xxix; and Zachariah of Mitylene, VIII, ii.

[4] *History of the Patriarchs*, I, xvi, Simon I, P.O., V, p. 35.

XI. THE RITUAL OF THE CONVERSION OF THE JEWS

It is equally difficult to assess with any accuracy the extent to which success attended the efforts of Christian preachers to convert actual Jews. For this purpose the existing disputations prove nothing. We know that from very early times collections of texts existed whose object was to prove to the Jew from his own scriptures the truth of the Christian gospel. But we do not know with what success they were used. We know that it was lawful for Jews to attend portions of the Christian services, but we do not know how many did so. We have in one or two of the catechetical addresses of Severus of Antioch the suggestion that he is speaking to Jews. But all this is extremely vague and leaves the main question unanswered.

Our collection of early liturgical uses is too scanty for us to know at what period special ritual was introduced for the conversion of the Jews. In the very beginning it was easier for a Jew to enter the Church than for a pagan. He already accepted much of the faith, and the only real question at issue was his acceptance of the claims of Jesus as interpreted by the Church. No special problem seems to have arisen until the beginning of anti-Jewish legislation introduced a class whose conversions were due to economic and social and not to religious motives. With this class we have already become familiar in the later Roman legislation[1].

With the emergence of such a class it is natural that the Church proceeded to make it harder, instead of easier, for a Jew to enter her fold, and both in the west and in the east immense and complicated forms of abjuration were devised in the attempt to secure the sincerity of the conversion[2]. The forms themselves exhibit an exquisite ignorance of things Jewish. To assert that the Jew solemnly and with hope awaited the coming of Antichrist was to be expected of Byzantine theologians. But to class together

[1] Cf. C.T., 9.45.2 and 16.8.3, laws of Honorius and Arcadius.

[2] Oriental and Visigothic forms of abjuration are given in Appendix 3.

'Sabbaths, superstitions, hymns, chants, observances and synagogues' indicates a somewhat muddled conception of Judaism[1].

XII. RELATIONS BETWEEN JEWS AND CHRISTIANS

These early centuries of Byzantine history are of extraordinary interest for the information which they give us of all things Jewish. The picture is full of variety, and at times astonishingly vivid. It reflects many different situations, and shows the Jews in varying lights. The general trend of the whole is certainly to show a progressively increasing hostility between the Jews and their Christian neighbours. But it is also possible to trace with a certain amount of precision the causes of this change. In the first place must come the increasing severity of Byzantine legislation, for, as we have seen again and again, it is not possible to create an inferior class and then to expect that individual enthusiasm will not overstep the bounds of legal permission. The general validity of this consequence is being abundantly proved in present day Germany. The second cause is the religious fanaticism of the oriental monastic orders, fanaticism from which the Jews were not the only sufferers. The third cause is the political situation caused by the Persian wars, and the difference of treatment accorded to Jews on the two sides of the eastern frontier of the Byzantine empire.

It is also evident that the political cause is secondary and the result of the first two causes, both of which are in their nature religious. And again it is impossible to get behind the religious cause to a secret economic hostility.

References to the economic activities of the Jews are practically non-existent, and the fact that a few Jews possessed immense fortunes is not enough to prove that all Jews lived by commerce[2], or that the considerable numbers who did so earned the hostility of their Christian neighbours thereby. It is noticeable that the description which Jacob

[1] On the whole subject of Jewish conversions see Juster, *op. cit.*, Vol. I, pp. 102-119.

[2] Cf. Theophanes, anno 620, for the story of a wealthy Jew of Caesarea, who was filled with hatred for the Christians; and Dionysius of Tel Mahre, ed. Chabot, p. 41, for a Jew of Emesa from whom the Moslems took 400,000 pieces of gold.

gives of his activities as a Jew before his conversion are entirely political, whereas if the Jews were notorious for exhibiting their hostility in business he would more likely have described his methods of overreaching Christians or harassing them in his commercial activities. But as a merchant he seems to have been above reproach[1]; in fact, they took him for a Christian until his unlucky fall down the stairs. The monks of Tomei have no complaint to make of the treatment which they received from the Jews from whom they bought their food. The friends of Theodore objected to the religion and not to the business of Abraham, and as a financier he showed himself far more generous than any of Theodore's Christian friends. Not only are there such passages where silence is legitimately used as an argument, but our information in general is too full and varied for the omission of all references to Jewish commercial activity to be an oversight.

To these facts must be added the evidence that, where there was no direct reason for the contrary, relations between Jews and Christians were not unfriendly. Local Christians did not necessarily approve of the doings of the monks, and the councils in the east as well as in the west had to cope with close social relationships between Jews and Christians. All references to Jews are not hostile. Anecdotes are retailed by various chroniclers showing their compassion for Christian suffering[2], their admiration for Christian piety[3], and their desire to assist Christians in distress[4].

If, therefore, there was a class which plagued the Church by fraudulently demanding baptism, and against which it was necessary to adopt severe measures, it does not seem that the ordinary Jew earned the hostility of the ordinary Christian by his behaviour. Left to themselves, they still got on well together. In the face of the legal hostility, the violence of the monks, and severe political tension lasting over a century, this could only have been the case if their daily relations, social and commercial, passed without any specific mark of hostility.

[1] Sargis d'Aberga in P.O., III.

[2] E.g. *History of S. Ahoudemmeh* in P.O., III, p. 43.

[3] *E.g.* Barhadbesabba 'Arbaia, *History of Basil of Caesarea*, P.O., XXIII, p. 287; or *ibid.*, *Life of Mar Abraham* in P.O., IX, p. 621.

[4] See Ch. VII, Section VIII.

CHAPTER NINE

CIVES ROMANI, RELIGIONE JUDAEI

BIBLIOGRAPHICAL INTRODUCTION

Although the histories of the Jews in western Europe mostly begin with the eleventh or twelth centuries, yet there are a certain number of studies of considerable value for the earlier period. The relevant references are collected, with a few exceptions, in the extracts of Aronius, accompanied in most cases by bibliographical notes. The sources themselves are primarily the *History of the Franks* by Gregory of Tours, the letters of Sidonius, the poems of Venantius, and certain lives of contemporary ecclesiastics to be found either in the *Patrologia Latina*, the *Acta Sanctorum* or the *Monumenta Germaniae Historica*. The last named also contains all the laws of the period, and the early chroniclers. The canons of the different councils are naturally to be found in the Collection of Mansi. In treating of the Arian period of southern French history, the Breviary of Alaric has been omitted, as it can more easily be considered in the next chapter in relation to the development of Visigothic law.

For the general history of the period it is not necessary to quote a long list of books. The history of Lot gives a general picture of conditions and also contains a full bibliography.

The study of specifically Jewish history in this period begins in the early nineteenth century with the inauguration by the Institut de France in 1821 of a competition for a work on the mediaeval history of the Jews in France, Spain and Italy. This formed the foundation for the books of Depping and Bedarride—the latter a work remarkable for the extent of its references and for the fact that the numbers in the text rarely correspond with the numbers in the notes. These two works were followed by two German contributions to the subject, which concentrated specially on the early laws affecting the Jews, the works of Scherer and Stobbe. A more general study is that of Abbott.

The economic conditions of the Jews at this period have also been the subject of special studies, especially the dissertation of Hahn, and the early chapters of the monumental work of Caro. But together with these works should be read the article of Bréhier on the Syrians if a correct proportion is to be preserved.

Finally the religious relations between Jews and Christians are traced by Newman, but he has little to say of the period preceding the Carolingian Renaissance, the study of which belongs properly to a work on the Middle Ages.

LIST OF BOOKS

ABBOTT, G. F. *Israel in Europe.* Macmillan, 1907.

ARONIUS, J. *Regesten zur Geschichte der Juden im Fränkischen und Deutschen Reiche bis zum Jahre* 1273. Berlin, 1902.

BEDARRIDE, I. *Les Juifs en France, en Italie et Espagne.* Paris, 1859.

BRÉHIER, L. *Les Colonies des Orientaux en Occident* in Byzantinische Zeitschrift, 1903.

CARO, G. *Sozial- und Wirtschaftsgeschichte der Juden im Mittelalter und der Neuzeit.* Leipzig, 1908.

COCHARD, CANON *La Juiverie d'Orleans du VIe au XVe siècle.* Orleans, 1895.

DEPPING, G. B. *Les Juifs dans le Moyen Age.* Paris, 1834.

DILL, S. *Roman Society in the Last Century of the Western Empire.* London, 1899.

GREGORY OF TOURS *History of the Franks.* Ed. O. M. Dalton. Oxford, 1927.

GROSS, H. *Gallia Judaica.* Paris, 1897.

HAHN, B. *Die Wirtschaftliche Tätigkeit der Juden im Fränkischen und Deutschen Reich bis zum 2, Kreuzzug.* Freiburg, 1911.

LEVI, I.	*Histoire des Juifs de France au Xe siècle* in: Rapport sur la Seminaire Israelite. Paris, 1903.
LOT, F.	*La Fin du Monde Antique et le Début du Moyen Age.* Paris, 1927.
MANSI	*Collectio Conciliorum Amplissima,* Vols. VIII, IX and X.
MONUMENTA GERMANIAE HISTORICA	Various volumes.
NEWMAN, L. I.	*Jewish Influence on Christian Reform Movements.* Columbia University Press, 1925.
RÉGNÉ, J.	*Etude sur la Condition des Juifs de Narbonne, du Vème au XIVème siècle.* Narbonne, 1912.
SAIGE, G.	*Les Juifs de Languedoc anterieurment au XIVe siècle.* Paris, 1881.
SCHERER, J. E.	*Die Rechtsverhältnisse der Juden in den deutschösterreichischen Ländern.* Leipzig, 1901.
SIDONIUS APOLLINARIUS	*Letters.* Ed. Baret, Paris, 1879, and O. M. Dalton, Oxford, 1915.
STOBBE, O.	*Die Juden in Deutschland während des Mittelalters, in politischer, sozialer und rechtlicher Beziehung.* Berlin, 1923.
VENANTIUS FORTUNATUS	*Carmina.* Ed. M.G.H. Scriptores, quarto, Vol. IV.

I. THE BARBARIAN INVASIONS

In dealing with the Theodosian Code in the west it has already been necessary to refer to the passage of power from the Roman emperors to their barbarian successors in Italy. In that country this passage left Roman law modified but not superseded. The same thing happened elsewhere. It is fortunately not necessary to trace the waves of invasion which swept over western Europe from the beginning of the fifth century onwards. Many of them passed too fast to have any effect upon the social structure of the society which they ravaged. Those alone which led to permanent settlement had any effect upon the position of the Jewish population. The taking of Rome by Alaric, the invasion of Attila, the whirlwind march of the Vandals across Europe into Africa—these events, catastrophic as they may have been, did not affect the Jew as Jew. They affected him as a member of a society in ruins, but they did not alter his position relative to other members of that society.

Four groups alone affected Jewish conditions, the Ostrogoths, the Visigoths, the Franks and the Burgundians. Of the Jews under the Vandals in Africa and under the Lombards in Italy we know nothing. The situation of the Jews under Theodoric the Ostrogoth has already been described, and the Visigoths are also treated in a separate chapter. But it is not entirely possible to make definite geographical divisions in treating the subject, for in some cases a situation was common to all western Europe, and in others different groups successively ruled the same territory. Thus the south of France was successively held by Ostrogoths, Visigoths and Franks. On the other hand, what is said in this chapter of the Syrians in Gaul would apply also to Italy, and possibly to Spain. Thus while primarily treating of the Jews under the Franks and Burgundians, this chapter also includes incidents occurring in the south of France during the Ostrogothic and early Visigothic period.

II. THE POSITION OF THE JEWS IN ROMAN GAUL

Of the Jews in Roman Gaul we know very little. They were sufficiently important in Cologne in the fourth century for Constantine to pass a special edict enforcing their participation in curial responsibilities[1]. They must also have been numerous farther south, and especially along the Mediterranean coast and in the cities of the Rhone valley. But all we know of their history is contained in a few anecdotes. The murder of a bishop of Clermont by an infuriated father whose son had become a convert has been recounted[2]. In addition we are told that in a rising against Stephen, Bishop of Avignon, at the end of the fourth century Jews took part[3]. This is the extent of our precise knowledge of them for the first few centuries of their settlement.

It is the fashion of many writers to proclaim that in the barbarian invasions the Jew alone made a profit. That he did not suffer exceptionally is perhaps true, though a class with many representatives in the towns and in commercial life is apt to be more affected than country dwellers by such incursions. But neither did he profit exceptionally. The picture of the Jew as a being apart, untouched by the burning of one town, since it meant nothing to him to move to the next; the conception of him as growing perpetually richer among the impoverished natives on a ceaseless flow through his hands of slaves and church plate, is a mythical one[4]. The essential factor about his position was that he was a Roman citizen. The main if not the only distinguishing mark which he possessed was his religion. To go further is to pass into the region of speculation unsupported by evidence.

[1] C.T., 16.8.3.

[2] Ch. IV, Section IV.

[3] Related from *Annales Avenion. Episcoporum* by Leon Bardinet in R.E.J., Vol. I, p. 266. But though he calls them a 'multitude considerable', the text as he quotes it says 'non parva seditiosorum et Judaeorum multitudo', *i.e.* the whole crowd was considerable, not necessarily the Jewish section of it.

[4] Cf., for example, Milman, *History of the Jews*, Vol. II, Bk. xxi, and Dill, *Roman Society in Gaul*.

III. THE SYRIANS IN WESTERN EUROPE

Even when the exaggerated picture of the Jew growing fat out of the profits of the collapse of Rome is avoided, it is often assumed that the Jew stood out as the only trader and banker of his time. His uniqueness is attributed to his economic situation, and not to his religion. But this is radically false. All Jews were not traders and the Jews were not the only traders. They were, perhaps, not even the chief traders of the period. Trade itself, naturally, declined enormously during such a period of chaos and poverty. But it still existed, and the aristocracy still demanded in Spain and Gaul their luxuries from Syria and the east. Bankers were still needed, and slaves were still bought. In all this the Jew had an extremely powerful rival, who both enjoyed the privilege of being a Christian, and also, if patristic writers are to be trusted, was infinitely more unscrupulous than the Jew is ever accused of being. This rival was the 'Syrian'. The Syrians have passed almost unnoticed by most historians. Georg Caro, in his Economic History of the Jews, scarcely mentions them[1]. Their significance was first fully revealed by a French scholar, Louis Bréhier, whose work is copiously supported by references in patristic literature and the evidence of inscriptions[2].

The evidence of patristic literature is of especial importance, for it enables us to weigh together the views of contemporary writers on the Jews and the Syrians, and thereby to correct the perspective of modern authors, who have assumed that what the Jew was in the fifteenth century he must also have been in the fifth. That Jerome was no friend of the Jews we know already. He draws occasional attention not only to their theological errors, but to their unpleasant habits. But his views of them are mild compared with his opinion of the Syrians. Of the latter he remarks that 'up to the present day they are passionately attached to commerce. They overrun the whole world in their passion for lucre; and such is their mania for business

[1] Caro, *op. cit.*, Vol. I, p. 97.

[2] Byzantinische Zeitschrift, 1903, *Les Colonies des Orientaux en Occident*.

that now, while the whole Roman world is the theatre of battle and massacre, their one interest is wealth, and the one thing they flee is poverty '[1]. The implications of the sarcastic remarks of Sidonius Apollinarius on Ravenna imply the same situation when he speaks of ' the priests practising usury and the Syrians singing hymns, the business men fighting, and the soldiers running business '[2]. At the same period Salvianus, writing from Marseilles on the appalling corruption of society, takes as his type of Christian the Syrian, for ' leaving the rest apart, let us look at the whole crowd of traders and Syrians who occupy the larger part of every city, and we shall see that their life is nothing but the plotting of fraud and the fabrication of lies, and that they think that words are utterly wasted which bring no profit to him who uses them '[3]. Compared with such utterances the occasional references to Jewish wealth are insignificant.

There existed corporations of Syrian merchants in the principal towns of Italy, Gaul, Spain and Africa, and in addition to introducing certain agricultural products they specialised in the products of Syria—glass, silk and dyes. In the third century there was a corporation of merchants of Gaza at Ostia[4], and of Tyrian merchants at Puzzoli, and the merchants of Damascus possessed a factory at Misenum; in 440 Valentinian expelled the ' graeci negotiatores ' from Rome, because of their competition with Roman merchants, but was compelled to allow them to return very shortly afterwards. The Syrians possessed a special quarter at Ravenna and another at Naples, and in both were important bankers. In Africa, at the time of the invasion of Belisarius, Gelimar the Vandal threw a large number of them into prison, suspecting their friendship with the Byzantines. In Spain there were two Syrian corporations at Malaga. In Gaul they existed in all parts, passing up the Rhone to Vienne and Lyons; spreading thence into the country regions east of it, they are found down the Seine and Loire, especially at Paris, Orleans and Tours. They penetrated

[1] Jerome, *On Ezekiel*, xxvii, 16; P.L., XXV, p. 266.

[2] Sidonius, Ep. i, 8.

[3] Salvianus, *De Gubernat. Dei*, IV, xiv; P.L., LIII, p. 87.

[4] For references to inscriptions see Bréhier, *op. cit.*

the Garonne to Bordeaux. Traces are even found on the Rhine. They were in regular communication from the French ports with Antioch and the east.

Moreover, they had one immense advantage over the Jews. They were Christians, and their religious penetration, especially in areas influenced from Byzantium, was as great as their commercial. There were various monasteries following the Syrian rule in Gaul, and numbers in Italy, especially at Rome and Ravenna, and they provided a number of Popes. Bréhier sums up their situation in the following words: ' the occupation of the west by orientals went on without interruption until the eighth century. . . . For more than eight hundred years Syrians, Armenians, Egyptians, Persians and Greeks, all soon included under the designation of " Syrians ", established themselves in the main cities of the western empire. Their aim was to acquire wealth by industry and commerce: they never came to the west simply to propagate their ideas. . . . (In the first period) they contented themselves with practising the special industries of Phoenicia, and had to submit to the competition of western industries which possessed a very strong organisation. After the fifth century, in the midst of the barbarians camped in the empire, they preserved the advantage of their ethnic separateness. . . . Instead of mixing with the rest of the population, they formed in each town a distinct group, preserving their Syrian language, and appearing as a corporation in public ceremonies. Their isolation led them to mutual co-operation. Different groups began to act in concert. Meanwhile, the western corporations, so powerful before the third century, had been crushed by state control, and in the fifth century disappeared. The Syrians quite naturally took their place. They and the Jews possessed the monopoly of industry and commerce. They profited by this situation to enrich themselves, and in the middle of barbarian society their wealth soon brought them social advancement. If in this society they could not occupy posts of political importance, they tried instead to gain a foothold in the Church. In Gaul and Italy they sometimes became bishops, and at Rome in the sixth and seventh century, they had almost exclusively the privilege of providing Popes '.

Forgetting the Jews altogether, Bréhier concludes by saying 'after the disappearance of the industrial corporations of the west, it was the Syrians who controlled the whole of economic life. In particular they monopolised the traffic in rare products, and in all the luxuries which the aristocracy of the barbarian period considered indispensable to their material comfort. From the fifth to the eighth century the Syrians were almost the only navigators of the Mediterranean sea, and the only industrialists of the barbarian world '[1].

Even if the last paragraph is an exaggeration, yet the Syrians were of at least equal importance with the Jews both as merchants and bankers. It has already been pointed out that in the mass of references to usury there is no place where ' Jew ' and ' usurer ' are connected, even when to make the connection, if it existed, would have seemed obvious; and the only explicit reference to a Jewish money-lender in the west is to Armentarius, who came to Tours to collect a debt owed him by two officials, and was murdered instead[2]. On the other hand there are, naturally, more references to Jewish traders than to Jewish slaves, peasants or landholders, though all these classes were represented among the Jews of these times and countries. Little is known of Syrian peasants in the west, and this is natural, for they had never had the wholesale expulsions or captivities to which the Jew had been subject; and Syria was far more fertile than Palestine.

It is probable that the Mahometan conquest of Syria contributed to the decline of the Syrians as a separate entity in western Europe, and the fact that they were not separated by religion from those around them would mean that, cut off from their base, they would tend to intermarry and so disappear. In any case before the eighth century we not only cannot speak of the Jew as the only trader of western Europe, but we have no evidence for assuming his importance to be equal to that of the Syrian. Religious distinction, not commercial aptitude, caused his survival when the Syrian disappeared.

[1] Bréhier, *Colonies*, pp. 18 and 37.

[2] Gregory of Tours, *Hist. Ecc. Franc.*, vii, 23.

IV. THE SIMPLIFICATION OF ROMAN LAW

Had the economic situation of the Jew been as exceptional as modern authors claim, there is no reason why restrictive legislation should not have made an early appearance. There were two forces which remained fairly constant and consistent among the warring kings and princelings of the period, the Church and, at its side as the chief secular force, the great landholders. Both had means of legislation, the Church through its council, and the landholders through the survival of Roman law for Roman citizens. But from neither source do we obtain any evidence of definite economic hostility towards the Jew in the centuries immediately following the barbarian invasions.

Ultimately it was from these two forces that mediaeval European society evolved. The system which they slowly perfected and the structure of rights and duties which grew around them, were very different from Roman society. The Catholic Christian religion came to be the exclusive basis of membership. As this happened, as Roman law was slowly replaced by feudal and ecclesiastical law, the last of the Roman citizens, the Jew, came to find himself without any rights whatever, and was forced to depend on the precarious favour of the different powers around him. As long as Roman law survived, so long only was the Jew a normal member of society, except for the restrictions in force in the Roman legislation of the Theodosian Code. The extra laws of Justinian were not valid in the west, and were not introduced until centuries later than our present period. But various modified and simplified recensions of the Code of Theodosius were circulated in western Europe, and formed the basis of legal authority for the indigenous populations.

The Ostrogoths in Italy, and the Papacy succeeding them, administered simply the Code itself. This is apparent again and again in the letters of Gregory the Great and in the edicts and judgments of Theodoric. An Arian Visigothic king, Alaric II, issued the most complete revision of the Code which has survived, and it is noticeable that, so far from having to accentuate the legislation affecting the Jews, he omitted most of the more violent outbursts of the beginning of the fifth century. The Franks and Burgundians contented themselves with a general edict that Roman citizens were to continue to live according to Roman law. The general decline in education makes it probable that it was not the full code, together with the great text books of Law, that was used in France and Burgundy. Here also simplified editions were probably in use, and there is nothing to warrant the supposition that the editions which have perished were more concerned with the Jews than those which have survived.

But as society reformed itself into more coherent and definable areas, general Roman law began to give way to different national codes, and the unity of the treatment of the Jew ceased. He might flourish in one country and be legally oppressed in another. During the time that the Visigoths of Spain were passing their most repressive laws, the Jews of France were living in comparative tranquillity. But it was also true that treatment might vary in a single country according to the enthusiasm or toleration of local authorities. In the old empire difference of treatment was usually due to violent and illegal action in particular places. Now a show of legality could be given to treatment in one place which differed radically from that in a neighbouring community or city. Thus when Avitus used his authority as bishop legally to expel them from Clermont, the neighbouring bishops left them in peace.

V. THE ARIAN PERIOD

The distinction between Goth, Frank or Burgundian and Roman was slow to disappear, and the process was made still slower by the fact that the conquerors were all Arians, while the Roman population was Catholic. The first of the barbarian conquerors to accept Catholicism was Clovis the Frank in 496. The Burgundians followed after their conquest by the Franks some thirty years later. The Visigoths of Spain remained Arian until the conversion of their king Reccared in 586. The last to surrender were the Lombards, living as neighbours to the Papacy itself.

This religious division meant that from the point of view of the central authority, the distinction between Gaul or Goth and Roman was more fundamental than the division between Christian and Jew. In the south of France not only were the Roman titles preserved, but the power was mainly left in the hands of the great Gallo-Roman families, who could wield it either as ecclesiastical or as secular authorities. In fact one could pass from one field to the other. Sidonius Apollinaris, the bishop of Clermont, was son-in-law of that emperor Avitus of whom Gregory of Tours charmingly says that the senate ' finding him somewhat wanton in his habits deposed him from the purple and had him consecrated bishop of Placentia '. Bishopric and Prefecture were parallel roads to the same destination —the authority necessary to the maintenance of order. What was happening at the same time in the empire of Justinian happened also in the west. The ecclesiastical power was being given secular responsibility, and this situation survived the unification of the different kingdoms under the Catholic Church. Not only did it survive but subsequent centuries saw it considerably increased. The power to protect brought the responsibility to govern, and the bishoprics followed the papacy in assuming territorial jurisdiction. As a natural result we shall find church councils passing legislation affecting the civil status as well as the religion of their flocks, and prescribing secular as well as ecclesiastical punishments.

Of the events of the Arian period little has survived, for it was only as times began to be more settled that literature in any form was likely to flourish, or that church councils were likely to be able to meet.

There are several incidents which reveal how much the Arian kings feared to annoy their Catholic subjects. Neither Theodoric nor Alaric thought of altering in favour of their own Church the law by which a new synagogue passed into the hands of the Catholics[1]. Alaric also was compelled to allow his Catholic subjects to meet in council at Agde, moved, it is suggested, by fear that if he refused they would desert to the Franks, whose king, Clovis, had just accepted the Catholic faith. The council of Agde passed two canons

[1] Cf. Ch. VI, Section III, and Breviary of Alaric, Nov. 3.

affecting the Jews. In the first, after expressing alarm at the number of Jews whose conversion had proved insincere, it laid down an eight months' catechumenate to test their sincerity before their admission to baptism[1]. In the other it repeated a canon of the council of Vannes in Brittany. This prohibited the clergy from eating with the Jews on the ground that it was acknowledging an inferior status to accept food from people who considered that the food eaten by Christians was impure, and who therefore would not return the compliment and eat with Christians[2]. The council of Agde adds one phrase to the canon of Vannes, and extends the prohibition to the laity[3].

It would be interesting to know the influence of contemporary Jews on Christians who treated Saturday with especial respect. They may simply have acted out of reverence for the Ten Commandments, but references to this ' Judaising ' habit are extremely frequent for several centuries to come. The twelfth canon of Agde prohibits the omission of fasting on the Saturdays of Lent, and may be a reflection of Jewish influence[4]. The giving and receiving of invitations to meals show that close relations did exist between Jews and Christians in the country, though the increase of false conversions suggests the beginning of a period in which there were advantages in not being a Jew.

There is only one other canon of the Arian Visigothic period which may refer indirectly to Jews, the sixth canon of Orange[5]. This was designed to prevent infuriated owners from claiming the slaves of the clergy when their own had taken refuge in a church and been confiscated. Any slave of a Jew might take refuge in a church and express his desire to become a Christian, on which his Jewish master, even if he followed him to baptism, lost all rights over him. But there was no special ground on which a Christian master lost his slaves if they took refuge in a church. Though it is much later, there is legislation of the

[1] Agde, Canon 34; M., VIII, p. 330.

[2] Vannes, Canon 12; M., VII, p. 954.

[3] Agde, Canon 40; M., VIII, p. 331.

[4] Cf. Orleans III, Canon 28, quoted below, p. 324.

[5] Orange, Canon 6; M., VI, p. 437.

time of Charlemagne forbidding persons to tempt slaves away from their Christian masters, and stating that it is the duty of the Christian to impress on the slave his duty to remain loyal to his master. Gregory the Great was also troubled by the idea that Christian slaves might be led away from their masters and induced to enter a monastic life, and with much hesitation expressed his disapproval of it, unless the slave had a very clear call. It seems then likely that the only classes who would be regularly affected by this canon would be pagan or Jewish owners, and the former were probably very few.

One interesting event is recorded of the Arian Visigothic period, the part played by the Jews at the siege of Arles by Clovis in 508. According to the Life of Saint Caesarius[1] they attempted to betray the city to the Frankish invaders. The story is, however, extremely suspicious. One day the Arlesians discovered a letter, tied to a stone and thrown from the Jewish section of the wall, which promised to deliver the town in return for the immunity of the Jews and their goods. But on the previous day serious suspicion had been thrown upon the bishop that he intended to do the same thing. An ecclesiastic, who was a near relation of his, deserted to the Franks, and Caesarius, who was already under a cloud because of some previous action, was suspected of being behind this desertion of his relative. An angry crowd confronted the bishop and imprisoned him. On the next day the fortunate discovery of the perfidy of the Jews caused a revulsion of popular opinion in his favour, and he was released. But while it is understandable that a Catholic bishop should have motives for belonging to the realm of the Catholic Clovis, rather than to that of the Arian Alaric, it is extremely difficult to see why a Jew should desire to make this change, since the Arians usually treated them better than the Catholics. The story throws a sidelight on another historical fact, whatever be the truth of the alleged treachery. It is evident that in spite of the law which did not allow the Jews to serve in the army, in case of siege they had their own quarter of the wall allotted them to defend.

A special Code was given by Gondebaud of Burgundy,

[1] Cyprianus, *Vita S. Caesarii*, I, iii, 21, 22; P.L., LXVII, p. 1011.

as by the other Arian kings, to his Roman subjects. Only one law refers explicitly to the Jews. It prohibits marriages between Jews and Christians[1]. But Gondebaud also added in his own law a paragraph dealing with them. In this paragraph Jews were forbidden to attack Christians with fist or foot or cudgel, or to pull their hair. The penalty was the loss of a hand, unless it was redeemed by a payment of 12 and a compensation of 75 solidi[2]. The council of Epaone, which was summoned after the conversion of the Burgundians to Catholicism, dealt only with Christians who accepted invitations to Jewish banquets[3].

A survey of the Arian barbarian period shows that the age was marked by increasing lawlessness. But even if they were a minority it does not seem that the Jews quietly accepted the attacks of their Christian neighbours. In fact, the law of Gondebaud, and the canon of Orange (if it refers to the Jews), suggest that they were prepared to give back violence for violence. Of their activities in other directions we know nothing, though it is certain that Marseilles was a great centre of Jewish commerce in the fifth and sixth centuries, as was also probably Narbonne. The council of Epaone shows that their relations with Christians in Burgundy were not entirely those of fisticuffs, and the great outburst of anti-Jewish legislation in Catholic Spain shows that in Arian Spain relations were friendly.

VI. THE JEWS AND THE FRANKISH COUNCILS

Our information on their situation after the conversion of Clovis to Catholicism is much fuller. Councils met with much greater regularity and reviewed the life of the people in considerable detail. Their canons were many, and were probably as effective as any legislation at that time. Different dioceses still had different usages; the era in which an attempt was made to introduce uniformity had not yet begun; collections of canon law were still non-existent, and as a result the treatment of the Jews is not everywhere the same, and laws enacted at one diocesan or provincial council

[1] Leges Romanae Burgundionum, M.G.H. folio, Leges, III, p. 609.

[2] M.G.H. folio, Leges, III, p. 573, Law cii.

[3] Epaone, Canon 15, M., VIII, p. 561.

are not necessarily in force throughout the country[1]. In addition to the councils we possess an invaluable source for the general conditions of the time in the *History of the Franks* of Gregory of Tours, and that author has a number of explicit references also to Jewish life. These two sources, together with occasional references in chroniclers, enable us to recreate a picture of Jewish life under the Franks more completely than we can for any other western kingdom. For in Visigothic Spain our immense collection of legal material is unaccompanied by any information on the actual life and conditions of the Spanish Jews of the epoch.

Yet with all our material on the subject the picture is still inevitably indistinct, and the very wealth and variety of the references make generalisations an easy temptation, and one to which most writers have succumbed. Unfortunately they have used as the basis for their generalisations not the decisions of courts and councils, but the picturesque anecdotes of Gregory and the chroniclers. From the former we can indeed make general deductions, but the latter we can only use legitimately as individual incidents. To generalise from them is merely to exhibit our prejudices. It is easy to say that because Armentarius of Tours was a money-lender this was a common or even universal trade among Jews. It would be just as scientific to say that there were no Jewish money-lenders in France after the sixth century, for since Armentarius was murdered on the only occasion on which (so far as we know) he collected a debt, therefore all money-lenders were murdered as soon as they tried to collect their debts[2].

The conversion of Clovis to Catholicism in 496 did not produce any anti-Jewish movement comparable to that introduced into Spain by the conversion a century later of Reccared. The French councils of Orleans, Clermont and Macon have none of the virulence of the councils of Toledo. The situation with which they deal is one which is well illustrated by two anecdotes of an earlier period, dealing with the two Hilaries. Of Hilary of Poitiers (d. 367) it is related that he was so ' cautious ' that he never accepted

[1] On the growth of canon law and uniformity in France see P. Fournier, *Histoire des collections canoniques en Occident*, Paris, 1931-2.

[2] On Armentarius, see below, p. 341.

food from a heretic or from a Jew. 'Indeed, this most holy man so detested the enemies of the Catholic faith that it is not enough to say that he refused to eat with them, for he refused even to reply to their salutations in the streets.'[1] The author adds of this abstinence from Jewish hospitality that it is something 'quod inter mortales adhuc valde videtur difficile'. Of Hilary of Arles (d. *c.* 450) it is said that he was so much beloved by the people of that city that at his funeral 'the Hebrew wailings of the Jews' were heard side by side with those of other citizens[2].

The comment of the biographer of Hilary of Poitiers and the situation described by the chronicler of the life of Hilary of Arles are shown to reflect a normal state of affairs by the fact that the first French canon which deals with the Jews is a canon of Vannes prohibiting the acceptance of Jewish hospitality by Christian clerics[3]. This prohibition was repeated no less than three times within the century, and it is noticeable that the repetitions come from very different areas, Vannes in Brittany, then Agde on the Mediterranean coast, and finally Orleans in the centre of the country.

Nor is this the only evidence of the intimacy of relationships between Jews and Christians at this period. Intermarriage also occupied the attention of the councils, and under grave ecclesiastical penalties three separate canons forbade such an offence to Christian feeling as marriage with Jews or Jewesses[4]. It is evident also that these close relationships went further than social intercourse or even marriage. Two canons deal with Jewish religious influence. The third council of Orleans refers to people who have been persuading the Christians that they ought to observe the Lord's day in the Jewish fashion, and abstain from all work upon it[5]. This is one of the many border-line cases which we find all

[1] *Life of Hilary of Poitiers* by 'Venantius' (probably Venantius Fortunatus), in P.L., IX, p. 187.

[2] *Life of Hilary of Arles* in P.L., L, p. 1243.

[3] Vannes (465), Canon 12; this canon is repeated in Agde, Canon 34, and Orleans III, Canon 13; M., IX, p. 15.

[4] Orleans II (533), Canon 19; M., VIII, p. 838; Clermont (535), Canon 6; M., VIII, p. 861; and Orleans III (538), Canon 13; M., IX, p. 15.

[5] Orleans III, Canon 28; M., IX, p. 19.

through the history of Jewish-Christian relationships, where we cannot say how far it is the influence of living Jews upon their Christian contemporaries, and how far that of the written word of the Torah upon some enthusiastic reader or hearer. In this case it is perhaps more probable that the action was due to the influence of living Jews, for we know of no Judeo-Christian sect in Gaul at this epoch. This is all the more likely in that we know that the Jews were making proselytes among various classes of slaves and servants. This question was handled by the following council of Orleans, which decreed that such a convert became free if he was either a foreigner (*advena*), or a man who had been converted to Christianity (*Christianus factus*), or a Christian concubine. But if he was himself a Christian, and had accepted Judaism on condition that he received his freedom if he remained steadfast in his Judaism, then the reverse was to happen. He was to be condemned to perpetual slavery for his desertion of Christianity, presumably in the service of a Christian master, for his Jewish master lost him for the crime of having converted him[1].

In the political situation of the Jews the councils took little interest. The matter did not lie outside their jurisdiction, but either they found Jewish officials tolerable or there were not enough of them to create a serious problem. References to Jewish officials are extremely rare. In fact, apart from the Jewish mayor in the letter of Severus of Majorca, there is only the Jewish judge in the mythical acts of Benedicta of Lyons[2]. But that such persons did exist is shown by the canon of Clermont, which repeats the law of Valentinian III issued a century earlier to the Prefects of the Two Gauls[3]. As a council would not be likely to deal with a non-existent situation, and as, on the other hand, our information is so scanty, and the conciliar prohibition was never repeated, we may perhaps conclude that Jewish officials were relatively rare, and that they were not distinguished by any unpleasant characteristics which brought them into notice, a situation which would agree with the general conditions of the times.

[1] Orleans IV (541), Canon 31; M., IX, p. 118.

[2] A.S., Oct. 8. The Bollandists themselves class the Acta as ' fabulosa '.

[3] Clermont (535), Canon 9; M., VIII, p. 861. Cf. *Const. Sirm.*, vi, *fin.*

Of more importance was the Jewish possession of Christian slaves. The problem was universal and continuous in the ancient world. But it is interesting to note that nowhere was the situation treated more mildly than in Gaul. No early councils attempted to put into force the full rigour of the Roman Code—a refusal which, as we have seen, caused great indignation to Gregory the Great[1]. Legally, they might have demanded the surrender of all Christian slaves in Jewish possession, but they never attempted to do so. The third council of Orleans only considered Christian slaves who received particular ill-treatment from Jewish masters. If they were ordered to perform an action which offended religious principles, if they were punished for an action for whose commission the Church had already imposed penance and given absolution, and if in either case they took sanctuary in a church, then the priest should only return them to their master if the value of each slave was deposited as a guarantee for his subsequent treatment[2]. The next council of Orleans, three years later, decided that under similar conditions the Jew should be forced to sell the slave if a Christian purchaser could be found, and this act of piety was specially commended to Christians[3]. The fifth council of Orleans took the matter up for the third time, and extended the scope of the legislation to deal with Christian masters also who ill-treated their slaves. If the slave of such a master took sanctuary in a church, then he was returned by the priest to the master, who had to swear not to ill-treat him. This was considered a sufficient guarantee, as the Church could impose ecclesiastical penalties in case of a renewal of the offence. But if the offender was not a Christian, then he had to produce Catholic guarantors who would undertake that the slave should be made to do nothing contrary to his religion[4].

It is evident that apart from the purely religious question involved in the conversion of Christian slaves to Judaism, the councils showed no desire to exhibit an unfriendly attitude towards Jewish ownership. This last canon classes

[1] See Ch. VI, p. 215.

[2] Orleans III (538), Canon 13; M., IX, p. 15.

[3] Orleans IV, Canon 30; M., IX, p. 118.

[4] Orleans V, Canon 22; M., IX, p. 134.

together Christian and non-Christian owners, and in its recognition that a Jew might persuade practising Christians to act as his sureties, it is an immense advance on Roman legislation with its interminable abuse of everything Jewish.

Another canon, which introduces a new restriction, is a final confirmation of the good relations existing between Jews and Christians at this time. The third council of Orleans forbade Jews to appear in the streets between Maundy Thursday and Easter Monday[1]. It may seem at first sight strange to quote this canon as evidence of good relations, but, in fact, it can legitimately be so used. We know from a Precept of Childebert that these days were days of particular licence, of drunkenness, and dance and song[2]. The bishops of the time were in some sense living in missionary dioceses, weaning the population slowly from heathen practices. Such festivities were probably connected with ancient festivals of spring, and were very likely obscene in their character. That at such a time the bishops should feel that it was well to keep Jewish influence out of the way was natural, but that Jews should participate at all in such popular festivities would at a later date have been incredible.

From the middle of the sixth century onwards a less friendly attitude prevails in the canons of the councils, and this corresponds to a certain increase of action against the Jews on the part of the secular and individual episcopal authorities. But the kings and even bishops went considerably farther than even the most hostile council would have allowed, and the forced baptisms which began to take place under royal or episcopal authority found no approval in canonical sanction. The subjects of legislation were still the same, with one exception. It was apparently unnecessary to return to the question of mixed marriages, and this may be in itself some sign that the Jewish and Christian population were drawing apart. But legislation was still needed against accepting Jewish hospitality[3].

[1] Orleans III, Canon 30; M., IX, p. 19.

[2] See below, Section VII.

[3] Macon (581), Canon 15; M., IX, p. 934; and Reims (624), Canon 11; M., IX, p. 596.

The legislation already recorded did not succeed in eliminating Jewish officials, and later councils become both more explicit in their definition of the offenders and more severe in their prescription of the penalties. The council of Macon forbade the appointment of Jews as judges or as collectors of those indirect taxes which constituted the main financial burden of the general population[1], on the grounds that these two positions gave undue authority to Jews over Christians. The addition to this explanation of the words 'quod Deus avertat' constitutes the first abusive phrase found in Gallic conciliar legislation[2]. Finding this unavailing, the council of Paris devised a punishment to fit the crime which is almost worthy of Gilbertian opera. Since only a Christian should exercise authority over Christians, if any Jew were found to have assumed, or even to have applied for, an official position, he was to be taken by the bishop of the town where the offence was committed and immediately baptised, together with his whole household. But whether thus safely set on the path of salvation he was to be allowed to keep his office the council neglected to decide[3]. Even this solution did not remove the difficulty, and the council of Reims ten years later returned to the attack, but lacking the humour of their Parisian colleagues they were content merely to repeat the prohibition and to insist upon its application to all 'actiones publicae'[4].

Later councils had again to deal with the question of the Jewish holding of Christian slaves. The council of Macon finally passed a law definitely prohibiting such ownership. That the canon was not effective is clearly shown by the letters of protest on this precise subject addressed by Gregory the Great to the Frankish sovereigns less than twenty years later. The bishops at Macon took their stand on previous legislation by which Jews were compelled to sell Christian slaves whom they had ill-treated, if a Christian purchaser could be found. After ascribing the possession of Christian slaves either to the

[1] 'Impots indirects ou tonlieux (*telonea*) comprenant les douanes, les péages et les taxes sur les objets vendus aux foires et marchés.'—Lot, *op. cit.*, p. 405.

[2] Macon, Canon 13; M., IX., p. 934.

[3] Paris (614), Canon 15; M., X, p. 542.

[4] Reims (624), Canon 11; M., X, p. 596.

fortunes of war or to 'Jewish fraud', they expressed their astonishment at hearing that in some cities the insolence of the Jews was such that they refused to sell their slaves even when Christian purchasers offered the price. Legally, however, the Jew was in his rights in refusing such a sale unless ill-treatment could be proved; since it is a fair presumption that later conciliar enactments overrode those of the original Theodosian Code when they dealt with the same subject, and the councils of Orleans only dealt with cases of ill-treatment. But the council of Macon extended this compulsory sale to all cases of Jewish ownership of Christian slaves, fixed a general price of twelve solidi for such a sale, and in case of Jewish refusal to accept the price, allowed the slave to leave his master and to settle where he willed among Christians[1]. It added a further canon to prevent the Jews from evading the laws by converting their Christian slaves to Judaism[2].

The council of Reims attempted to get nearer the root of the trouble by preventing Christian slaves from ever falling into Jewish hands. Christians were to be sold to neither Jews nor pagans, and if a Christian master was forced to sell his Christian slaves, he could only do it to another Christian. If he sold them to a Jew or a pagan he was to be himself excommunicated, and the sale was to be considered invalid[3]. This was as far as it was possible for the legislation to go at the time, and if it could have been carried out completely it would have solved the whole problem. The difficulty of carrying it out is revealed in the letter of Gregory the Great[4] on the slave trade in Naples. When a batch of slaves was offered for sale, it was impossible to know if among them there were Christians. Finally, the council of Chalons sur Saone forbade all sales of captives outside the kingdom of Clovis, and thereby prevented the sale of slaves to pagan and Jewish masters abroad[5]. After these two canons we hear no more from the councils, and we hear little of Jewish possession of Christian slaves, so

[1] Macon, Canon 16; M., IX, p. 935.

[2] Macon, Canon 17; M., IX, p. 935.

[3] Reims, Canon 11; M., X, p. 596.

[4] See Ch. VI, p. 216.

[5] Chalons (*c.* 650), Canon 9; M., X, p. 1191.

that it may be considered that by thus attacking the root of the matter, the sale of the slaves, the Gallic bishops had solved the problem which had always beaten Roman legislators.

Other legislation of the later councils is of less importance. The council of Macon, in renewing the law affecting Jewish appearance in the streets over Easter, added a clause forbidding them to sit in the presence of the clergy, and ordered the civil judges to assess their punishment according to the rank of the cleric in whose presence the offender had seated himself[1]. A local council of Auxerre passed legislation affecting the observance of Sunday which may have been of great importance for the Jews of the diocese, though we have no means of judging. All work, agricultural or other, was completely forbidden, but the law does not specify whether it is to be applied to Jews[2]. The almost contemporary canon of Narbonne in Visigothic Spain mentions them expressly, but whether the absence of this explicit reference in the council of Auxerre means that they were not included, or that it was taken for granted that they were included, and therefore not mentioned, is a matter of taste. For the sake of completeness in this picture of conciliar enactments, it may be added that Jews visiting nunneries on business were forbidden to linger there, to have any private conversations, or to show any familiarity to the inmates[3]. But this matter concerns rather the morality of nuns than the disabilities of Jews.

VII. THE JEWS AND THE FRANKISH KINGS

Fortunately for the Jews it was more customary for the kings of the sixth century to ratify the canons of the councils than for the councils to ratify the edicts of the kings. In fact, it is only on the Easter question that the councils refer to the kings at all, and in this matter they might equally well have referred to the council of Orleans. It must be admitted that there is not the air of impartiality and 'gravity' in

[1] Macon, Canon 14; M., IX, p. 934.

[2] Auxerre (578 or 582), Canon 16; M., IX, p. 913.

[3] Macon, Canon 2; M., IX, p. 934.

royal and episcopal action that there is in the most unfavourable decisions of the councils. That the disabilities under which the Jews suffered should increase rather than diminish was unfortunately to be expected, for such is always the case when discrimination against a group begins and nothing occurs definitely to swing the pendulum in the opposite direction. But the councils can fairly be said to have been behind and not ahead of others in imposing them, and when they did act they may have acted with severity, but they certainly cannot be said to have acted with either violence or spite, and they were no harder on Jews than on the sinners of their own flocks.

We do not hear anything in France of the Jews being forbidden to build new synagogues until the council of Meaux in the ninth century when Agobard, bishop of Lyons, had already inflamed opinion against them. And on only two occasions do we know of synagogues being destroyed by popular violence. We are told that the synagogue of Tours was destroyed a short time before the visit of King Guntram in 585[1]. The Jews obviously intended to petition him for its reconstruction out of public funds, but this the king 'admirabili prudentia' absolutely refused to allow. But there is no statement that they were not to be allowed to rebuild it themselves. It may or may not be significant that the same passage of Gregory speaks of the welcome given to the king by the population, 'including Syrians, Romans, and even Jews'. Syria was the home of synagogue destruction in this century, and the penetration of the Syrians into France was a penetration of monks as well as of traders. This exceptional incident may, therefore, owe its origin to external persuasion rather than to local hostility. Such a suggestion is not entirely without support, for we know of no popular molestation of the Jews at this period except under the inspiration of some particular provocation. For the other case was at Clermont in the time of Avitus.

With an active episcopacy and an effective system of councils, it is natural that there was little direct royal action concerning the Jews. Such precepts and instructions as there are cover the same ground as that covered

[1] *Hist. Franc.*, Bk. VIII, i.

by the councils and are generally issued in confirmation of them. Childebert I repeated the conciliar canon forbidding the Jews to appear in the streets at Easter, and added a clause that they only did so to mock at the Christians. The necessity for this action is revealed in a general precept of his about the disgraceful conduct of Christians at these seasons: 'We have received a complaint that many sacrilegious actions take place among the people, whence God is injured, and the people commit mortal sin: we hear of nights spent in drunkenness, scurrility and singing, and even on the sacred days of Easter, Christmas and the other feasts of the Church and on Sundays dancers (?) circulate in the "villas".' It can well be imagined that such occasions gave opportunities for Jews to poke fun at the ceremonies involved[1].

Both Guntram and Childebert II issued orders forbidding all work on Sunday, but again there is no direct mention of the Jews[2]. There is no trace of any royal enactment following the letters of Gregory the Great to Theodoric, Theodobert and Brunhild, expressing his horror at their allowing Jews to possess Christian slaves. The sovereigns seem to have been content to follow Gallic tradition, and to prohibit only conversion. Clothaire II in 614 renewed the exclusion of the Jews from all public services. He added a further clause forbidding them to associate themselves with someone for some purpose, but unfortunately the manuscript has a tear at this point, and exists in only one copy[3]. Two royal edicts for compulsory baptism will be considered later. No Frankish Breviary of the Theodosian Code survives, though the councils frequently refer to the paragraphs of the Code, and Clothaire II about 560 issued a general order that Romans were to live according to Roman Law[4]. This general statement would have included

[1] *Epistola data per ecclesias vel omni populo*. The passage, however, is a restoration from the canon. M.G.H., Leges, I, 1, and *Preceptum Childeberti* in M.G.H. quarto, Leg. II, Vol. 1.

[2] Guntram, M.G.H. quarto, Leg. II, Vol. 1, 11. Childebert, *ibid.*, p. 17.

[3] Clothaire II, Oct. 18, 614, M.G.H. quarto, Leg. II, Vol. 1, p. 22. The defective passage runs: 'Quicumque se . . . tuos . . . dine sociare presumpserit, severissimam legem ex canonica sententia incurrat'.

[4] M.G.H. quarto, Leg. II, Vol. 1, p. 19.

the Jews, except in so far as their position had been modified by royal or conciliar enactment—not a very serious addition, for it amounted only to their exclusion from the streets at Easter and the warning not to dally in nunneries.

VIII. COMPULSORY BAPTISMS IN FRANCE

If the kings spent little time on the Jews in their legislation, yet from the middle of the sixth century onwards there are a number of cases of extra-legal action towards them for which sometimes the sovereigns, and sometimes the bishops, were responsible. These actions generally took the form of baptisms or expulsions. From the point of view of Code and council such actions were clearly illegal; but the increasing frequency with which they occurred shows that the law was becoming an ever slenderer reed for the support of Jewish rights. For it is needless to say that it would have been useless for the Jews to have appealed either to Roman or to ecclesiastical law for protection against the personal action of king or bishop. Their only possible protector would be the Pope himself, and we do not know of any papal intervention in their favour except from Gregory the Great. Most ecclesiastical authorities would follow the line taken by the chronicler of the forced baptisms of Sisebut, that it was ' not according to knowledge, . . . but, as it was written, by opportunity or by truth, Christ is preached '[1], and would certainly not carry their disagreement to the length of open protection of the Jews.

The first recorded example of compulsory baptism took place at the instance of Childebert I in the diocese of Ferreol of Uzès in 558. His biographer relates that he was solicitous for the conversion of the numerous Jews in Uzès, and often invited them to his table and made them presents. He tried to urge them to baptism in friendly conversation. Unfortunately this was misrepresented at Paris, and the bishop was accused of holding this close intercourse with them for treasonable purposes. (Uzès lying in the hills above Nîmes was not far from the Visigothic frontier.) He was summoned to Paris and kept there until after three years his innocency

[1] Isidore, *Hist. Goth. Anno DCL.*, M.G.H. quarto, Chron. Min., II, 291.

was admitted. On his return he changed his tactics, and, after holding a council of his diocese to secure approval for his action, he forced them to accept either baptism or expulsion. Large numbers were baptised[1]. The rest migrated elsewhere. Twenty years later, in 576, Bishop Avitus of Clermont succeeded (after lengthy preaching) in converting one Jew, but as his convert was passing through the gate in a procession of catechumens, an unconverted Jew poured rancid oil all over him. The people, infuriated, tried to stone the offender, but the bishop intervened. On Ascension Day the mob rushed and burnt the synagogue. After some hesitation the bishop offered baptism or exile, and, after deliberation, Jews to the numbe rof five hundred were baptised. The rest went to Marseilles[2]. The event inspired one of the poems of Venantius Fortunatus. He describes it in graphic detail, and with no sympathy for the Jews. His poem is notable as containing the earliest known reference to a familiar mediaeval legend, that of the smell of the Jew and its immediate change on baptism. Venantius may have meant it to be taken metaphorically, though the wealth of detail suggests easily its direct application. He begins by explaining:

> 'Christicolis Judaeus odor resilibat amarus,
> Obstabatque piis impia turba sacris.'

But after baptism

> 'abluitur Judaeus odor baptismate divo,
> Aspersusque sacro fit gregis alter odor.'

An ambrosian aroma filled the air. . . . One may doubt if it was entirely metaphorical in the mind of Venantius[3].

In 582 Chilperic ordered the baptism of a large number of Jews, probably in or around Paris, and himself acted as godfather to many of them[4]. Here the events of Clermont were reversed. Instead of the Jew insulting the convert, Priscus, the king's jeweller, who was on intimate terms with him, evaded the baptism and was murdered by one of

[1] *Gallia Christiana*, 1739, Vol. VI, p. 613.

[2] Gregory of Tours, *Hist. Franc.*, Bk. V, vi (xi).

[3] *Carmina*, V, 5.

[4] Gregory of Tours, *Hist. Franc.*, Bk. VI, x (xvii).

the newly baptised[1]. Gregory of Tours remarks that many of the 'converts' continued to observe Jewish customs. In 591 Gregory the Great writes to the bishops of Arles and Marseilles, reasoning with them gently for having followed the same policy of forced baptisms in their dioceses. In 624(?) Dagobert, at the request of the Emperor Heraclius, who had received a warning that he would be overthrown by the circumcised, is said to have baptised or expelled all the Jews of his kingdom 'summo studio'[2].

The last recorded victims of compulsory baptism in this period were the Jews of Bourges, at the hands of the bishop Sulpicius, some time between 620 and 644[3].

It is possible, and perhaps even probable, that other cases occurred, and that they were either not recorded, or else the records have perished. The history of the Jews in France in the seventh and eighth centuries is completely obscure. But by these seven cases we can see that we are entering already into the transition from a situation in which Jewish rights were firmly based on the common law of the Roman Codes, governing all the citizens alike, to the mediaeval position where the Jews existed only by toleration, and were outside the normal operation of the law. So far they were still technically 'cives Romani', and on the whole this position seems to have given them adequate protection; but it can only have been because there was no general ill-feeling between them and the rest of the population, for we can see already how slight is their security when anything occurs to challenge it. The Codes protected them only so long as it was not necessary to appeal to them. If an appeal had to be made, then the appeal of bribery or flattery was more powerful, and from the entry of Guntram into Tours onwards for many centuries bribery and flattery were frequently their only protection.

[1] Gregory of Tours, *Hist. Franc.*, Bk. VI, v.

[2] Fredegarius Chron. 65, Gesta Dagoberti, xxv; P.L., XCVI, p. 1405. It is possible that the absence of all data on Jewish life in France for one hundred and fifty years after this event is due to this expulsion. But our general information for this period is also slight, and it is likely that considerable numbers of Jews fled from Spain to France during this century. A lengthy and relatively complete absence of Jews from France during the period of silence seems to me, therefore, improbable.

[3] *Vita Sulpicii*, i, 14; P.L., LXXX, p. 573.

IX. THE JEWS IN LITERATURE

In the west as in the east it became the fashion of religious romancers to embroider their legends with stories of the superiority of Christianity over Judaism. Belief in improbable miracles increased as the intellectual level of the population decreased. In the early days there was often colouring and exaggeration, but there is less evidence of pure imagination. The stories follow in the main the line of eastern literature, but they exhibit less literary power and imagination.

Two stories are told of the power of Germanus, bishop of Paris, over the Jews. On one occasion he met a young slave, presumably a Christian, being led along the road in chains by some Jews. The boy states that he is thus chained because he has refused to accept Judaism. The bishop makes the sign of the cross over the chains, and they fall off[1]. On another occasion he miraculously heals the wife of a Jew who accepts baptism with her husband. As a result a large number of other Jews accept baptism[2].

Gregory of Tours relates a story of a certain archdeacon of Bourges, Leunast, which has a clear didactic purpose. The archdeacon lost his sight, and had it restored by touching the relics of S. Martin of Tours. But, not completely satisfied with the cure, he went to a Jewish doctor on his return, and, very properly to the mind of Gregory, immediately became completely blind again[3]. Such a story would serve as an admirable warning against the use of Jewish doctors. A story with a doctrinal purpose is related in the Chronicle of Bernold. A blind Jew of Rome disputed the doctrine of the Virginity of the Virgin Mary. As a proof of her power he received his sight but, oddly enough, neither he nor the Jews with him were converted[4].

Gradually it became the fashion to attribute some miraculous contact with Jews to every well-known saint, and to make use in the west as in the east of Jewish anecdotes, or

[1] *Vita S. Germani*, lxv; P.L., LXXII, p. 74.

[2] Venantius Fortunatus, *Vita S. Germani*, lxii, in M.G.H. Script, II, p. 24.

[3] *Hist. Franc.*, Bk. V, iv (vi).

[4] *Bernoldi Chron. anno* 609, M.G.H. Script, Vol. V, p. 414.

supposed Jewish actions, to confirm disputed doctrines, and to enforce rules of conduct.

To look to the literature of the period for any fresh views of the Jews and Judaism is useless. Literature and theology were at a very low ebb, and remained so until the renascence under Charlemagne. But the writers of his epoch belong not to the old Roman world, but to the beginnings of mediaeval Europe. It is necessary to consider the Carolingian legislation in this chapter, but to treat of its literature would be to trespass on the second period of Jewish relationships with Christianity, a subject outside the scope of the present volume.

X. THE LAWS OF CHARLEMAGNE

From the time of Sulpicius of Bourges (644) to the time of Charlemagne there is complete silence as to the history of the Jews in France, but with the latter our information, though still scanty, is enough to give us some picture of their situation. The great emperor was no enemy of the Jews, and even employed a Jew on a diplomatic mission to Haroun al Rashid[1], and is said to have requested Haroun to send him a learned Jew in order to establish a Jewish seminary in Narbonne. This only rests on later information, and is less likely to be true. It would probably have stirred up so much feeling among the clergy that we should have some information from a contemporary on the subject[2].

There are five genuine laws of Charlemagne affecting the Jews, and two whose authenticity is suspect. In 806 he issued a stern order to the ecclesiastical authorities that they were not on any account to sell any of their church treasures to merchants, Jews or others, and he added that both Jews and other merchants were boasting that they had no difficulty in buying anything that they wanted from the churches[3]. Eight years later he issued four ordinances together[4]. The

[1] *Einhardi Annales* 801; M.G.H. Chron., Vol. I, 190. Aronius, 68 and 71.

[2] See Aronius, 70. On the various stories of Charlemagne and the Jews of Narbonne see Régné, p. 13 ff.

[3] *Capitulare Duplex ad Niumagen*; M.G.H. folio, Leg. I, 144. Aronius, 72.

[4] *Capitula de Judaeis*; M.G.H. folio, Leg. I, 194. Aronius, 76, 77.

first repeated the previous prohibition and extended it to receiving church property in pawn. But, whereas the previous law had only punished the clergy who sold, this punished severely the Jew who bought. He suffered the loss of his possessions and the amputation of his right hand. By the second, no Jew was allowed to take the person of a Christian in pledge either from another Jew or from a Christian, lest his honour should be insulted. If he did so he lost the pledge and the debt of which the Christian was the pledge. By the third the Jews were forbidden 'to have money in their houses', and to sell wine and corn or other things. The meaning of this prohibition is obscure. Among the Jews were certainly merchants in considerable numbers. It is possible, and in fact probable, that the emphasis is on 'in their houses', and that the meaning is that the Jews may only carry on their businesses in the recognised markets, to whose organisation Charlemagne paid considerable attention. The fourth ordinance deals with the form of oath to be taken by Jews in a suit with a Christian. Having crowned and surrounded himself with sorrel, and having taken in his right hand the Pentateuch in Hebrew, or in Latin if the Hebrew were not available, he swore as follows: 'As God is my help, God who gave the law to Moses on Mount Sinai, and as the leprosy of Naaman the Syrian may not come upon me as it came upon him, and as the earth may not swallow me as it swallowed Dathan and Abiron, have I in this case planned no evil against you.' A further law is much more explicit, but its authenticity is doubtful[1]. According to it a Jew in a case with another Jew used his own law, but against a Christian he had to submit to the trial by ordeal, either by swearing upon a reliquary, or by holding red-hot iron or by other specified methods. A Jew convicted of an offence against a Christian was tied in a sack and drowned like a parricide. It is unlikely that such a law dates from the time of Charlemagne.

Finally, if a Jew wished to give evidence against a Christian he had to produce either three Christian witnesses, or four, seven or nine Jewish witnesses according to circumstances. If the Jew were summoned by the Christian, then three witnesses on either side sufficed. This was an advance on

[1] Aronius, 78.

the previous law by which they were not allowed to give evidence against a Christian at all. In this form it had been published by Charlemagne himself in the beginning of his reign in the collection of canons which he received from the pope Hadrian[1]. The new law may therefore not be of Charlemagne, but of Louis the Pious. The legislation of the latter was much fuller, and indeed constituted the basis of the mediaeval status of the Jews. Charlemagne himself left their basic status unchanged, and only legislated on particular issues that needed settlement. Thus he marks the end of the old period, and the transition to the new. Technically, perhaps, the Jews were still ' cives Romani ', in that they enjoyed the position they had held in Roman times with modifications. But the modifications had become so extensive that it was necessary to make a fresh start in the time of his successor.

XI. THE ECONOMIC POSITION OF THE JEWS

We have seen that on the whole it was a period in which there was no evidence of extensive hostility between Jews and Christians. Incidents there were, and outbreaks at times, but grounds for believing in anything approaching the mediaeval situation there are none. The councils show some decrease in friendliness as they follow each other in the sixth century. But in the ninth century we shall still find plenty of evidence that the general population lived peaceably together, or that, at least, Christians showed no special hostility to the Jews.

So many modern theories of antisemitism attempt to explain the phenomenon in purely economic terms, that it is wise to review the evidence already given, and to study such references to the economic life of the Jews as survive, to see if they support the supposition that such hostility as there was at that time had its root in their economic position. Was the Jew of Milman a real person?

The main charge of the modern writer is always the slave trade, and it was also one of the main preoccupations of ancient Christian legislators. It is often assumed that the

[1] *Cap. Aquisgran.*, 45; M.G.H. folio, Leg. I, 61.

Jews possessed a monopoly of this unpleasant traffic. All our references to slave traders are to Jews. But it is also true that all our references to Jewish slavers are to the religious question involved in the possession of a Christian by a Jew. Only one canon deals with slaves in general, and it does not mention Jews except as one of the alternative fates of a captive sold out of the country. And its objection to such a sale is religious. We can do more than hint at the probability of slave traders who, being Christians, raised no issue which needed legislation. For, as the century absolutely accepted slavery, it could not have prohibited Jews engaging in the traffic without recognising that, the Jews excluded, there were other sources from which slaves could be obtained[1]. That they were the main slavers at the end of the period under discussion is probable, and their preponderance in the traffic is likely to have increased with the Mahometan conquests, for it was easier for them to penetrate into Mahometan countries. But though we may reprobate them altogether for indulging in a trade against which we revolt, we must realise that the sixth century saw only a religious issue, the exclusive possession of one whom Christ had redeemed by one of those who had slain Him[2].

They certainly also dealt in the trade in precious objects. Priscus, the friend of Chilperic, has already been mentioned. It is even possible that he had the right of coining gold coins[3]. Cautinus, the wicked bishop of Clermont, was a familiar friend of Jewish merchants, whom he invited to dinner; and when they had adroitly flattered him, they sold him objects for more than their worth—the only accusation of dishonesty in the records of the period, and a slender peg on which to hang the conventional ' as usual '[4]. Eufrasius tried to obtain the same see by buying costly objects from the Jews to bribe the king[5]. Outside France there was their attempt, recorded by Gregory the Great[6], to buy the church

[1] Reims, Canon 11.

[2] Macon, Canon 16.

[3] *Description Raisonée des Monnaies Merovingiennes* by the Vicomte P. d'Amécourt, quoted in R.E.J., Vol. X, p. 237.

[4] Gregory of Tours, *Hist. Franc.*, Bk. IV, viii (xiii).

[5] *Ibid.*, Bk. IV, xxxv.

[6] See p. 218.

plate of Venafro, and in one of the edicts of Charlemagne 'Jews *and others also*' were accused of doing the same thing[1]. Apart from these references, we have notices of Jewish merchants and shipowners, but no statement about their particular traffic. Evidence of hostility to the Jews on this score there is none, and a rascally bishop overreached after a good dinner is small evidence on which to 'indict a nation'. We have frequent references to business dishonesty, but among the Syrians, not among the Jews.

The third charge is money-lending. We know of one money-lender. But the only time that we know that he tried to collect a debt, he and his companions were all murdered by the debtors[2]. Armentarius came to Tours to collect a debt owed by the ex-vicarius Injuriosus and the ex-comes Eunomius; and he was accompanied 'cum uno sectae suae satellite et duobus Christianis'. It is generally assumed, as the narrative is mostly in the singular, that the Christians were in a subordinate position, and that the only money-lender was Armentarius. But after their murder, 'parentes eorum' attempted to bring the murderers, that is the ex-vicarius and ex-comes, to trial, but failed for lack of witnesses. It does not seem likely that if the Christians were only servants, and not living in Tours, their relations would have been able to attempt to bring two such powerful persons to trial. It is more fitting to the facts as we have them to assume the Christians to have been business associates of Armentarius. This is all the more likely in that we know that the main money-lenders of the time were Syrians, and that almost every council had to prohibit money-lending on the part of clerics[3]. The forged canons of Nicaea, which are an oriental collection of about this period, specifically forbid Christians to go into partnership with Jews for business purposes[4]: the obliterated charter of Childebert refers to some kind of Jewish association with others: there is thus no reason to assume it to be impossible that a Jew should be in association with two Christians in such a business. Our evidence for Jewish money-lenders is

[1] *Capitulare Duplex ad Niumagen*; M.G.H., Leg. I, 144.

[2] Gregory of Tours, *Hist. Franc.*, Bk. VII, xxiii.

[3] *E.g.* Arles II, 14; Tours, 13; Orleans III, 27.

[4] Canon 52, to be found with the Canons of Nicaea in Harduin, Vol. I.

thus extremely slight, and is made still more so by the fact that Charlemagne two centuries later, when the Syrians had become less important in western Europe, legislated on lending without any mention of Jews at all[1].

Two interesting indirect allusions confirm this impression that the Jew was not noticeable economically in the community. Julian of Toledo expressed his violent dislike of France in an account of the unsuccessful rebellion of Paul, governor of Narbonne, against Wamba, the Visigothic king of Spain. He described France as ' a country of lack of faith (or perfidy), of obscene works, of fraudulent business, of venal judges, and, what is worst of all, a brothel of Jews blaspheming our Saviour and Lord '[2]. In a ' Defiance against the Tyrant of Gaul ' appended to the work by his own or another's hand, there is a somewhat similar picture of the friendship existing in France with Jews[3]. But in neither case are the Jews considered anything but a religious menace. It is the Franks, not the Jews, who are dishonest, a characteristic which is repeated in an amusing ninth-century collection of national attributes, which gives to the Franks ' commercia Gallorum ' or ' gula Gallorum ', while to the Jews it ascribes ' invidia '[4].

The only real crime of the Jews was ' perfidia ', and perfidia means ' want of faith ', and not moral worthlessness.

XII. RELATIONS BETWEEN JEWS AND CHRISTIANS

It is clear from the variety of the references to Jews that they were widely scattered throughout the country. They were to be found not only in the Rhone valley and the south-west, but also on the Loire and Seine. The Visigothic persecutions caused an immigration into France, and it is possible that throughout the period there was also an immigration from other Mediterranean countries. Early mediaeval records show them to be living in almost every

[1] *Capitula*, M.G.H., Leg. I, 144.

[2] Hist. reb. adv. Wambam, v; P.L., XCVI, p. 766.

[3] Insullatio, i and ii; P.L., XCVI, p. 797.

[4] *De Proprietatibus Gentium* in M.G.H. quarto, Chron. Min., Vol. II, p. 389.

important centre in the north as well as in the south of the country, and it is probable that many of these settlements existed long before the time of our present records. We can safely say that the Jew was not a rare and abnormal feature in the life of the towns of the Merovingian period, and that relations between Jews and Christians must have been frequent and have touched many aspects of life.

This being so, we can clearly assume that throughout the country as a whole the relations between the two peoples were not bad. Since all our records are written by churchmen, and since what hostility there was came on every occasion from the clergy, it is not surprising that we do not actually find complimentary reference to Jewish life and qualities. And yet even these are not completely lacking. The letters of Sidonius Apollinarius, written in the second half of the fifth century, contain several kindly references to Jews. On two occasions he sends a letter by a Jew 'who would be dear to my heart if it were not for his abominable religion '[1]. In one of his letters he recommends a Jew to the good offices of Bishop Eleutherius. After expressing his regret for the error which is causing his involuntary destruction, he adds that 'it is wrong to condemn any man alive, since as long as he lives he has a chance of conversion '. But in any case, whatever his theology, in matters of earthly affairs and business he considers them 'honestas habere causas ', and therefore to be worthy of episcopal support[2].

If it is difficult to give direct evidence of the attitude of individual Christians to the Jews, it is still more difficult to give direct evidence of the attitude of individual Jews to Christians. We can only say that since the general evidence is that the Christians were friendly to the Jews, the reverse must hold good, and that the individual Jews must have enjoyed friendly contacts with their Christian neighbours. It is no bad record of Jewish conduct throughout these centuries which is presented to us. Two murders, a pail of slops, the outwitting of a rascally bishop, this is the tale of Jewish misdeeds over several centuries. It is not impressive when compared with the number of references to them. Nor does it gain additional weight from a number of general

[1] Ep. III, iv; IV, v.

[2] Ep. to Bp. Eleutherius. Ep. VI, xi.

attacks upon their character as a people, for such are entirely absent.

The period was not Elysian. Security was by no means perfect. Violent outbreaks occurred. Even the right of religious freedom as guaranteed by the law was occasionally violated. But robbery and violence were in the spirit of the times, and it was not to be expected that the Jew alone should escape. Even the particular disabilities from which he suffered as a Jew were not extensive. And other classes also had their particular disabilities. The cumulative effect through the centuries of actions which at this time were spasmodic, and of attitudes which were still but half expressed and rarely practised, created in the end sinister results which it is easy but inaccurate to anticipate.

While he lived with the substantial background of the Roman Codes, and while he was distinguished by few characteristics from the rest of the population so far as daily life was concerned, his situation was easily tolerable, and his life, considering the period, can legitimately be called normal and agreeable. To shed tears over his sufferings or to grind one's teeth over his iniquities is to ignore all the evidence—and it is considerable—which we possess.

CHAPTER TEN

THE JEWS IN VISIGOTHIC SPAIN

BIBLIOGRAPHICAL INTRODUCTION

It is an extraordinary fact that in spite of the immense collection of legislation, Arian and Catholic, secular and conciliar, which the Visigothic period has bequeathed to us, we are almost entirely without knowledge of the conditions of the Jews of the time. The anecdotal side of history is entirely untreated, and of the three apologists who wrote against the Jews not one shows the slightest sign of any knowledge of contemporary Jewish conditions. Chroniclers and historians alike are lacking, and all that we possess is a certain knowledge of the behaviour of the Jews during the rebellion against Wamba, and an *ex parte* statement of their responsibility for the final downfall of the kingdom.

In these conditions the different modern studies of the subject are inevitably merely a *réchauffée* of the same meagre source—material dressed according to the views of the author. It is best, therefore, to go to the most modern, the works of Dubnow and Juster, since Bedarride or Graetz had no different material on which to work, and Dubnow and Juster add only a more modern approach, and no new material. The question which has been much interesting modern scholars, the relationship between custom and law in the evolving Teutonic societies brought into contact with the formal nature of Roman law, does not touch the situation of the Jews, since no Teutonic 'customs' governed Jewish behaviour. In consequence the whole of the legislative activity of the Visigoths on Jewish questions owes its inspiration to the traditions of the Roman Church and State and not to the fastnesses of Teutonic barbarism. Non-Roman influence can at most be traced in their affection for pulling out the hair of offenders.

The relative weight of responsibility to be laid on the Church and the Monarchy forms the main point around which controversy can turn. All that can be said for the Church will be found in the work of Ziegler, a book which impresses the more in that it does not attempt to disprove too much.

LIST OF BOOKS

LEX ROMANA VISIGOTHORUM (The Breviary of Alaric)	Ed. G. Haenel. Leipzig, 1849.
LEGES VISIGOTHORUM	Ed. K. Zeumer, in M.G.H. quarto, Leges, Sect. 1, i. Hanover and Leipzig, 1902.
ACTA CONCILIORUM AMPLISSIMA	Ed. Mansi, Vols. IX to XII.
JUSTER, J.	*La Condition legale des Juifs sous les Rois Visigoths.* Paris, 1912.
LUKYN WILLIAMS, A.	*The Jews and Christian Apologists in Early Spain*, in the Church Quarterly Review, 1925.
MELICHER, T.	*Der Kampf zwischen Gesetzes- und Gewohnheitsrecht im Westgotenreich.* Weimar, 1930.
ZIEGLER, A.	*Church and State in Visigothic Spain.* Catholic University of America, Washington, D.C., 1930.

I. THE VISIGOTHIC PERIOD

After their various wanderings across Europe the Visigoths finally settled in Spain, and succeeded in conquering the greater part of the country by the second half of the fifth century. Their territory extended across the Pyrenees to the rich province of Narbonne, whose possession involved them in constant wars with the Franks. But for more than a century their history is relatively unimportant for two reasons. They were Arians, and living as a small military minority in the midst of a large and apparently fanatically Catholic population. Real unity and development were therefore impossible. Secondly, the royal line of the Balts was extinguished in the person of Alaric II in 507, and thereafter the throne was held by a succession of usurping nobles who enjoyed none of the prestige of the old and semi-divine ruling house. The few incidents of this period have already been related in the previous chapter. The only other event of importance to record is the publication by Alaric II, a year before his death, of the shortened edition of the Code of Theodosius known as the Breviary of Alaric.

The succession of royal nonentities came to an end in 570, when a king arose capable of consolidating the royal power; but the real change came when his son Reccared accepted Catholicism. Acting from motives of statesmanship rather than religious fervour, he succeeded in doing it in such a way that the majority of the Visigothic nobility followed in his footsteps. Those who resisted were easily crushed. The conversion of the king and aristocracy completely changed the balance of the different parties of the kingdom. The king could now choose his allies. He could appeal to the nobles against the bishops, or to the bishops against the nobles, or he could side with the people against both bishop and noble. As the kingship was still in itself weak (for it was still elective, and only eight of the twenty-three Visigothic monarchs were sons of their predecessors), it was nearly always necessary for the king to rely on one or other of these groups. The other group naturally went into opposition, so that in the hundred and twenty years which preceded the Moorish conquest history was largely made up of an unedifying series of internal intrigues and murders.

As the succession mostly went by usurpation, and as the usurper had to collect forces to support his pretensions, it is natural that there was a fairly regular pendulum movement of alliances between the bishops, the nobles and the people. For a usurper would look to the opposition to secure his election. It is perhaps significant that almost all the legislation affecting the Jews comes from those kings who were in close alliance with, or the tools of, the clerical party—Reccared, Sisebut, Chintila, Recceswinth, Erwig and Egica.

This unhappy situation inevitably ruined the country, and the last quarter of the seventh century presents a miserable picture. The class of small free proprietors had almost completely disappeared before the encroachments of those who needed to be rewarded for their support of royal claimants, whether bishops or nobles; the trade of the country was in ruins, and the Church in a state of collapse; and it is not surprising that a single battle, and an army of less than twenty thousand Arabs, sufficed for the complete overthrow of the Visigothic power.

II. CONDITIONS OF THE JEWS IN SPAIN

Although no other country provides us with anything like so complete a legislative array as does Visigothic Spain through both the royal and the ecclesiastical laws, we remain extremely ignorant of the state of life and the general conditions of the country. We have nothing to compare with the fulness of the chronicles of Gregory of Tours, and we have practically no correspondence or other contemporary literature. The only names to be recalled are Isidore of Seville and Julian of Toledo, but the information which they give us is extremely scanty. Particularly is this so with regard to Jewish affairs, for though anecdotes in themselves are dangerous as a basis for generalisations, a code which by its excess and its repetition reflects rather the enthusiasm of the legislators than any particular qualities in its objects, presents practically no concrete picture of conditions whatsoever. And this is the situation with regard to the Jews in Spain. They were numerous, they were powerful, they were wealthy. They indulged in all pursuits, agriculture as well as trade. They were to be found in all classes. So much we can deduce, and we can safely add that they bewildered the simple Visigoth by the wiliness with which they evaded his ponderous legislative efforts. From the success with which they secured the help for these evasions from bishops, clergy and nobility we can deduce at will either that their power of bribery was incredibly vast or that they were not generally unpopular. If we incline to the first view, we must regretfully accept a very low standard of morality among the clergy, for bishops themselves were suspected by pious kings of favouring the Jews; but the very extent of the royal suspicion would, perhaps, justify a Jew in parodying the words of Burke, and professing his inability to bribe a whole people. The improbability that the Jews could have been wealthy enough to indulge in all the bribery with which they are credited, together with the fact that there is absolutely no record of any popular movement against them, make the second alternative more probable, that the Jews were not necessarily unpopular with the rank and file of the population, or with the ordinary provincial and ecclesiastical authorities. This view finds some support in the fact that it was those who were popular with the common people who passed no measures against the Jews, or allowed them to evade the restrictions of their predecessors; whereas it was those who were allied to the ecclesiastical and noble parties who most violently oppressed them. To attack the Jews was not, therefore, an accepted method of securing popular favour.

Our ignorance of life in Visigothic Spain is nowhere more unfortunate than in the realm of commerce. The immense mass of Visigothic Law pays practically no attention to commercial life. Apart from a small section, entirely composed of reproductions of ancient laws[1], and dealing with foreign trade, neither the word ' negotiator ' nor the word ' mercator ' occurs in the Code. On the other hand Roman Spain was a wealthy province, and the Visigoths must have found an ancient and well-established commercial life in operation. It is unlikely that this entirely disappeared under their rule, though the descriptions of Egica suggest that at the end of the seventh century the country was in a desolate

[1] Bk. XI, tit. 3.

condition. As we are ignorant of the general economic conditions, so are we still more ignorant of the rôle of the Jews in economic life. The section dealing with international trade makes no special mention of them. In the Book devoted to them economic affairs come in only occasionally and indirectly, and always in the form of the restriction of the trading privileges of Jews who refused baptism, or, being baptised, lapsed.

It has already been suggested[1] that in Gaul a large part of the trade was in the hands of the Syrians. We have references to Syrians in Septimania, and it is a reasonable presumption that there were also many of them in Spain. It would be very surprising if it were not so, since we know them to be scattered in every other commercial centre of western Europe. But of the division of trade between them, the Jews, and the rest of the population we know absolutely nothing, and we have no real data for forming a valid judgment. We cannot go beyond the statement already made that the Jews were clearly both wealthy and powerful. The absence of reference to the Syrians or other traders, since they were Christians, does not prove that other groups were not equally wealthy and powerful.

We are on safer ground in presuming that the Jews were numerous. It is improbable that a small group would either have attracted so much legislative attention or have been so competent to evade its results. Their settlement in Spain was also an ancient one, and many Jews are said to have gone there after the destruction of the Temple. The fact that Paul proposed to visit it suggests the existence of large Jewish communities. Moreover, they were very numerous in Arab Spain after the conquest of the country. Allowing for some considerable reduction of their population through voluntary or compulsory exile during the Visigothic Catholic period, we can assume that they formed a considerable proportion of the total population in the fifth and sixth and probably also the seventh centuries.

Any study of their relations with the rest of the population is confused by the fact that so many Jews were nominally Christians, that prohibition of intercourse, or of Judaising, has not the same significance as it would have elsewhere.

[1] Ch. IX, Section III.

We cannot say if the frequent denunciation of people who corrupt the faith has any reference to Gentile Christians, for it has such an obvious significance if applied to Jews who had accepted baptism, and whom their still unconverted relations tried to draw back to the Jewish fold. There is one law of Chindaswinth on Judaising Christians, prohibiting the sons of Christian parents from being circumcised. But here again it is far more likely that the Christian parents were of Jewish stock than that they were pure Gentiles. Forced baptisms had begun at least thirty years earlier, so that this interpretation is the natural one.

We are thus left entirely to the laws for our picture of the life of a people, and no situation could be more unsatisfactory. The deduction that the normal relations between Jews and Christians were not unfriendly is the one which corresponds most to the facts we possess. It is certainly true for the earlier period. That relations deteriorated in the second half of the century is probable, and if we believe that the Jews were responsible for the Arab invasion which put an end to Visigothic power, it is certain. But it is equally certain that the violence of the laws did not reflect any universal reprobation of the Jews by the general public.

III. THE BREVIARY OF ALARIC

Being Romans the Jews of the Visigothic dominions lived under the Code of Theodosius, supplemented by conciliar enactments, until the time of Alaric II. Owing to the decline in the intellectual level of even the Roman section of the population, Alaric found it necessary to issue a simplified version of the Roman Code, eliminating laws which were redundant, inconsistent, or made unnecessary by the change of circumstances. The laws affecting the Jews were reduced from over fifty to ten, to which must be added the third Novella of Theodosius and two Sentences of Paul.

In the main these left the Jewish position unchanged. Intermarriage between Jews and Christians was still identified with adultery, and information could be laid by anyone[1]. Lawsuits which did not affect religious questions were to be

[1] Breviary, 3.7.2 and 9.4.4.

dealt with in the Roman courts, unless both parties agreed to submit to a Jewish judge as arbitrator. On the other hand, no actions were to be brought against Jews on their religious holidays[1]. While all the abusive and petulant phraseology of Theodosius II on relations between Jews and Christians was omitted, the actual content of his laws remained. Jews were not to build new synagogues, and if they did, they were, strangely enough, to be handed over to the *Catholic* authorities[2]. That it was not the Arians who received them suggests that Alaric employed Roman, and therefore Catholic, lawyers to compose the Breviary, and that they saw no reason to change the terms of the Theodosian edition. If Jews tried to convert others to their own faith the penalty was intestability[3]. The apostate forfeited his property[4]. But if a Jew became a Christian, then the Jews were not to molest him[5]. The exclusion from office remained in force. Jews could still only fulfil the burdensome portions of the decurionate, and the duties of guard. They were excluded from all honours[6]. They were particularly excluded from prison governorship[7]. They were not allowed to buy or acquire a Christian slave as a gift, but might inherit him or possess him as trustee[8]. If they circumcised him, they were put to death[9]. The slave was to be set free[10]. It is not possible to say whether in all circumstances the slave was set free without compensation to the owner, for the Breviary contains two contradictory laws on this subject[11].

It will be seen from this summary that there are only a few important modifications of their position under Theodosian law. No privileges were given to Jewish clergy. The privilege of fixing their own market prices was withdrawn.

[1] Breviary, 2.1.10 and 2.8.3.

[2] Novella 3, paras. 3 and 5.

[3] Breviary, 16.2.1.

[4] *Ibid.*, 16.3.2.

[5] *Ibid.*, 16.3.1.

[6] Novella 3, 2.

[7] *Ibid.*, para. 7.

[8] Breviary, 3.1.5.

[9] *Ibid.*, 16.4.2 and Nov. 3, 4.

[10] Breviary, 16.4.1.

[11] *Ibid.*, 16.4.2 and 3.1.5.

Jews forcibly baptised were not allowed to return to Judaism. But, on the other hand, the diversion of the aurum coronarium to the treasury ceased, and though the Patriarchate no longer existed, Jews could presumably, if they wished, remit money to Palestine. The restrictions on their movements during Easter also disappeared, and there were no expressed limitations to the right of sanctuary[1]. The best tribute to the efficiency of the government of Alaric is that all the laws forbidding violence against the Jews were omitted. The little we know of the period is sufficient for us to say that this was not due to an anti-Jewish bias on the part of the Visigoths, but to the fact that under a strong government such violence did not need special legislation. Had there been any special oppression during this time we should certainly have had a hint of it from some document.

The only other events of the Arian period of Visigothic history which are of importance have already been referred to in the previous chapter[2]. Of events in Spain itself at this time we have no knowledge.

IV. LAWS AND COUNCILS OF THE FIRST HALF OF THE SEVENTH CENTURY

It has already been indicated how the advent of Reccared changed the whole situation, and it is natural that this new alliance between king and people was the signal for a great increase in the legislation affecting the Jews. Their main privileges continued to be those granted by the Breviary of Alaric, but royal decree and ecclesiastical council alike co-operated to circumscribe and finally nullify such status as they possessed, until, when finally the Breviary was revoked by Recceswinth, they had little to trust in except the fact that they had been 'cives Romani'.

Of the legislation of Reccared himself we have no complete record. One law only is preserved, in which the ancient prohibition against the ownership of Christian slaves is repeated[3]. This was confirmed by the third Council of

[1] Cf. *Leges Visigoth.*, 9.3.1, which is called 'Antiqua', *i.e.* dating from the period before the composition of the Code of Recceswinth.

[2] Ch. IX, Section V.

[3] *Leg. Vis.*, 12.2.12.

Toledo[1]. The two editions do not completely correspond. If a Jew buys or receives a Christian servant as a gift, he loses him without compensation. If he circumcises him, he forfeits also his property. Thus far the law. The council is milder and only prescribes liberation in cases of circumcision or perversion to Judaism. Each has also a special clause. The council deals with all relations between Jews and Christian women, and prohibits such, ordering the children of such unions to be baptised. It also forbids Jews (or the children above mentioned) to hold any public office over Christians. The law, on the other hand, allows all servants of Jews, who declare they are not Jews, to obtain their freedom. We have here, probably, only the relics of a more complete legislation, for there is a letter to Reccared from Gregory the Great[2], in which he congratulates him 'Constitutionem quandam contra Judeorum perfidiam dedisse', and the existing laws are neither very new nor sufficiently exceptional to explain why the Jews, to avoid them, offered the king a large bribe, which Gregory congratulates him on refusing. The decision of a combined ecclesiastical and secular council under Sisebut[3] also refers to the *Constitutio* of Reccared, though the precise reference is to this law.

In the same year as that of the third council of Toledo, there was a council at Narbonne, which also dealt with various Jewish matters, but on questions of detail rather than principle. The Jews were strictly forbidden to work on Sunday. They were prohibited from singing psalms at their funerals, and they were punished if they harboured or consulted any kind of sorcerer or fortune teller[4]. It is evident that there is still a distinction between Septimania and the part of the kingdom beyond the Pyrenees. Legislation upon such trifling details is very different from the sweeping attacks upon vital points which began to emanate from Toledo. In the seventh century, however, it is probable that the status of the Jews was similar on both sides of the mountains, for Visigothic councils are held almost exclusively at Toledo, and bishops from Septimania occasionally attend.

[1] Toledo III, Canon 14.

[2] Ed. Hartmann, ix, 228.

[3] *Leg. Vis.*, 12.2.13.

[4] Narbonne, Canons 4, 9, 14.

Selva, Metropolitan of Narbonne, appears to have been Vice-President of the important fourth council of Toledo, and he presided over the sixth.

The next king to take action affecting his Jewish subjects was Sisebut (612-620), who in the first year of his reign passed still stricter measures against the Jewish possession of Christian slaves and servants. Apparently the law of Reccared had, as one might expect, been evaded, and some Jews claimed written authority for their continued possession of Christian slaves. This is the first sign of the conflict between royal and episcopal authority on the one hand, and an intelligent group, aided by the open or purchaseable sympathy of local authorities, on the other. Sisebut ordered the cancellation of all the written authorisations to which the Jews laid claim, and laid down that all Christian slaves so held, together with all those since acquired, should be set at liberty with suitable gratuities, or sold within six months. The sales themselves were strictly controlled. The purchaser had to be a Christian, and the slave could not be sold away from the district in which he lived. Irregular sales were heavily punished, in order to prevent the Jew going through a formal transaction with a dummy Christian, which left him the effective ownership of the servant. Various other crimes and penalties were added, and the death sentence was enforced against proselytising either a man or a woman[1]. We learn from a law of Recceswinth that Sisebut was compelled to issue a decree against those Christians who in any way defended the Jews from the operation of the laws or assisted them in their evasion[2].

As these measures failed to suppress them, the king cut the Gordian knot by ordering all Jews within his kingdom to accept baptism or to depart. Many, as a result, fled to France, and waited for a turn of the tide in Spain[3]. Isidore of Seville, while condemning this action, yet considered that those who had become Christian should remain so, and applied to the situation the remark of Paul to the Philippians that ' whether in pretence or in truth, Christ is proclaimed ', and rejoiced thereat. It is, however, certain from the

[1] *Leg. Vis.*, 12.2.13 and 14.

[2] *Ibid.*, 12.2.15.

[3] Isidore, *Hist. Goth. anno* DCL. in M.G.H., Chron. Min., ii, p. 291.

difficulties which future law-makers encountered with lapsed Christians that a very large number accepted nominal conversion and remained Jews at heart. The period of oppression did not on this occasion last for long. In 621 a king of a very different character mounted the throne in the person of Swinthila, and proceeded to recall the Jews from exile, and to allow those who had relapsed to do so openly[1].

Such a permission was inevitably disagreeable to the Church party, and under his successor, Sisinand (631-636), the fourth council of Toledo devoted considerable attention, and no less than ten canons, to the Jews. Meeting under the presidency of Isidore of Seville, it began by affirming its disapproval of forced baptism. But it insisted that those who had received the Christian sacraments must not be allowed to dishonour them by reverting to unbelief. Those who had remained Jews were to be led to the Christian faith of their own free will. It then concentrated most of its attention on the punishments to be meted out to those who had been baptised and lapsed. Any Christian, from the bishop downwards, who had connived at these lapses was to be severely punished. The punishment of the lapsed themselves was entrusted to the bishops and not to the magistrates. The children of the lapsed, if they had been circumcised, were to be taken away from their parents and handed over to genuine Christian families for education. If they had remained Christian they were not to be disinherited. If lapsed Christians had circumcised their slaves, the latter were to be set free. They were not to frequent unconverted Jewish friends. If they did they were to be reduced to slavery, and the unconverted friend was to be publicly flogged. In a mixed marriage the non-Christian partner must accept Christianity or be separated. The children were to be brought up as Christians. The lapsed might not give evidence. They might not hold office.

In comparison with this the lot of those who had managed to evade the formality of baptism was comparatively light. They also might not hold office, and they might neither buy nor possess Christian servants. But the really severe attack upon them (and, indeed, if it was carried out it was a mortal one), was that they were to be deprived of their

[1] Joseph Hacohen, quoted in Juster, *op. cit.*, p. 6, n. 2.

children[1]. These were to be brought up in a monastery or a Christian home, as Christians[2]. While thus avoiding the shameful guilt of forcing conversion, the council provided a happy lesson of what might be done, which Recceswinth, a generation later, was to show that he had aptly studied.

The Christian theologians, accustomed as they were to a particular method of biblical exegesis, were in a certain dilemma in regard to the Jews, a dilemma which we have already noted, but which comes out very clearly in the book which Isidore of Seville wrote for the benefit of his sister, an Abbess[3]. It was perhaps meant to aid her in the bringing up of Jewish children. The dilemma was a simple one. It was clearly stated in Scripture that the Jews would not be converted until the end of the world, and it was pleasantly easy to infer that even then but few of them would be benefited by the occasion offered[4]. There was, therefore, no hope that success would really crown their efforts to keep those Jews who had accepted baptism in the narrow paths of Christian orthodoxy (and, indeed, scripture made it quite clear that they were exceptionally hard-hearted and would always backslide). Unless, therefore, the end of the world was at hand, there was little scriptural reason for expecting success to crown their efforts to baptise those who had so far eluded them. Moreover, it is evident from Isidore that the Jews were efficient defenders of their position, and knew how to parry many of the quotations produced for their discomfiture. He mentions specifically that they parried the blessing of Judah in Genesis xlix with the statement that they still had a king of the tribe of Judah reigning in Babylon, and that they insisted on translating the passage of Isaiah in support of the Virgin Birth with the word ' young woman '. After extensive proofs from the Old Testament that Jesus was the Messiah, Isidore devoted most of his time to proving that all the Jewish ceremonies were superseded, and that the

[1] The Canon (60) refers to *Judaei*, but it is just possible that it refers to baptised Jews.

[2] Toledo IV, Canons 57-66.

[3] *De Fido Catholica ex vetere et novo Testamento, contra Judaeos*, Migne, P.L., LXXXIII, p. 419.

[4] *Op. cit.*, Bk. II, v and vii.

Christian sacraments were alone efficacious for salvation. The book is of some importance, for it not only probably influenced Recceswinth, but it was also early translated into various Germanic languages and seems to have had a wide circulation in western Europe, taking the place of the collections of proof texts in use in the earlier Church[1].

Chintila, the successor of Sisinand, reverted to the solution of Sisebut, and 'would allow no one to remain in his kingdom who was not a Catholic'. This was confirmed by the sixth council of Toledo in 638[2]. There exists in the archives of Leon a 'Placitum' or 'declaration of faith' which he exacted from the Jews of Toledo, in which they undertake to be sincere in their Christian faith, to forswear all Jewish rites and observances, to eat everything which is eaten by Christians, except when a physical and not a religious repugnance prevents them, to have no relations with and not to marry unbaptised Jews, to hand over all Jewish books in their possession, including the Talmud and Apocrypha, to denounce to the king, Church or magistrates any of their own number who transgresses his declaration, and to stone him themselves if he is guilty. The council passed a canon that every king on ascending the throne should first swear to enforce all the laws in operation against the Jews, and itself confirmed all those passed by previous councils[3]. At the conclusion of the council the bishops assembled wrote to the Pope Honorius, and expressed their grave concern at hearing that he was allowing lapsed Jewish Christians to remain in their Jewish ways, and protested that they would not do so in Spain[4].

Such is the shortness of human permanence that the very successor of Chintila, the aged and competent general Chindaswinth (641-649) apparently allowed the Jewish Christians to revert, and the unbaptised to return from exile. In the one council held in his reign, Toledo VII, there is no mention of the Jews. All that he insisted on was that those who were born Christians should, if they practised

[1] See the edition of Weinhold, Paderborn, 1874.

[2] Canon 3.

[3] *Ibid.*

[4] The letter is quoted in the R.E.J., Vol. II, 137. It is not in the collection of Mansi.

circumcision, be put to death, ' conspiratione et zelo catholicorum novis et atrocioribus poenis adflicti '[1]. It is not likely that this is a law against the Judaising of Gentile Christians, as Juster takes it, for by 640 it is perfectly natural that a generation should be growing up who were—technically, at least—born the Christian children of Christian parents, parents who had been forcibly baptised by Sisebut or who had accepted Christianity even earlier.

V. LAWS AND COUNCILS OF RECCESWINTH

If Chindaswinth was independent of the Church, his son, Recceswinth, was the exact opposite. Moved by the legal disorder which existed, he issued a completely new and comprehensive Code for all his subjects, whereby the Jews, if they had not already ceased to be Roman citizens in the lost constitution of Reccared, forfeited all privileges which were not allowed in the new Code. This new law considerably increased the powers given to the clergy. It dealt exhaustively with the Jewish question, and eleven of its laws survive.

The main problem confronting Recceswinth was the situation of those Jews who had so far evaded baptism, for theoretically all the Jews in his dominions were baptised Christians, unless they had gone into exile in the time of Chintila and only returned with the permission of Chindaswinth. It is certain that he did not in so many words order their violent baptism. Graetz has held that he allowed Jews who professed to be Jews to practise their religion openly, and he secures this result by always taking the word ' Judaeus ' in his laws to apply exclusively to baptised Jews. Juster, on the other hand, states that he allowed Jews to remain Jews provided they did not follow the practices of Judaism[2]. In fact, it appears as if the dilemma of Isidore of Seville is reproduced in the laws of Recceswinth. The purpose of his legislation was: ' ut fideles in religionis pace possederim, atque infideles ad concordiam religiosae pacis

[1] *Leg. Vis.*, 12.2.16.

[2] The arguments of Juster and a summary of those of Graetz will be found in the former, *op. cit.*, pp. 10 ff.

adduxerim[1]. To this the eighth council of Toledo, to which he had appealed for severity against the Jews, added that it was wrong for an orthodox prince to rule over blasphemers and to pollute his faithful subjects with the society of unbelievers[2]. It is clear then that the intention of king and council was to get rid of the Jews in one way or another. The council actually did not do more than confirm the canons of the fourth council of Toledo, but the king was much more explicit. The argument that he only allowed Jews to remain Jews at the cost of exile rests upon the following points from the actual laws:

12.2.2.—No one is *even in his heart* to have the slightest doubts about the Catholic faith. If he has, he is to go into exile until he thinks differently.

12.2.3—All the laws in force against the Jews are to be observed. (Does this not include that of Chintila that no one was to remain in the country who was not a Catholic?)

12.2.15.—No unbaptised Jew may remain '*in suae observationis detestanda fide et consuetudine*'.

To these explicit points may be added the query: What is a Jew who is uncircumcised, who does not observe the Sabbath, who eats pork, who celebrates marriage in Christian fashion, who observes no Jewish feasts and who believes explicitly in the Christian gospel in his heart? It is evident that such a Jew does not exist, and that in the last phrase Recceswinth had evolved an early form of the ' psychological tests ' beloved of American colleges for limiting the numbers of their Jewish students. Without saying so in so many words, Recceswinth forced all Jews who remained in Spain to accept conversion. In his laws, however, there is one explicit reference to rights of unbaptised Jews. Jews, whether baptised *or unbaptised*, are not allowed to give evidence[3] against Christians, but are allowed to go to law among themselves[4]. If it be thought necessary to defend the absolute consistency of a Visigothic prince, then the only solution is that such persons were foreign Jews with whom

[1] *Leg. Vis.*, 12.2.1.

[2] Toledo VIII, Canon 12.

[3] 12.2.10.

[4] 12.2.9.

Spanish Jews were in contact, and this explanation is not in itself extravagant. In any case, the right to go to law with another Jew is not one of the essentials of Judaism, so that it still remained true that it was impossible for a Jew, as such, to remain in the country.

The purpose of Recceswinth was, then, to force baptised Jews to remain faithful to their Christian profession, and unbaptised ones to leave the country. This purpose is carried out in very great detail. No baptised Jew may openly or secretly impugn the Christian faith. He shall not try by flight to evade his Christian duties. He shall not conceal any other transgressor[1]. Similarly, no Christian, of whatever rank, ecclesiastical or official, shall attempt to get any special indulgence for any Jew, or protect him in any way. This applies to bishops and the highest dignitaries[2]. That such a law was necessary is again an indication of the actual situation. Moreover, the law is ordained for all time, and future monarchs are forbidden to weaken it. Every Jew was required to sign a *placitum* of enormous length, swearing to forsake all Jewish observances[3]. This itself is reinforced by explicit laws forbidding every kind of Jewish observance[4].

Finally, if any Jewish Christian did revert to Jewish observances, the other Jewish Christians pledged themselves to stone the offender.

It is evident that such a law could only be very imperfectly carried out, and it is not surprising to find that a year later, in 655, the ninth council of Toledo was irresistibly impelled to go into still more extravagant detail in the attempt to make it workable. All baptised Jews were ordered to spend in the actual presence of the bishops all Jewish and Christian feast days. The bishop could thus see for himself that they did not observe the one and did observe the other[5]. When the last opportunity for evasion seemed finally removed, the council of the following year was not unnaturally horrified to find that on such important points as the ownership of slaves, and marriage with

[1] 12.2.4.

[2] 12.2.15.

[3] 12.2.17. See Appendix Three.

[4] 12.2.5-8.

[5] Toledo IX, Canon 17.

Christians, the Jews were not only evading the law, but actually finding priests and ecclesiastics who were willing to sell them Christian slaves with complete indifference as to whether such slaves subsequently were converted to Judaism[1]. Such an admission on the part of the council throws doubt on the success of the whole of the scheme of the king and bishops, and makes one wonder whether, except in the immediate surroundings of some enthusiast, the law was ever anything more than a dead letter.

Even so its very existence was enough to inconvenience the Jews to a serious extent, for so long as it existed, and so long as the king who promulgated it was reigning, there was always the danger that it would be applied to catch this or that individual. Further, it gave every unscrupulous official the opportunity to extract blackmail from a Jew under threat of carrying out the law against him. It is not, then, surprising to find that when under Wamba, the successor of Recceswinth, there was a rebellion in Septimania, the Jews were easily won over to the side of the rebels by the promise of freedom to follow their own observances. How large a part the Jews played in the rebellion we have no means of knowing, but when it was crushed by Wamba, who was an energetic ruler, they were expelled from Narbonne[2].

VI. LAWS AND COUNCILS OF ERWIG

Wamba was succeeded by Erwig, who issued a new revision of the Code of Laws left by Recceswinth. This involved, naturally, a rewriting of the laws affecting the Jews. Having completed his task, he submitted the Code to the bishops in council at Toledo, and secured their approval of the work[3]. Erwig was less scrupulous than his predecessors on the subject of compulsory baptism. Having studied the text that ' the kingdom of heaven suffereth violence, and the violent take it by force ', he came to the conclusion that if they refused to do so they might legitimately be forced to take it by violence. He refused even to allow them the

[1] Toledo X, Canon 7.

[2] Julian of Toledo, *History of the Rebellion against Wamba*, Chs. v and xxviii; M.G.H. quarto, SS. Mer., v.

[3] Toledo XII, Canon 9.

straight alternative of exile. Those who refused baptism for themselves or for their households were to be publicly flogged and to have their hair pulled out, before they were even permitted to tread the stony path of exile. The utmost concession he would allow was a year's grace to make up their minds as to the alternative to choose[1].

He made two important modifications in the laws in force at his accession. He refused to allow Jews who were forced to give up their Christian slaves to do so by setting them free. For he considered it an insult to a Christian to receive even his liberty at the hands of a Jew. Such slaves were to be sold, and sold under the eye of clergy who would watch to see there was neither evasion nor injustice. Sixty days from the proclamation of the edict were allowed for this sale, and during that time the Jew could, if he wished, make a claim to the retention of his slaves, on the ground that his conversion to Christianity had been a sincere conversion. If he succeeded in convincing the bishop that he had really been baptised, and that since his baptism he had not lapsed, then upon his signing a *placitum* before a bishop and a magistrate, and swearing to it on oath, he was allowed to retain his slaves. If the owner in question was a Christian who had lapsed, or a Jew who had never been baptised, then he was compelled to proceed to the sale within the statutory sixty days. If he failed to sell them within this period they were to be confiscated[2]. Harsh penalties were imposed for any infraction of the law, especially in the case where a Jew made the declaration and then lapsed. If a Christian slave neglected to declare his Christianity he was also exposed to severe punishment[3].

The second modification was the abolition of the death sentence for any Jewish offences. This he supported by both legal and scriptural argument. The laws abrogated are those imposing the death sentence on any who circumcise Christians, passed by Chindaswinth, and that compelling Jews to stone any member of their community who transgressed his *placitum*, passed by Recceswinth[4]. Extravagant

[1] *Leg. Vis.*, 12.3.3.

[2] *Ibid.*, 12.3.1, 12 and 13.

[3] *Ibid.*, 12.3.13 and 16.

[4] *Ibid.*, 12.2.16 and 12.2.11.

as is much of the legislation of Erwig, he is entitled to some respect for this action. His religious reasons appear sincere, and his legal argument, that it ignores the relative severity of different offences, is a sound one.

Having ordered all unbaptised Jews to leave his kingdom, he was presumably referring to Christians of Jewish origin in speaking of ' Judaei ' in the rest of his Code. In the main, the laws followed the preceding series. His favourite penalty was the lash, and the plucking out of the hair. To this in any serious offence was added the confiscation of the offender's property, and exile, either permanent or till the offender repented. There is the usual series of prohibitions against Jewish customs, meats and feasts[1]. Insulting the Christian faith, or seeking to evade its discipline or even being cognisant of the commission of such offences by others, was punished by confiscation and banishment[2]. Working on Christian feast days was punished with flogging or a fine. This law is mainly interesting in that it specifies especially agricultural work, showing that a considerable proportion of the Jews must have been on the land[3].

Then follows a series of laws regulating the position of the Hebrew Christians in the general community. It has already been said that they might only hold Christian servants if they had an absolutely blameless past. The same also applied to pagan or Jewish servants who wished to become Christians[4]. This is somewhat inconsistent with the order that every Jew *must* have his whole household baptised. It is presumably a reference to all future acquisitions. No Jew was to hold any kind of office without special royal consent[5]. He was not to be bailiff of any Christian property[6]. A rigorous system governed his right to travel. He had to set out armed with a passport of orthodoxy given by his local priest, and with a letter of introduction to the clergy of all places he was going to visit. Each had to endorse this letter with the

[1] *Leg. Vis.*, 12.3.4 and 5 passover, other feasts and circumcision; 7, meats; 8, marriage; 11, use of Jewish books.

[2] 12.3.2 and 9.

[3] 12.3.6.

[4] 12.3.18.

[5] 12.3.17.

[6] 12.3.19.

time of his arrival and departure, and a statement of his orthodoxy during his stay. All Jewish or Christian feast days he had to pass in the presence of the clergy. He was liable to severe punishment if he altered his route[1]. Not only travellers but all Jews were compelled to pass certain days in the presence of the bishop or his representative, and this they had to do ' not only washed but in a suitable frame of mind '. Even with this guarantee it must have been rather trying for the bishop. If there were no ecclesiastic in the neighbourhood, they were imposed upon some Christian whose orthodoxy was indisputable. This is in itself a surprisingly stiff piece of legislation, but the difficulties which beset the royal path in dealing with Jews were apparently as nothing compared with the problem set by Jewesses, who were strictly forbidden to come into the presence of the priest—lest he be tempted to commit misconduct with them! They were to spend the same day in the presence of reputable Dorcases[2]. Christian laymen who had Jews in their employment were responsible for seeing that their attendance at the bishop's was strictly carried out[3].

Erwig, like his predecessors, was justifiably afraid that local authorities would not carry all these laws into execution, and that the Jews would find means of evading them, or would plead ignorance of their scope. To prevent the latter, he had all Jews brought together to hear the laws read to them, after which a written copy was to be given to the Jewish community, so that no one could plead that he was ignorant of them through not being present at the reading. Further, the declaration of faith which every Jew had to sign was to be carefully conserved in the ecclesiastical archives[4]. To compel the authorities to carry out the law, not only were heavy penalties imposed for any connivance with its evasion, but every official was in some sense made a spy over the others. A higher official could only escape if a lower one had not reported to him a case with which he had not dealt himself. The king showed clearly that he had no real confidence in the integrity even of his bishops and

[1] 12.3.20.

[2] 12.3.21.

[3] 12.3.22.

[4] 12.3.28.

higher magistrates. Bishops were allowed to confiscate each other's sees if they could detect each other in indifference. Fines and excommunications menaced offenders high and low[1]. That he was more suspicious of the secular authorities was not only to be expected, but is shown by a special law which allows a secular judge to try cases under these laws only in the presence of the bishop or someone directly deputed by him. He could only act on his own in districts where no clergy were available[2]. Even to himself Erwig only allows the prerogative of pardon for first offences. No second condemnation could avoid the full rigour of the law[3].

Such is the Code of Erwig, and it carries the seal of its impracticability in its violence against those whose duty it was to enforce it. The royal power was far too weak, and local feeling far too strong, for such legislation to have any chance of success unless the local authorities themselves really wished to carry it out, and Erwig admitted that he knew that this was not the case. Moreover there were far too many pressing problems in existence for a conscientious magistrate to be able to spend his time on such unprofitable nonsense. By the end of the seventh century the whole kingdom was falling into decay. The incompetence of the kings and the rapacity of the bishops and nobility had combined to destroy it, and it is highly probable that this perpetual harassing of the Jews had much to do with the decline.

VII. LAWS AND COUNCILS OF EGICA

General conditions had been steadily going from bad to worse. They came to a crisis in the reign of Egica, the successor of Erwig. According to his own statements he had done all that he could to alleviate the lot of the Jews, and had allowed them even to possess Christian slaves[4]. There were, officially, no Jews still living in Spain at this time, and it would seem, therefore, that he was speaking

[1] 12.3.10, 23, 24 and 26.

[2] 12.3.25.

[3] 12.3.27.

[4] Toledo XVII, Royal Opening Address; M., XII, p. 94.

of those who had lapsed from the Christian faith and had repented, or who had in some other way transgressed the laws of Erwig. This permission may well have had a genuine economic motive, for in the collapse of Rome Honorius followed the same course[1]. Similar economic necessity may also have been the basis for his ' gentleness and kindness in urging them into the Christian fold '[2].

Unhappily for his reputation, these expressions of generosity have left no trace in the records of history. Nor can we be certain of his motives, for if he were moved by a desire to restore the prosperity of his kingdom by encouraging the economic activities of the Jews, something or someone must have succeeded in effecting a complete change in his opinions. For he followed these actions with the promulgation of a law which could only have led to the complete economic ruin of the Jews. By this law no one but a true Christian was to carry on any commerce whatever or to travel for any purposes of trade[3]. By Christian must again be meant Gentile Christians or Jews whose Christian record was without blemish. But it gave the latter no more security than Marranos were to enjoy a thousand years later. It was possible for any Gentile to impugn the sincerity of the conversion of a Jew, and it was practically impossible for the Jew to prove it unless the court was disposed in his favour. Moreover, as it would clearly be to the interest of the Christian rival to make such an accusation, this law can be fairly considered a fundamental attack upon the commercial section of the Jewish population in its entirety. Any unknown Christian arriving in a place for trading purposes was to open the proceedings by reciting the Lord's Prayer or the Apostles' Creed before witnesses, and by eating a dish of pork. Jews were only allowed to trade with other Jews, and within the kingdom: they might not travel abroad. All their property which had once been in Christian possession, real estate and otherwise, was to be turned into the treasury, and compensation would be given therefor. The compensation, unless the royal treasury was a very unusual one, could not with the best will in the world

[1] C.T., 16.9.3.

[2] Toledo XVII, *ibid.*

[3] *Leg. Vis.*, 12.2.18. Cf. Toledo XVI, Royal Address.

have been very extensive if the confiscation was really carried out. Any Christian trading with a Jew was to be suitably punished.

Within a year this law bore fruit. The Jews were convinced that the situation was intolerable, and prepared for desperate measures. Correspondence was discovered which seemed to the authorities to reveal the preparation of a plot to overthrow the Visigothic power. The Jews were alleged to be in communication with the Moors and to be inviting them to invade the country. The treason was said to have been confirmed by confessions of the guilty parties. The king brought the question before the seventeenth council of Toledo, contrasted the ingratitude of the Jews with his own great generosity, and implored the council to take stern measures against them. How much truth there was in the accusation it is impossible for us to know. That desperate men should revolt against their persecutors is human nature. That the Visigothic kingdom lay an obvious prey to Moorish conquerors without the need for any invitation or treason is also obvious.

In any case, the council considered that violent measures would be justified, and by a single act all the Jews of the kingdom were reduced to the status of slaves. Their property was confiscated and handed over to one of their Christian slaves to administer. We learn indirectly that there was a special Jewish tax in existence, since the administrator had to continue its payment to the treasury. Their children, from the age of seven, were taken from them and placed in Christian families, and subsequently married to Christians.

Such was the end of the first Spanish Jewish community, a foreshadowing of the greater tragedy which was to befall their successors nearly eight hundred years later. For some peculiar reason Spain has always been the European land of the greatest Jewish prosperity and the deepest Jewish tragedy. The Marranos of the later mediaeval period and after had their prototypes in the Jews of the Visigothic times. Both seem to have shown an equal fidelity to their traditions, and an equal skill in evading the measures destined for their extermination. That in the end the Visigothic Jew welcomed the Arab invader, and perhaps even invited him[1], was but the natural consequence of the treatment which he had received. To say with H. S. Chamberlain that 'under the rule of that thoroughly Western Gothic king (Egica), who had showered benefits upon them, they invite their kinsmen the Arabs to come over from Africa, and, not out of any ill-feeling, but simply because they hope to profit thereby, they betray their noble protector '[2], is to distort the whole of the facts which are contained not in documents of Jewish propaganda, but in the pages of Christian councils and Visigothic laws themselves.

VIII. REASONS FOR THE PERSECUTION OF THE JEWS IN SPAIN

There is no evidence that the Jews were inspired by such motives in calling in their 'kinsmen' against the noble-hearted Aryan, but is there any evidence that the motive which had actuated their persecution during a century was itself based on economic grounds? There is a certain class of historian who, if a rich group is persecuted, will immediately see only economic jealousy as the cause, and it is a reasonable presumption that some Jews were rich. In the absence of all the 'anecdotal' side of the history of the Jews under the Visigoths, it is extremely difficult to know what were the relations between the Jews and the average Christian, though reasons have already been given for believing they were not unfriendly. But now that we have considered the laws themselves, we can go a little further. Not only do they not in the least suggest an attack on Jewish wealth, but if such was their motive, they were even more inefficient than they appear at first sight. A law which appeared curious when taken in its apparent sense, might reveal its true purpose if we applied the economic motive to it, but here, if we take that as the true objective, the laws make no sense at all. Firstly, apart from the eternal question of slaves, there is no reference whatever to economics and economic disabilities until the very end, the time of Erwig

[1] For a discussion on the extent to which this was so, see Juster, *op. cit.*, p. 24, where all the sources are quoted.

[2] English Trans., Vol. I, p. 342.

and Egica. But secondly, even when there were economic issues at stake, the law says *explicitly*[1] that if their Christian faith be beyond reproach they are to enjoy all the privileges of other Christians in the carrying on of business. Persecution from jealousy of their wealth would have left them Jews and restrained their activities, as was done in later ages. It would certainly never have forced their conversion and left them in the enjoyment of all their supposed wealth. Thirdly, it is to be noted that no special Jewish tax appears to exist before the time of Egica, although the Theodosian Code gave admirable precedent for such a tax. Alaric omitted it in the Breviary, but the persecuting kings could easily have restored it. Lastly, if we have no anecdotes, we have an unrivalled collection of abusive terms, both in the councils and in the laws, but above all in the royal addresses to the councils. In all the rich variety of epithet which enlivened Visigothic oratory, there is no single term which suggests other than religious hostility. Not even such a phrase as 'exploiters of Christians', or 'vaunters in the goods of this world', slips in by accident in the rounded phrases so dear to their hearts. Jealousy is supposed to develop a certain low cunning. If it were jealousy which animated the Visigoths, it produced the unusual phenomenon of religious mania.

[1] *Leg. Vis.*, 12.2.18.

CHAPTER ELEVEN

THE FOUNDATIONS OF ANTISEMITISM

In the passage of the eight centuries reviewed in the previous chapters of this book we have seen the laying of the foundations of modern antisemitism. At times the ancient legislation itself has an appallingly modern ring in its very phraseology. With Leo and Charlemagne the curtain rings down upon the first act. The second act takes us up to the Reformation: the third act is still upon the stage. But it is an act of the same play, and can be explained only in the light of what has preceded it. Our interpretation of the first act is, therefore, no academic question, but the means by which we can understand what is passing before our eyes.

To some the interpretation begins with the formation of the Jewish people themselves. They point to the troubles of the Jews in Egypt and in the Roman Empire before the coming of Christianity into power, and find there the explanation. It is racial. It is some quality in Jewish blood strengthened by the inhuman provisions of the Jewish law.

Here it has been necessary to treat somewhat summarily the history of the relations between the Jews and the various peoples of the Graeco-Roman world, but enough has been said to show that this first interpretation is false. Without reverting to the plagues of Egypt, we can see that such hostility as existed in the Graeco-Roman world, especially at Alexandria, had reasonable historical causes, and needs no semi-mystic explanation. The adjustment of a monotheistic people to a polytheistic world was not an easy one. It is hard to blame the Jew for his monotheism. Nor will a modern patriot find anything criminal or abnormal in the revolts of the Jews against Rome. What trouble there was came from one of these two causes, monotheism or the harshness of the Roman domination. The significant fact for subsequent history is that when these two causes were removed, the problem remained. When Christianity became the religion of the state, monotheism was no longer abnormal. With the scattering of the Jews from Palestine in the second century, Jewish rebellions came to an end. But the Jewish problem remained. Either we are forced to revert to the explanation already rejected, and find some mystical racial reason, or we must find a new cause for its survival.

The most popular cause for modern scholars is an economic one, and they have sought to interpret Jewish relationships with their neighbours in economic terms. To-day, and indeed in the later Middle Ages, economic questions play a large rôle in the Jewish problem, but all the documents of the centuries reviewed in this work fail to find a single genuine economic cause for the phenomenon. Apart from the famous Alexandrian letter with its warning to 'keep clear of the Jews', it is impossible to find a single reference to, or sign of interest in, the economic position of the Jews, whether in Rome, Byzantium or in western Europe. There are indeed references to single wealthy Jews, to particular Jewish traders, but nowhere is the general term 'Jew' coupled with any term of economic significance, and nowhere do we find cases of economic hostility or maladjustment between the Jews of a locality and their neighbours. Even if considerable numbers of Jews were traders yet Jews were also represented in every class of society from slave to millionaire, from soldier to official, from artisan to peasant. And in the east as well as in the west our evidence all tends to show that they lived on good terms with their neighbours.

It is true that it was not an age which attributed events easily to economic causes, but that is not to say that it was ignorant of economic facts. We find plenty of abuse of this or that class or people. Greeks are called traders, Syrians are called worse, Egyptians are called soothsayers. But no one name covers the Jews. Emperors legislated to deal with the economic menace of particular groups. They never so dealt with the Jews, though frequently occupied with them. Even on the question of slavery it is solely the question of the ownership of a Christian by a Jew which moved them to pass laws. And if we review our documents impartially, the only possible conclusion is that there is no reference to, or interest in, the economic situation of the Jews, because in actual fact there was nothing of any interest or significance in that situation. They were neither a menace nor even a problem. They were a normal portion of society.

The new factor was not economic. It was religious. Christianity began as a Jewish sect. Its original adherents were loyal Jews, observing the whole Law. But when after twenty years a considerable number of Gentiles joined the new sect the question of their relation to the Jewish Law became acute. But the points at issue were connected with the ceremonial law, and not with the fundamentals of Judaism, fundamentals which lay behind the teaching of Jesus, and were shared by all His Jewish followers. But at the same time Jesus had added something new to their experience. They found in Him something they lacked in Judaism, the 'grace', which forms so large a part of Paul's message, and which he contrasts with the powerlessness of the Law to do more than convict him of sin. Jewish scholars have rightly pointed out that there is a doctrine of 'grace' in Judaism, a doctrine of repentance, and of reception back into the covenant of God. But whatever his attitude to this doctrine, Paul found something in his Christian experience which he personally had not found in Judaism. Such is the historical setting for what followed. At the end of the century the leadership of the Church was already passing into Gentile hands. Gentile congregations were powerful and numerous. Any compromise on the ceremonial law had been completely rejected. Had this been all, Judaism and Christianity might still have come together again after a period of tension. There were 'liberals' among the Jews who would have been ready to discuss the question of Gentile observance of the ceremonial law. The hardening of Judaism is a result, not a cause, of the separation. But, whether through the influence of Paul, or, more likely, through the misunderstanding of him by Gentile successors, the issue had gone much deeper, and the entirety of the religious conceptions of Judaism as proclaimed in the Old Testament was rejected as superseded by the Church. Such a claim made the acceptance of Jesus by the Jews impossible, and there follows the bitter period of hostility at the end of the first and the beginning of the second centuries which has been related.

It is in this conflict and its issue that modern anti-semitism finds its roots. For the Gentile Church the Old Testament no longer meant a way of life, a conception of the relation of a whole community to God, but a mine from which proof texts could be extracted. Instead of being the history of a single community, and the record of its successes and failures, it became the record of two communities, the pre-Incarnation Church symbolised by the 'Hebrews', and the temporary and rejected people of the Jews. Out of this artificial separation of history into two parts, on the simple principle that what was good belonged to one group and what was bad to the other, grew the caricature of the Jew with which patristic literature is filled.

The Christian theologian did not set out deliberately to blacken the character of his Jewish opponent, nor did he deliberately misrepresent his history. He cannot be said to have been actuated simply by hatred and contempt. His mistake was due to his belief in the verbal inspiration of the Scriptures which he read on the basis of the two separate communities. This is apparent in the whole volume of the literature of the time, with its complete silence about contemporary Jewish life. It is always the historical picture of the Jews in the Old Testament which moves the eloquence of the writers, never the misdoings of their living Jewish neighbours. After the period of violence at the end of the first century we have no evidence of any intensive campaign of Judaism against Christianity. We have, on the contrary, copious records of the friendship between the two peoples. Not only were there sects representing every shade of religious belief from orthodox Judaism to orthodox Christianity, but conciliar legislation in east and west alike is full of prohibitions of close social intercourse and even of participation in Jewish religious observances.

There is nothing abnormal in such conflicts as did occur. The Jews were an ordinary group of human beings with all the failings of humanity, and the Christians were the same. Each at times provoked the other, though the battle was unequal, for Judaism soon numbered fewer adherents than her rival. Occasional outbursts, caused by sudden religious inflammation or political disagreements, are normal in the life of a people. They form in themselves no explanation of a problem which has lasted nearly two thousand years. Moreover, if we had to explain events on the basis of casual happenings alone, we should be forced to the conclusion that there was far more reason for the Jew to hate the Christian than for the Christian to hate the Jew—and this on the evidence of Christian sources alone.

There is no other adequate foundation than the theological conceptions built up in the first three centuries. But upon these foundations an awful superstructure has been reared, and the first stones of that superstructure were laid, the very moment the Church had power to do so, in the legislation of Constantine and his successors. If we leave out ecclesiastical and secular legislation in the history of Jewish-Christian relations up to the eighth century there is almost nothing left. And if we add to legislation acts clearly due to religious fanaticism—forced baptisms or burnings of synagogues by Christians, and riotous observation of Purim or sudden acts of violence by Jews—then we have nothing left at all except the incidents accompanying the Persian wars, which have their own evident political explanation.

It is possible that Jewish association with certain heresies may have added somewhat to the vigour of the picture of the Old Testament Jew, but the evidence therefor is exceedingly slight. It is possible again that memories of the Jewish wars disposed the Roman population to believe ill of the Jew. It is possible even that a certain resentment of the old pagan population against this new Jewish religion, which was so much more of a menace than Judaism itself, may have turned to dislike of the Jews as the original authors of it. But all these three factors are at best minor, and the main responsibility must rest upon the theological picture created in patristic literature of the Jew as a being perpetually betraying God and ultimately abandoned by Him.

Up to the end of the period reviewed in this book the Jew himself shows no signs of the abnormalities which are noticeable in the later mediaeval period, and which are still evident to-day. By adopting the principle of using legislation to coerce a religious opposition, the first steps are already taken both in the east and in the west which will ultimately make those abnormalities inevitable. In the Byzantine empire, in France, and in the rest of Christendom it has become impossible for him to hold public offices. Other careers are also slowly being closed to him. Certain restrictions on his liberty have been enacted. It is still only the beginning. There is as yet no ghetto, no Jewish badge, no concentration into one or two professions, but the beginning has been made. More sinister for the future than the restrictions in force in the eighth century was the immunity enjoyed by those who violated such rights as the Jew officially possessed. A Theodoric and a Gregory might see that his rights were not ignored, but usually bishops, kings and barons were free to do what they willed. There was no appeal against them.

The ninth century begins a new act in both east and west. The Basilica of Basil the Macedonian contain the laws governing Jewish life in eastern Europe down to the present century, and in the west the charters of Louis and the fulminations of Agobard begin the story of the Middle Ages. But the new act follows directly from the first, and is rooted in the same causes. Fresh crimes were added to the historic crimes of the Old Testament. Ritual murder, the poisoning of wells, the profanation of the Host, all these are natural growths from the picture created by a Chrysostom or a Cyril. And the old falsification of Jewish history itself persisted, and has persisted up to the present time in popular teaching. Scholars may know to-day of the beauty and profundity of the Jewish conception of life. They may know that '*some* Jews' were responsible for the death of Jesus. But the Christian public as a whole, the great and overwhelming majority of the hundreds of millions of nominal Christians in the world, still believe that 'the Jews' killed Jesus, that they are a people rejected by their God, that all the beauty of their Bible belongs to the Christian Church and not to those by whom it was written; and if on this ground, so carefully prepared, modern antisemites have reared a structure of racial and economic propaganda, the final responsibility still rests with those who prepared the soil, created the deformation of the people, and so made these ineptitudes credible.

APPENDICES

APPENDIX ONE

LEGISLATION AFFECTING THE JEWS FROM A.D. 300 to 800

LAWS OF THE UNDIVIDED EMPIRE

Laws of Constantine

C.T., 16.8.1; to Evagrius, 18.x.315.
On converts to Judaism and to Christianity.
C.T., 16.8.3; to the Officials at Cologne, 11.xii.321.
With certain exceptions Jews are to be called to the Decurionate.
C.T., 16.8.2; to Ablavius the Pretorian Prefect, 29.xi.330.
On the relation of Jews to the Decurionate.
C.T., 16.8.4; to the Jewish Priests, Rabbis, Elders and other authorities, 1.xii.331.
Immunities of synagogue authorities.
C.T., 16.8.5; to Felix, P.P., 22.x.335.
On molesting Jewish converts to Christianity.
C.T., 16.9.1; to Felix, P.P., 22.x.335.
Circumcision of non-Jewish slaves.

Laws of Constantius

C.T., 16.9.2; to Evagrius, 13.viii.339.
Purchase and circumcision of non-Jewish or Christian slaves.
C.T., 16.8.6; to Evagrius, 13.viii.339.
Marriage between Jews and members of the imperial factories.
C.T., 16.8.7; to Thalassius, P.P., 3.vii.352 or 357.
Apostasy to Judaism.

Laws of Valentinian

C.T., 7.8.2; to Remigius Mag. Off., 6.v.368, 370 or 373.
Violation of synagogues.

Laws of Gratian

C.T., 12.1.99; to Hypatius, P.P., 18.iv.383.
On the relation of Jews to the Decurionate.
C.T., 16.7.3; to Hypatius, P.P., 21.v.383.
Intestability for apostates to Judaism.
C.T., 3.1.5; to Cynegius, P.P., 22.ix.384.
Possession or purchase of Christian slaves.

Laws of Theodosius the Great

C.T., 3.7.2 or 9.7.5; to Cynegius, P.P., 14.iii.388.
Intermarriage between Jews and Christians.
C.T., 13.5.18; to Alexander, Prefect of Egypt, 18.ii.390.
Questions of maritime transport.
C.T., 16.8.8; to Tatianus, P.P., 17.iv.392.
Jewish right of excommunication.
C.T., 16.8.9; to Addeus, Commander-in-Chief of the Eastern Command, 29.ix.393.
Judaism is a lawful sect.
C.J.,[1] 1.9.7; to Infantius, Governor of the Eastern Provinces, 30.xii.393.
Jews may only marry according to Christian table of affinity.

[1] *The text of this law is not to be found in the Codex Theodosianus.*

Laws of the Western Provinces of the Empire

Laws of Honorius

C.T., 12.1.157; to Theodorus, P.P., 13.ii or ix.398.
Jewish duty in the Decurionate.
C.T., 12.1.158; ditto.
C.T., 16.8.14; to Messala, P.P., 11.iv.399.
Confiscation of the *aurum coronarium*.
C.T., 16.8.16; to Romulianus, P.P., 22.iv.404.
Exclusion of Jews from military and court functions.
C.T., 16.8.17; to Hadrian, P.P., 25.vii.404.
Permission to send *aurum coronarium* restored.
C.T., 16.5.44; to Donatus (in Africa), 24.xi.408.
Jews and heretics must not disturb sacraments.
C.T., 16.5.46; to Theodore, P.P., 15.v.409.
Laws against Jews and heretics to be strictly enforced.
C.T., 16.8.19; to Jovius, P.P., 1.iv.409.
The ' Caelicoli ' are to be suppressed.
C.T., 8.8.8 or 2.8.26; to Johannes, P.P., 26.vii.409 or 412.
Jews to be left undisturbed on Sabbaths and Feast Days.
C.T., 16.8.20; to Johannes, P.P., 26.vii.412.
Synagogues and Sabbaths to be left undisturbed.
C.T., 16.9.3; to Annatus Didascalus and the Elders of the Jews, 6.xi.415.
Jews may own Christian servants if they do not convert them.
C.T., 16.8.23; to Annatus Didascalus and the Elders of the Jews, 24.ix.416.
Jewish converts to Christianity may revert to Judaism.
C.T., 16.8.24; to Palladius, P.P., 10.iii.418.
Jews may not enter government service or army. They may follow law, liberal professions and decurionate.

Laws of Valentinian III

Const. Sirm. 6 fin. to Amatius, Governor of Gaul, 9.vii.425.
Jews to be excluded from government service.
C.T., 16.8.28; to Bassus, P.P., 8.iv.426.
Converted children of Jews to inherit from their parents.

Laws of the Eastern Provinces of the Empire up to the Publication of the Theodosian Code

Laws of Arcadius

C.T., 16.8.10; to the Jews, 27.ii.396.
Jews to fix their own prices.
C.T., 16.8.11; to Claudianus, Governor of the Eastern Provinces, 24.iv.396.
The Patriarch not to be insulted.
C.T., 9.45.2; to Archelaus, Prefect of Egypt, 17.vi.397.
Jews not to become Christians from economic motives.
C.T., 16.8.12; to Anatolius, Prefect of Illyricum, 17.vi.397.
Jews and their synagogues are to be protected.
C.T., 16.8.13; to Caesarius, P.P., 1.vii.397.
Jewish clergy to have the same privileges as Christian clergy.
C.T., 2.1.10; to Eutychianus, P.P., 3.ii.398.
Jews to follow Roman Law except on religious questions.

C.T., 12.1.165; to Eutychianus, P.P., 30.xii.399.
Jews to serve in Decurionate.
C.T., 16.8.15; to Eutychianus, P.P., 3.ii.404.
The Patriarch to retain his privileges.

Laws of Theodosius II

C.T., 16.8.18; to Anthemius, P.P., 29.v.408.
Jews not to mock the Cross at Purim.
C.T., 16.8.22; to Aurelian, P.P., 20.x.415.
Degradation of the Patriarch.
C.T., 16.9.4; to Monaxius, P.P., 10.iv.417.
Various regulations on the possession of Christian slaves.
C.T., 16.8.21; to Philip, Governor of Illyricum, 6.viii.412.
Jews are not to be attacked or synagogues burnt, but they must not outrage Christianity.
C.T., 16.8.25; to Asclepiodotus, P.P., 15.ii.423.
Synagogues not to be pulled down or confiscated. New ones not to be built.
C.T., 16.8.26; to Asclepiodotus, P.P., 9.iv.423.
Laws to be enforced, synagogues not to be pulled down, Jews to be exiled for circumcising non-Jews.
C.T., 16.9.5; to Asclepiodotus, P.P., 9.iv.423.
Jews not to purchase Christian slaves.
C.T., 16.8.27; to Asclepiodotus, P.P., 8.vi.423.
New synagogues not to be built, old ones not to be confiscated.
C.T., 16.10.24; to Asclepiodotus, P.P., 8.vi.423.
Peaceable Jews not to be offended.
C.T., 15.5.5; to Asclepiodotus, P.P., 1.ii.425.
Jews to observe seasons of fast and feast.
C.T., 16.8.29; to John, Count of the Sacred Largesse, 30.v.429.
All special Jewish taxes to be confiscated to Charity Fund.
Novella 3; to Florentius, P.P., 31.i.438.
No Jew to hold office; new synagogues not to be built; proselytising to be punished with death; new synagogues to be confiscated; burdensome public office to be undertaken; Jewish law to be followed in private cases only.

Councils of the Empire up to the Time of the Publication of the Theodosian Code

Elvira (Spain), c. 300

Canon 16. Intermarriage with Jews.
49. Blessing of fields by Jews.
50. Sharing feasts with Jews.
78. Adultery with Jewesses.

Antioch, 341

Canon 1. Eating Passover with the Jews.

Laodicea, 360

Canon 16. Gospels to be read on Saturday.
29. Christians to work on Sabbath.
37. Gifts for feasts from Jews, and sharing feasts with Jews, prohibited.
38. Unleavened bread not to be accepted from Jews, and Jewish feasts to be avoided.

The Apostolic Canons

Canon 61. Denying Christianity through fear of Jews.
63. Entering a synagogue prohibited.
69. Feasting or fasting with Jews prohibited.
70. Oil not to be taken into synagogue for feasts.

Barbarian Recensions of the Theodosian Code

The Breviary of Alaric

2.1.10=C.T., 2.1.10; Jews to use Roman courts except on religious questions or by agreement.
2.8.3=C.T., 2.8.26; Sabbath not to be disturbed.
3.1.5=C.T., 3.1.5; Jews not to possess Christian slaves.
3.7.2 and 9.4.4=C.T., 3.7.2 and 9.7.5; intermarriage.
16.2.1=C.T., 16.7.3; apostates to be punished with intestability.
16.3.1=C.T., 16.8.5; converts to Christianity not to be molested.
16.3.2=C.T., 16.8.7; apostates to Judaism.
16.4.1=C.T., 16.9.1; circumcised slaves.
16.4.2=C.T., 16.9.4; possession of Christian slaves.
Novella 3=Novella 3, public office, building of synagogues, perversion of Christians.

Roman Law of the Burgundians

Law of Gondebaud, 19.4. Intermarriage.

Roman Law of the Franks

Clothaire II, Constitutio Generalis 4. Lawsuits between Romans to be conducted according to Roman Law.

Roman Law of the Ostrogoths

Theodoric, Cap. 143. Jews to retain privileges allowed by Law.

Lex Romana Raetica Curiensis

2.1.8; extent and limitations of judicial autonomy.
3.1.5; purchase of Christian slaves.
3.7.2; intermarriage.

Law of the Lombards

2.56.1; Roman citizens to live according to Roman Law.

Legislation of the Western Kingdoms: the Visigoths

Laws of Reccared I of 588

12.2.12. Purchase, possession and circumcision of non-Jewish slaves.

Laws of Sisebut of 612

12.2.13. Christian slaves of Jews to be freed; converts to Christianity to inherit; other legislation affecting slaves.
12.2.14. Liberation of Christian slaves; mixed marriages; irrevocability of this law.

Laws of Chindaswinth of between 641 *and* 652

12.2.16. Christians Judaising.

Laws of Recceswinth of c. 652

12.2.2. Christian doctrine not to be criticised.
12.2.3. Laws are to be considered irrevocable and strictly enforced.
12.2.4. Apostasy not to be permitted.
12.2.5. Passover and Jewish feasts not to be observed.
12.2.6. Marriage only by Christian tables of affinity.
12.2.7. Circumcision prohibited.
12.2.8. Distinctions of foods prohibited.
12.2.9. Actions or evidence against Christians prohibited.
12.2.10. Evidence against Christians prohibited.
12.2.11. Lawbreakers to be stoned or enslaved.
12.2.15. Jews on no account to be protected by clergy.

Laws of Erwig of c. 680

12.3.1. Owing to Jewish evasions all laws to be re-enacted, except those concerning manumission and capital punishment.
12.3.2. Blasphemy against Christian doctrine to be punished.
12.3.3. All Jews to submit to baptism.
12.3.4. Practice of Jewish customs to be punished.
12.3.5. Celebration of Jewish feasts to be punished.
12.3.6. Work on Sunday to be punished, and special feasts to be observed.
12.3.7. Distinctions of meats prohibited, except for those physically unable to eat pork.
12.3.8. Marriage to be according to Christian customs.
12.3.9. Blasphemers and apostates to be punished.
12.3.10. Jewish bribes not to be accepted.
12.3.11. Jewish books and teaching to be suppressed.
12.3.12. Jews not to own Christian slaves.
12.3.13. Jews to sell their Christian slaves or prove their own orthodoxy.
12.3.16. Treatment of apostate slaves.
12.3.17. No Jew to exercise authority over Christians.
12.3.18. Slaves desiring to become Christians to be free to do so.
12.3.19. No Jew to be appointed bailiff of Christian property.
12.3.20. Regulations affecting Jewish travellers.
12.3.21. Feast days to be spent in presence of bishop, or suitable Christian.
12.3.22. Jewish employees to be obliged to obey regulations.
13.3.23. Clergy to see to carrying out of these laws.
12.3.24. Penalties for corruption or laxity.
12.3.25. Lay judges not to act without ecclesiastical supervision.
12.3.26. Local religious authorities responsible for strict enforcement.
12.3.27. Limitation of royal prerogative of pardon.
12.3.28. Method of publication of this legislation.

Laws of Egica of c. 690

12.2.18 Regulations of Jewish traders, Jewish taxes, and Jewish leases of Christian property.

Councils of the Visigoths

Agde, 506[1]

Canon 12. Fasting in Lent on Saturdays.
34. Special conditions for Jewish catechumens.
40. Clergy and laity to avoid Jewish feasts.

[1] *These councils were held by the Catholics (i.e. Roman citizens) at a time when their Visigothic masters were Arians.*

Valencia, 524[1]

Canon 16. Jews, heretics and pagans to be allowed in church up to the missa catechumenorum.

Toledo III, 589

Capit. 14. Intermarriage; Christian slaves; children of mixed marriages; public office; proselytising, and circumcision.

Narbonne, 589

Canon 4. Jews not to work on Sunday.
9. Psalms not to be sung during Jewish funerals.
14. Jewish fortune-tellers not to be consulted.

Toledo IV, 633

Canon 57. Jews not to be compelled to be baptised.
58. Jewish bribes not to be accepted by Christians.
59. Apostates to be punished.
60. Children of Jews to be brought up by Christians.
61. Children of apostates to inherit.
62. No communication to be allowed between baptised and unbaptised Jews.
63. In mixed marriages unconverted partner must be baptised and children brought up Christians.
64. Apostates not to be allowed as witnesses.
65. Jews and Jewish Christians to be excluded from public office.
66. Jews not to own Christian slaves.

Toledo VI, 638

Canon 3. Jews remaining in Spain must be baptised.

Toledo VIII, 653

King's Speech (Recceswinth). Denunciation of apostates.
Canon 10. Future sovereigns must be orthodox.
12. Jews remaining in Spain must be baptised.
Included in this council is a Placitum. See Appendix 3, A.i.

Toledo IX, 655

Canon 17. Jews to pass Jewish and Christian festivals in presence of ecclesiastical authorities.

Toledo X, 656

Capit. 1. Easter must be celebrated uniformly.
7. Christian slaves not to be sold to Jews.

Toledo XII, 681

King's Speech (Erwig). Implores action on Jewish apostasy and delinquency.
Canon 9. Confirmation of the Laws of Erwig. (See above.)

Toledo XVI, 693

King's Speech (Egica). Appeal for confirmation of all previous laws, together with prohibition of unconverted Jews trading, and converted Jews being taxed specially.
Capit. 1. Confirmation of King's Speech.

[1] *These councils were held by the Catholics (i.e. Roman citizens) at a time when their Visigothic masters were Arians.*

Toledo XVII, 694

King's Speech (Egica). Jewish plot against Spanish security. All Jews except those of Septimania to be reduced to slavery.

Canon 8. Confirms King's request.

Legislation of the Western Kingdoms: the Burgundians

Gondebaud

Law 102. Punishment of Jewish assault on Christians.

Council of Epaone, 517

Canon 15. Attendance at Jewish banquets prohibited.

Legislation of the Western Kingdoms: the Franks

Childebert, *c.* 554

Letter to clergy and people. Jews not allowed in street between Holy Thursday and Easter.

Clothaire II, 614

Edict. Jews not to hold office.

Charlemagne

Cap. Acquisgran. 15 (=Laodicea, Canon 29) 789. Christians to work on Sabbath.

Cap. Acquisgran. 45 (=Carthage IV, Canon 196) 789.
Jews not to give evidence.

Cap. dup. ad Niumagen, 806.
Clergy not to allow sale of church plate to Jews or others.

Cap. de Jud. 1, 814.
Jews not to receive Church property in pledge.

Cap. de Jud. 2, 814.
Christians not to be taken in pledge.

Cap. de Jud. 3, 814.
Jews not to mint or trade privately.

Cap. de Jud. 814.
4a. Oath to be taken by Jew in giving evidence.
4b. Oath to be taken in pleading not guilty.

Councils of the Franks

Vannes, 465

Canon 12. Clergy to avoid Jewish feasts.

Orleans II, 533

Canon 19. Intermarriage.

Clermont, 535

Canon 6. Intercourse between Christian and Jew.
9. Jewish judges.

Orleans III, 538

Canon 13. Regulations for Christian servants of Jews; intermarriage; attending Jewish festivities.
28. Sunday not to be observed in Jewish fashion.
30. Jews not to mix with Christians between Holy Thursday and Easter.

Orleans IV, 541

Canon 30. Christian slaves of Jews to be redeemed on request.
31. Conversion of servants to Judaism prohibited.

Orleans V, 548

Canon 22. Conditions to be observed when slaves take refuge in churches.

Macon, 581

Canon 2. Jewish conversation with nuns.
13. Jews not to be judges or tax collectors.
14. Jews not to mix with Christians between Holy Thursday and Easter.
15. Christians not to take part in Jewish festivities.
16. Christian slaves to be redeemed.
17. Attempted conversion of slave to Judaism to be punished.

Paris, 614

Canon 15. Jews seeking positions of authority to be baptised.

Reims(?), 624

Canon 11. Christians not to be sold to Jews; Jews not to hold office. Jewish slanders against Christianity to be refuted.[1]

Chalons sur Saone, 650

Canon 9. Slaves not to be sold beyond frontiers, so as not to fall into hands of Jews.

' *Canons of Carthage* ', *or* ' *of the African Church* '

Canon 84. Jews, heathen and heretics to be allowed into church up to the missa catechumenorum.
89. Judaising to be suppressed.
196. Jews and others not to give evidence.

Councils of the Papacy

Rome, 743

Canon 10. Intermarriage.

Legislation of the Eastern Empire

The Code of Justinian contained certain laws from the Code of Theodosius. These are marked with an asterisk. Except where noted, they were unchanged.

**Laws of Constantine*

C.T., 16.8.1=C.J., 1.9.3.

**Laws of Constantius*

C.T., 16.8.7=C.J., 1.7.1.
C.T., 16.8.6 is combined with 16.9.1 (of Constantine), 16.9.2 (of Constantius) and 16.9.4 (of Theodosius II) and ascribed to Constantius, as C.J., 1.10.1.

[1] *This last may be a scribe's error for:* ' *Jewish banquets not to be attended* ', *reading* ' *convivia* ' *for* ' *convicia* '. *It is so given in* Concilium Clippiacense *in M.G.H. quarto, Conc. I, p.* 199.

**Laws of Valentinian*

C.T., 7.8.2=C.J., 1.9.4.

**Laws of Gratian*

C.T., 12.1.99=C.J., 1.9.5.
C.T., 16.7.3=C.J., 1.7.2.

**Laws of Theodosius the Great*

C.T., 3.7.2=C.J., 1.9.6.
C.J., 1.9.7 has no counterpart in the Theodosian Code.

**Laws of Honorius*

C.T., 12.1.157=C.J., 10.32.49.
C.T., 16.8.19=C.J., 1.9.12.
C.T., 8.8.8=C.J., 1.9.13, adding that on Jewish feasts Jews shall not be entitled to summon Christians.

**Laws of Arcadius*

C.T., 16.8.10=C.J., 1.9.9.
C.T., 9.45.2=C.J., 1.12.1.
C.T., 2.1.10=C.J., 1.9.8.
C.T., 12.1.165=C.J., 1.9.10.

**Laws of Theodosius II*

C.T., 16.8.18=C.J., 1.9.11.
C.T., 16.8.22=C.J., 1.9.15, including only the paragraph dealing with Jewish juridical competence.
C.T., 16.9.4=C.J., 1.10.1.
C.T., 16.8.21=C.J., 1.9.14.
C.T., 16.8.26=C.J., 1.9.16.
C.T., 16.10.24=C.J., 1.11.6.
C.T., 15.5.5=C.J., 3.12.6.
C.T., 16.8.29=C.J., 1.9.17.
Novella 3=C.J., 1.5.7, 1.7.5, and 1.9.18.

Laws of Marcian

C.J., 1.1.4; to Palladius, P.P., 7.ii.452.
Christianity not to be discussed in public.

Laws of Justin and Justinian

C.J., 1.5.12 of 527.
'Heretics are all such as do not belong to the Catholic faith'—including Jews. They are not to hold any office; or follow profession of law. Heavy penalties for connivance with evasion.

Laws of Justinian

C.J., 1.5.13, no date or address.
Orthodox children not to be disinherited by Jewish parents.
C.J., 1.5.17, no date or address.
Complete destruction of Samaritan synagogues ordered.
C.J., 1.3.54, no date or address.
No Jew to possess Christian slaves, or slaves desiring to become Christian.
C.J., 1.10.2, no date or address.
No Jew to own a Christian slave.

C.J., 1.9.2, no date, (?) addressed to the Jews.
Sabbath not to be disturbed.
C.J., 1.5.21, to Johannes, P.P., 28.vii.531.
Jews may not give evidence against orthodox, but may do so against each other. They may witness documents.
Nov. 37, to Salomon, Governor of Africa, 1.viii.535.
Jews not to be allowed to attend church services; or to own Christian slaves. Their synagogues are to be turned into churches.
Nov. 45, to Johannes, P.P., 1.ix.537.
Jews are to perform decurionate without its honours; may, in a suit involving orthodox persons, only give evidence for them or for the state.
Nov. 131, to Peter, P.P., 545.
Jews may not lease orthodox property; they may not build new synagogues.
Nov. 146, to Areobindus, P.P., 8.ii.553.
(*Owing to its importance the text is given in full as Appendix* 2.)

Laws of Leo the Isaurian

Ecloga, App. 4.6.
Jews to hold no public office.
Ecloga, App. 4.7.
Either Jewish parent may desire the children to be educated as Christians.
Ecloga, App. 4.13.
Samaritan synagogues to be destroyed.
Ecloga, App. 4.16.
Apostasy to Judaism to be punished.
Ecloga, App. 4.24.
Proselytising to Judaism to be punished.
Ecloga, App. 6.26.
Jews neither to possess nor circumcise Christian slaves.
Ecloga, App. 6.27.
No Jew to possess Christian slave.
Ecloga, App. 6.28.
Slave of Jew desiring to become Christian to be freed.
Ecloga, App. 6.30.
Circumcision of Christian to be punished.

Councils of the Eastern Empire

Chalcedon, 451

Canon 14. Marriageable members of clergy not to wed Jew.

Trullanum, 692

Canon 11. No Christian to eat unleavened bread with Jew, use them as doctors or bathe with them.

Nicaea II, 787

Canon 8. Baptised Jews who lapse are to be treated as Jews.

'*Forged*' *Canons of Nicaea*

Canon 52 (56). Clergy are not to eat or have business associations with Jews.

APPENDIX ONE, PART TWO

LAWS AFFECTING THE JEWS

According to their Subject

Admission to Church, C.J., Nov. 37; Carthage IV, 84; Nicaea II, 8; Valencia, 16.

Adultery with Jews, Clermont, 6; Elvira, 78; Orleans IV, 31.

Apostasy of converted Jews, L.V., 12.2.4; L.V., 12.2.11; L.V., 12.2.16; L.V., 12.3.9; L.V., 12.3.11; L.V., 12.3.15; Agde, 34; Nicaea II, 8; Toledo IV, 57; Toledo VIII, King's Speech.

Attacks on Christianity, C.T., 16.8.21; C.J., 1.1.4; L.V., 12.2.2.; L.V., 12.3.2; L.V., 12.3.9; Reims, 11.

Attacks on Christians, C.T., 16.8.1; C.T., 16.8.5; C.T., 16.5.44; C.T., 16.5.46; Gondebaud, 102; Can. Apost., 61.

Attacks on Jews, C.T., 16.8.26; C.T., 16.10.24.

Aurum Coronarium, C.T., 16.8.14; C.T., 16.8.17; C.T., 16.8.29.

Burial, ceremonies of Jewish, Narbonne, 9.

Caelicoli, C.T., 16.8.19; C.J., 1.9.12.

Children of Jewish marriages, Ec. Leo. App. 4, 7; Toledo IV, 60.

Children of mixed marriages, L.V., 12.2.14; Toledo III, 14; Toledo IV, 63.

Church property, Jewish possession of, Charlemagne, Cap. dup., Charlemagne, Cap. Jud.

Circumcision (see also Slaves), C.T., 16.8.26; L.V., 12.2.7; L.V., 12.3.4; Toledo XII, 9.

Clergy, respect for, Macon, 14.

Clergy, responsibility of, C.J., 1.5.12, xii; C.J., 1.3.54; L.V., 12.3.20, 21, 22, 23, 24, 25, 26, 28; Toledo XII, 9.

Confirmatory Laws, C.T., 16.5.46; C.T., 16.8.26; C.T., 16.8.27; C.J., 1.5.12; L.V., 12.2.14; L.V., 12.2.3; L.V., 12.2.11; L.V., 12.3.1; L.V., 12.3.23; L.V., 12.3.26; Toledo VIII, 12; Toledo XII, King's Speech.

Connivance in Jewish evasions, C.T., 16.5.46; C.J., 1.3.54, xi; C.J., 1.5.12; L.V., 12.2.15; L.V., 12.3.1; L.V., 12.3.9, 10; L.V., 12.3.22, 23, 24, 25; Toledo IV, 58; Toledo IV, 65; Toledo VI, 3; Toledo VIII, 10; Toledo XII, 9.

Converts to Christianity (voluntary), C.T., 16.8.1; C.T., 16.8.5; C.T., 16.8.28; Brev., 16.3.1; L.V., 12.2.14; Agde, 34.

Converts to Christianity (compulsory), L.V., 12.2.15; L.V., 12.3.3; Toledo IV, 57; Toledo VI, 3.

Converts to Christianity (false), C.T., 9.45.2; C.T., 16.8.23; Nicaea II, 8.

Converts to Christianity (evasion of), L.V., 12.2.15; L.V., 12.3.3; L.V., 12.3.10; L.V., 12.3.16; L.V., 12.3.22; Toledo XII, 9.

Converts to Judaism, C.T., 16.8.1; C.T., 16.8.7; C.T., 16.7.3; Nov. T., 3; Ecloga, 4.16; Ecloga, 4.24; Brev., 16.2.1; Brev., 16.3.2; Brev., Nov. 3; L.V., 12.2.14; L.V., 12.3.4; Orleans IV, 31 ; Toledo XII, 9.

Curial Responsibility, C.T., 16.8.3, 2, 4; C.T., 12.1.99; C.T., 16.8.13; C.T., 12.1.157, 158, 165; C.T., 16.8.24; Nov. T., 3; C.J., 1.5.12; Nov. J., 45.

Doctors, Trullanum, 11.

Easter, celebration of, C.T., 16.10.24; L.V., 12.2.5; Antioch, 1; Can. Apost., 69; Carthage IV, 89; Toledo X, 1.
Easter, appearance of Jews during, Childebert, epist.; Macon, 14; Orleans II, 30.
Evidence, right of Jews to give, C.J., 1.5.21; Nov. J., 45; Ec. Priv. Auct., xv, 7; L.V., 12.2.9, 10; Charlemagne, Cap. Acg. 45; Carthage IV, 196; Carthage VII, 2; Toledo IV, 64.
Excommunication, right of Jewish, C.T., 16.8.8; C.J., Nov. 146, ii.

Feasts (Jewish), C.T., 16.8.18; C.T., 15.5.5; L.V., 12.3.1, 4, 5, 20, 21; Toledo XII, 9.
Feasts (Christian), attendance at of Jews, L.V., 12.3.6; Toledo IX, 17; Toledo X, 1; Toledo XII, 9.
Feasts (Jewish), attendance at of Christians, Antioch, 1; Laodicea, 37, 38; Can. Apost., 69; Agde, 40.
Fields, blessing of, Elvira, 49.
Foods, distinction of, L.V., 12.2.8; L.V., 12.3.7; Toledo XII, 9.
Fortune Tellers, Carthage IV, 89; Narbonne, 14.

Gifts, acceptance of, L.V., 12.3.10; Can. Apost., 69; Laodicea, 37, 38.

Heresy, defence of, C.J., 1.1.4; L.V., 12.2.2; L.V., 12.3.1, 2.
Hospitality accepted, Agde, 40; Elvira, 50; Epaone, 15; Macon, 15; Orleans III, 13, ii; Trullanum, 11; Vannes, 12.
Hospitality of Jews accepted by converted Jews, Toledo IV, 62.

Inheritance, C.T., 16.8.28; C.J., 1.5.13; Ec. Priv. Auct., vii, 18; L.V., 12.2.13; L.V., 12.3.8; Toledo IV, 61.
Intermarriage with Jews, C.T., 16.8.6; C.T., 3.7.2; C.T., 9.7.5; Brev., 3.7.2.; Brev., 9.4.4.; L.V., 12.2.14; L.R. Burg., 19.4; L.R.R.C., 3.7.2; Chalcedon, 14; Elvira, 16; Orleans II, 19; Orleans III, 13, ii; Rome, 10; Toledo III, 14; Toledo IV, 63; Toledo X, 7.

Judaising, L.V., 12.2.16; Toledo IV, 59. (See also Easter, Sabbath.)
Judaism, legality and protection of, C.T., 16.8.9, 12, 13, 20, 24; Theodoric, Cap. 143; L.R.R.C., 2.1.8.
Judicial autonomy, C.T., 2.1.10; C.T., 16.8.22; Nov. T., 3; Brev., 2.1.10; L.V., 12.2.9; L.R.R.C., 2.1.8; Theodoric, Cap. 143; Clothaire II, Const. Gen., 4.

Lawsuits against Christians, C.J., 1.9.5; L.V., 12.2.9.
Legal Profession, C.T., 16.8.24; C.J., 15.5.12.

Maritime Duties, C.T., 13.5.18.
Marriage by Jewish Law, C.J., 1.9.7; L.V., 12.2.6; L.V., 12.3.8; Toledo XII, 9.

Nuns, conversation with, Macon, 2.

Oath, Jewish, Charlemagne, Cap. de Jud., 4a.
Official and military positions, C.T., 16.8.16; C.T., 16.8.24; Const. Sirm., 6; Nov. T., 3; C.J., 1.5.12; Nov. J., 36; Ecloga, 4.6; Brev., Nov. 3; L.V., 12.3.17; Clothaire II, Edict; Clermont, 9; Macon, 13; Paris, 15; Reims, 11; Toledo III, 14; Toledo IV, 65; Toledo XII, 9.

Partnership with Jews, Forged Nicaea, 52.
Patriarch, The, C.T., 16.8.11, 14, 15, 17, 22.
Placita, L.V., 12.2.4; L.V., 12.2.11; L.V., 12.3.12; L.V., 12.3.13; L.V., 12.3.28; Toledo XII, 9.

Pledges, Christians not to be taken as, Charlemagne, Cap. Jud., 2.
Pork, L.V., 12.3.7.
Property, Jewish Occupation of Christian, Nov. J., 131; Toledo XII, 9.

Sabbath, Observation of, by Christians, L.V., 12.2.5; L.V., 12.3.20, 21; Charlemagne, Cap. Acg., 15; Agde, 12; Carthage IV, 89; Laodicea, 16; Laodicea, 29; Orleans III, 28; Toledo XII, 9.
Sabbath, Protection of, C.T., 2.8.26; C.T., 8.8.8; C.T., 16.8.20; C.J., 1.9.2; Brev., 2.8.3.
Samaritans, C.T., 16.8.16; C.J., 1.5.17; Ecloga, 4,13.
Slaves, not to be sold abroad, L.V., 12.2.14; Chalons, 9.
Slaves, Jews reduced to, L.V., 12.2.11; Toledo XVII, 8.
Slaves, Christian, acquisition of, C.T., 16.9.2; C.T., 3.1.5; C.T., 16.9.4, 5; C.J., 1.10.1; Ecloga, 6.26; Ecloga, 6.27; Brev., 3.1.5; Brev., 16.4.2; L.V., 12.2.12, 13; L.R.R.C., 3.1.5.
Slaves, apostasy of, C.T., 16.9.4; C.T., 12.2.13, 14; Ecloga, 4.16; L.V., 12.3.16; Orleans IV, 31; Toledo XII, 9.
Slaves, circumcision of, C.T., 16.9.1; C.T., 3.1.5; C.T., 16.8.22; C.T., 16.8.26; Nov. T., 3; C.J., 1.10.1; Ecloga, 6.26; Ecloga, 6.30; L.V., 12.2.12, 13,14; Macon, 17; Orleans IV, 31; Reims, 11; Toledo III, 14.
Slaves, liberation of, C.T., 3.1.5.; Ecloga, 6.28; L.V., 12.2.14; L.V., 12.3.1; L.V., 12.3.12; Macon, 16; Orleans IV, 30.
Slaves, possession of, prohibited, C.T., 3.1.5; C.J., 1.3.54; C.J., 1.10.2; Ecloga, 6.26; Ecloga, 6.27; Brev., 3.1.5; L.V., 12.2.12.; L.V., 12.2.13, 14; L.V., 12.3.1; L.V., 12.3.13; Orleans III, 13, i; Toledo IV, 66; Toledo XII, 9.
Slaves, possession of, allowed, C.T., 16.9.3; Toledo XVI, King's Speech.
Slaves, Christian, concealment of their Christianity by, C.T., 16.9.4; L.V., 12.3.16.
Slaves, Christian, sale of, to Jews, L.R.R.C., 3.1.5; Reims, 11; Toledo X, 7.
Slaves, non-Jewish, acquisition of, C.T., 16.9.1, 2.
Slaves, circumcision of, C.T., 16.9.1, 2; C.T., 16.8.22; Brev., 16.4.1; Orleans IV, 31.
Slaves seeking baptism, possession of, C.J., 1.3.54; Ecloga, 6.28; L.V., 12.2.13; L.V., 12.3.18; Toledo XII, 9.
Sunday, observance of, by Jews, L.V., 12.3.6; Narbonne, 4.
Synagogue, building and repair of, C.T., 16.8.22; C.T., 16.8.25; C.T., 16.8.27; Nov. T., 3; Nov. J., 131; Brev., Nov. 3.
Synagogue, confiscation of, Nov. J., 37, viii.
Synagogue, entering of, by Christians, Can. Apost., 63; Can. Apost., 70.
Synagogue, services of, Nov. J., 146.
Synagogue, violation of, C.T., 7.8.2; C.T., 16.8.12; C.T., 16.8.20, 21; C.T., 16.8.25, 26, 27.

Talmud, suppression of (deuterosis), Nov. J., 146; L.V., 12.3.11; Toledo XII, 9.
Taxation, Jewish (see also aurum coronarium), Toledo XVI, King's Speech.
Testamentary rights (see also inheritance), C.T., 16.7.3.
Trade right of (see also travel), C.T., 16.8.10; L.V., 12.2.18; Charlemagne, Cap. Jud., 3; Toledo XVI, King's Speech.
Travel, regulation of, L.V., 12.3.20; L.V., 12.2.18; Toledo XII, 9.

APPENDIX TWO

NOVELLA 146 OF JUSTINIAN

8.ii.553. Nov. 146. Justinian to Areobindas, P.P.

A Permission granted to the Hebrews to read the Sacred Scriptures according to Tradition, in Greek, Latin or any other Language, and an Order to expel from their community those who do not believe in the Judgment, the Resurrection, and the Creation of Angels.

Preface. Necessity dictates that when the Hebrews listen to their sacred texts they should not confine themselves to the meaning of the letter, but should also devote their attention to those sacred prophecies which are hidden from them, and which announce the mighty Lord and Saviour Jesus Christ. And though, by surrendering themselves to senseless interpretations, they still err from the true doctrine, yet, learning that they disagree among themselves, we have not permitted this disagreement to continue without a ruling on our part. From their own complaints which have been brought to us, we have understood that some only speak Hebrew, and wish to use it for the sacred books, and others think that a Greek translation should be added, and that they have been disputing about this for a long time. Being apprised of the matter at issue, we give judgment in favour of those who wish to use Greek also for the reading of the sacred scriptures, or any other tongue which in any district allows the hearers better to understand the text.

Ch. I. We therefore sanction that, wherever there is a Hebrew congregation, those who wish it may, in their synagogues, read the sacred books to those who are present in Greek, or even Latin, or any other tongue. For the language changes in different places, and the reading changes with it, so that all present may understand, and live and act according to what they hear. Thus there shall be no opportunity for their interpreters, who make use only of the Hebrew, to corrupt it in any way they like, since the ignorance of the public conceals their depravity. We make this proviso that those who use Greek shall use the text of the seventy interpreters, which is the most accurate translation, and the one most highly approved, since it happened that the translators, divided into two groups, and working in different places, all produced exactly the same text.

i. Moreover who can fail to admire those men, who, writing long before the saving revelation of our mighty Lord and Saviour Jesus Christ, yet as though they saw its coming with their eyes completed the translation of the sacred books as if the prophetic grace was illuminating them. This therefore they shall primarily use, but that we may not seem to be forbidding all other texts we allow the use of that of Aquila, though he was not of their people, and his translation differs not slightly from that of the Septuagint.

ii. But the Mishnah, or as they call it the second tradition, we prohibit entirely. For it is not part of the sacred books, nor is it handed down by divine inspiration through the prophets, but the handiwork of man, speaking only of earthly things, and having nothing of the divine in it. But let them read the holy words themselves, rejecting the commentaries, and not concealing what is said in the sacred writings, and disregarding the vain writings which do not form a part of them, which have been devised by them themselves for the destruction of the simple. By these instructions we ensure that no one shall be penalised or prohibited who reads the Greek or any other language. And their elders,

Archiphericitae and presbyters, and those called magistrates, shall not by any machinations or anathemas have power to refuse this right, unless by chance they wish to suffer corporal punishment and the confiscation of their goods, before they yield to our will and to the commands which are better and dearer to God which we enjoin.

Ch. II. If any among them seek to introduce impious vanities, denying the resurrection or the judgment, or the work of God, or that angels are part of creation, we require them everywhere to be expelled forthwith; that no backslider raise his impious voice to contradict the evident purpose of God. Those who utter such sentiments shall be put to death, and thereby the Jewish people shall be purged of the errors which they introduced.

Ch. III. We pray that when they hear the reading of the books in one or the other language, they may guard themselves against the depravity of the interpreters, and, not clinging to the literal words, come to the point of the matter, and perceive their diviner meaning, so that they may start afresh to learn the better way, and may cease to stray vainly, and to err in that which is most essential, we mean hope in God. For this reason we have opened the door for the reading of the scriptures in every language, that all may henceforth receive its teaching, and become fitter for learning better things. For it is acknowledged that he, who is nourished upon the sacred scriptures and has little need of direction, is much readier to discern the truth, and to choose the better path, than he who understands nothing of them, but clings to the name of his faith alone, and is held by it as by a sacred anchor, and believes that what can be called heresy in its purest form is divine teaching.

Epilogue. This is our sacred will and pleasure, and your Excellency and your present colleague and your staff shall see that it is carried out, and shall not allow the Hebrews to contravene it. Those who resist it or try to put any obstruction in its way, shall first suffer corporal punishment, and then be compelled to live in exile, forfeiting also their property, that they flaunt not their impudence against God and the empire. You shall also circulate our law to the provincial governors, that they learning its contents may enforce it in their several cities, knowing that it is to be strictly carried out under pain of our displeasure.

APPENDIX THREE

PROFESSIONS OF FAITH EXTRACTED FROM JEWS ON BAPTISM

(A) Visigothic Professions

i. Of Recceswinth, *from Leg. Vis.* 12.2.17.

To our most merciful and tranquil lord Recceswinth the King, from us the Jews of Toledo as witnessed or signed below. We well remember how we were long and rightly constrained to sign this Declaration promising in the name of King Chinthila's holy memory to support the Catholic faith; and we have done so. However, because our pertinacious lack of faith and the ancient errors of our fathers held us back from believing wholly in Our Lord Jesus Christ or accepting the Catholic truth with all our hearts, we therefore make these promises to your greater glory, on behalf both of ourselves and our wives and children, through this our Declaration, undertaking for the future not to become involved in any Jewish rites or customs nor to associate with the accursed Jews who remain unbaptised. We will not follow our habit of contracting incestuous unions or practising fornication with our own relatives to the sixth degree. We will not on any pretext, either ourselves, our children or our descendants, choose wives from our own race; but in the case of both sexes we will always link ourselves in matrimony with Christians. We will not practise carnal circumcision, or celebrate the Passover, the Sabbath or the other feast days connected with the Jewish religion. We will not keep to our old habit of discrimination in the matter of food. We will do none of the things which the evil tradition of long custom and intercourse urges upon us as Jews. Instead, with utter faith and grace in our hearts, and with complete devotion towards Christ the Son of the Living God, as the apostolic tradition enjoins, shall we believe on Him and confess Him. Every custom of the holy Christian religion, feast days, marriage, and what is lawful to eat, indeed every ceremony thereof, we shall faithfully hold and embrace with all our hearts, reserving no hint within ourselves of resistance, no suspicion of deception, whereby we may come to repeat those errors we now deny, or fulfil with little or no sincerity that which we now promise to do. With regard to swines' flesh we promise to observe this rule, that if through long custom we are hardly able to eat it, we shall not through fastidiousness or error refuse the things that are cooked with it. And if in all the matters touched on above we are found in any way to transgress, either presuming to work against the Christian Faith, or promising in words to perform actions suitable to the Catholic religion, and in our deeds deferring their performance, we swear by that same Father, Son and Holy Ghost, who is One God in Three, that whoever of us is found to transgress shall either perish by the hands of our fellows, by burning or stoning, or if your splendid piety shall have spared our lives, we shall at once lose our liberty and you shall give us along with all our property to whomever you please into perpetual slavery, or dispose of us in any other manner that seems good to you. To this end you have free authority, not only on account of your royal power, but also arising out of the stipulations of this our guarantee. This Declaration is given at Toledo in the name of the Lord, on the 18th of February in the sixth year of your glorious reign.

ii. Of Erwig, *from Leg. Vis.* 12.3.14.

I do here and now renounce every rite and observance of the Jewish religion, detesting all its most solemn ceremonies and tenets that in former days I kept and held. In future I will practise no rite or celebration connected with it, nor any custom of my past error, promising neither to seek it out nor to perform it. Further do I renounce all things forbidden or detested by Christian teaching; and,

(Here follows the Nicene Creed)

In the name of this Creed, which I truly believe and hold with all my heart, I promise that I will never return to the vomit of Jewish superstition. Never again will I fulfil any of the offices of Jewish ceremonies to which I was addicted, nor ever more hold them dear. I altogether deny and reject the errors of the Jewish religion, casting forth whatever conflicts with the Christian Faith, and affirming that my belief in the Holy Trinity is strong enough to make me live the truly Christian life, shun all intercourse with other Jews and have the circle of my friends only among honest Christians. With them or apart from them I must always eat Christian food, and as a genuinely devout Christian go often and reverently to Church. I promise also to maintain and embrace with due love and reverence the observance of all the Lord's days or feasts for martyrs as declared by the piety of the Church, and upon those days to consort always with sincere Christians, as it behoves a pious and sincere Christian to do.

Herewith is my profession of faith and belief as given by me on this date.

iii. Of Erwig, *from Leg. Vis.* 12.3.15.

I swear first by God the Father Almighty, Who said, ' By Me shall ye swear, and ye shall not take the Name of the Lord your God in vain, Who made Heaven and earth, the sea and all things in them ', and set bounds to the ocean, saying ' So far shalt thou come and here shall thy proud waves be stayed ', Who said, ' Heaven is my home, the earth my footstool ': Who first cast forth from Heaven the Archangel in his overweening pride, before Whose sight the host of Angels stand in fear, Whose gaze lays bare the abyss and Whose anger wastes away mountains: Who put the first man Adam in Paradise, giving him the law that he should not eat of the forbidden apple tree. He ate of it and was cast forth from Paradise, and bound himself, together with the human race, in the chains of error. And by Him Who gladly received the offerings of Abel and justly rejected the unworthy Cain; Who, when they were about to die, took Enoch and Elijah to Paradise in the body of this life, and shall bring them back to the world at the end of this age; Who thought fit to save Noah with his wife and three sons and their wives and all the animals, birds and reptiles in the Ark at the time of the Flood, whereby every species was preserved; Who from Shem the son of Noah saw fit to give issue in Abraham, and from him the people of Israel; Who chose Patriarchs and Prophets, and blessed the Patriarchs of Abraham's line, Isaac and Jacob; Who promised holy Abraham, saying, ' In your seed shall all mankind be blessed ', giving him the sign of circumcision as the seal of His promise for ever. I swear by Him Who overthrew Sodom and turned Lot's wife, when she looked back, into a statue of salt; and by Him Who wrestled with Jacob, and touching a sinew made him lame, saying, ' Thou shalt be called not Jacob but Israel '. I swear also by Him who freed Moses from the waters, and appeared to him in a flaming bush, and by his hand brought ten plagues upon the Egyptians, and freed the people of Israel from the Egyptian slavery, making them to cross dry through the

Red Sea, where against natural law the water stood up in a solid wall. I swear by Him Who drowned Pharaoh and his army in the Red Sea. I swear by Him Who led the people of Israel by a pillar of cloud by day and of fire by night. I swear by Him Who gave to Moses on Mount Sinai the law written by His own fingers on tables of stone. I swear by Him Who made that mountain to smoke in the sight of all Israel. I swear by Him Who chose Aaron for His first priest and consumed his sons by fire in their tent, because they had dared to offer strange fire before the Lord. I swear by Him Who in His justice ordered Dathan and Abiram to be swallowed alive by the earth. I swear by Him Who changed the bitter waters into sweet by the casting in of the trunk of a tree. I swear by Him Who, when the people of Israel thirsted in Horeb, caused Moses to smite the rock with his rod and bring forth great streams of water. I swear by Him Who for forty years fed the people of Israel in the wilderness, and preserved their garments so that they wore not out with use; and kept them safe in every way. I swear by Him Who decreed once and for all that no Israelite should enter the Promised Land, because they had doubted the Lord's word, excepting only Joshua and Caleb, whom He promised should enter. I swear by Him Who told Moses that if he raised his hands on high, the people of Israel should be victors against the Amalekites. I swear by Him Who ordered our Fathers by the hand of Joshua to cross the Jordan and raise twelve stones from that river in witness thereof. I swear by Him Who enjoined upon all Israel that having crossed the river Jordan they should circumcise themselves with stone knives; and by Him Who overturned the walls of Jericho. I swear by Him Who adorned David with the glory of kingship, and saved him from the hands of Saul and of his son Absalom. I swear by Him Who at the prayer of Solomon filled the Temple with cloud, and poured His blessing therein. I swear by Him Who, raising the Prophet Elijah through a whirlwind in a chariot of fire, brought him from earth to the seats of Heaven; and by Him Who, at the prayer of Elisha, divided the waters of Jordan when Elisha smote them with the robe of Elijah. I swear by Him Who filled all His Prophets with the Holy Spirit, and freed Daniel from hungry and monstrous lions. I swear by Him Who saw fit to preserve three boys in the fiery furnace, under the eyes of a hostile king; and by Him 'Who keeps the key of David, closing what no man has opened, opening what no man has closed'. I swear by Him Who brings about all wonders, virtues and signs to Israel and other peoples. I swear also by the Ten Commandments. I swear also by Jesus Christ, His ascent to Heaven, His glorious and terrible coming, when He shall come to judge the living and the dead, showing Himself gentle to the just and terrible to sinners; and by the revered Body and precious Blood of Him Who opens the eyes of the blind, makes the deaf to hear and brings back the paralysed to the use of their limbs: Who loosens the tongues of the dumb, cleanses the devil-ridden, makes the lame to run, and rouses the dead: Who walked over the waters, and brought back Lazarus, freed from death, when his flesh was already in corruption, to life and safety, changing grief to joy: Who is the Creator of time, the Principle of life, the Author of salvation: Who illumined the world with His rising, and redeemed it by His Passion: Who alone among the dead was free, and death could not hold Him: Who undermines the gates of Hell, and by the majesty of His power draws the souls of the blessed up from the shades: Who having vanquished death has taken the body which He assumed upon earth into Heaven with Him after His victory over the world, and sits at the right hand of God the Father Almighty, receiving from Him the power of eternal sway. I swear also by all the heavenly virtues, and by the relics of all the Saints and Apostles, and also by the four holy Gospels, on which I lay this Declaration upon the sacred altar which I hold with my hands. Since I have taken care to note well everything in my profession of Faith, and have been able to put it together, I give my signature to you, my Lord Bishop, and affirm everything in all sincerity, with no reservations or deception as to what is meant. With absolute sincerity, as I have said in my profession, I have abjured all Jewish rites and observances, and with my whole heart shall believe in the Holy Trinity, never returning in any way to the vomit of my former error, or associating with the wicked Jews. In every respect will I lead the Christian life and associate with Christians. The meaning which I have discerned in what I have signed concerning the observance of the holy Faith I will guard with all the purity of my faith, so that I shall live from now henceforth according to the Apostolic tradition and the law of the holy Creed. If I wander from the straight path in any way and defile the holy Faith, and try to observe any rites of the Jewish sect, or if I shall delude you in any way in the swearing of this oath, so that I appear to swear sincerely, yet do not perform my promises in the spirit in which I have heard and understood them from you while I made my profession; then may all the curses of the law fall upon me as they are promulgated by the lips of the Lord against those who despise the commandments of God. May there fall upon me and upon my house and all my children all the plagues which smote Egypt, and to the horror of others may I suffer in addition the fate of Dathan and Abiram, so that the earth shall swallow me alive, and after I am deprived of this life I shall be handed over to the eternal fire, in the company of the Devil and his Angels, sharing with the dwellers in Sodom and with Judas the punishment of burning; and when I arrive before the tribunal of the fearful and glorious Judge, Our Lord Jesus Christ, may I be numbered in that company to whom the glorious and terrible Judge with threatening mien will say, ' Depart from Me, evil-doers, into the eternal fire that is prepared for the Devil and his Angels '.

(B) Profession of Faith, from the Church of Constantinople

From Assemani, Cod. Lit., I, p. 105.

As a preliminary to his acceptance as a catechumen, a Jew ' must confess and denounce verbally the whole Hebrew people, and forthwith declare that with a whole heart and sincere faith he desires to be received among the Christians. Then he must renounce openly in the church all Jewish superstition, the priest saying, and he, or his sponsor if he is a child, replying in these words:

'I renounce all customs, rites, legalisms, unleavened breads and sacrifices of lambs of the Hebrews, and all the other feasts of the Hebrews, sacrifices, prayers, aspersions, purifications, sanctifications and propitiations, and fasts, and new moons, and Sabbaths, and superstitions, and hymns and chants and observances and synagogues, and the food and drink of the Hebrews; in one word, I renounce absolutely everything Jewish, every law, rite and custom, and above all I renounce Antichrist, whom all the Jews await in the figure and form of Christ; and I join myself to the true Christ and God. And I believe in the Father, the Son and the Holy Spirit, the Holy, Consubstantial and Indivisible Trinity, and the dispensation in the flesh and the descent to men of the Word of God, of the one person of the Holy Trinity, and I confess that he was truly made man, and I believe and proclaim that after the flesh in very truth the Blessed Virgin Mary bore him the son of God; and I believe in, receive, venerate and embrace the adorable Cross of Christ, and the holy images; and thus, with my whole heart, and soul, and with a true faith I come to the Christian Faith. But if it be with deceit and with hypocrisy, and not with a sincere and perfect faith and a genuine love of Christ, but with a pretence to a be Christian that I come, and if afterwards I shall wish to deny and return to Jewish superstition, or shall be found eating with Jews, or feasting with them, or secretly conversing and condemning the Christian religion instead of openly confuting them and condemning their vain faith, then let the trembling of Cain and the leprosy of Gehazi cleave to me, as well as the legal punishments to which I acknowledge myself liable. And may I be anathema in the world to come, and may my soul be set down with Satan and the devils.'

(c) Profession of Faith of uncertain Eastern origin, attached to the Clementine Recognitions

From P.G., I, p. 1456.

It is my desire to-day to come from the Hebrews to the Christian faith. I have not been brought by any force, necessity, fear, annoyance or poverty; nor because of a debt, or of an accusation lodged against me; nor for the sake of worldly honours, of advantages, of money or property which has been promised me by anyone; nor for the sake of its useful consequences, nor to obtain human patronage; nor because of any quarrel or dispute which I have had with people of my own religion; nor for secret purposes of revenge on the Christians, by a feigned admiration for their law, nor because I have been wronged by them; but I have been brought by a whole-hearted love of Christ and of faith in Him.

I renounce the whole worship of the Hebrews, circumcision, all its legalisms, unleavened bread, Passover, the sacrificing of lambs, the feasts of Weeks, Jubilees, Trumpets, Atonement, Tabernacles, and all the other Hebrew feasts, their sacrifices, prayers, aspersions, purifications, expiations, fasts, Sabbaths, new moons, foods and drinks. And I absolutely renounce every custom and institution of the Jewish laws.

Moreover, I place under anathema the heresies among the Jews, and the heretics themselves. I anathematise the Sadducees, who are called just, who blaspheme the Holy Spirit, who attack the resurrection of the dead, and deny the existence of angels. I anathematise the Pharisees, the separate ones, who fast on the second and fifth days, who pretend to sexual abstinence at definite times, and afterwards despise all continence, who foretell the future, and waste their time on astrology. I anathematise the Nazareans, the stubborn ones, who deny that the law of sacrifices was given by Moses, who abstain from eating living things, and who never offer sacrifice: I anathematise the Osseans, the blindest of all men, who use other scriptures than the Law, and reject most of the prophets, and who boast in a man as master, one Elxai, that is 'the hidden virtue', and who worship, as Gods, two women of his offspring, Marthonis and Marthana: I anathematise the Herodians, who worship as Christ a foreign king of the Jews, Herod, who was eaten of worms. I anathematise the Hemerobaptists, who believe as do the Pharisees, but also teach that a man cannot be saved without daily washing. I anathematise the scribes, or doctors of the Law, who are not content to live according to the Law, but of their own free will perform more than is prescribed in the Law, and devising washing of vessels and cups and platters and other articles of furniture, and frequently wash their hands and their pots;

and who call all these many traditions they have added to the Law 'Deuteroses', as though they were a second series of Divine Laws, and they falsely ascribe the first to Moses, and the second to Rabbi Akiba, and the third to Annas who is also called Judas, and the fourth to the sons of the Hasmoneans who even violated the Sabbath in battle.

Together with all these Jewish heresies and heresiarchs, deuteroses and givers thereof, I anathematise those who celebrate the feast of Mordecai on the first Sabbath of the Christian fast, hanging the effigy of Haman on a gibbet, and mingling the sign of the cross therewith, and burning all together, and subjecting the Christians to every kind of curse and anathema.

II. Together with the ancients, I anathematise also the Chief Rabbis and new evil doctors of the Jews, to wit, Lazarus the inventor of the abominable feast which they call Monopodaria, and Elijah who was no less impious, and Benjamin, Zebedee, Abraham, Symbatius and the rest of them. Further I invoke every curse and anathema on him whose coming is expected by the Jews as the Christ or Anointed, but is rather Anti-Christ, and I renounce him and commit myself to the only true Christ and God. And I believe in the Father, the Son and the Holy Spirit, the Holy Consubstantial and Indivisible Trinity; I confess the Incarnation and the coming to man of one of the Holy Trinity, to wit, the only begotten Son and Word of God, begotten of the Father before all the centuries, through Whom all things were made. I believe Him to be the Messiah foretold by the Law and the prophets; and I am convinced that He has already come into the world for the salvation of mankind; that He was truly made man, and did not surrender His Divinity, that He is truly God and truly man, without confusion, change or alteration, of one person and two natures. I believe that He suffered all things of His own will, and was crucified in the flesh, while His Divinity remained impassable, and was buried, and rose again on the third day, and ascended into heaven, and shall come again in glory to judge both the living and the dead.

And I believe and profess the Blessed Virgin Mary, who bore Him according to the flesh, and who remained a virgin, to be truly and actually the Mother of God, and I venerate and honour her truly as the Mother of God Incarnate, and as the Lady and mistress thereby of all creation.

I am convinced and confess and believe that the bread and the wine which is mystically consecrated among Christians, and which they take in their sacred rites, is the very body and blood of the Lord Jesus Christ, transmuted by His Divine power reasonably and invisibly, in His own way beyond all natural understanding, and I confess that in taking the sacrament I am taking His very body and blood, to the gaining of life eternal and the inheritance of the Kingdom of Heaven which belongs to those who receive them in perfect faith.

Finally, I beg for Christian baptism, out of a pure and spotless heart and mind, and a sincere faith, truly persuaded that it is the true spiritual washing, and the regeneration of soul and body.

III. I receive, honour and accept as symbols and indications of their prototypes, the venerable Cross of the true Christ and God, no longer the instrument of death and crime, but of liberty and eternal life, and the sign of victory over death and Satan; likewise I receive the hitherto venerated images both of the Word of God according to the flesh among men, and likewise of the most pure and ineffable Mother of God, of the holy angels, and finally of all the saints.

I honour and venerate with the honour due to them the blessed angels and all the saints, not only the patriarchs and prophets, but the apostles, martyrs, confessors, doctors, saints, all indeed who pleased Christ when He came, as His servants and faithful followers.

Wherefore with my whole heart and mind and with deliberate choice I come to the Christian faith.

But if I make this statement falsely and deceitfully, and not on the witness of my whole conviction and in love for the Christ who has already come, but because of some compulsion, necessity, fear, loss, poverty, debt, accusation brought against me, worldly honour, dignity of any kind, money, promised gifts, or to serve some end, or for human protection, or because of dispute and quarrel with some of my own faith, or to revenge myself thus on the Christians, feigning respect for their law, or if I pretend to become a Christian because of some injuries suffered from them, and then revert to Judaism, or be found eating with the Jews, or observing their feasts and fasts, or speaking secretly with them, or defaming the Christian faith, or visiting their synagogues or oratories, or taking them under my protection, and do not rather confute the said Jews and their acts openly, and revile their empty faith, then may there come upon me all the curses which Moses wrote in Deuteronomy, and the trembling of Cain, and the leprosy of Gehazi, in addition to the penalties by law established, and may I be without any hope of pardon, and in the age to come may I be anathema and doubly anathema, and may my soul be set down with Satan and his demons.

APPENDIX FOUR

SPECIAL PRAYERS TO BE ADDED IN THE DEDICATION OF A CHURCH, WHEN THE BUILDING HAS BEEN A SYNAGOGUE

From the Liber Sacramentorum Romanae Ecclesiae, *Assemani, Cod. Lt. IV, ii, p.* 91.

XCIII. Oratio et Preces in Dedicatione loci illius ubi prius fuit synagoga.

Deus qui absque ulla temporis mutabilitate cuncta disponis; et ad meliorandum perducis quae eligis esse mutanda: respice super hanc Basilicam in honore Beati *Illius* nomini tuo dicatam: ut, vetustate Iudaici erroris expulsa, huic loco Sancti Spiritus novitate Ecclesiae conferas veritatem: per Dominum Nostrum.

Omnipotens sempiterne Deus, qui hunc locum, Judaicae superstitionis foeditate detersa, in honore Beati *Illius* Ecclesiae tuae dignatus es pulchritudine decorare, Per Dominum.

Praesta, quaesumus, Domine, ut illa fides hic fulgeat quae signo Crucis erecta, mortem subegit, et salutem nobis contulit et triumphum. Per Dominum.

Secreta. Deus vita credentium et origo virtutum, reple, quaesumus, hoc templum tuae gloria maiestatis in honore Beati *Illius*; fiat domus orationis quod perditum fuerat ante latibulum; et quia infidelium turba in isto loco conveniebat adversa, populus tuus oblationibus suis te hic semper mereatur invenire propitium. Per Dominum.

Post Comm. Gratias tibi, referimus, Domine, sacro munere vegetati, tuam misericordiam deprecantes; ut dignos eius nos participatione perficias. Per Dominum.

Ad Populum. A plebe tua, quaesumus, Domine, spiritales nequitiae repellantur, et aerearum discedat malignitas Potestatum. Per Dominum.

APPENDIX FIVE

MARTYRDOMS OF THE FIRST CENTURY ASCRIBED TO JEWS

(To illustrate Ch. IV)

These cases illustrate that there was a *common tradition* of Jewish responsibility in the persecution of individual Christians during the first century of Christianity, but that there was no *precise knowledge* of the actual fate of the individual concerned. In some cases the person concerned is historical, but various fates are ascribed to him, in others the person himself is imaginary, or only known to us as a name in some chance reference.

Agabus, the prophet referred to in Acts xxi, 10, was seized by the Jews of Jerusalem and stoned. A miracle accompanying his death led to the conversion of a woman who was standing by. She was stoned also. (S.A.J., Jan. 29.) Alternatively, he was killed by Jews and Greeks, at a place unmentioned, together with another preacher, Rufus. (S.C., April 8.)

Ananias, bishop of Damascus, converted many Jews and Greeks at Eleutheropolis. The governor had him stoned. (S.A.J., June 21 and 28.) (Greek MSS., Jan. 25.) Alternatively, he was stoned at Damascus by the Jews. (S.A., April 9.)

Ananias, a Jew who recognised Christ on the Cross, was immediately stoned and afterwards burnt by the chief priests. (Coptic Gospel of Twelve Apostles, P.O., ii, 167.)

Andrew the Apostle, was executed by Herod at Bethlehem according to western tradition. (A.S., Feb. 10.) Alternatively, he was killed by heathen priests at Patras. (S.E. in P.O., xv, 583.)

Aristobulus, the brother of Barnabas, and one of the seventy, suffered much from Jews and Greeks, and was finally stoned by them. (S.A.J., March 15.) Alternatively, he died in peace. (S.A., same date.) According to A.S. (same date) he was the first bishop in Britain, and died there.

Barnabas was, according to all accounts, killed in Cyprus, at the instigation of the Jews, and in some accounts by them also. (A.S., June 11; S.A.J., Dec. 17; S.A., June 11.)

Bartholomew, after a life of preaching among the Copts, is killed by King Agrippa. (S.A.J., Aug. 29.) Alternatively, he is crucified in eastern Armenia by the natives. (S.A., Aug. 24, and A.S., Aug. 25.)

Carpus, with whom Paul left his cloak at Troas, after a life of preaching to the Jews, was mercilessly slain by them. (S.C., May 26.)

Cleophas, the friend of Christ, was murdered by the Jews. (A.S., Sept. 25, embodying various ancient martyrologies.)

Eutychus, a disciple of Saint John, is successful in converting many Jews and Greeks, and is finally killed by the latter. (S.A.J., Aug. 24; S.E., Sept. 7.) This is one of the few cases where a man is said to have converted many ' Jews and Greeks ', but where his death is so definitely ascribed to the Greeks. A.S. records a number of different traditions.

Fouros, one of the seventy, was much persecuted by Jews and Greeks, but died peacefully. (S.A.J., May 25.)

Herodion, a cousin or follower of Paul, was taken by the Jews and pagans, and blinded, lynched and beheaded. (S.C., March 27; A.S., April 8.) His martyrdom is not definitely implied by S.A. (March 29).

James, the son of Alphaeus, who, according to the Acts of the Apostles, was killed by Herod (xii, 1), is accused of preaching another king to Claudius the governor, and stoned by his orders. (S.A.J., Feb. 4.) Alternatively, he is stoned by the Jews (S.C., Oct. 9) or stoned together with the scribe Hosiah, who first accused and afterwards was converted by him. (S.A., April 30.) Or, again, he is caught by the Jews just before he should have left for Spain, and they make Herod kill him. (Also S.A., but Feb. 21.)

James, the first bishop of Jerusalem, is similarly described in all the martyrologies.

Joseph of Arimathea was immured by the Jews in prison, and left to die of starvation. He is found, in perfect health, forty years later by Titus on the capture of Jerusalem. (A.S., March 17.) Alternatively, he is released by Christ Himself, and continues preaching. (S.E., August 7.) S.A. does not know of his imprisonment, but in one account states that the Jews tried to poison him. (S.A., Feb. 24.)

Judas Cyriacus, the last Jewish bishop of Jerusalem, was killed by the Jews in the war with Hadrian. (A.S., May 1.) Alternatively, he was martyred by Julian. (A.S., same date.)

Longinus, the centurion present at the Crucifixion, is a popular figure with all the martyrologies. According to one account he was bribed by the Jews to make sure that Christ was killed on the cross, and therefore pierced His side with a spear. Pilate finds out that he has become a Christian, and informs Tiberius, who orders his execution. (S.A.J., July 18, and S.E., July 30.) Alternatively, the Jews bribe Pilate to kill Longinus because he has become a Christian, and his head is brought to Jerusalem as proof of his death. (A.S., March 15, and S.A., Oct. 16.) The two stories are also blended by making Pilate show his head to the Jews in order to please them, although they had not asked him to secure his death. (S.A.J., second version, Nov. 1.)

Luke, after the death of Paul, preached in Rome, and a crowd of Jews and idolators complained of him to Nero, who sentenced him to death. (S.A.J., Oct. 19.) A number of variations are given in A.S., Oct. 18.

Manean, foster brother of Herod, preached to Jews and Gentiles, and was martyred by them. (S.A., April 9.)

Marcian, first bishop of Cyprus, was killed by the Jews through jealousy. (S.C., Oct. 31.) Alternatively, he was thrown from a tower. (A.S., June 14.)

Mary, the mother of Jesus, was much persecuted by Annas and Caiaphas, but when they tried to burn down her house, they were themselves burnt. At the Ascension the Jews tried to stone her, but they killed fifty of each other instead. (S.A., Aug. 15, and various apocryphal works.)

Mary, Martha and Lazarus (and sometimes some others) were put in a boat at Jaffa, in order to drown them. (A.S., various dates, but see Aug., Vol. iv, 592; S.A., April 9.)

Mary Magdalen suffered many outrages from the Jews but finally died in peace. (S.A.J., July 22; S.E., Aug. 4.) Alternatively, she followed Saint John to Ephesus, and was buried outside the cave of the seven sleepers. (S.A., July 22.)

Matthew, after escaping from the cannibals to whom he had been preaching, returned to Palestine and 'died a beautiful death', which, apparently, does not mean martyrdom. (S.A.J., March 6.) The same collection on a different date (Oct. 9) says that he was beheaded by Festus. Alternatively, the Jews secured two witnesses against him, and condemned and stoned him. (A.S., Feb. 22.)

Nathanael, after drawing from the Law and the prophets grave reproaches against the Jews, died at their hands. (S.A., April 9.) A.S. considers him to be probably the same as Bartholomew. (A.S., Jan. 10.)

Nicanor, the deacon, was killed by Vespasian, or alternatively with many thousand others at the same time as Stephen. (S.A., July 29.)

Nicodemus was much persecuted by the Jews, but finally died in peace and was buried with Stephen and Gamaliel. (S.A., April 9.)

Parmenas, with two thousand Christians, was killed on that occasion. (Also S.A., but Aug. 2.)

Paul is warned by the Christians of Rome that the chiefs of the Jews have implored Nero to send a letter to all his dominions ordering him to be executed wherever found. (S. Georgian, P.O., xix, 734.)

Simeon, bishop of Jerusalem, was, according to Eusebius, betrayed by heretics as a Christian, and put to death by Domitian (*Hist. Ecc.* iii, 32), by Hadrian (S.A.J., July 3) or Trajan (S.E., July 9). Alternatively, Domitian released him, and on his return to Jerusalem the Jews strangled him. (S.A., April 17.)

Simon of Cyrene believes in Jesus and is forthwith crucified by the Jews. (S.A., March 1.)

Temedrius, a deacon, one of the seventy, was stoned by the Jews for Christ. (S.A., April 9.) He is probably the same as Demetrius, in A.S. for the same date, who was a deacon, but of unknown century, and no details are known of his death.

Thaddeus, after suffering many torments from Gentiles (S.E., July 9), or Jews and Gentiles (S.A.J., June 26), died in peace. Alternatively, he is martyred in Persia. (A.S., Oct. 28.)

Timothy is finally killed by a mob of Jews and Greeks at Ephesus. (S.A.J., Jan. 18.) Alternatively, he is killed by the worshippers of Diana. (A.S., Jan. 24.)

Urbanus, a disciple of Andrew, is murdered in Macedonia, by Jews and Greeks, together with many others. (S.C., Oct. 30; A.S., Oct. 31.)

INDICES

I. BIBLICAL QUOTATIONS
II. PATRISTIC LITERATURE
III. CHRONICLERS AND HISTORIANS
IV. SECULAR LEGISLATION
V. CHURCH COUNCILS
VI. GENERAL INDEX

INDEX ONE

BIBLICAL QUOTATIONS

page

Genesis
xlix, 13 .. .. 6, 357

Deuteronomy
xxi, 23 98
xxviii, 66 281
xxx, 19 113
xxxii, 21 .. .. 148, 277
xxxiii, 18–20 6

Judges
v, 17 6

I Samuel
v, 1–5 165

I Kings
ix, 26 6
x, 28–29 6
xi, 31–33 9
xxii, 48 6

II Kings
v, 18 62
xiii, 21 .. .. 112, 295

Isaiah
xl, 4 113
lxv, 15 289
lxv, 17 113

Jeremiah
ii, 8 277
ii, 20 113
vii, 11 164

Hosea
ii, 19 113
xi, 9 113

Zecheriah
xii, 10 282

I Maccabees
viii, 22 .. .. .. 7, 8

II Maccabees
vii 105

Matthew
iii, 5–7 43
vi, 2, 5, 16 44
viii, 5 ff. 44
ix, 4, 13, 34 44
xii, 24 44

page

Mark
i, 22 38
27 38
44 38
ii, 6–7 .. .. 38, 43
17 39
19–22 39
27 39
iii, 2–6 40
12 41
21–29 41
vi, 4 43
vii, 1–23 41
9-13 44

Luke
iii, 7 43
iv, 28 43
v, 17, 21 43
vii, 36 43
xi, 37 43
xiii, 31 43
xiv, 1 43

John
i, 11 82
ii, 13 ff. 82
iii, 2 82
iv, 1, 3 82
v, 16, 18 83
39, 40 83
45, 46 83
vii, 13 83
1, 19, 25, 30, 45 .. 83
viii, 19 165
44 83
ix, 22 83
x, 31, 39 83
xi, 53 83
xix, 31 64

Acts of the Apostles
ii, 23 47
iii, 13, 17 47
iv, 21 48
27 47
v, 38–39 48
vi, 7 48
9 61
14 48
vii, 39 48

page

Acts of the Apostles, *contd.*
vii, 51 48
viii, 1–3 48
x, 1–47 49
xi, 1–18 49
19 48
xii, 1–3 69
xiii, 42 50
45 50
50 65
xiv, 1 ff. 50
5 65
19 65
xvii, 5 .. .. 52, 65
xviii, 4–7 52
6 65
12 ff. 65
19 52
xix. 8–9 52
xxi, 20 ff. 56
xxii, 3 68
xxiii, 1 68
9 56
xxiv, 5, 6 56
14 68
xxv, 11 68
xxvi, 5, 22 68
xxviii, 17 68
22 68

Romans
i, 16 53
iii, 1–2 53
20 53
21 54
31 54
iv, 1–24 54
10–12 54
vii, 12 53
14–25 53
ix, 3, 4 53
6 ff. 54
19 ff. 53
31 53
xi, 1–24 54
1 55
2 ff. 55
11 54
15–24 .. .. 53, 55

page

I Corinthians
vii, 18–20 56
ix, 19 56

II Corinthians
iii, 11, 15 54

Galatians
ii, 3 ff. 51
14 50
19 51
21 51
iii, 13 .. .. 98, 287
23, 24 54
iv, 22 51

I Thessalonians
ii, 14 ff. 52, 69
15 69

II Thessalonians
i, 8 52

Hebrews
ii, 2 59
vii, 1–28 59
18, 19 59
viii, 5 59
8–13 59
x, 1–18 59
1–39 59
xi, 1–40 59
13 60
15 60

I Peter
i, 12 58
18 58
ii, 12 86
iv, 15, 16 88

Revelation
vi, 9 88
vii, 4–8 57
14 88
xii, 11 88
xiii, 15 88
xvi, 6 88
xvii, 6 88
xviii, 24 88
xx, 4 88

INDEX TWO

REFERENCES TO AND QUOTATIONS FROM PATRISTIC LITERATURE

page

Altercations (anonymous)
Athanasius and Zacchaeus 118
Doctrina Jacobi nuper Baptizati (*Sargis of Aberga*), 264, 285, 286, 287, 306
Gregentius and Herbanus .. 284, 285
The Trophies of Damascus 282, 287, 288, 289
Ambrose
Epistles, I
xl and xli 166
xl, 23 187
Sermo vii 192
De Tobia 192
Ambrose-Ps.
Commentary on Romans, ix, 27 102
Anastasius of Sinai
Disputatio contra Judaeos
i 281
ii 281
iii.. .. .. 281, 282
Parvus Dialogus 282
Anonymous
Ep. to Diognetus
iii.. 101
iv.. .. .. 84, 101
xi.. 97
Didascalia Apostolorum
II, xxi 82
Aphraates
Demonstratio
V 278
VI, xx 278
X, i 277
XI 278
XII 278
XII, iii 277
XII, vii 277
XIII 278
XIV, xxvi 277
XV, ii 277
XV, viii 277
XVI 279
XVII 277, 278
XVIII 278
XIX 279
XXI 278

page

Athanasius
Encyclical Epistle, iii .. 186
Athanasius-Ps.
Sermon read at Conc. Nic. II 293
Athenagoras
Plea for the Christians
i 157
ii 111
xxxii 111
Augustine
De Catechezandis, vii, xx, xxv, xxvii 172
Epistolae, xxviii, xl, lxxv, lxxxii 96
Epistola, cxcvi 203
Augustine-Ps.
Altercatio Synagogae et Ecclesiae 239
Barnabas, Epistle of, iv .. 84
Basil
Homily on Psalm xiv .. 192
Cassiodorus
Expositio in Psalterium
Ps. xlix 209
Ps. lxxxi 209
Varia
II, xxvii 209
IV, xxxiii 209
IV, xliii 208
V, xxxvii .. 208, 267
Chromatius
In Evan. Matt., Tract. X 191
Chrysostom
Adversus Judaeos
i, 3 .. .. 164, 165
i, 5 165
i, 6 .. .. 164, 165
ii, 3 164
iii, 5 165
iv, 6 165
v, 1 165
vi, 1 165
vi, 2 164
vi, 3 .. .. 164, 165
vi, 6 165
vi, 8 165
vii, 1 166
viii, 3 166

page

Clement
  Epistle, I, vi 88
  Pedagogue, I, v 117
  Stromata, II, v 117
Clementine Recognitions, I, liii 94
Cyprian
  Testimonies against the Jews 99
Cyprian-Ps.
  Adversus Judaeos 106
Cyril of Jerusalem
  Catechetical Addresses
    iv, 2 172
    x, 2 172
Cyril-Ps.
  Sermon on Penitence .. 292
Ephrem the Syrian
  Rhythm against the Jews .. 276
Epiphanius
  Adversus Haereses 102, 169
Eusebius of Alexandria
  Sermon on the Resurrection 300
  Sermon xv 299
Eusebius of Caesarea (see also Index of Chroniclers)
  On Isaiah, xviii, 1 .. 80
  Preparatio Evangelica 161 f.
    I, ii-v 97
    XII, i 118
Eusebius of Caesarea
  Demonstratio Evangelica 161 f.
    I, ii 162, 172
Gaudentius
  In Laudem Philastrii .. 171
  Sermon iv 132
  Sermon xiii 192
Gregory the Great
  Epistles
    I, x (II, vi) .. 213, 215
    I, xxxv (I, xxxiv) 212, 213
    I, xlvii (I, xlv) 211
    I, lxviii (I, lxvi) .. 218
    I, lxxi (I, lxix) 213
    II, xxxii (II, xxxviii) .. 212
    III, xxxviii (III, xxxvii) 218
    IV, ix 215
    IV, xxi 215
    IV, xxxiii (IV, xxxi) .. 212
    V, viii (V, vii) 212
    V, xx (V, xxxvii) .. 302
    VI, xxxii (VI, xxix) .. 217
    VI, xxxiii (VI, xxx) .. 215
    VII, xxiv (VII, xxi) .. 217
    VII, xliv (VII, xli) .. 213
    VIII, xxi 215
    VIII, xxiii 213
    VIII, xxv 214

page

    IX, vi (IX, cxcv) 213, 214
    IX, xxxvi (IX, civ) .. 216
    IX, lv (IX, xxxviii) .. 214
    IX, cxxii (IX, ccxxviii) 354
    IX, lvi (IX, xl) 214
    IX, cix (IX, ccxiii) .. 215
    IX, cx (IX, ccxv) .. 215
    IX, cxxii (IX, ccxxviii) 218
    XI, lxvii (XI, lii) .. 302
    XIII, xii (XIII, xv) .. 214
  Commentary on Ezekiel, I, Hom. xii 220
  Commentary on Job
    iii, 1 220
    xlii, 11 220
Gregory of Nazianzen
  Sermon iv. and v. 188
Gregory of Nyssa
  Catechetical Address .. 172
  Sermon against Usury .. 192
  Epistle to the Bishop of Melitene 269
Hadrian, Pope
  Epistle to the Bishops of Spain 223
  Canons sent to Charlemagne 222
  Epistle to Charlemagne .. 186
Hilary of Poitiers
  Commentary on Psalms, li, 6, 161
  Commentary on Matthew, xiii, 22 160
  Life of 160, 324
Hippolytus
  Adversus Judaeos 101
    i and v 104
  Commentary on Genesis, xlix 101
  Refutation of All Heresies, IV, xiii ff. 99
Hippolytus-Ps.
  Discourse on Last Things, xxviii 99
Ignatius
  Epistle to the Ephesians, xii 88
  Philadelphians, vi, 1 .. 84
Irenaeus
  Contra Haereses
    III, xxi 106
    IV, v 84, 117
Isai the Doctor
  Treatise on the Martyrs 143
Isidore of Pelusium
  Epistles, I, cxli; III, xciv; IV, xvii 172
Isidore of Seville
  De Fide Catholica 357
    II, v and vii 357

page

Jacob of Serug
Homily against the Jews 108, 279
i, 283 .. .. 99, 279
Taunt Song .. 258, 280
Jerome
Commentary on Psalms
cviii 192
Commentary on Isaiah
ii, 8 191
iii, 2 10
v, 18 78
vi, 9 159
14 159
xi, 6 154
xviii, 2 80
xxvi, 11 159
xlviii, 22 159
xlix, 1 159
lviii 154
lix, 19 159
lxv, 13 159
on Jeremiah
xviii 159
xxviii 16
on Ezekiel
xxvii, 16 .. 191, 314
xxxvii, 1 173
xxxviii 154
on Amos, i, 22 132
on Hosea, Preface .. 191
on Matthew, xxiii, 6 .. 119
Contra Rufinum, III, xxv 154, 173
Translation of Origen, on Ezekiel, vii 155
Epistles
cxii 154
cxxi .. 101, 154, 191
Epistle of the Synod of Jerusalem 173
John of Antioch
Epistle to Proclus 239
Justin Martyr
First Apology
xxxi 93, 126
Dialogue with Trypho
viii 101
x 111
xvi .. 80, 84, 119, 126
xix–xxii 101
xxix 97
xxxviii 80
xliii 109
xlvi 101
xlvii 70, 80, 96
lxxi–lxxiii 109

page

lxxxix 98
xcii 99
xciv 99
xcv 80
cviii 80
cxxiii 100
cxxxiii 80
Lactantius
Divine Institutions, IV, x .. 98
Maximus Confessor
Epistle, xiv 262
Mercator, M.
On the heresy and books of Nestorius, I 302
Nicetas of Aquileia
Explanation of the Creed, V, ix 172
Nilus
Epistles, lvii 172
Origen
Commentary on Genesis, viii 117
on Numbers, x, 2 .. 115
on Psalms, xxxvi 126, 148
on Ezekiel, Hom. vii .. 155
Contra Celsum
I, xxxii; xxxviii; lxii .. 109
VI, xxvii 80, 111
Exhortation to Martyrdom 148
Paulinus of Nola
Epistle, xxix, 9 117
Philastrius
On Heresies 102
Salvianus
On Avarice, Bks. I–IV .. 192
On the Government of God, IV, xiv 314
Severus of Majorca
Epistle on the Jews 204
Severus of Antioch
Catechetical Address, lxx 269, 299
Homily lvi 303
Epistles
xv and xvi 244
xlvi 303
lii 245
Conflict of Severus 303
Sidonius Appolinaris
Epistles
I, viii 314
III, iv; IV, v; VI, xi .. 343
Simeon
Epistle on the Himyarite Jews 258
Sophronius
Ode 260

page

Stephen VI, Pope
Epistle to Aribert of Narbonne 221

Tatian
Address to the Greeks, xxxi and xxxvi–xl 98

Tertullian
Answers to the Jews
iii.. 104
x 117
xiii 85
Apology, xxi 99
To the Nations, I, xiv 110, 150
On the Scorpion's Bite, x .. 126
On theatrical Displays, xxx 110

Theodoret
Questions on Genesis xlix, cx 299

Theophilus
Epistle to Autolycus, II, xxxiii, and III, iv .. 98

Venantius Fortunatus
Carmina, V, v 334

Zeno
Tractate xiv 182

INDEX THREE

BIOGRAPHERS, CHRONICLERS AND HISTORIANS

(*Page references preceded by an asterisk are to the pages of the edition referred to in brackets after the title of the work*)

page

Acts of the Council of Constantinople 243
Agapius
  Universal History (P.O.)
    Constantine, *V, 645 .. 298
    Theodosius, *VIII, 408 234
    Justinian, *VIII, 427 .. 259
    Maurice, *VIII, 439 .. 293
    Phocas, *VIII, 449 .. 259
    Mahomet, *VIII, 466 .. 261
    Yezid ibn 'Abd el Malik, *VIII, 504 265
Annales Avenionensium Episcoporum, I, ii, 138 .. 312
Anonymous lives of the Fathers
  Ahoudemmeh, vii 306
  Basil of Caesarea, ii .. 296
  Germanus of Paris, lxv .. 336
  Hilary of Arles 324
  Sulpicius of Bourges, I, xiv 335
Anonymous stories
  History of the Likeness of Christ 293
  De maximo miraculo .. 293
  De Salvatoris Imagine dicta Antiphonetes 294
  Passio S. Salsae 187
Anonymous
  De Proprietatibus Gentium 342
Anonymus Valesianus, XVI, lxxx 207
Antoninus Placentius
  Itinerarium, v 259
Arabic History of the Patriarchs of Alexandria (P.O.)
  4th Preface, *I, 122 103, 193, 287, 290
  I, viii, *I, 419 .. 103, 299
    *I, 467 251
  I, xvi, *V, 35 303
Barhadbesabba 'Arbaia
  Ecclesiastical History (P.O.)
    Life of Mar Abraham, *IX, 626 .. 264, 306
    Life of Basil of Caesarea, *XXIII, 287 306
    Life of Gregory of Neocaesarea, *XXIII, 260 296

page

Barhebraeus
  Chronography, X 265
Bernoldus
  Chronicon, anno 609 .. 336
Carmen de Synodo Ticinensi 209
Celsus
  Vita Innocentii .. 187, 188
Chronicon Anonymum
  (C.S.C.O., S.S., III, iv, 2)
    *23 261
    *27 264
  (C.S.C.O., S.S., III, iv, 4)
    *161 301
Chronicon Edessenum, anno 723 236
Chronicon Pascale
  anno 484 244
  anno 530 259
Cyprian
  Life of S. Caesarius, I, iii, 21, 22 321
Dionysius of Tel Mahre
  Chronicle
    anno 928 265
    anno 1040 262
    anno 1046 265
    anno 1057 305
  Chronicle, R.O.C., *II, 462 244
Einhard
  Annales, anno 801 .. 337
Ekkehard
  Universal Chronicle, anno 723 266
Ephraem the Monk
  Liber Imperatorum et Patrum 245
Eusebius
  Chronicle, anno 356 .. 187
  Ecclesiastical History
    I, iv 100
    I, ix 110
    II, xxiii 129
    V, i 127
    V, xvi, 2 126
    VI, xii 145
  Martyrs of Palestine, viii .. 135
Eutychius
  Annals (P.G., CXI)
    *1083 260
    *1084 262

page

Eutychius, *contd.*
Annals (P.G., CXI), *contd.*
*1089 261
Evagrius
Ecclesiastical History
I, xiii 238
III, xiv 243
IV, xxxvi 296
Fredegarius
Chronicle, lxv 335
George Hamartolus
Chronicle
IV, ccxxii 296
IV, ccxxvii 260
IV, ccxlviii 291
IV, ccl 266
Gesta Dagoberti, xxiv (xxv) 265, 335
Gregory of Tours
Glory of the Martyrs, I, xxii 292
History of the Franks
IV, viii (xiii) 340
IV, xxxv 340
V, iv (vi) 336
V, vi (xi) 334
VI, v 335
VI, x (xvii) 334
VII, xxiii .. 316, 341
VIII, i 331
Miracles of the Saints, I, x 296
Isidore of Seville
History of the Goths, sub anno 650 .. 333, 355
John of Asia
Ecclesiastical History (R.O.C., II), *458 303
John of Ephesus
History
III, xxvii 259
III, xxxi 264
Lives of the Eastern Saints
v 264
xvi 274
xlvii 263
John of Nikious
Chronicle
lxxxix 244
xc 258
xci 294
xcix 265
cxviii 263
cxx 262
Joshua Stylites
Chronicle
xlvii 250
lviii 258

page

Julian of Toledo
History of the Rebellion against Wamba
v 342, 362
xxviii 362
Defiance of the Tyrant of Gaul, i and ii 342
Landolfus
Chronicle, XVIII, xvi .. 259
Malalas
Chronography (P.G.,XCVII)
XV, *568 244
XVI, *585 244
XVIII, *652 251
XVIII, *656 259
Mar Sabas, monk of
Letter on Capture of Jerusalem 261
Metaphrastes
Life of Simeon Stylites .. 238
Michael the Syrian
Chronicle
VI, x 236
VII, v 186
VII, vii 181
VIII, xii 303
IX, vi 243, 244
IX, xiv 303
IX, xxix 303
IX, xxxi 259
X, xiii 243
X, xxv 245
XI, i 260, 261
XI, iv 265
XI, ix 262
XI, xii 265
XI, xix 265
XI, xx 302
XI, xxii 251
Nestorian History
xix 186
xxvii 142
xxxiv 299
liii 297
cii 262
Nicephorus of Constantinople
De Rebus post Mauricium gestis, P.G., C, *925 .. 264
Antirrhetus, iii 291
Nicephorus Callistus
Ecclesiastical History, XVII, xxv 296
Procopius
De Aedificiis, VI, ii .. 250
History of the Wars, V, viii, ff. 209

page

Sebeôs
History of Heraclius
xxiii 260
xxiv 260, 261
xxx 261
xxxi 262

Sigbert
Chronicle
sub anno 724 291
sub anno 765 293

Socrates
Ecclesiastical History
II, xxxiii.. 187
III 188
VII, xiii 235
VII, xvi 234
VII, xxxviii 233

Sozomen
Ecclesiastical History
II, ix 142
II, xii 142
V 188

Sulpicius Severus
Chronicle, II, xxx 87

page

Theodoret
Ecclesiastical History
III 188
IV, xviii 186
IV, xix 186
Religious History, vi .. 292

Theophanes
Chronicle
sub anno 442 238
548 259
601 245
606 260
620 .. 261, 305
714 266
715 265
749 262

Venantius Fortunatus
Vita S. Germani, lxii .. 336

Zachariah of Mitylene
Chronicle
III, vi 243, 296
VII, viii 301
VIII, ii 303
IX, vi 260
IX, viii 259
IX, xxiv 244

INDEX FOUR

CODES AND SECULAR LAWS

page

(i) *Roman Law*

Codex Theodosianus
- 2.1.10 .. .. 232, 246
- 2.8.26 .. .. 203, 250
- 3.1.5 182
- 3.7.2 182
- 4.14.1 249
- 7.8.2 .. .. 189, 250
- 8.8.8 203
- 9.7.5 182
- 9.40.16 242
- 9.45.2 202, 232, 247, 304
- 9.45.4 202
- 11.30.57 242
- 12.1.99 181
- 12.1.157 200
- 12.1.158 200
- 12.1.165 232
- 13.5.18 189
- 16.3.1 242
- 16.3.2 242
- 16.4.4 243
- 16.4.5 243
- 16.4.6 243
- 16.5.1 183
- 16.5.4 184
- 16.5.5 .. .. 184, 241
- 16.5.6 184
- 16.5.8 184
- 16.5.13 184
- 16.5.14 184
- 16.5.21 184
- 16.5.25 240
- 16.5.27 240
- 16.5.29 240
- 16.5.30 240
- 16.5.33 240
- 16.5.34 240
- 16.5.36 240
- 16.5.37 241
- 16.5.44 203
- 16.5.46 203
- 16.5.53 240
- 16.5.66 240
- 16.7.3 .. .. 181, 250
- 16.8.1 .. .. 179, 250
- 16.8.2 .. .. 178, 246
- 16.8.3 .. 178, 304, 312
- 16.8.4 179
- 16.8.5 179
- 16.8.6 180
- 16.8.7 .. .. 180, 250
- 16.8.8 .. .. 189, 246
- 16.8.9 .. 189, 246, 266
- 16.8.10 231
- 16.8.11 231
- 16.8.12 231
- 16.8.13 .. .. 232, 246
- 16.8.14 200
- 16.8.15 231
- 16.8.16 201
- 16.8.17 200
- 16.8.18 234
- 16.8.19 203
- 16.8.20 .. .. 203, 246
- 16.8.21 .. 231, 236, 250
- 16.8.22 .. 182, 232, 235
- 16.8.23 .. .. 202, 221
- 16.8.24 201
- 16.8.25 .. .. 182, 236
- 16.8.26 237
- 16.8.27 237
- 16.8.28 205
- 16.8.29 235
- 16.9.1 .. .. 179, 247
- 16.9.2 .. .. 180, 247
- 16.9.3 .. 202, 215, 367
- 16.9.4 .. 215, 235, 247
- 16.9.5 237
- 16.10.24 .. .. 237, 250
- Nov. 3 .. .. 238, 240
- Const. Sirm. 4 179
- 6 .. 205, 325

Breviary of Alaric
- 2.1.10 352
- 2.8.3 352
- 3.1.5 352
- 3.7.2 351
- 9.4.4 351
- 16.2.1 352
- 16.3.1 352
- 16.3.2 352
- 16.4.1 352
- 16.4.2 352
- Nov. 3 .. .. 319, 352

Leg. Rom. Burgond. Gondebaud 322

Theodoric, Edict 143 .. 207

Leg. Rom. Raet. Cur.
- 2.1.8 210

page

3.1.5 210
3.7.2 210

(ii) *Barbarian Law*

Leg. Burgond. Gondebaud, CII 322

Leg. Franc.
Childebert I
Praeceptum 332
Epistola 332
Guntram 332
Childebert II 332
Clothaire II 332
Charlemagne
Cap. Acg. 45 339
Cap. de Jud. 337
Cap. dup. ad Neum. 337, 341
Cap. de Usuriis 342
Canons 222

Leges Visigothorum
9.3.1 353
11.3 349
12.2.1 360
12.2.2 360
12.2.3 360
12.2.4 361
12.2.5 361
12.2.6 361
12.2.7 361
12.2.8 361
12.2.9 360
12.2.10 360
12.2.11 363
12.2.12 353
12.2.13 .. .. 354, 355
12.2.14 355
12.2.15 .. 355, 360, 361
12.2.16 .. .. 359, 363
12.2.17 .. .. 361, 394
12.2.18 367
12.3.1 363
12.3.2 364
12.3.3 363
12.3.4 364
12.3.5 364
12.3.6 364
12.3.7 364
12.3.8 364
12.3.9 364
12.3.10 366
12.3.11 364
12.3.12 363
12.3.13 363
12.3.14 .. .. 361, 395
12.3.15 .. .. 361, 395

page

12.3.16 363
12.3.17 364
12.3.18 364
12.3.19 364
12.3.20 365
12.3.21 365
12.3.22 365
12.3.23 366
12.3.24 366
12.3.25 366
12.3.26 366
12.3.27 366
12.3.28 365

(iii) *Byzantine Law*

Syrian Roman Law Book
45 (Arab.) 249, 266
53 (Armen.) .. 249, 266

Codex Justinianus
1.1.4 243
1.3.26 243
1.3.32 242
1.3.54 .. .. 215, 247
1.5.1 255
1.5.2 255
1.5.3 255
1.5.4 255
1.5.5 .. .. 194, 255
1.5.6 255
1.5.8 .. .. 240, 255
1.5.10 256
1.5.12 .. 248, 249, 256
1.5.13 248
1.5.17 259
1.5.18 256
1.5.20 256
1.5.21 .. 177, 248, 256
1.5.22 256
1.7.1 250
1.7.2 .. .. 248, 250
1.9.2 .. .. 180, 250
1.9.3 250
1.9.4 250
1.9.6 250
1.9.7 .. .. 182, 250
1.9.9 248
1.9.13 250
1.9.14 250
1.9.15 246
1.9.18 .. .. 248, 250
1.10.2 247
1.11.6 250
1.12.1 247
1.12.2 202
1.55.8 204
7.39.3 249

page

Codex Justinianus, *contd.*
Nov.
37 250
45 248
131 .. .. 247, 256
146 .. .. 251 ff.
Digest
27.1.15, vi 247
48.8.11 63
Codex Justinianus, laws taken from the Codex Theodosianus, *q.v.*
1.5.7, see C.T. Nov. 3, para. 6
1.7.1 16.8.7
1.7.2 16.7.3
1.7.5 Nov. 3, para. 4
1.9.3 16.8.1
1.9.4 7.8.2
1.9.5 12.1.99
1.9.6 3.7.2 and 9.7.5
1.9.8 2.1.10
1.9.9 16.8.10
1.9.10 12.1.165
1.9.11 16.8.18
1.9.12 16.8.19
1.9.13 8.8.8 or 2.8.26
1.9.14 see C.T. 16 8.21
1.9.15 16.8.22
1.9.16 16.8.26
1.9.17 16.8.29
1.9.18 Nov. 3, para. 2, 3, 5
1.10.1 16.9.4
1.11.6 16.10.24
1.12.1 9.45.2
3.12.6 15.5.5
10.32.49 12.1.157

page

Leo the Isaurian
Ecloga
App. iv, 7 267
App. vi, 16, 24 268
App. vi, 26–30 267
Mosaic Supplement .. 268
Eclog. Priv. Auct.
vii, 18 267
xv, 7 267
Ecloga ad Procheiron Mutata, xxviii (xxvi), 14 .. 267
Epanagoge, xl, 33, 34 .. 267

Basil the Macedonian
Basilica, 21.1.45 267

INDEX FIVE

CANONS OF THE CHURCH COUNCILS

page

African Church, 196 232
Agde
  34 .. .. .. 320, 324
  40 320
Antioch, 1 175
Apostolic Canons
  61 176
  63 176
  69 176
  70 176
Arles II, 14 341
Auxerre, 16 330
Carthage IV
  84 .. .. .. 176, 250
  89 .. .. .. 173, 203
  196 176
Carthage VI, 2 176
Chalons, 9 329
Clermont
  6 324
  9 325
Elvira
  16 174
  49 175
  50 174
  78 .. .. .. 174, 221
Epaone, 15 322
Laodicea
  16 175
  29 .. .. .. 175, 222
  37 .. .. .. 175, 222
  38 .. .. .. 175, 222
Macon
  2 330
  13 328
  14 330
  15 327
  16 .. .. .. 329, 340
  17 329
Narbonne
  4 354
  9 354
  14 354
Nicea (forged) 52 .. 269, 341
Nicea, II
  8 268
  Actio IV 293
  Actio V 291
Orleans
  II, 19 324
  III, 13 .. .. 324, 326
  III, 27 341
  III, 28 .. .. 320, 324
  III, 30 327
  IV, 30 326
  IV, 31 325
  V, 22 326
Orange, 6 320
Paris, 15 328
Reims, 11 327, 328, 329, 340
Rome, 10 223
Toledo
  III, 14 354
  IV, 57–66 357
  VI, 3 358
    Ep. to Pope Honorius .. 358
  VIII, 12 360
  IX, 17 361
  X, 7 362
  XII, 9 362
  XVI, King's speech .. 367
  XVII
    King's speech .. 366, 367
    Canon 8 368
Tours, 13 341
Trullanum
  1 301
  11 268
  33 268
  99 268
Vannes, 12 .. .. 320, 324

GENERAL INDEX

Names in italics are those of authors whose works are discussed in the text or chapter bibliographies

A

Abbot, G. F., xvii, 308

Abdul Masih, 125, 144, 274

Abraham, as pre-incarnation Christian, 162

Abrahams, I., 137

Acts of the Apostles, 27, 47, 128

Acts of Heathen Martyrs, 2

Africa, Councils in, 175 f.; Jews in, 202 f., 250

African Church, Canons of, 232

Agabus, 402

Agapius, 293, 298

Agatha of Catania, 145

Agde, Council of, 319

Agricola and Vitalis, 145 n. 6

Alaric II, *Breviary* of, 307, 317, 347, 351

Alexandria, Jews of, in Ptolemaic times, 15, 17; in Roman times, 1, 13, 18; confiscation of synagogues in, 251; miraculous box at, 294; mockery of crucifix at, 234, 292; persecution of Christians at, 147; relations with Moslems in, 262; riots in time of Athanasius in, 147, 186; riots in time of Cyril in, 193, 235; source of hostile stories of the Jews, 15, 371

Allard, P., 122, 125, 149

Alphius of Leontini, 134

Altercations, Christian reports of, x, 112, 239, 276 ff., 280 ff.; Jewish reports of, x, 113, 283

Ambrose, 153, 166 ff., 185, 188, 192

Ananias, Bp. of Damascus, 402

Ananias, a Jew, 402

Anastasius, P. of Antioch, 245

Anastasius of Sinai, 281 f.

Andrew, 129, 402

Antherius, Bp. of Chersonese, 133

Antichrist expected by the Jews, 99, 304

Antioch, anti-Christian excesses at, 243, 245; anti-Jewish excesses at, 238, 244; Council of, 176; disputations at, 113; expulsion of Jews from, 293; Jewish gardens at, 181; profanation of image at, 293; sermons of Chrysostom at, see *Chrysostom*

Antisemitism, in Roman world, 1, 371; lack of economic causes for, 26, 256, 339, 369, 372; theological origin of, 26, 95 ff., 158 ff., 305, 372 ff.
(see also *Jews, attitude of Christians to*)

Aphraates, *Demonstrations of*, 117, 154, 276 ff.; on persecution of Christians, 142

Apion, 25

Apocryphal New Testament, Jews in, 94 ff., 102, 114, 297 ff.; *Miracles of Jesus*, 298; *Hebrew Gospel of Matthew*, 114; *Acts of Peter*, 95; *Gospel of Peter*, 102; *Preaching of Peter*, 102; *Acts of Philip*, 94, 103; *Acts of Pilate*, 103, 298; *Gospel of Twelve Apostles*, 103, 298; *Assumption of the Virgin*, 103

Apollonius Molon, 16

Apologies for Christianity, 92, 110.

Apostasy, see *conversion*

Apostolic Canons, 176

Aqiba, 78, 93

Arcadius, legislation of, 200, 231, 240, 242

Arians in western Europe, 318, 347; attitude to Catholics of, 319, 352; attitude to Jews of, 147, 321

Aribert of Narbonne, 221

Aristobulus, 129, 402

Arles, forced baptism at, 211, 335; Jews during siege of, 321

Armentarius of Tours, 323, 341

Aronius, 307

Asceticism, 155

Assemani, 122

Athanasius, 171, 186

Athanasius and Zacchaeus, Dialogue of, x, 118, 280

Augustine, 96, 153, 171, 202

Augustine-Ps., Dialogue of, xi, 239

Aurum Coronarium, 10, 19, 200, 235, 246, 353
Austremonius, 133
Auxerre, Council of, 330
Avengillayon, 109
Avignon, riot at, 312
Avitus of Clermont, 134, 334
Avitus, Emp., 319

B

Baptism, forced, in Antioch, 245; Arles, 335; Borion, 250; Bourges, 335; Chersonese, 133; Clermont, 134, 334; Dertona, 188; Marseilles, 211, 335; Minorca, 205; Ravenna, 207; Terracina, 211; Uzès, 333
  ordered by Chilperic, 334; Chintila, 358; Dagobert, 265, 335; Erwig, 362; Heraclius, 265, 285; Justinian, 250; Leo the Isaurian, 265; Lombards, 209; Maurice, 265; Phocas, 245, 265; Recceswinth, 359; Sisebut, 355
  disapproval of, 211, 327, 333, 355
Barbarian invasions, 199, 201, 311, 312
Barcochbar, 78, 93, 126
Bardy, G., 271
Barnabas, 129, 402
Barnabas, Epistle of, 84, 97
Barsauma, 233, 236, 238
Bartholomew, 402
Basil of Caesarea, 195
Basil of Cheronese, 133
Basilica, The, 225, 246, 267, 376
Basnage, J. C., xiv
Beaulieu, A. Leroy, xvii
Bedarride, I., xvi, 307, 345
Beirut, synagogues collapse in, 250; miraculous image of, 293
Benedicta of Lyons, 140
Berrhoea, Jewish outrages at, 244
Billerbeck, P., 29
Birkath-ha-Minim, 77, 80, 91, 93
Bischoff, E., 29
Bishops, civil authority of, 247, 254, 319; conduct of, 156
Boleslav of Kalish, 120
Bollandists, The, 121, 128
Bonosus and Maximilian, 140
Borion, Jews of, 250
Bourges, blind archdeacon at, 336; forced baptism at, 335
Branscomb, B. H., xvi, 29
Bréhier, L., 313
Burgundy, legislation of, 318, 321
Burkitt, F. C., 27
Buxdorf family, xvii
Byzantine literature, 273

C

Caelicoli, 203
Caesarea, martyrdom of Carterius at, 139; reported betrayal to Moslems of, 260; riots in, 20
Caesarea in Cappadocia, 262
Caesarius of Arles, 321
Caglieri, synagogue of, 214
Callinicum, synagogue of, 166 ff.
Caro, G., 308, 313
Carpus, 402
Carterius, 139
Carthage, Councils of, 203; Jewish insult in, 150
Cassiodorus, 207, 209
Catechumens, explanation of creed to, 172; Jewish influence on, 95, 172, 303
Cautinus of Clermont, 340
Cedrenus, 225
Chalcedon, Council of, 256
Chalons, Council of, 329
Chamberlain, H. S., xiii, 158, 369
Charlemagne, attitude to Jews of, 337; legislation of, 321, 337, 342, 371
Childebert I, 327, 332
Childebert II, 332
Chilperic, 334
Chindaswinth, 351, 358
Chintila, 358
Christianity, antiquity of, 77, 97 ff.; 161; attitude of Roman authorities to, 85 ff.; charges of immorality against, 80, 110 f.; effect of admission of Gentiles to, 49; Jewish view of, 79, 106 ff.; a religio illicita, 89; seperation from Judaism of, 47, 61, 77 ff., 149; task of in fourth century, 153 ff., 157f.; the True Israel, 84, 100; variety of sects in, 94, 183, 194, 374
Christians, the new nation, 288, 289
Chromatius, 191
Chrysostom, sermons of at Antioch, 79, 119, 157, 163 ff., 231, 232, 245; attitude of Epiphanius to, 168
Church plate, bought by Jews, 218, 262, 337

Chwolson, D. A. xvii
Circumcision, Christian gibes at, 83, 104, 278; prohibition of, 24, 62
(see also *Conversions to Judaism,* and *App. I, ii*)
Clearchus, 14
Clemens and Domitilla, 87, 90, 91
Clement, Epistle of, 88, 90
Clementine Recognitions, 71, 94
Cleophas, 402
Clermont, Council of, 323, 324, 325
(see also *Avitus, Austremonius, Cautinus* and *Ubricius*)
Clothaire II, 332
Clovis, conversion of, 321, 323
Codex Justinianus, 225, 246, 317
Codex Theodosianus, 177, 199, 214, 225, 246, 317
Cohen, J., xv
Cologne, Jews in, 312
Constantine, legends of, 186; legislation of, 178 ff.
Constantine the monk, 296
Constantinople, confiscation of synagogue in, 238, 294; miracle of glass-blower's son at, 296; miracle in S. Sophia at, 293; rioting in, 264
Constantius, legislation of, 179 ff.
Conversion to Christianity, xvii, 133, 134, 171, 213, 214, 216; ritual for, 304; stories of, 291 ff., 336
Conversion to Judaism, 25, 62, 81, 107, 154, 171, 287, 325; prohibited, 179, 180, 181, 182, 247, 267, 355
(see also *App. I, ii*)
Converts to Christianity, allowed to return, 202, 221, 356, 358; attitude of Gregory to, 210 ff.; forced to remain Christians, 353, 355, 356, 360 ff.; not to be molested, 179, 213, 219; suspected, 268, 304, 319, 334, 356
(see also *App. I, ii*)
Converts to Judaism, death-bed repentance of, 176, 269
Corban, discussion of, 44
Corluy, J., 125, 149
Councils, attitude to Jews of, 174, 177, 325, 327, 331
Crete, false Messiah of, 233
Crucifixion, apocryphal stories of, 103; not cause of seperation, 33 f., 45, 69; gibes on offering vinegar at, 104; Gospel accounts of, 42, 45 f.; impossible death for Messiah, 98; Jewish petition to Marcian on, 303; Jewish story of, 46; Peter's account of, 47; Paul's account of, 50, 52, 69; Stephen's view of, 48
Cumberland, R., xv
Curial responsibilities, 177, 178, 181, 200, 232, 248, 352
(see also *App. I, ii*)
Cyprian, 72, 99
Cyril of Alexandria, 193, 235
Cyril of Jerusalem, 157, 231

D

Dagobert, 265, 335
Decurionate, see *curial responsibilities*
Delehaye, H., 2, 122
Demetrius of Thessalonica, 144
Democritus, 16
Depping, G. B., xvi, 307
Deuterosis, 154, 252
Dickens, C., xv
Didascalia Apostolorum, 71, 82
Dio Cassius, 87, 90, 91
Diocaesarea, attempted rising at, 187; martyrs of, 135
Diogenes Laertius, 14
Disputations, see *altercations*
Doctrina Jacobi nuper baptizati, 285 ff., 306
Dohm, C. W., xiv
Dominicans in Middle Ages, xii
Donatists, The, 202
Donatus of Istria, 112, 295
Drumont, Ed., xiii, 158
Dubnow, S., xvi; 345

E

Easter, celebration with Jews of, 119, 175, 221, 222; date of, 119; exclusion of Jews from streets during, 327, 330, 332
(see also *App. I, ii*)
Easton, B. S., 29
Eclogues, see *Leo the Isaurian*
Edersheim, A., xviii
Edessa, attempted rising of Jews at, 186; confiscation of synagogue at, 236; Jews refuse to receive Heraclius at, 261
Egica, 366
Egyptian story of Exodus, 15

Eisenmenger, J. A., xii
Elijah, bones of, 299
Eliphius, 140
Elisha, bones of, 295
Elliot, George, xv
Elvira, Council of, 174, 221
Emancipation of the Jews, xiii
Entawos the Amorean, 295
Epaone, Council of, 322
Ephrem the Syrian, 117, 276
Epiphanius, conversion of, 168, 295, 296; writings on heresy of, 168 ff., 251
Erwig, abolition of death sentence by, 363; legislation of, 362
Eucharist, Jews converted by, 296
Euphrasius, 340
Eusebius of Alexandria, 299
Eusebius of Caesarea, 80, 110, 118, 126, 160 ff.
Eusebius of Emesa, 299
Eutychus, 402
Evidence, right of Jews to give, 176, 222, 232, 248, 267, 338, 360 (see also *App. I, ii*)
Excommunication, Jewish right of, 62, 64, 189
Expulsion of Jews, by Avitus, 334; Constantine, 186; Chintila, 358; Dagobert, 335; Erwig, 363; Recceswinth, 360; Sisebut, 355; Wamba, 362
from Antioch, 293; Clermont, 334; Dertona, 188; France, 335 n. 2; Narbonne, 362; Spain, 355, 358, 360, 363; Uzès, 334

F

Feasts to be spent in presence of Bishop, 361, 365
Ferreol of Uzès, 333
Fields, not to be blessed by Jews, 175
Fiscus Judaicus, 62
Foakes Jackson, F. J., 69
Fouros, 402
Franks, character of, 342; laws of, 318
Friedländer, M., 2

G

Gamaliel, defence of Peter by, 48
Gamaliel, Patriarch, 235
Gaudentius, 192
Generalisations, danger of, 312, 339
Genizeh fragments, 113
Genoa, Jews of, 208
Germanus of Paris, 336
Germany, National-Socialist policy in, 200
Gospels, synoptic, attitude to Jews in, ix, 33
Gothofredus, 203 n. 5
Graetz, H., xvi, 345, 359
Gratian, legislation of, 180, 181, 184
'Greens, The' 244
Gregentius and Herbanus, Dialogue of, 283 ff.
Gregory the Great, attitude to Jews of, 210 ff.; attitude to slave-owning of, 215 ff., 321; as a Biblical commentator, 219; interest in conversion of Jews of, 210, 335; letters to Frankish kings of, 215, 222, 326, 332; letters to Reccared of, 218, 354
Gregory of Nazianzen, 188
Gregory of Neocaesarea, 296
Gregory of Nyssa, 268
Gregory of Tours, *History* of, 307, 323; story of miraculous image in, 292 n. 2
Gregory III, Pope, 221
Guntram, legislation of, 332

H

Habib of Edessa, 145
Hadrian, Emp., 13, 19
Hadrian, Pope, 222, 339
Hagada in Church Fathers, xi, 108, 117, 154, 277
Hagadists, The, 108
Hahn B., 308
Harnack, A., xvi, 125, 149
Harris, Rendell, 71, 99 n.
Hebrews, distinct from Jews, 161, 374
Hebrews, Epistle to the, 52, 58 ff.
Hecataeus, 15
Helbo, R., 107
Hemerobaptists, 169 f.
Heraclius, 261, 265
Heretics, Epiphanius' description of, 168 ff.; Jews treated as, 102, 249, 256, 300; list of, 194; treatment of, 155, 183, 190, 239 ff., 255 ff.
Herford, R. T., xvi, 29, 37, 57
Hermes, Aggaeus and Caius, 145 n.
Hermippus, 14
Herodians, 156, 169

Herodion, 403
Hilarion, 192
Hilary of Arles, 324
Hilary of Poitiers, 160 ff., 323
Hild, J. A., 2
Himyarite Jews, 258
Hippolytus, 72, 99, 104
Hodgkin, T., 197
Honorius, Emp., Legislation of, 200, 232
Honorius, Pope, 221, 358
Hoshaye, R., 113
Hospitality, Jewish, 174, 268, 320, 322, 324, 327
(see also *App. I, ii*)
Host, profanation of, 207 n. 2

I

Iconoclastic controversy, 291 ff.
Ignatius, 84
Images, Jews converted by, 292 ff.
Inmestar, crucifixion of boy at, 234
Innocentius of Dertona, 187
Intermarriage with Jews, 174, 180, 182, 223, 250, 256, 322, 324, 351, 354
(see also *App. I, ii*)
Irenaeus, 106, 117
Isaac, as alternative to Jesus, 116
Isaac of Troki, x
Isai the Doctor, 142
Isbozetas, 143
Isidore of Pelusium, 283
Isidore of Seville, x, 276, 348, 355, 356, 357, 359

J

Jacob of Serug, 99, 279
Jacobs, Joseph, xvi
James, Epistle of, 58
James, son of Alphaeus, 403
James the brother of John, 130
James the Just, 129, 403
James of Nisibis, 296
Jamnia, a Jew of, 214
Jason and Papiscus, Dialogue of, x, 71, 280
Jerome, 78, 80, 96, 108, 117, 119, 153, 159, 173, 233, 253, 313
Jerusalem, bishops of, 93; capture of by Heraclius, 261; capture of by Moslems, 262; capture of by Persians, 260; capture of by Titus, 77, 82, 149; Jews present at sermons in, 173; massacre of Christians in, 260 ff.; massacre of Jews in, 238, 261
Jesus, apocryphal miracles of, 298; attitude to Torah of, 38 ff.; conflict with Pharisees of, 34 ff., 37, 38 ff.; historicity of, 97; Jewish attitude to Messianic claims of, 45, 80, 114; Jewish stories of life of, see *Sepher Toldoth Jeshu;* Jewish view of resurrection of, 80; as one of twenty-two elders, 290; teaching of, 34 ff., 373
Jewesses, danger of to Spanish clergy, 365
Jews:
I. *History of the Jews*
Entry into Palestine, 5
Relations with Greco-Roman world, 8, 19, 371
Contacts with Rome, 7, 20, 22
The Jews as Roman citizens, 10, 199, 208, 312, 317, 332, 335, 339, 344, 353, 359
The Jews in Persia, 141, 257
The Jews in the fourth century, 157, 177 ff.
The Jews in fifth-century Palestine, 233
The Jews under the Byzantines, 257, 274; the Franks, 199, 222, 312, 318, 323, 335, 342; the Lombards, 209; the Moslems, 262; the Ostogroths, 199, 206 ff., 317; the Visigoths,, 199, 222, 345, 350
The Jews in the Middle Ages, 199, 254, 376
Perversions of Jewish history in patristic literature, 96 ff., 105, 158, 160
II. *Occupations of the Jews*
Occupations in Alexandria, 17 ff.; in eastern provinces, 274; in Roman empire, 12 ff., 119 ff., 192; in Persia, 274; in Spain, 175, 348 ff., 369; in the west, 339
Doctors, 336; Farmers, 6, 12, 175, 219, 221, 348, 364; Financiers, 13, 192, 316, 323, 341, Jewellers, 340; Lawyers, 201, 248; Officials, 140, 204, 325; Slave-traders, 216, 219, 329, 340; Soldiers, 6, 10, 201, 260; Traders, 12, 17, 305, 313, 338, 341, 348, 372

Missionary activity of the Jews, 6, 23, 62, 107, 120

III. *Relations of Jews with non-Jews*

Relations with the general population, 20, 118

Friendly relations with Christians, 118 ff., 164, 189, 269, 305 ff., 322, 324, 339, 342, 349, 369

Business relations with Christians, 269, 332, 341

Relations with Christian scholars, 117 ff., 277

IV. *Pagan view of the Jews*

as ass worshippers, 16

as beggars, 23

as misanthropes, 14, 20, 23

as philosophers, 14, 23

as worshippers of Sabazius, 21

Egyptian view of the Jews, 15 ff.

V. *Christian view of the Jews*

Christian view based on Matt. xv, and not on crucifixion, 33 f., 45, 69; at time of destruction of Temple, 77; at time of separation, 45, 69, 81, 83, 149; in fourth century, 158

The Jews as apostates, 102 ff., 298; as devils, 164; as frivolous or repulsive, 101, 153, 191; as hated by God, 101 n. 4, 165, 279; as heretics, 102, 249, 256, 300; as idolators, 164, 299; as ignorant of God, 102; as litigious, 192; as possessing special smell, 334; as responsible for crucifixion, 33 ff., 45, 69

Epithets applied to the Jews in laws, 185, 237 f., 370

The restoration of the Jews, 77, 165, 279, 284, 288

The ultimate destination of the Jews, 54, 159, 185, 220, 300, 357

Admission to church services, 173, 176, 269, 304

For the Christian view of Jewish history, see *History of the Jews*

VI. *Christian attacks on the Jews*

The Jews attacked in Antioch, 238; Illyricum, 231; Jerusalem, 236, 238; Mesopotamia, 259; Palestine, 236, 238; Tella, 258; Tyre, 262

see also *Synagogues, destruction of*

VII. *Jewish attitude to Christianity*

Jewish attitude to Peter, 48; to Paul, 64 ff.; in Jerusalem, 77; in the first century, 48, 61, 69; at the time of separation, 48, 61, 81, 149; in the second century, 108, 149; in the fourth century, 156 f.; to crucifixion, 46; to doctrine of Trinity, 108, 269

Power of Jews over early church, 63

Defamation of Christianity by Jews, 79, 125, 150, 243

Influence of Jews on catechumens, 95, 172, 303

Influence on heretics, 95, 324, 375

Jewish reply to Christian claims, 80, 108, 277, 357

Secret respect for Christianity, 115, 287, 290

VIII. *Jewish attacks on the Christians*

Jews accused of betraying Arles, 321; Caesarea, 260; Diocaesarea, 262; Tella, 257; Visigothic Spain, 368

Jews attack Christians in Alexandria, 147, 186, 235; Africa, 202; Antioch, 243 f.; Arabia, 258, 263; Avignon, 312; Berrhoea, 244; Caesarea, 259; Diocaesarea, 187; Edessa, 187, 261; Jerusalem, 93, 260 ff.; Mesopotamia, 259; Palestine, 233, 259; Tyre, 262; in time of Julian, 167, 188

Jews, converts to and from, see *conversion*

'Jews', as a term of abuse, 239, 300 ff.

'Jews', Christians calling themselves, 194, 203

Jochanan, R., 109, 116

John, Gospel of, ix, 28, 33, 60, 82 ff.

John the Baptist, preaching of, 43; bones of, 299

John of Ephesus, 263, 271

John of Nikious, 225, 262, 294
Joseph of Arimathea, 298, 403
Josephus, 110
Joshua the Stylite, 225
Jovian, 181
Judaising, in Africa and the east, 175, 203, 278; in Armenia, 268; in Byzantine empire, 268; in Gaul, 222, 320, 324; in Visigothic Spain, 350, 359
Judaism, Alexandrian view of, 15; Christian view of, 100 ff., 373; view of Recceswinth of, 360 f.
Judaism, antiquity of, 98; early history of, 5 f.; dispersion of, 25; in first century, 34, 81; in second century, 115; in fourth century, 153 ff.
Roman toleration of, 25; legality of, 8, 62, 181, 183, 189, 246, 249, 266; situation of as monotheism, 9, 24, 25, 155, 371
Judaism, asceticism in, 155; doctrine of mediator in, 116; doctrine of forgiveness in, 115
Judaism, attitude of Jesus to, 38 ff.; attitude to Gentiles of, 6, 23, 24, 62, 107, 120; causes of Christian separation from, 34
Judas Cyriacus, 403
Judas Iscariot, 192
Judeo-Christians, 56, 58, 72, 77, 78, 92 ff., 106, 110, 154, 169 ff.
Judicial autonomy, 8, 232, 352
Julian, attitude of Jews to, 298; attitude to Jews of, 20, 188, 190; frees Jews from decurionate, 180; Jews offer crown of idols to, 299; reign of, 181, 190
Julian of Toledo, 276, 342, 348
Julius Caesar, 8, 10, 21, 24
Juster, J., xvi, 1, 345, 359
Justin Martyr, 72, 96, 117; *Dialogue with Trypho of*, 71, 82, 98, 99 ff., 111; accuses Jews of responsibility for persecution, 79, 126, 132; attitude of to Christians who keep Law, 70 n., 96
Justinian, abolishes legality of Judaism, 249, 266; legislation of, 245 ff., 254; regulation of synagogue services by, 251 ff.
Juvenal, 21, 23

K

Klausner, J., xvi
Krauss, S., 225

L

Labourt, M. J., 122
Lactantius, 97
Lake, Kirsopp, 28
Laodicea, murder of acrh-deacon of, 239; synagogues collapse in, 251; Council of, 175
Law, The, see *Torah*
Lazare, B., xvii
Leclercq, H., 125
Legal profession, Jews and, 201, 248
Legislation, purpose of, 155, 185
Lemann, Abbé J., xiii
Lenz, H. K., 151
Leo the Isaurian, forced baptism ordered by, 265; Eclogues of, 225, 246, 267, 371
Leo of Patara, 139
Leontini, Jews of, 134
Lessing, T., xiv
Letters to the synagogues, The, 79 ff.
Lévêque, N., xvii
Levi, Israel, 107
Lex Romana Raetica Curiensis, 199, 209
Liturgy, attitude to Jews in, 173, 304
Lombards, Jews under the, 209
Longinus the Centurion, 130, 403
Lot, F., 197, 307
Louis the Pious, laws of, 339, 376
Lucas, L., 151
Luke, *Gospel of*, 42; story of crucifixion in, 47; story of death of, 403
Lukyn Williams, Canon, xi
Lyons, martyrs, of, 127
Lysimachus, 16

M

Macon, Council of, 323 ff.
Mancius, 134
Manean, 403
Manetho, 15, 25
Mar Kadagh, 142
Mar Maris, 112
Marcian, Emp., Jewish petition to, 303; legislation of, 240
Marcian, Bp. of Cyprus, 403
Marciana, 144

Mark, Gospel of, attitude to Jews in, 38 ff., 82; historicity of, 27, 42; story of crucifixion in, 47
Marmorstein, Dr., 113, 115
Marr, W., xiii
Marseilles, forced baptism at, 211; Jewish trade at, 322; refugees from Clermont received at, 334
Martial, 23
Martyrs, burial in Jewish cemeteries of, 145; collections of lives of, 121, 127; eastern Acta of, 275; Jewish hostility to, see Ch. IV; Jews prayed for by, 135; Jewish sympathy with, 139, 144, 306; tradition of in first century, 130, 402
Mary, Martha and Lazarus, 403
Mary Magdalen, 403
Mary the Virgin, 403; *Assumption of,* 103
Matrona, 134
Matthew, death of, 404
Matthew, Gospel of, attitude to Jews in, 33, 41, 43, 60; story of crucifixion in, 45
Maurice, Emp., orders baptism of Jews, 265
Meaux, Council of, 331
Meir of Jabne, R., 109
Mellito of Sardis, 90
Mendelssohn, M., xiv
Merchant of Venice, eighth century version of, 293
Merrill, E. T., 88 ff.
Messiah, Jewish refusal of, 281
Messianism, in first century, 22, 25; in Crete, 233; in Mesopotamia, 264; in Sicily, 218; in Syria, 264
Metuentes Deum, The, see *Conversion to Judaism*
Michael of Saba, 291
Michael the Syrian, 225, 265
Mieses, M., xvii
Milan, Jews of, 208
Minim, The, 78, 110
Minorca, Jews in, 203 ff.
Miracle Plays, xi
Miracles, conflict for superiority in, 112, 295; practical and theological use of, 295 ff., 336
Mnaseas, 16
Molinier, 226
Monasticism, oriental, 189, 234, 242, 263 f., 275, 305, 331
Monophysite controversy, 296, 300
Montanists, not persecuted by Jews, 126
Montefiore, C., xvi, 29, 57 n.
Moore, G. F., 29
Moslems, relations with Jews of, 262; Christian altercations with, 291
Murawski, Bp., 151, 166

N

'Name, The', 85, 86, 88
Naples, interference with Jews of, 214; Jews during siege of, 209; Jewish slave trade at, 216, 217, 329
Narbonne, Council of, 330, 354; Jews in, 217, 221; Jews expelled from, 362; rebellion against Wamba in, 342, 362
Nathanael, 404
Nau, Dr., 236
Navicularii, 189
Nazareans, 169 f.
Nazarenes, 78
Nero, persecution of Christians by, 86, 89, 91, 125, 146
Nestorian controversy, 239, 241, 243, 300 f.
Neumann, T., xvii
Newman, L. I., 308
Nicaea, second council of, 268, 291; forged canons of, 269
Nicanor, 404
Nicodemus, 404
Nicomedia, martyrs of, 143
Nisibis, Jews of, 264
Novella, 146, 251 ff., 392
Nunneries, behaviour in, 330

O

Oath, Jewish, 222, 238
Official positions, exclusion from, 201, 204, 205, 238, 248, 325, 328, 332, 352, 364
(see also *App. I, ii*)
Old Testament, adoption of by Christians, 96 ff., 104 f.; alleged Jewish falsification of 118, 253, 298; method of interpretation of, 98 ff., 149, 158, 173, 200, 251, 275, 281, 374; promises of cannot be fulfilled twice, 279
(see also *Torah* and *Promises*)

Orange, Council of, 320
Origen, 71, 72, 105, 117; accuses Jews of responsibility for persecution, 110, 126, 147
Orleans, Council of, 323
Ossenes, 169 f.

P

Palermo, confiscation of synagogues in, 213
Palestine, different religions allowed in, 5; few Christians in fifth century in, 233; Jewish settlement in, 5
Papacy, attitude to Jews of, xiv, 210, 223, 254, 317, 333
Paris, Council of, 328
Parmenas, 404
Passover, Christian attendance at, 165, 175, 176
Patriarch, The Jewish, 10, 11, 62, 231, 235
Patriarchs, The, as Christians, 104, 162
Paul, at Corinth, 65 ff.; at Rome, 68; attitude of Jews to, 56, 64, 77, 92; attitude to Law of, 28, 51 ff., 55, 57, 69, 373; attitude to the Promises of, 54 f.; career of, 50 ff., 55, 63, 64; death of, 298, 404; preaches in synagogues, 50, 52; remains a Jew, 51, 55
Paul, Epistles of, 28, 58
Paul, Valentinian and Thea, 135
Persecution, Christians accept shelter of synagogue during, 144 f.
Jewish share in, during apostolic age, 64, 128 ff.; in first century, 128, 149; from the second to fourth centuries, 133 ff.; under Julian, 140; in Persia, 140 ff., 186; in Vandal Africa, 147; in Moslem Spain, 147; according to patristic literature, 126, 148; according to modern scholars, 122, 125, 150
Roman responsibility for, 133
Persia, persecution under Shapur in, 140, 186; war with Byzantium of, 257, 305
Peter, attitude to Jewish authorities of, 47; betrayal of by Jews, 298; reception of Gentiles by, 49
Peter, Acts of, 95
Peter, Epistle of, 58, 87, 89
Peter, Gospel of, 102
Pfefferkorn, xii
Pharisees, attitude to Rome of, 22; conflicts with Jesus of, 38 ff.; friendship with Jesus of, 43, 44; not mentioned in crucifixion narratives, 45; support Paul, 56; teaching of, 35, 38, 40, 49, 54, 169; warn Jesus of danger, 43
Philastrius, 171, 251
Philip of Alexandria, 290
Philip of Heraclea, 127, 139
Philip, Acts of, 94, 103
Philo, 18, 154
Phocas, baptism of Jews ordered by, 245, 265
Phylacteries, use of by Christians, 119
Pilate, 46, 102 ff.
Pionius, 127, 137, 144, 147
Placita, 304, 358, 361, 363, 365, 394 ff.
Polycarp, 127, 136, 147
Polygamy, 182, 250
Pompey, 21
Pontius, 127, 143
Pork, necessity of in commercial transactions, 367; readiness to eat, 299; reasons for non-use of, 282; regret for failure to eat, 289
Portugal, slave martyred in, 134
Poseidonius, 16
Priscus, 334, 340
Promises, The, Christian attitude to, 57, 58 ff., 84, 96, 253; Pauline attitude to, 53; Pharisaic attitude to, 54; not to be shared with Jews, 84
Psychological tests, Visigothic substitute for, 360
Purim, regulations for, 234, 250; Christian boy killed during, 234

R

Rabbulas, 236
Radin, Max, xvi, 1
Ramsay, Sir W., 85 ff.
Raven, C. E., 28, 29
Rawlinson, A. E. J., 27
Reccared, conversion of, 347; legislation of, 353 ff.; letter of Gregory to, 218, 354
Recceswinth, definition of Judaism by, 360; legislation of, 358, 359 ff.

Reims, Council of, 327, 328
Reuchlin, xii
Revelation, Book of, 57, 88, 89
Ritual Murder, xiii, 16; 234 n. 2
Rohling, A., xii, xiii, xvi
Roman Law, of the Burgundians, 318; of the Franks, 318; of the Lombards, 209; of the Ostrogoths, 207; of the Raetians, 209; of the Visigoths, 317
Romanus of Antioch, 112
Rome, attitude to Judaism of, 21, 25; blind Jew at, 336; Council of, 223; expulsion of Jews from, 21, 24; knowledge of Christianity of Jews in, 68; persecution of Church by, 85 ff., 91; state of Empire in fourth century, 177
Rösel, G., 122
Ruinart, 121

S

Sabbath, Christians to work on, 175, 222, 320; Gospels to be read on, 175; Jesus' attitude to, 39; Jews not to be disturbed on, 203, 250, 352; Jews not to be served on, 176; Pharisaic attitude to, 40
Sadducees, 169, 252
Salvador, J., xv
Salvianus of Marseilles, 314
Samaritans, hatred of Christians of, 258; laws affecting, 258; risings of, 233, 243, 258; synagogue of at Rome, 208
Sanctuary, exclusion from, 201, 232, 247, 353
Sargis of Abergra, see *Doctrina Jacobi*
Scherer, J. E., 308
Schürer, E., xvi, 1
Scribes, 36, 169
Sebeôs, 225
Seneca, 23, 25
Sepher Toldoth Jeshu, xi, 46, 80, 109, 114, 191
Septimania, rising in, 362
Sergius of Amida, 263
Severianus of Philadelphus, method of argument of, 297
Severus of Antioch, catechetical addresses of, 269, 304; *Letters of,* 244; moderation of, 29; view of Nestorius of, 303
Severus of Majorca, 203 ff.
Shammai, R., 107
Shapur II, 140 ff.
Sidonius Apollinaris, 307, 314, 319, 343
Simeon bar Sabbae, 141
Simeon, Bp. of Jerusalem, 404
Simeon Stylites, 238
Simeon the Mountainer, 274
Simlai, R., 113
Simon of Cyrene, 404
Sira, the Persian martyr, 142
Sisebut, 354, 355
Sisinand, 356
Slave trade, 216, 219, 231, 329, 340
Slaves, martyrs among, 134; number of Christians from, 180; right to possess Christian, 202, 215, 367
(for all legal questions affecting slaves see *App. I, ii*)
Smyrna, 136
Sombart, W., xiv
Spain, commercial situation in, 349 f.; correspondence of Pope Hadrian with, 222; situation of Jews in, 276, 348
Stähelin, F., 2
Stephen, relics of in Minorca, 204; speech of, 48, 61
Stephen VI, Pope, 221
Stobbe, O., 308
Strack, H., xvi, 29
Sulpicius of Bourges, 335
Sunday, no work to be done on, 330, 332
Swintila, 356
Synagogue, collapse of buildings of, 238, 250; regulations of services of, 251; ritual for consecration of, 401
Synagogues, confiscation of, in Africa, 250; at Alexandria, 251; at Antioch, 238; at Borion, 250; at Caglieri, 214; at Constantinople, 238, 294, 303; at Edessa, 236; at Palermo, 213; at Terracina, 213; at Tipasa, 187
by John of Ephesus, 263; by Sergius of Amida, 263
Synagogues, destruction of, at Amida, 263; at Callinicum, 166 ff., 187; at Clermont, 331, 334; at Daphne, 244; at Dertona, 187; in Eastern Empire, 235; in Illyricum, 231; in Min-

orca, 204 f.; in Palestine, 236; at Ravenna, 207; at Rome, 187, 207; in Syria, 235; at Tours, 331
Synagogues, laws affecting, see *App. I, ii*
Syrian Roman Law Book, 249, 266
Syrians, The, 191, 313, 341, 350

T

Tacitus, 15, 16, 20, 23, 25, 86, 89
Talmud, attacks on, xii, 78, 253, 254; compilation of, 191, 275; references to Jesus in, 109; references to Christianity in, 106, 108, 171; surrender of, xii, 358
(see also *Altercations, Crucifixion, Isaac, Jesus, Minim, Paul*)
Tarbula, 142
Tarphon, R., 109
Taxes, Jewish, 368, 370
(see also *aurum coronarium*)
Tella, betrayal of, 257
Temedrius, 404
Terracina, Jews in, 211; synagogue at, 213
Tertullian, 72, 99, 104, 117, 150; accuses Jews of responsibility for persecution, 85, 111, 126, 147
Testimonies, ix, 71, 99; Teutonic edition of, x, 358
Thaddeus, 404
Theodoret of Cyr, 188, 283, 292, 299
Theodoric, 206 ff., 267
Theodorus of Alexandria, 147 n. 1
Theodorus of Cyrene, 145
Theodorus of Mopsuestia, 297
Theodosius I, 166, 185, 199, 241
Theodosius II, 233, 236, 242
Theodosius the priest of the Jews, 290, 297
Theophilus and Simon, Dialogue of, 280
Tiberias, collapse of synagogues in, 251; story of image at, 292 n. 3
Timothy, 404
Timothy and Aquila, Dialogue of, x, 280
Titus, circumcision of, 51
Titus, Emp., council of before Jerusalem, 87, 91
Toledo, Councils of: IIIrd, 354; IVth, 355, 356, 360; VIth, 221, 358; VIIth, 358; VIIIth, 360; IXth, 361; Xth, 361 f.; XIIth, 362; XVIIth, 366
Tomei, Conversion of Jews of, 289 f., 306
Torah, attitude of Peter to, 50; attitude of Paul to, 50 ff., 69; Christian view of, 37, 50, 57, 96, 162; meaning of, 33, 35, 37; observation of by Christians, 49, 50, 92
Toussenel, A., xiii
Trade restrictions, 367
Travel, control of, 364
Trinity, Doctrine of, 108, 155, 172, 269, 278
Trophies of Damascus, 287
Trullanum, Council, 268
Trusteeship, 247
Tyre, plot of Jews in, 262

U

Ubricius of Clermont, 133
Uhlmann, F., 122
Urbanus, 404
Usury, canons on, 269, 341; Jews and, 13, 192; Laws on, 192, 342; sermons on, 192
Uzès, forced baptism at, 333

V

Valentinian and Valens, legislation of, 181
Valentinian III, legislation of, 205
Vannes, Council of, 320, 324
Vasilief, A. A., 226
Venantius of Arles, 145
Venantius Fortunatus, 334
Vincent and Orantius, 145 n.
Visigoths, in Illyricum, 232; in Spain, 347 ff.; conception of kingship among, 347

W

Wagenseil, J. S., xi
Wamba, 362
Wilcken, U., 2
Willrich, H., 1

Z

Zeno, Emp. Henoticon of, 243; views on Jews of, 244
Zeno of Verona, 182
Ziegler, A., 346
Zionism, xiv